Security Without Obscurity

Public Key Infrastructure (PKI) is an operational ecosystem that employs key management, cryptography, information technology (IT), information security (cybersecurity), policy and practices, legal matters (law, regulatory, contractual, privacy), and business rules (processes and procedures). A properly managed PKI requires all of these disparate disciplines to function together – coherently, efficiently, effectually, and successfully. Clearly defined roles and responsibilities, separation of duties, documentation, and communications are critical aspects for a successful operation. PKI is not just about certificates, rather it can be the technical foundation for the elusive "crypto-agility," which is the ability to manage cryptographic transitions. The second quantum revolution has begun, quantum computers are coming, and post-quantum cryptography (PQC) transitions will become PKI operation's business as usual.

Jeff Stapleton is the author of the *Security Without Obscurity* five-book series (CRC Press). He has over 30 years' cybersecurity experience, including cryptography, key management, PKI, biometrics, and authentication. Jeff has participated in developing dozens of ISO, ANSI, and X9 security standards for the financial services industry. He has been an architect, assessor, auditor, author, and subject matter expert. His 30-year career includes Citicorp, MasterCard, RSA Security, KPMG, Innové, USAF Crypto Modernization Program Office, Cryptographic Assurance Services (CAS), Bank of America, and Wells Fargo Bank. He has worked with most of the payment brands, including MasterCard, Visa, American Express, and Discover. His areas of expertise include payment systems, cryptography, PKI, PQC, key management, biometrics, IAM, privacy, and zero trust architecture (ZTA). Jeff holds a Bachelor of Science and Master of Science degrees in computer science from the University of Missouri. He was an instructor at Washington University (St. Louis) and was an adjunct professor at the University of Texas at San Antonio (UTSA).

W. Clay Epstein currently operates a cybersecurity consulting company Steintech LLC, specializing in Cybersecurity, Encryption Technologies, PKI, and Digital Certificates. He has international experience developing and managing public key infrastructures primarily for the financial services industry. Clay has worked as an independent Cybersecurity and PKI consultant for the past 11 years. Previously, Clay was the VP and Technical Manager at Bank of America responsible for the Bank's global Public Key Infrastructure and Cryptography Engineering Group. Prior to Bank of America, Clay was CIO and Head of Operations at Venafi, a certificate and encryption key management company. Prior to Venafi, Clay was Senior Vice President of Product and Technology at Identrus, a global identity management network based on PKI for international financial institutions. Previously, Clay also served as Head of eCommerce Technologies for Australia and New Zealand Banking Group (ANZ) and was the CTO for Digital Signature Trust Co. Clay holds a Bachelor of Science in Computer Science degree from the University of Utah and a Master of Business Administration in Management Information Systems degree from Westminster College.

Security Without Obscurity
A Guide to PKI Operations

Second Edition

Jeff Stapleton and W. Clay Epstein

CRC Press
Taylor & Francis Group
Boca Raton London New York

CRC Press is an imprint of the
Taylor & Francis Group, an **informa** business

Designed cover image: ©Shutterstock Images

Second edition published 2024

by CRC Press
2385 NW Executive Center Drive, Suite 320, Boca Raton FL 33431

and by CRC Press
4 Park Square, Milton Park, Abingdon, Oxon, OX14 4RN

CRC Press is an imprint of Taylor & Francis Group, LLC

© 2024 Jeff Stapleton and W. Clay Epstein

First edition published by CRC Press 2021

ISBN: 978-1-032-54522-6 (hbk)
ISBN: 978-1-032-54525-7 (pbk)
ISBN: 978-1-003-42529-8 (ebk)

DOI: 10.1201/9781003425298

Typeset in Times New Roman
by Apex CoVantage, LLC

Contents

Preface

Most of the books on public key infrastructure (PKI) seem to focus on asymmetric cryptography, X.509 certificates, certificate authority (CA) hierarchies, or certificate policy (CP), and certificate practice statements (CPS). While algorithms, certificates, and theoretical policies and practices are all excellent discussions, the real-world issues for operating a commercial or private CA can be overwhelming. Pragmatically, a PKI is an operational system that employs asymmetric cryptography, information technology, operating rules, physical and logical security, and legal matters. Much like any technology, cryptography, in general, undergoes changes: sometimes evolutionary, sometimes dramatically, and sometimes unknowingly. Any of these can cause a major impact, which can have an adverse effect on a PKI's operational stability. Business requirements can also change such that old rules must evolve to newer rules, or current rules must devolve to address legal issues such as lawsuits, regulatory amendments, or contractual relationships. This book provides a no-nonsense approach and realistic guide for operating a PKI system.

In addition to discussions on PKI best practices, this book also contains warnings against PKI bad practices. Scattered throughout the book are anonymous case studies identifying good or bad practices. These highlighted bad practices are based on real-world scenarios from the authors' experiences. Often bad things are done with good intentions but cause bigger problems than the original one being solved.

As with most new technologies, PKI has survived its period of inflated expectations, struggled through its disappointment phase, and eventually gained widespread industry adoption. Today, PKI, as a cryptographic technology, is embedded in hardware, firmware, and software throughout an enterprise in almost every infrastructure or application environment. However, it now struggles with apathetic mismanagement and new vulnerabilities. Moore's law continues to erode cryptographic strengths, and, in response, keys continue to get larger and protocols get more complicated. Furthermore, attackers are becoming more sophisticated, poking holes in cryptographic protocols, which demands continual reassessments and improvements. Consequently, managing PKI systems has become problematic. The authors offer a combined knowledge of over 50 years in developing PKI-related policies, standards, practices, procedures, and audits with in-depth experience in designing and operating various commercial and private PKI systems.

Errata

Our sincere thanks to readers who spotted a few errors in previous books, and recognitions to our reviewers for this book: Ralph S. Poore, Bill Poletti, and Richard M. Borden. Also, special appreciation to Ralph, who has steadfastly reviewed multiple drafts of every book and provided excellent comments, not only the mundane typos and punctuation but far more importantly brilliant discourse on a wide variety of information security topics including my favorites: cryptography and key management. Without him, there would be far more errors.

SECURITY WITHOUT OBSCURITY: A GUIDE TO CONFIDENTIALITY, AUTHENTICATION, AND INTEGRITY

- As far as we know, no errors have been reported.

SECURITY WITHOUT OBSCURITY: A GUIDE TO PKI OPERATIONS

- Saliha Lallali e-mailed me on March 17, 2017: I'm reading your book *Security Without Obscurity: A Guide to PKI Operations*, and on page 28 I think there is a small mistake: "the receiver uses the sender's public key to verify the signature versus its own public key to *decrypt* the data." Good spotting, it should read: the receiver uses the sender's public key to verify the signature versus its own public key to *encrypt* the data.
- Note this error has been corrected in this Second Edition.

SECURITY WITHOUT OBSCURITY: A GUIDE TO CRYPTOGRAPHIC ARCHITECTURES

- In the Annex: XOR Quick Reference there are a few errors in Table 2.1:
- The correct result is: 5 (0101) XOR 9 (1001) = C (1100)
- The correct result is: 5 (0101) XOR C (1100) = 9 (1001)
- The correct result is: 9 (1001) XOR A (1010) = 3 (0011)

SECURITY WITHOUT OBSCURITY: FREQUENTLY ASKED QUESTIONS (FAQ)

- As far as we know, no errors have been reported.

Hopefully, there are no errors in this book: *A Guide to PKI Operations*, Second Edition

1 Introduction

Public key infrastructure (PKI) is an operational system that employs key management, cryptography, information technology (IT), information security (cybersecurity), legal matters, and business rules as shown in the Venn diagram in Figure 1.1 called PKI Cryptonomics.[1] While certainly there are business, legal, security, technology, and cryptography areas within any organization that function outside of a PKI, the fact is that a properly managed PKI requires all of these disparate disciplines to function effectively. The lack of one or more of these factors can undermine a PKI's effectiveness and efficiency. Furthermore, all of these disciplines must interact and complement each other within a PKI framework.

Cryptography includes asymmetric and symmetric encryption algorithms, digital signature algorithms, hash algorithms, key lifecycle management controls, cryptographic modules, and security protocols. Asymmetric cryptography provides digital signatures, encryption, and key management capabilities to establish symmetric keys. Symmetric cryptography provides legacy key management, encryption, and Message Authentication Codes (MAC). Legacy key management suffers from a fundamental problem of how to securely establish an initial key that asymmetric cryptography overcomes. Hash algorithms enable keyed Hash MAC (HMAC) and digital signatures. Key lifecycle management includes generation, distribution, installation, usage, backup and recovery, expiration, revocation, termination, and archive phases. Cryptographic modules include software libraries and specialized hardware. Security protocols establish cryptographic keys and enable data protection schemes.

IT involves mainframes, midrange, personal computers, mobile devices, local area networks, wide area networks, the Internet, applications, browsers, operating systems, and network devices. Application server platforms include hardware, firmware, operating systems, and software applications. End-user platforms include hardware, firmware, operating systems, applications, browsers, widgets, and applets. Networks include switches, routers, firewalls, network appliances, and network protocols.

Information security, also called cybersecurity, involves entity identification, authentication, authorization, accountability, access controls, activity monitoring, event logging, information analytics, incident response, and security forensics. Logging tracks event information such as who, what, where, when, how, and hopefully why. Many aspects of security rely on cryptography and key management for data confidentiality, data integrity, and data authenticity. For details, refer to the book *Security Without Obscurity: A Guide to Confidentiality, Integrity, and Authentication* [B.7.2].

Legal matters address privacy, intellectual property, representations, warranties, disclaimers, liabilities, indemnities, terms, termination, notices, dispute resolution, national and international governing law, and compliance. While many of these issues may be incorporated into the CPS or related agreements such as the CSA or RPA for public consumption, others might be addressed in separate documents such as contractual master agreements, statements of work, or an organization's standard terms and conditions. The application environments, third-party business relationships, and geopolitical locations often influence the various legal implications.

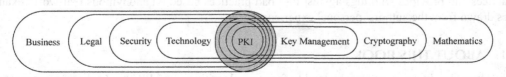

FIGURE 1.1 PKI cryptonomics.

DOI: 10.1201/9781003425298-1

Business rules involve roles and responsibilities for the registration authority (RA), the certificate authority (CA), subscribers (also known as key owners), relying parties, applications, fees, revenues, risk management, and fraud prevention. RA services include certificate requests, revocation requests, and status queries. CA services include certificate issuance, certificate revocation list (CRL) issuance, and Online Certificate Status Protocol (OCSP) updates. The CA business rules are defined in a variety of documents including a certificate practice statement (CPS), certificate subscriber agreement (CSA), and relying party agreement (RPA). Furthermore, the CA will typically provide some documents for public consumption, some proprietary with disclosure under a nondisclosure agreement (NDA) or contract, while others are confidential for internal use only.

PKI is also a subset of the broader field of cryptography, which in turn is a subset of general mathematics, also shown in Figure 1.1. Cryptography has its own unique set of risks, rules, and mathematics based on number theory, which essentially creates its own set of operating laws, and so can be called cryptonomics. PKI Cryptonomics incurs growth as more applications, cloud services, and microservices are available online, including mobile apps and Internet of Things (IoT), incorporating cryptography. Cryptonomics also suffers from a type of inflation as Moore's law continues to increase computational and storage capabilities [B.7.1]. NIST describes "cryptographic strength" as the amount of work either to break a cryptographic algorithm or to determine a key, which is expressed as the number of bits relative to the key size [B.5.19]. Simplistically, as computers get faster, keys must get larger. Cryptonomics further demonstrate lifecycle differences for various symmetric, asymmetric, and now post-quantum cryptography (PQC) algorithms. Accordingly, PKI Cryptonomics embodies all of the general cryptography characteristics and the additional managerial traits and issues from IT, business, and legal domains.

For the purposes of this book, cryptographic agility (Crypto-Agility) is defined as the capability of a PKI to easily switch between cryptographic algorithms, encryption key strengths, and certificate contents in response to changing system and enterprise needs. See Section 7.7 "Crypto-Agility," for details.

The X9.24–2 [B.1.2] defines Crypto-Agility as "a practice used to ensure a rapid response to a cryptographic threat. The goal of Crypto-Agility is to adapt to an alternative cryptographic standard quickly without making any major changes to infrastructure."

This is a good working definition that has a focus on a PKI's "infrastructure." The PKI infrastructure is an important part but not the only part of an overall PKI operation. Other important components of Crypto-Agility include the PMA's approval process and Legal's input as critical components of the PKI. Another essential component includes the risk analysis of any changes that a new cryptographic algorithm may have. All of these components and the responsive infrastructure are required for a PKI to operate in a crypto-agile environment.

Also, for this book, a Cloud PKI is defined as either the migration of a PKI-enabled application or the relocation of the PKI itself to a cloud environment. See Section 7.8 "Cloud PKI," for further discussion. Note that a Cloud PKI can be operated with in-house resources or in conjunction with cloud provider resources.

This book provides realistic guidelines for operating and managing PKI systems, including policy, standards, practices, and procedures. Various PKI roles and responsibilities are identified, security and operational considerations are discussed, incident management is reviewed, and aspects of governance, compliance, and risks (GCR) are presented. This book also both discusses PKI best practices and provides warnings against PKI bad practices based on anonymous real-world examples drawn from the authors' personal experiences.

1.1 ABOUT THIS BOOK

While most books on cryptography tend to focus on algorithms, and PKI books discuss certificates, this book addresses governance, risk, and compliance issues of PKI systems for issuers, subjects, and relying parties. The scope of this book includes both X.509 certificates and other PKI credentials, as well as various certificate authority (CA) and registration authority (RA) hierarchies, including pyramid architectures, hub and spoke topologies, bridge models, and cross-certification schemes. Furthermore, this book addresses PKI policy, standards, practices, and procedures, including certificate policy and certificate practice statements (CP and CPSs).

The intended audience for this book includes technicians, administrators, managers, auditors, corporate lawyers, security professionals, and senior-level management, including chief information officers (CIOs), chief technology officers (CTOs), and chief information security officers (CISOs). Each of these roles can benefit from this book in a variety of ways. A common benefit to the reader is general education and awareness of PKI systems, cryptography, and key management issues.

- Senior managers are responsible for making strategic decisions and supervising managers. The more senior managers know about the underlying technologies supported by their subordinate managers and their respective teams, the better they can manage the overall business. Making unknowledgeable strategic decisions is a bad practice that can adversely affect staffing, systems, and profitability.
- Managers are responsible for making tactical decisions and supervising personnel including technicians, administrators, auditors, and security professionals. The more managers know about the underlying technologies supported by their teams, the better they can manage their staff. Making unknowledgeable tactical decisions is a bad practice that can adversely affect staffing, systems, and productivity.
- Administrators are responsible for installing, configuring, running, monitoring, and eventually decommissioning network or system components inclusive of hardware devices, firmware modules, and software elements. Extensive knowledge of PKI systems is needed by administrators to properly manage cryptographic features, functionality, and associated cryptographic keys.
- Auditors are responsible for verifying compliance to information and security policy, standards, practices, and procedures. Risk can be better identified and managed when the evaluator has a solid understanding of general cryptography, specifically PKI, and related key management. Furthermore, compliance includes not just the organization's internal security requirements but also external influences such as regulations, international and national laws, and contractual responsibilities.
- Security professionals are responsible for assisting other teams and developing security policy, standards, practices, and procedures. However, security professionals are expected to have an overall knowledge base with expertise typically in only a few areas, so this book can be used as a reference guide and refresher material. For example, the (ISC)2 CISSP® program is organized into eight domains with cryptography included in one of them, cryptography and key management is no longer its own domain area, and further the CISSP certification only requires emphasis in two of the domains.
- Corporate lawyers are responsible for legal practices and interpretations within an organization. Consequently, having a basic understanding of PKI enhances their ability to advise on warranty claims, disclaimers, limitations, liabilities, and indemnifications associated with the issuance and reliance of public key certificates.
- Subscribers are responsible for protecting their cryptographic keys and using them properly in accordance with CA and RA policies, standards, practices, agreements, and procedures. Accordingly, having both a fundamental understanding of all PKI roles and responsibilities and specific awareness of the subscriber duties is important.
- Relying parties are responsible for validating and using digital certificates and their corresponding certificate chain in accordance with CA policy, standards, practices, agreements, and procedures. Hence, having both a fundamental understanding of all PKI roles and responsibilities and knowledge of the relying party obligations is paramount.

In addition to operational responsibilities, senior managers and managers need to address risk and compliance issues. Compliance might focus primarily on regulatory or other federal, state, or local laws, but contractual obligations must also be addressed. Relative risks also need to be evaluated for determining acceptable losses due to fraud, identity theft, data theft, potential legal actions, or other cost factors. Risks might be detectable or preventable, compensating controls might help mitigate issues, or backend controls might lessen the overall impacts.

The chapters in this book are organized as a learning course and as a reference guide. As a learning course approach, each chapter builds on the information provided in the previous chapters. The reader can progress from chapter to chapter to build their PKI knowledge. From a reference guide perspective, the chapters are structured by major topics for easy lookup and refresher material.

- Chapter 1, "Introduction," provides an overview of the book and introduces security basics and associated standards organizations as background for Chapter 2, "Cryptography Basics," and Chapter 3, "PKI Building Blocks."
- Chapter 2, "Cryptography Basics," provides details on symmetric and asymmetric cryptographic solutions for encryption, authentication, nonrepudiation, and cryptographic modules. The cryptography details establish connections between the associated security areas for confidentiality, integrity and authentication, and nonrepudiation.
- Chapter 3, "PKI Building Blocks," builds on the general cryptography basics provided in Chapter 2, "Cryptography Basics," providing details of PKI standards, protocols, and architectural components. The PKI building blocks provide a knowledge base for the remainder of the chapters.
- Chapter 4, "PKI Management and Security," builds on the information provided in Chapter 3, "PKI Building Blocks," to establish the groundwork for documenting and managing the PKI system and application components. The methodology is organized in a top–down approach, beginning with policy, then practices, and finally procedures.
- Chapter 5, "PKI Roles and Responsibilities," identifies the various PKI roles and corresponding responsibilities including positions, functions, jobs, tasks, and applications. The information presented in this chapter provides a reference baseline used in subsequent chapters.
- Chapter 6, "Security Considerations," discusses various security considerations that affect the operational environments of the CA, the RA, the subscriber, and the relying party. Subscribers and relying parties include individuals using workstation applications or server applications running on midrange or mainframe platforms.
- Chapter 7, "Operational Considerations," discusses operational issues for PKI roles identified in Chapter 5, "PKI Roles and Responsibilities," balanced against security issues described in Chapter 6, "Security Considerations."
- Chapter 8, "Incident Management," discusses various types of events and methodologies for handling atypical or unusual occurrences that have security or PKI operational implications. Incidents can originate from insider threats or external attacks, system or application misconfigurations, software or hardware failures, zero-day faults, and other vulnerabilities. Components of incident management include monitoring, response, discovery, reporting, and remediation.
- Chapter 9, "PKI Governance, Risk, and Compliance," addresses organizational issues such as management support, security completeness, and audit independence. Management support includes the policy authority for managing the CP and CPS, facility and environmental controls, asset inventory, application development, system administration, vendor relationships, business continuity, and disaster recovery. Security completeness includes planning and execution, data classification, personnel reviews, physical controls, cybersecurity, incident response, access controls, monitoring, and event logs. Audit independence

includes assessments, evaluations, and reviews that are reported to senior management without undue influence from operational teams.

- Chapter 10, "PKI Industry," provides an overview of the industry including standards and groups that manage or influence PKI operations, with special attention on the Financial PKI.

The remainder of this chapter introduces security disciplines (i.e., confidentiality, integrity, authentication, authorization, accountability, nonrepudiation) and provides background on various standards organizations (e.g., ANSI, ISO, NIST) and related information security standards focusing on cryptography and PKI. These discussions establish connections with symmetric and asymmetric cryptographic methods and the associated standards referenced throughout the book, in particular Chapter 3, "PKI Building Blocks," along with a historical perspective of cryptography and PKI referenced throughout the book.

1.2 SECURITY BASICS

Most security practitioners are familiar with the basic security tenets of confidentiality, integrity, authentication, and nonrepudiation. In addition to authentication, authorization and accountability are also important, and the three are sometimes referred to as the "AAA" security controls. The book *Security Without Obscurity: A Guide to Confidentiality, Integrity, and Authentication* [B.7.2] includes authorization and accountability as part of authentication, but for the purposes of this book, we separate and offer the following basic definitions of security:

- Confidentiality is the set of security controls to protect data from unauthorized access when in transit, process, or storage. Transit occurs when data is transmitted between two points. Process occurs when data is resident in the memory of a device. Storage occurs when data is stored on stationary or removable media. Note that the states of transit, process, and storage align with the PCI Data Security Standard (DSS)^2 for cardholder data.
- Integrity is the set of security controls to protect data from undetected modification or substitution when in transit or storage. Data in process is a necessary unstable state where data is being intentionally changed; however, this is where software assurance plays an important role.
- Authentication is the set of security controls to verify an entity and potentially grant access to system resources, including data and applications. There is a distinction between regular data and authentication data, also called authentication credentials. Authorization and accountability are sometimes included as part of authentication controls, but for the purposes of this book we treat all three of these security areas as separate controls.
- Authorization is the set of security controls to validate permissions for accessing system or network resources to read or write data, or to read, write, or execute software. Such approvals are based on authentication occurring first to verify the requestor, followed by authorization to validate that the requestor is allowed access.
- Accountability is the set of controls to monitor and analyze the three "W" facts: who did what and when they did it. This includes log management for generating, collecting, storing, examining, alerting, and reporting events.
- Nonrepudiation is the set of security controls to prevent refusal by one party to acknowledge an agreement or action claimed by another party. This is accomplished by having both data integrity and authenticity provable to an independent third party.

Confidentiality can only be partially achieved using access controls. System administrators can restrict access to files (data in storage) and systems (data in process), and under certain conditions limit access to network components (data in transit). Files or memory might contain system configurations, cryptographic parameters, or application data. However, only encryption can provide confidentiality for data in transit between communication nodes. Additionally, encryption can also offer confidentiality for data in storage and in some cases even data in process. Because of the role data encryption keys play in providing confidentiality data, encryption keys must also be protected from disclosure or unauthorized access; otherwise, if the key is compromised, then the encrypted data must be viewed as similarly compromised.

Integrity can be achieved using various comparison methods between what is expected (or sent) versus what is retrieved (or received). Typically, integrity is validated using an integrity check value (ICV), which might be derived cryptographically or otherwise. In general, the ICV is calculated when a file is about to be written or a message is about to be sent, and it is verified when the file is read or the message is received. If the previous (written or sent) ICV does not match the current (read or received) ICV, then the file (or the ICV) has been modified or substituted and is untrustworthy. However, a noncryptographic ICV can be recalculated disguising the attack, whereas the use of a cryptographic key to generate and validate the ICV deters the attacker, who must first obtain the cryptographic key in order to recalculate a valid ICV for the changed file or message.

Authentication methods for individuals and devices differ. Individual authentication methods include the three basic techniques of something you know (called knowledge factors), something you have (possession factors), and something you are (biometrics), and arguably a fourth method, something you control (cryptographic keys), often included as a possession factor. Conversely, device authentication can only use possession or cryptography factors, as devices cannot "remember" passwords or demonstrate biological characteristics. Some hardware devices have unique magnetic, electromechanical, or electromagnetic characteristics that can be used for recognition. Regardless, once an entity has been authenticated and its identity has been verified, the associated permissions are used to determine its authorization status. Furthermore, logs are generated by various network appliances, system components, and application software for accountability.

All the authentication methods have the prerequisite that an initial authentication must be achieved before the authentication credential can be established. The individual or device must be identified to an acceptable level of assurance before a password can be set, a physical token can be issued, a person can be enrolled into a biometric system, or a cryptographic key can be exchanged. If the wrong entity is initially registered, then all subsequent authentications become invalid. Similarly, if a digital certificate is issued to the wrong entity, then all succeeding authentications are based on a false assumption. Thus, if "Alice" registers as "Bob" or if Bob's authentication credential is stolen or his identity covertly reassigned to Alice's authentication credential, then basically "Alice" becomes "Bob," resulting in a false-positive authentication.

Nonrepudiation methods are a combination of cryptographic, operational, business, and legal processes. Cryptographic techniques include controlling keys over the management lifecycle. Operational procedures include information security controls over personnel and system resources. Business rules include roles and responsibilities, regulatory requirements, and service agreements between participating parties. Legal considerations include warranties, liabilities, dispute resolution, and evidentiary rules for testimony and expert witnesses.

For more details on confidentiality, integrity, authentication, and nonrepudiation, refer to the book *Security Without Obscurity: A Guide to Confidentiality, Integrity, and Authentication* [B.7.2]. The book organizes security controls into three major areas, confidentiality, integrity, and authentication, which were chosen as the primary categories to discuss information security. While data confidentiality and integrity are fundamental information security controls, other controls such as authentication, authorization, and accountability (AAA) are equally important. The book also addresses nonrepudiation and privacy to help round out the overall discussion of information security controls. And since cryptography is used in almost every information security control such as data encryption, message authentication, or digital signatures, the book dedicates an entire chapter to key management, one of the most important controls for any information security program and unfortunately one of the most overlooked areas.

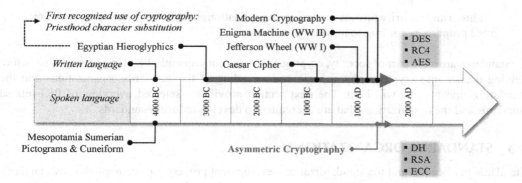

FIGURE 1.2 Selected history of cryptography.

PKI incorporates both symmetric and asymmetric cryptography along with many other security controls. Symmetric cryptography includes data encryption, message integrity and authentication, and key management. Asymmetric cryptography includes data encryption, message integrity and authentication, nonrepudiation, and key management. Asymmetric key management is often used to establish symmetric keys. However, symmetric cryptography has been around for a long while, whereas asymmetric cryptography is rather recent. Figure 1.2 shows a comparison between the history of symmetric and asymmetric cryptography.

In the known history of the world, cryptography has been around for at least 4,000 years beginning with the substitution of hieroglyphics by the Egyptian priesthood to convey secret messages [B.7.3]. The top arrow shows the 4,000-year history of symmetric cryptography. Interestingly, the earliest known human writings are Sumerian pictograms and cuneiform in Mesopotamia, which are only a thousand years older than cryptography. Substitutions ciphers are a form of symmetric cryptography since the mapping between cleartext and ciphertext characters represents the symmetric key. For example, a simple substitution cipher maps the English alphabet of 26 letters to the numbers 1–26, and the key would be the relative position of each letter, for example, A is 1, B is 2, and so on.

Better-known symmetric algorithms include the Caesar cipher,[3] used by Julius Caesar in Rome; the Jefferson wheel,[4] designed by Thomas Jefferson but still used as late as World War I; and the infamous German Enigma machine,[5] ultimately defeated by the Allies of World War II. Furthermore, World War II ushered in modern cryptography, which today includes symmetric algorithms (e.g., DES, RC4, and AES) and asymmetric algorithms (e.g., DH, RSA, and ECC).

In comparison to symmetric ciphers, asymmetric cryptography has only been around since the 1970s depicted by the short bottom arrow showing its short 50-year history. So, in comparison, symmetric cryptography has been around for thousands of years whereas asymmetric cryptography has only been around for decades.

In order for the wide variety of symmetric and asymmetric algorithms to be properly implemented, and for the two cryptography disciplines to properly interoperate within secure protocols, applications, and business environments, standardization is necessary. Standards can provide consistency and continuity across product lines, among vendors, and for intra- or inter-industry segments. Many different participants rely on standards.

- Developers and manufacturers rely on standards to build secure software, firmware, and hardware products.
- Implementers and service providers rely on standards for products and protocols to securely interoperate.
- Managers and administrators rely on the underlying standards to safely operate applications and systems that incorporate cryptographic solutions.

- Auditors and security professionals expect applications to execute properly and to be managed properly according to industry standards.

Standards are a big part of security, cryptography, and consequently PKI Cryptonomics so before delving deeper into cryptography, a basic understanding of the standards organizations and the standardization process will help. The next section provides a selected overview of PKI-related standards and the organizations that are accredited to develop industry standards.

1.3 STANDARDS ORGANIZATIONS

Standards publication and the standardization development process are accomplished by standards organizations. Some standards development groups are formally recognized internationally, some are formal national groups, while others are self-recognized or more informal groups. Figure 1.3 provides an overview of informal, formal international, and formal U.S. national standards organizations. There are several international formal groups, notably ISO[6] (pronounced "eye-so," derived from the Greek prefix isos, meaning equal), which was established in 1946 by delegates from 25 countries. The United States is one of the 164 country members of ISO, whose mandatory national standards body is the American National Standards Institute (ANSI†). ANSI does not develop standards; rather, it accredits standards developers within industry segments and designates technical advisory group (TAG) to international groups.

- INCITS – For example, the International Committee for Information Technology Standards[7] (INCITS), originally named "X3," is an ANSI-accredited standards developer organization (SDO) for the Information and Communications Technologies (ICT) industry. INCITS is also the designated U.S. TAG to the Joint Technical Committee 1 (JTC1), which is the international standards developer for ICT established mutually by ISO and the International Electrotechnical Commission (IEC). Within JTC1 is Subcommittee 27 for Information Security (SC27), which has Cyber Security (CS1) as its U.S. TAG. INCITS standards are labeled and numbered using either INCITS or its original name X3.
- ASC X9 – Another example is the Accredited Standards Committee X9[8] (ASC X9) for the financial services industry, which retained its original "X9" name. In addition to being the U.S. TAG to Technical Committee 68 Financial Services, X9 is also the TC68 Secretariat. Within TC68 is Subcommittee 2 for Information Security (SC2), which has the X9F Data and Information Security Subcommittee as its U.S. TAG. X9 standards are labeled and numbered using its X9 name, for example, X9.79 versus ISO 21188.

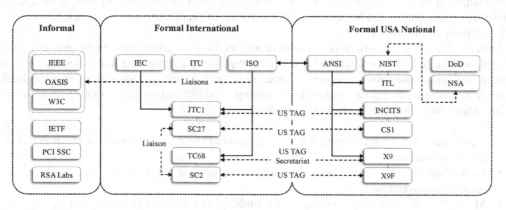

FIGURE 1.3   Standards organizations.

From an international perspective, JTC1/SC27 and TC68/SC2 maintain a liaison relationship, sharing information but developing separate and independent standards. TC68 standards are labeled and numbered as ISO, whereas JTC1 standards are labeled ISO/IEC and numbered accordingly. Domestically within the United States, both INCITS and X9 memberships are managed at the company level, but the groups do not share a similar relationship status beyond having some of the same members. INCITS and X9 standards are accredited and therefore are ANSI standards.

- TC68 – One of the many groups within ISO is Technical Committee 68 Financial Services,[9] whose scope is standardization in the field of banking, securities, and other financial services. Membership consists of 34 participating countries, 50 observing countries, and 8 liaison relationships to other standards groups. This committee has three standing subcommittees: SC2 Information Security, SC8 Reference Data, and SC9 Information Exchange. The committee has several Advisory Groups (AG) and Study Groups (SG) including SG5 Central Bank Digital Currency (CBDC).
- JTC1 – Another ISO group is Joint Technical Committee One,[10] whose scope is standardization in the field of information technology. Membership consists of 34 participating countries, 66 observing countries, and 31 liaison relationships to other standards groups. This committee has 22 subcommittees, including SC27 Information Security, Cybersecurity, and Privacy Protection, whose focus includes PKI.
- NIST – The National Institute of Standards and Technology[11] develops Federal Information Processing Standards (FIPS) and Special Publications, along with various other technical specifications.[12] All of these are U.S. government documents and are not affiliated with ANSI or ISO. However, the Information Technology Laboratories (ITL) within NIST is an ANSI-accredited standards developer. NIST also works with the National Security Agency[13] (NSA) within the Department of Defense[14] (DoD) on many standards issues, including cryptography and key management.
- ITU – The International Telecommunication Union[15] (ITU) is the United Nations specialized agency in the field of telecommunications and Information and Communications Technologies (ICT) and whose developer group is designed as ITU-T for Telecommunications Recommendations.[16]

ITU-T Recommendations include the "X" series for data networks, open system communications, and security, which includes the recommendation X.509 Information Technology – Open Systems Interconnection – The Directory: Public Key and Attribute Certificate Frameworks, more commonly known as X.509 certificates. While most PKI-enabled applications support X.509 certificates, there are other PKI formatted credentials in use today, such as PGP-type products, EMV payment smart cards, and numerous others.

Within the realm of less formal standards groups, there are several notable organizations that have developed numerous cryptography standards that either extend or rely on PKI.

- IEEE – The Institute of Electrical and Electronics Engineers[17] (IEEE), pronounced "Eye-triple-E," has roots as far back as 1884 when electrical professionalism was new. IEEE supports a wide variety of standards topics and has liaison status with ISO. Topics include communications, such as the 802.11 Wireless standards, and cryptography, such as the 1363 Public Key Cryptography standards. Note that the IEEE Standards Association, an arm of IEEE, is an ANSI-accredited Standards Developing Organization (SDO).
- OASIS – The Organization for the Advancement of Structured Information Standards[18] (OASIS), originally founded as "SGML Open" in 1993, is a nonprofit consortium that has liaison status with ISO. OASIS focuses on Extensible Markup Language (XML) standards, including the Digital Signature Services (DSS), Key Management Interoperability Protocol (KMIP) specification, and Security Assertion Markup Language (SAML) specifications.

- W3C – The World Wide Web Consortium[19] (W3C) is an international community to develop web standards including Extensible Markup Language (XML) security such as the XML Signature, XML Encryption, and XML Key Management standards. W3C also has liaison status with ISO and collaborates frequently with OASIS and the IETF.
- IETF – The Internet Engineering Task Force[20] (IETF) is an international community and the protocol engineering and development arm for the Internet. The IETF has various active and concluded security workgroups such as IP Security (IPsec) Protocol, Public Key Infrastructure X.509 (PKIX), Simple Public Key Infrastructure (SPKI), and Transport Layer Security (TLS). The IETF is not affiliated with ISO.

The Internet Architecture Board[21] (IAB), which formally established the IETF in 1986, is responsible for defining the overall architecture of the Internet, providing guidance and broad direction to the IETF. The Internet Engineering Steering Group[22] (IESG) is responsible for technical management of IETF activities and the Internet standards process. In cooperation with the IETF, IAB, and IESG, the Internet Assigned Numbers Authority[23] (IANA) is in charge of all "unique parameters" on the Internet, including Internet Protocol (IP) addresses.

- PCI SSC – The Payment Card Industry Security Standards Council[24] (PCI SSC) is a global forum established in 2006 by the payment brands: American Express, Discover Financial Services, JCB International, MasterCard Worldwide, and Visa Incorporated. China Union Pay (CUP) joined PCI in 2020. PCI develops standards and supports assessment programs and training, but compliance enforcement of issuers, acquirers, and merchants is solely the responsibility of the brands. The PCI standards include the Data Security Standard (DSS), Point-to-Point Encryption (P2PE), and Personal Identification Number (PIN). The PCI programs include Qualified Security Assessors (QSA), Qualified PIN Assessors (QPA), Approved Scanning Vendors (ASV), Internal Security Assessors (ISA), and others. The PCI SSC is not affiliated with ISO but is an active member of ASC X9.
- RSA Labs – RSA Laboratories is the research center of RSA, the Security Division of DELL EMC, and the security research group within the EMC Innovation Network. The group was established in 1991 within RSA Data Security, the company founded by the inventors (Rivest, Shamir, Adleman) of the RSA public key cryptosystem. RSA Labs developed one of the earliest suites of specifications for using asymmetric cryptography, the Public Key Cryptography Standards (PKCS).

While this discussion of standards organizations is not all-encompassing, it does provide an equitable overview of groups that have developed or maintain cryptography standards. These groups and their associated cryptography standards, specifications, and reports are referenced throughout this book. Technical and security standards are developed at various levels.

- Algorithm standards can define cryptographic processes. An algorithm can be defined as a process or set of rules to be followed in calculations or other problem-solving operations, especially by a computer. An algorithm standard defines the inputs, processes, and outputs, including successful results and error codes. Examples include FIPS 180 Secure Hash Algorithm (SHA), FIPS 186 Digital Signature Algorithm (DSA), FIPS 197 Advanced Encryption Standard (AES), and their successors.
- Protocol standards might incorporate the use of cryptographic algorithms to define cryptographic protocols for establishing cryptographic keying material or exchanging other information. For example, X9.24 defines three key management methods for establishing a PIN encryption key used to protect personal identification numbers (PINs) entered at a point-of-sale (POS) terminal or ATM during transmission from the device to the corresponding bank for cardholder authentication. Other key establishment examples include

X9.42 using discrete logarithm cryptography (e.g., Diffie–Hellman), X9.44 using integer factorization cryptography (e.g., RSA), and X9.63 using elliptic curve cryptography (ECC).

- Application standards could define how cryptographic algorithms or protocols are used in a particular technological environment to protect information, authenticate users, or secure systems and networks. For example, X9.84 defines security requirements for protecting biometric information (e.g., fingerprints, voiceprints), and X9.95 provides requirements and methods for using trusted time stamps. While neither standard deals with business processes for using such technologies, they do address how to make business applications more secure.
- Management standards often provide evaluation criteria for performing assessments to identify security gaps and determine remediation. They may also offer exemplars for policy or practice statements. In addition to policy or practice examples, management standards might also provide guidelines for security procedures. Examples include X9.79 and ISO 21188 Public Key Infrastructure (PKI) Practices and Policy Framework.

Ironically, many consider security standards as best practices, such that any subset of a standard is sufficient; however, most standards represent minimally acceptable requirements. Standards include mandatory requirements using the reserved word "shall" and recommendations using the term "should" to provide additional guidance. The "shall" statements represent the minimal controls and the "should" statements are the best practices.

The standardization process varies slightly between organizations, but many are similar or equivalent. For example, the ASC X9 procedures are modeled after the ISO processes, so we will selectively compare the two. The six stages of an ISO standard are shown in Figure 1.4. The process begins when a new work item proposal (NWIP) is submitted to one of the ISO technical committees for consideration as a new standard. The NWIP might be an existing national standard submitted for internationalization or a proposition of a brand-new standard. The NWIP ballot requires a majority approval of the technical committee membership, and at least five countries must commit to actively participate. Once approved, an ISO number is allocated and the work item is assigned to either an existing workgroup within a subcommittee or possibly a new workgroup is created. Occasionally, a new subcommittee might be created.

Once the workgroup is established, a working draft (WD) is created. The goal of the WD is to identify the technical aspects of the draft standard. When the workgroup determines the WD is ready to be promoted, it can issue a committee draft (CD) ballot. If the CD fails the ballot, then the workgroup resolves the ballot comments and can attempt another CD ballot. Otherwise, the draft is considered a CD, and the workgroup continues to develop the remaining technical and supportive material. When the workgroup determines the CD is ready for promotion, it can issue a draft international standard (DIS) ballot. If the DIS ballot fails, the workgroup can resolve the comments and attempt another DIS ballot; otherwise, the DIS is considered stable and is prepared for its Final DIS (or FDIS) ballot. Upon completion of the FDIS ballot, an ISO audit is performed to ensure the ISO procedures were followed, and the International Standard (IS) is published. Multiple CD ballots or DIS ballots are permitted; however, sometimes interest wanes to the point that an insufficient number of ISO members remain active, and the work item is eventually canceled.

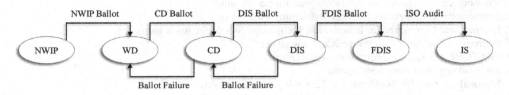

FIGURE 1.4 ISO ballot process.

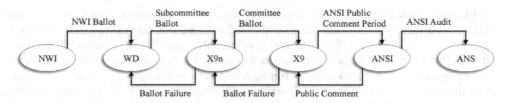

FIGURE 1.5 X9 ballot process.

The equivalent six stages of an X9 standard are shown in Figure 1.5. Similar to ISO, the X9 process begins when a new work item (NWI) with at least five member sponsors is submitted as consideration for a new standard. The NWI ballot is at the full X9 committee level, and if approved an X9 number is allocated and the work item is assigned to either an existing workgroup within a subcommittee or possibly a new workgroup is created. Again, comparable to the ISO process, a new subcommittee might be created.

The draft standard is similar to the ISO WD, and once the workgroup decides the standard is ready, it is issued for a subcommittee (e.g., X9A, X9B, X9C, X9D, or X9F) ballot. If the ballot is disapproved, then the workgroup resolves the comments and a subcommittee recirculation ballot is issued, especially when technical changes are made. But even if the ballot is approved, the workgroup still resolves comments. Regardless, once the subcommittee ballot is approved, the draft standard is then submitted for its full X9 committee ballot, the same ballot process as for the original NWI ballot. If the X9 ballot is disapproved, the workgroup resolves the comments and a committee recirculation ballot is issued. And again, even if the ballot is approved the workgroup still resolves comments. Once the committee ballot is approved, the final draft standard is submitted to ANSI for a public comment period. All public comments, if any, are resolved by the workgroup, and the final draft is submitted again to ANSI for an audit to ensure the ANSI procedures were followed, and finally the American National Standard is published.

The ISO and ANSI consensus process helps ensure industry representation by interested participants. The standards process is often referred to as the "alphabet soup," which is understandable due to the many organizations and numbers. However, the standards process is important for industry consistency, continuity, and interoperability. This is especially important for cryptography and PKI Cryptonomics as parties need to establish trusted relationships. If one party cannot trust the cryptographic keys and particularly the public key certificates of the other, then the data and interactions cannot likewise be trusted.

NOTES

1. Cryptonomics originated in the first edition *Security Without Obscurity: A Guide to PKI Operations* in 2016 but since then has been adopted by others.
2. Payment Card Industry (PCI) Security Standards Council (SSC). Data Security Standard (PCI DSS v3.1): Requirements and security assessment procedures, www.pcisecuritystandards
3. https://en.wikipedia.org/wiki/Caesar_cipher
4. www.monticello.org/site/research-and-collections/wheel-cipher
5. www.bbc.co.uk/history/worldwars/wwtwo/enigma_01.shtml
6. International Organization for Standardization, www.iso.org.
7. International Committee for Information Technology Standards, www.incits.org.
8. Accredited Standards Committee X9, www.x9.org.
9. ISO TC69, www.iso.org/committee/49650.html
10. www.iso.org/committee/45020.html
11. National Institute for Standards and Technology, www.nist.gov
12. Computer Security Resource Center of NIST, csrc.nist.gov/publications
13. National Security Agency, www.nsa.gov

14. Department of Defense, www.dod.gov.
15. International Telecommunications Union, www.itu.itl
16. ITU Telecommunications Recommendations, www.itu.int/en/ITU-T/Pages/default.aspx
17. Institute of Electrical and Electronics Engineers, www.ieee.org
18. Organization for the Advancement of Structured Information Standards, www.oasis-open.org
19. World Wide Web Consortium, www.w3c.org
20. Internet Engineering Task Force, www.ietf.org
21. Internet Architecture Board, www.iab.org
22. Internet Engineering Steering Group, www.ietf.org/iesg/index.html
23. Internet Assigned Numbers Authority, www.iana.org
24. Payment Card Industry Security Standards Council, www.pcisecuritystandards.org

2 Cryptography Basics

The security basics, confidentiality, integrity, authentication, authorization, accountability, and nonrepudiation were discussed in Chapter 1, "Introduction." In this chapter, we discuss how cryptography can help achieve many of these controls. We will apply these concepts to the operations of PKI and how PKI can deliver on the promise of these controls. From a cryptographic point of view, as shown in Table 2.1, some security basics have equivalent cryptography basics, while some of the security basics merge into a single cryptography basic, and we need to add some new cryptography basics.

Cryptography is literally defined as the process of writing or reading secret messages,[1] whereas cryptanalysis is the breaking of those secret messages. However, the term "cryptography" has evolved from its origins of just data confidentiality (secret messages) to include methods for integrity, authenticity, and nonrepudiation. A common misnomer is interchanging the terms "encryption" and "cryptography" – they are not equivalent, as encryption is one of many cryptographic mechanisms. As was provided in Chapter 1, "Introduction," for security basics and for the purposes of this book, we provide the following basic definitions of cryptography:

- Algorithms are a set of rules for mathematical calculations or other problem-solving operations including cryptographic processes. Ciphers are a method for making information secret, which includes encryption algorithms, but not all cryptographic algorithms are necessarily ciphers, and some provide authentication, nonrepudiation, or key management services.
- Encryption is the process of transforming original information called "cleartext" to an undecipherable format called "ciphertext," which provides data confidentiality. The reverse process is called "decryption," which changes ciphertext back to cleartext for recovering the original information. The cryptographic key is commonly called the encryption key regardless of if the cleartext is being encrypted or the ciphertext is being decrypted. Without access to the encryption key, cleartext cannot be encrypted and ciphertext cannot be decrypted by any other party.

TABLE 2.1

Security and Cryptography Basics

Security Basics	Cryptography Basics	Rationale
Confidentiality	Encryption	Confidentiality and encryption controls are essentially equivalent methods.
Integrity	Cryptographic Signature	Cryptographic signatures include symmetric and asymmetric signatures.
Authentication	Cryptographic Authentication	Cryptographic authentication is based on security protocols using cryptographic methods.
Authorization	Cryptographic Credential	Cryptographic credentials include X.509 public key and attribute credentials.
Accountability	Log Management	Log management is an information technology control applied to cryptographic methods.
	Key Management	Key management is specific to cryptography.
	Cryptographic Module	Cryptographic hardware and software modules are specific to cryptography.
Nonrepudiation	Nonrepudiation	Nonrepudiation is based on digital signatures.

DOI: 10.1201/9781003425298-2

- Cryptographic authentication is the process of deriving an authentication token from original information, sometimes just called a "token" or "authenticator." The token is a cryptographic pseudonym of the original data. The corresponding process verifies the token that provides both authentication and data integrity to a "relying" party. In this use case, the cryptographic key is commonly called an authentication key. Without access to the authentication key, the token cannot be generated or verified by any other party.

  This type of cryptographic authentication should not be confused with the three basic authentication methods: something you know (knowledge factor), something you have (possession factor), and something you are (biometrics). While some methodologies include cryptographic keys as possession factors, this book considers cryptography as a fourth "something you control" factor. However, symmetric keys and asymmetric private keys should never be known – see Section 2.4, "Key Management," for a discussion on the key management lifecycle.

- Nonrepudiation is the process of deriving a nonrepudiation token from original information, usually called a "signature." Similar to an authentication token, the signature is a cryptographic pseudonym of the original data, and the corresponding process is also verification to a relying party.

  The additional attribute for nonrepudiation is that the authentication and integrity are provable to an independent third party, such that the signer cannot refute a legitimate signature. It is important to understand this is a technical definition of nonrepudiation, and many lawyers will argue the legal definition of the term; for the purposes of this book, we will be using the technical definition and not the legal one. Nonrepudiation and legal considerations are discussed further in Chapter 9, "PKI Governance, Risk, and Compliance."

  This type of signature should not be confused with an "electronic signature" that is defined in the Electronic Signatures in Global and National Commerce Act (the ESign Act) of 2000 as an electronic sound, symbol, or process attached to or logically associated with a contract or other record and executed or adopted by a person with the intent to sign the record. However, the ESign "process" definition allows for cryptographic signatures, commonly called digital signatures, which can be used for nonrepudiation services. Electronic signatures and nonrepudiation services are discussed further in Chapter 9.

- Key management is the process of securely managing cryptographic keys over their lifecycle, including key generation, distribution, usage, backup, revocation, termination (which includes key destruction), and archive phases. Generation is when keys are created for a specific algorithm, purpose, strength, and lifetime. Distribution occurs when keys need to be established at more than one location beyond their generation site. Usage is when and where keys are employed per their intended purpose. Backup is done for business continuity or disaster recovery to reestablish keys due to various failures. Revocation is done only when keys are no longer viable prior to their original expiration date. Termination is the removal of previously established keys upon their end of life or revocation. Archival is for retaining certain keys past their usage period for various legal or contractual reasons.

- Cryptographic modules include both hardware and software implementations. The National Institute of Standards and Technology (NIST) describes a cryptographic module as including, but not limited to, hardware components, software or firmware programs, or any combination thereof [B.5.3]. Cryptographic keys are used with cryptographic algorithms and functions embodied in software, firmware, or hardware components.

In general, cryptographic algorithms are divided into symmetric and asymmetric algorithms. Symmetric ciphers use the same key to encrypt and decrypt data, whereas asymmetric ciphers use two different keys. Figure 2.1 shows a functional diagram with two inputs (parameters and key) and one output (results). The nomenclature and graphics used in Figure 2.1 are used for all diagrams used in this book. The function is a cryptographic operation based on a cryptographic algorithm, for

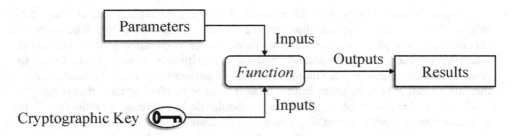

FIGURE 2.1 Cryptographic functions.

example, a cryptographic algorithm might include encryption and decryption functions. The request parameters typically include a command, the data, and associated options. The cryptographic key instructs the algorithm as to how it manipulates the input data. The results provide the output data and usually include a return code indicating success or an error.

Symmetric and asymmetric algorithms and functions are discussed in Section 2.1, "Encryption," Section 2.2, "Authentication," and Section 2.3, "Nonrepudiation." Where, when, and how cryptographic keys are stored are in Section 2.4, "Key Management." Where and how functions are accessed by applications when using cryptographic algorithms are discussed in Section 2.5, "Cryptographic Modules." This book refers to various standards and specifications that define cryptographic algorithms, modes of operations, and associated options, but it does not provide process details or descriptions of the underlying mathematics [B.7.4].

2.1 ENCRYPTION

When describing a symmetric algorithm, sometimes called a symmetric cipher, it is easiest to consider the overall process between a sender and a receiver. Figure 2.2 shows a sender encrypting the cleartext and sending the ciphertext to the receiver and then a receiver decrypting the ciphertext to recover the original cleartext. Both parties use the same cryptographic algorithm and key, but the sender uses the encrypt function, while the receiver uses the decrypt function. Since the same key is used for both encryption and decryption, this is called a symmetric algorithm with a symmetric key.

Furthermore, any interloper without access to the same symmetric key cannot decrypt the ciphertext, and therefore the encryption provides data confidentiality. An outsider might attempt an exhaustive key attack, that is, try every possible key until the right one is determined. There are no protections against an exhaustive attack except for the huge number of possible keys provided by the size of the symmetric key used to encrypt the cleartext; given enough time and resources, the symmetric key can theoretically be found.

In fact, there is always a nonzero probability that a key can be found, and it is actually possible but highly unlikely that the first guess happens to be the correct key. In comparison, a winning lottery ticket with 6 out of a possible 100 numbers is $100 \times 99 \times 98 \times 97 \times 96 \times 95 = 858{,}277{,}728{,}000$

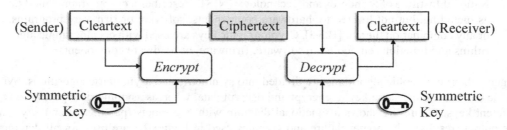

FIGURE 2.2 Symmetric encryption.

or one chance in about 858 billion (a billion is 10^9 or 9 zeroes), which is better than one chance in a trillion (or 10^{12} or 1 with 12 zeroes after it). A modern symmetric algorithm using a 128-bit key has more than 340×10^{36} possible keys, which is a number that has 27 more zeroes than the lowly lottery ticket's chance of winning.

Thus, the huge number of possible symmetric keys typically makes an exhaustive attack impractical. In addition, if the key can be found within someone's lifetime, the value of the recovered cleartext is likely expired or useless. For example, if it takes 30 years to determine a key used to encrypt a password that was only valid for 30 days, the attack is essentially a waste of time. Furthermore, changing the key periodically is a common countermeasure, such that the time needed to exhaustively determine a symmetric key often far exceeds its actual lifetime.

However, there are far easier attacks to get the symmetric key. For example, in order for the sender and receiver to exchange the encrypted information (ciphertext) and decrypt it, they must first exchange the symmetric key, which, if not done in a secure manner, might allow an outsider to get the key. Furthermore, in order for the sender to encrypt and the receiver to decrypt, they must have access to the same key. Inadequate key storage protection might allow an outsider to hack into the systems and get the key or an unauthorized insider to access the systems and provide the key to the outsider. Related vulnerabilities, threats, and risks are discussed in more detail in Section 2.4. However, insider threats are more likely to occur than outsider threats. The Ponemon Institute[2] and Raytheon released a 2014 study on insider threats including both adversarial and inadvertent security breaches:

- Eighty-eight percent of respondents recognize insider threats as a cause for alarm but have difficulty identifying specific threatening actions by insiders.
- Sixty-five percent of respondents say privileged users look at information because they are curious.
- Forty-two percent of the respondents are not confident that they have enterprise-wide visibility for privileged user access.

The 88% of respondents who recognize a cause of alarm toward insider threats seem justified by other studies such as the Carnegie Mellon University and Software Engineering Institute study on insider threats in the U.S. Financial Services Sector,[3] which provides a damage comparison between internal and external attacks. The study was based on 80 fraud cases between 2005 and 2012. On average, the actual internal damage exceeded $800,000, while the average internal potential was closer to $900,000. In comparison, the actual average external damage was over $400,000, and the potential average external damage was closer to $600,000. The study indicates that insider damage is doubled (or 100% greater), while its potential is a third higher (or about 33% greater).

When describing an asymmetric algorithm, also called an "asymmetric cipher," it is easier to consider the overall process between a sender and a receiver, as we did for symmetric algorithms. Figure 2.3 shows a sender encrypting cleartext using the receiver's public key, sending the ciphertext

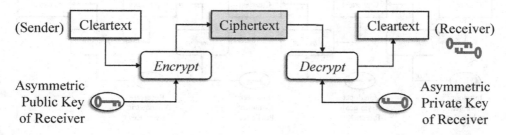

FIGURE 2.3 Asymmetric encryption.

to the receiver, and then the receiver decrypting the ciphertext using its private key to recover the cleartext. The receiver generates an asymmetric key pair consisting of the private key and the public key and sends its public key to the sender. Similar to symmetric ciphers, both parties used the same cryptographic algorithm but with this example, each used a different key. Since different keys are used, the public key for encryption and the private key for decryption, this is called an asymmetric algorithm with an asymmetric key pair.

The cleartext encrypted using the public key can only be decrypted using the corresponding private key. Thus, any sender with a copy of the public key can encrypt cleartext but only the receiver can decrypt the ciphertext. Thus, any interloper with a copy of the receiver's public key cannot decrypt the ciphertext so the data confidentiality is maintained. Furthermore, the distribution of the asymmetric public key does not require secrecy as does a symmetric key. On the other hand, the asymmetric private key is as vulnerable to outside hackers or insider threats as any symmetric key. In general, the same key management controls used for symmetric keys are equally needed for asymmetric private keys. However, as we dig deeper into PKI operations further in the book, it will become readily apparent that the strongest controls are needed for asymmetric private keys.

With respect to asymmetric public keys, we mentioned earlier that they do not need to be kept secret; however, they do require authenticity. Otherwise, without the sender being able to authenticate the receiver's public key, asymmetric cryptography is susceptible to a "man-in-the-middle" (MITM) attack as shown in Figure 2.4. Consider the same scenario of a sender sending ciphertext to the receiver by encrypting the cleartext with a public key. The MITM attack occurs when an interloper convinces the sender that its public key belongs to the receiver. The sender encrypts the cleartext with the interloper's public key, thinking it is using the receiver's public key, and sends the ciphertext to the receiver, which the interloper intercepts. The interloper decrypts the ciphertext using its private key to recover the original cleartext, then re-encrypts the cleartext using the actual receiver's public key and sends the ciphertext onto the receiver. The receiver decrypts the ciphertext using its private key to recover the original cleartext, unaware that the interloper has accessed the message.

The sender falsely believes it is securely exchanging information with the receiver as shown by the dotted line, but the interloper is the man in the middle. Furthermore, the interloper not only sees the original cleartext from the sender but also changes the cleartext such that the sender sends one message but the receiver gets a completely different message, and neither of them is aware of the switch. Often, asymmetric encryption is not used for exchanging data but rather for exchanging symmetric keys, which are subsequently used to encrypt and decrypt data. So, a MITM attack would capture the symmetric key again allowing the interloper to encrypt and decrypt information. To avoid a MITM attack, the sender must be able to validate the public key owner, namely, the receiver, which is discussed in Section 2.2.

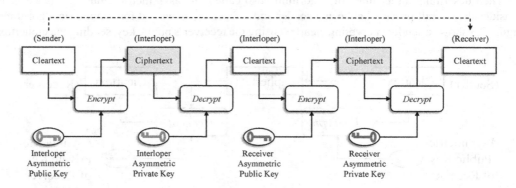

FIGURE 2.4   Asymmetric man-in-the-middle (MITM) encryption.

2.2 AUTHENTICATION

We now continue the sender and receiver discussion from Section 2.1, "Encryption," when using symmetric and asymmetric ciphers for authentication and integrity.

Figure 2.5 shows a sender generating a Message Authentication Code (MAC) using a symmetric encryption function. The MAC is generated using a specific cipher mode of operation called cipher block chaining (CBC). Basically, the cleartext message is divided into chunks of data, each chunk is encrypted such that the ciphertext from the previous encryption is used with the next encryption, and the MAC is the first half of the last ciphertext block [B.4.9] and [B.4.3]. Both parties use the same cryptographic algorithm, the same symmetric key, and the same encrypt function.

The sender generates the MAC from the cleartext and sends both the cleartext message and the MAC to the receiver. The receiver generates its own MAC from the cleartext message and compares the received MAC to the newly generated MAC. If the two match, then the receiver has validated that the cleartext message (and the MAC) has not been altered, and therefore the message integrity has been verified. Furthermore, since only the sender and the receiver have access to the MAC key and the receiver did not send the cleartext message, the MAC also provides message authentication. Additional services are discussed in Section 2.3, "Nonrepudiation."

Figure 2.6 shows a sender generating a keyed Hash Message Authentication Code (HMAC) using a hash algorithm instead of a symmetric cipher. In general, a hash function maps data of an arbitrary large size to data of a smaller fixed size, where slight input differences yield large output differences. A cryptographic hash function must be able to withstand certain types of cryptanalytic attacks. At a minimum, cryptographic hash functions must have the following properties:

- Preimage resistance is with regard to a known message: it must be infeasible to determine the original message m from just the hash result h, where h = hash (m).
- Second preimage resistance is with regard to a known message and an unknown message: it must be infeasible to find a second message g that yields the same hash result as message

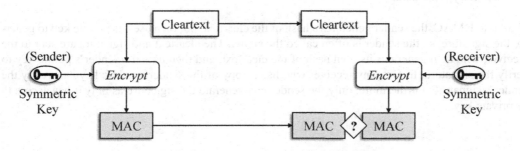

FIGURE 2.5   Symmetric Message Authentication Code (MAC).

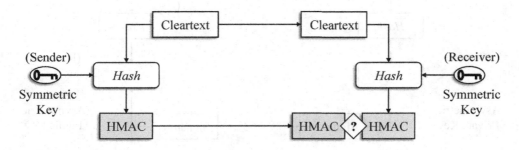

FIGURE 2.6   Symmetric Hash Message Authentication Code (HMAC).

m, where h = hash (m) = hash (g). This resistance deters an attacker from finding a second message that might be used to counterfeit the first message.

- Collision resistance is with regard to two unknown messages: it must be infeasible to find any two messages m and g that yield the same hash results h, where h = hash (m) = hash (g). This resistance is analogous to the birthday paradox, finding two individuals with the same birthday within a room of people.

If any of these conditions are not met, then an interloper might be able to determine another cleartext message and substitute it for the original message. A sender or a receiver might also be able to determine another message claiming it was the original message and so repudiate the message. Otherwise, similar to the MAC, the HMAC algorithm [B.5.7] incorporates a symmetric key with the cryptographic hash function used by the sender and the receiver.

The sender generates the HMAC from the cleartext and sends both the cleartext message and the HMAC to the receiver. The receiver generates its own HMAC from the cleartext message and compares the received HMAC to the newly generated HMAC. If the two match, then the receiver has validated that the cleartext message (and the HMAC) has not been altered, and therefore the message integrity has been verified. Since only the sender and the receiver have access to the HMAC key, and the receiver did not send the cleartext message, the HMAC also provides message authentication. Additional services are discussed in Section 2.3, "Nonrepudiation."

Figure 2.7 shows a sender generating a digital signature, sometimes just called a signature, using a combination of a hash function and a digital signature algorithm.

The differences between asymmetric encryption (see Section 2.1) and digital signatures include the following:

- The sender uses its own private key to generate the signature versus the receiver's public key to encrypt data.
- The receiver uses the sender's public key to verify the signature versus its own public key to encrypt the data.

Similar to HMAC, the sender generates a hash of the cleartext, but then uses its private key to generate the signature, so the sender is often called the signer. The cleartext and signature are sent to the receiver, who then generates its own hash of the cleartext, and then uses the sender's public key to verify the signature. In fact, any receiver who has a copy of the sender's public key can verify the sender's signature. Furthermore, only the sender can generate the signature as only it has access to its private key.

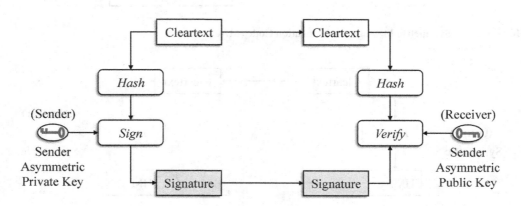

FIGURE 2.7   Asymmetric digital signature.

The sender (or signer) generates a hash from the cleartext and uses its asymmetric private key to generate the digital signature. The cleartext message and the digital signature are sent to the receiver. The receiver generates its own hash from the cleartext message and verifies the signature using the sender's public key. If the signature verifies, then the receiver has validated that the cleartext message has not been altered, and therefore the message integrity has been verified. Since only the sender has access to the private key, the signature also provides message authentication. Additional services are discussed in Section 2.3.

As mentioned in Section 2.1, "Encryption," asymmetric public keys do not need to be kept secret; however, they do require authenticity. Otherwise, without the receiver being able to authenticate the sender's public key, asymmetric cryptography is susceptible to a MITM attack as shown in Figure 2.8. Consider the same scenario of a sender sending a signed message to the receiver by hashing the cleartext and generating the signature using its private key. A MITM attack occurs when an interloper convinces the receiver that its public key belongs to the sender. The sender generates the digital signature using its private key, which the interloper cannot counterfeit. However, the interloper intercepts the cleartext message and generates a new digital signature using its private key. The interloper sends the re-signed message to the receiver. The receiver uses the interloper's public key, believing it is the sender's public key, and successfully verifies the digital signature.

The receiver thinks it has verified a signed message from the sender, unaware that the interloper is the man in the middle. The interloper can modify or substitute the cleartext message such that the sender signs one message but the receiver verifies another, and neither of them is aware of the switch. To avoid a MITM attack, the receiver must be able to validate the public key owner, namely, the sender. This is accomplished by encapsulating the sender's public key in a PKI credential, commonly called public key certificate, sometimes called a digital certificate or just certificate, signed and issued by a trusted third party (TTP) called a certificate authority (CA). The standards that define the certificate contents and the CA operations are discussed in Section 3.1, "PKI Standards Organizations," but here, we introduce the basic concepts regarding the authenticity and integrity of the public key.

Let's review Figure 2.7, where the sender signs a cleartext message using its asymmetric private key and sends the original cleartext and signature to the receiver for verification using the sender's asymmetric public key. Let's also reconsider Table 2.2 using the same scenario. It is important to recognize that there are two very different signatures – the signature for the cleartext message generated by the sender and the signature for the certificate generated by the issuer. And as we will explain, the receiver will need to verify both signatures in the overall authentication and integrity validation.

- Subject name is the public key owner's name, in this case the sender.
- Subject public key is the subject's public key, in this case the sender's public key.

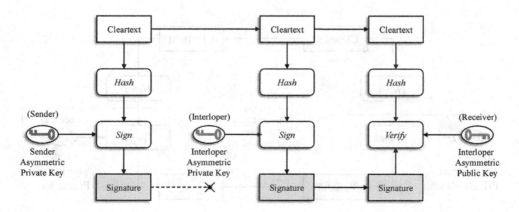

FIGURE 2.8 Asymmetric man-in-the-middle (MITM) signature attack.

- Issuer name is the certificate signature signer's name; in this case, we introduce another entity, the CA.
- Issuer signature is the issuer's digital signature, in this case the CA's signature generated by the CA's asymmetric private key. This signature encapsulates the certificate information like an envelope; that is, the subject, the public key, and the issuer fields are hashed, and the issuer's asymmetric private key is used to generate the certificate signature.

Furthermore, the receiver is the relying party using the sender's public key to verify the sender's signature on the cleartext message, but not until after the receiver uses the CA's public key to verify the signature on the certificate. As shown in Table 2.2, the certificate signature is over the certificate fields, which provides cryptographic bindings between the sender's name and public key and between the sender's name and the CA's name. Thus, the receiver can rely on the sender's public key to verify the cleartext message because the sender's certificate has been validated using the CA's public key (Figure 2.9). However, the validation process for verifying the sender's certificate and related CA certificates, called the certificate chain, shown in Figure 2.10 is discussed in the succeeding text.

Since hashing the cleartext is always part of generating the digital signature, for the remainder of this chapter, the hash step will not be shown. We also introduce two important concepts for confirming a digital signature – verification versus validation:

- Verification is the partial confirmation consisting of a single cryptographic object, such as a digital signature or a digital certificate. For example, an individual signature can be verified using a public key; however, without proper validation, the public key cannot be trusted as it requires authentication.
- Validation is the complete end-to-end confirmation of the certificate chain, including the end-user certificate, the intermediate CA certificates, and the root CA certificates, as well as the checking of the validity dates and status of each certificate.

TABLE 2.2
Selected Certificate Fields

Certificate Fields	Certificate Fields Description
Subject name	Subject is the public key owner's name.
Subject public key	Public key is the subject's public key.
Issuer name	Issuer is the TTP signer's name.
Issuer signature	Signature is the TTP digital signature of the certificate.

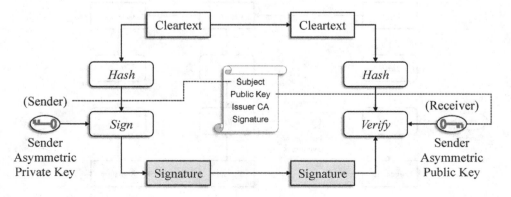

FIGURE 2.9 Certificate basics.

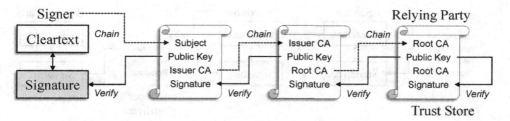

FIGURE 2.10 Basic certificate signature verification.

Figure 2.10 demonstrates a signed cleartext message, the signer's certificate, an issuer CA certificate, and a root CA certificate. In order for the relying party to verify the signed message, it must validate the certificate chain, consisting of the subject (signer), issuer CA, and root CA certificates.

However, in order to validate the certificate chain, the relying party must first determine the certificate chain. This is accomplished by walking the certificate chain in the following manner – refer to the dotted line from left to right:

(1) The relying party matches the signer's name with the subject name in the signer's certificate to find the signer's public key. This presumes the relying party has a means by which to identify the signer's name, also called an identity.

(2) The issuer CA name in the signer's certificate is then matched with the issuer CA name in the issuer CA certificate to find the issuer CA's public key.

(3) The root CA name in the issuer CA certificate is then matched with the root CA name in the root CA certificate to find the root CA's public key.

Once the certificate chain is determined and each participant's public key has likewise been established, the relying party can then walk the chain in reverse and verify the signature on each certificate in the following manner – refer to the solid line from right to left:

1. The root CA public key is used to verify the signature on the root CA certificate. It is important to note that since the root CA is the apex of the hierarchy, there is no other entity to sign the root CA certificate, and therefore it is a self-signed certificate. Root CA certificates are installed in a reliable and secure storage, often called a trust store, to ensure and maintain its authenticity and integrity. Once the certificate signature has been verified, its public key can be used to verify the next certificate in the chain.

2. The root CA public key is then used to verify the signature on the issuer CA certificate, such that once the certificate signature has been verified, its public key can be used to verify the next certificate in the chain.

3. The issuer CA public key is then used to verify the signature on the subject certificate, such that once the certificate signature has been verified, its public key can be used to verify the next certificate in the chain.

The subject public key can then be used to verify the signature on the cleartext message, which authenticates the signer and provides message integrity. It is important to note that Table 2.2 and Figure 2.10 do not list all of the fields in a standard certificate. Individual certificate verification and certificate chain validation are more complex than discussed so far. In addition to signatures, validity dates and certificate status must also be checked. Refer to Chapter 3, "PKI Building Blocks," for certificate formats and Chapter 5, "PKI Roles and Responsibilities," for more details.

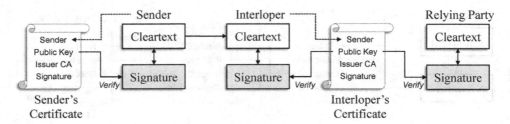

FIGURE 2.11   Subject self-signed certificates.

SPECIAL NOTE 2-1 SELF-SIGNED CERTIFICATES

Relying on self-signed certificates is a bad practice since they do not authenticate the subject of the certificate and because the contents are unreliable.

Except for root CA certificates that are installed and protected in trust stores to ensure and maintain their authenticity and integrity, subject self-signed certificates are unreliable. An example is shown in Figure 2.11 with the signer sending a signed cleartext message. The left side shows the legitimate sender signing the cleartext that can be verified using the sender's self-signed certificate. However, on the right side, an interloper has resigned modified cleartext but substituted a counterfeit self-signed certificate that contains the sender's name but the interloper's public key. The relying party verifies the signature on the substituted cleartext unknowingly using the interloper's certificate. Both the interloper's certificate and signed message verify because they were signed by the interloper's private key, but the relying party cannot distinguish between the sender's real certificate and the interloper's certificate. Thus, the content of a subject self-signed certificate is unreliable.

The discussions on certificate verification and certificate chain validation employed examples where the subject's public key was used to verify signed cleartext messages. It is important to recognize that a subject's asymmetric private key and certificate can be used for many other purposes including data encryption discussed in Section 2.1, "Encryption," key encryption discussed in Section 2.4, "Key Management," code signing, e-mails, and time stamps. Digital signatures for achieving nonrepudiation are discussed in Section 2.3, "Nonrepudiation," and cryptographic modules to protect asymmetric keys are discussed in Section 2.5, "Cryptographic Modules."

2.3 NONREPUDIATION

As described earlier, nonrepudiation is the process of deriving a nonrepudiation token from original information, usually called a signature. First, let's discuss why some of the other integrity and authentication mechanisms cannot provide nonrepudiation services.

Let's reconsider Figure 2.5, where the sender sends both the cleartext message and the MAC to the receiver for message integrity. Since only the sender and the receiver have access to the MAC key and the receiver did not send the cleartext message, the MAC also provides message authentication. However, since both the sender and the receiver have access to the MAC key and can generate the MAC, either might have also created the message, so the authentication and integrity are not provable to an independent third party, and therefore the MAC cannot provide nonrepudiation.

Arguably, a symmetric cipher scheme might be used for nonrepudiation. For example, as shown in Figure 2.12, if an authentication system enforced the use of two separate MAC keys, one for sending and the other for receiving, then this might meet third-party provability. But, unlike asymmetric ciphers, the key separation controls are not inherent within the cryptography but rather part of the application. Thus, the MAC keys are generated and exchanged with send-only and receive-only controls strictly enforced. For example, Party A might generate its send-only key, and when exchanged with Party B, the key is installed as a receive-only key. Likewise, Party B would generate a different send-only key, and when exchanged with Party A, the key is installed as a receive-only key. Clearly, additional access and execution controls are needed for this scenario. Regardless, while the cryptography scheme is an important aspect of the overall nonrepudiation services, it is not the only consideration.

Likewise, let's reconsider Figure 2.6, where the sender sends both the cleartext and HMAC to the receiver for message integrity. Since only the sender and the receiver have access to the HMAC key and the receiver did not send the cleartext message, the HMAC also provides message authentication. However, since both the sender and the receiver have access to the HMAC key and can generate the HMAC, either might have also created the message, so the authentication and integrity are not provable to an independent third party, and therefore the HMAC cannot provide nonrepudiation. Arguably, using two separate HMAC keys, one for sending and the other for receiving, might meet third-party provability, but again the cryptographic scheme is not the only consideration for nonrepudiation services.

Now let's reconsider Figure 2.7, where the sender sends both the cleartext and signature to the receiver for message integrity. Since only the sender has access to the private key, the signature also provides message authentication. Because the signature can only be generated using the private key, the authentication and integrity are provable to an independent third party, and therefore the signature can provide nonrepudiation. But once again, the cryptographic scheme is not the only consideration for nonrepudiation services.

Another method involves a combination of cryptographic hashes and digital signatures shown in Figure 2.13. Here, we provide an overview of trusted time stamp technology and the use of a Time Stamp

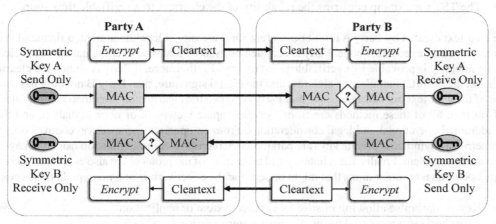

FIGURE 2.12   Message Authentication Code (MAC) nonrepudiation.

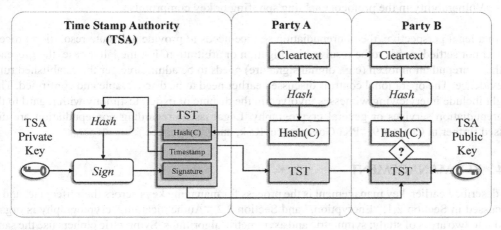

FIGURE 2.13   Time Stamp Token (TST).

Authority (TSA). The first step occurs when Party A generates a hash of its cleartext denoted hash(C) and provides it to the TSA, requesting a Time Stamp Token (TST). The TSA operates independently of Party A as either an external organization or a service encapsulated within a cryptographic module. Furthermore, the TSA never has access to the original cleartext, only the hash(C) of the cleartext [B.1.15].

The second step takes place when the TSA generates a Time Stamp Token (TST) by adding a time stamp to the submitted hash(C) and generating a signature over both elements. The TSA generates its own hash of the hash(C) and the time stamp and applies its private key to generate the signature. The time stamp is from a clock source that is calibrated to the International Timing Authority (ITA). Calibration means the time difference between the TSA clock and the ITA clock is registered; the clocks are not synchronized, as that would change the TSA clock. Other cryptographic mechanisms such as hash chains, MAC, or HMAC might be used; however, for the purposes of this book, we only refer to digital signatures. The TSA returns the TST to Party A.

The third step happens when Party A provides its cleartext message and the corresponding TST to Party B. Party B regenerates hash(C) from the cleartext and matches it to the hash(C) in the TST. Party B then verifies the TST signature using the TSA's public key. The TSA signature cryptographically binds the original hash(C) to the time stamp such that when Party B validates the TST, the following has been proved:

- The TST signature authenticates that the TST was generated by the TSA.
- The TST hash(C) confirms the integrity of the cleartext provided by Party A.
- The TST time stamp confirms the reliability of the cleartext to a verifiable time source.

The cleartext created by Party A might be content for a website, a legal document, a financial statement, or even an executable code. Party B can then be assured that whatever the nature of the cleartext, its integrity is provable to a verifiable point in time. Furthermore, if Party A signed the cleartext such that the hash(C) includes the cleartext and the digital signature, then Party B not only has assurance of the cleartext but can also prove that Party A signed the cleartext no later than the time stamp.

However, all of these methods are from a cryptographic viewpoint of nonrepudiation, and there are additional operational and legal considerations. From an operation perspective, controls over the symmetric or asymmetric private keys are paramount. Controls over the application using the keys are likewise as important. Finally, the reliability and robustness of the protocol are also essential. There are many operational considerations that might undermine the effectiveness of a nonrepudiation service:

- Key compromise allowing misuse by another system or application
- Unauthorized access to the key allowing system misuse
- Unauthorized access to the application allowing operational misuse
- Vulnerability in the protocol enabling spoofing or key compromise

From a legal perspective, the nonrepudiation service needs to provide a dispute resolution process and, if not settled, needs to be resolved in litigation or arbitration. For the latter case, the presence of the nonrepudiation token (e.g., digital signature) needs to be admissible per the established rules of evidence. The operational controls discussed earlier need to be discoverable and confirmed. This might include interviewing witnesses involved in the dispute or expert testimony with regard to the nonrepudiation services or general cryptography. Legal issues regarding nonrepudiation are discussed further in Chapter 9, "PKI Governance, Risk, and Compliance."

2.4   KEY MANAGEMENT

As described earlier, key management is the process for managing keys across their lifecycle, and as discussed in Section 2.1, "Encryption," and Section 2.2, "Authentication," cryptography is organized into two areas of study: symmetric and asymmetric algorithms. Symmetric ciphers use the same key for related functions, and asymmetric ciphers use different keys (public and private) for related functions. For symmetric ciphers, we discussed the following cryptographic operations:

- Encryption and decryption of data using a symmetric data encryption key (DEK).
- Generation and verification of a Message Authentication Code (MAC) using a symmetric MAC key.
- Generation and verification of a keyed Hash Message Authentication Code (HMAC) using a symmetric HMAC key.

For asymmetric ciphers, we discussed the following cryptographic operations:

- Encryption and decryption of data using an asymmetric key pair, where the data are encrypted using the public key and decrypted using the associated private key.
- Signature generation and verification using an asymmetric key pair, where the signature is generated using the private key and verified using the corresponding public key.

In addition to the aforementioned operations, we now discuss additional key management functions for both symmetric and asymmetric algorithms:

- Encryption and decryption of other keys using a symmetric key encryption key (KEK).
- Encryption and decryption of symmetric keys using an asymmetric key pair, where the key is encrypted using the public key and decrypted using the associated private key.
- Negotiation of symmetric keys using asymmetric key pairs; both parties use their private key, their public key, and the public key of the other party to derive a shared value.

In general, when a symmetric key is generated by one party and transmitted as ciphertext to the other party, this is called key transport. Conversely, when both sides negotiate the symmetric key without having to transmit it as ciphertext, this is called key agreement. Key transport and key agreement are collectively called key establishment. Figure 2.14 shows the encryption, transmission, and decryption of a symmetric key.

The sender generates a random symmetric key, encrypts it using a symmetric KEK, and transmits the ciphertext to the receiver. The receiver decrypts the ciphertext using the same KEK to recover the newly generated symmetric key. The KEK would have been previously established between the sender and the receiver and used exclusively for key encryption. There are several methods to establish a KEK including asymmetric key transport or key agreement protocol, or manual methods including key components or key shares, commonly called key splits in this book. Each of these methods has strengths and weaknesses, which are discussed further in more detail. The most important aspect of establishing a KEK, especially when using manual methods, is having documented procedures with good practices that are followed and kept as an audit log for subsequent review and confirmation.

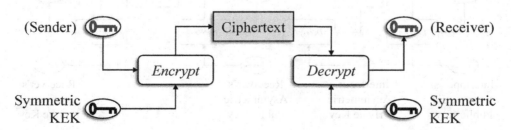

FIGURE 2.14   Symmetric key transport.

The purpose of the exchanged symmetric key is indeterminate without a bilateral agreement between the sender and the receiver or additional information transmitted along with the ciphertext. Such information about the exchanged symmetric key might be included as part of a key exchange protocol. For example, in Figure 2.12, we identified the scenario of exchanging not only a MAC key but also the key's directional usage (send vs. receive) as part of its control mechanisms. Some key establishment protocols provide explicit key exchange parameters, while others are implicit. Some data objects such as digital certificates or encrypted key blocks include explicit key usage information that applications are expected to obey. Some cryptographic products enforce key usage controls, while others do not. And sometimes the key exchange purpose is merely a contractual agreement between the participating parties with manual procedures that might require dual controls.

Figure 2.15 also depicts the encryption, transmission, and decryption of a symmetric key. Examples of key transport schemes include RSA Optimal Asymmetric Encryption Padding (OAEP) and the RSA Key Encapsulation Mechanism and Key Wrapping Scheme (KEM-KWS) methods [B.1.6] based on the paper "Method for Obtaining Digital Signatures and Public Key Cryptosystems" [B.7.5], published in 1976.

The sender generates a random symmetric key, encrypts it using the asymmetric public key of the receiver, and transmits the ciphertext to the receiver. The receiver decrypts the ciphertext using its asymmetric private key to recover the newly generated symmetric key. The receiver's public key would have been previously provided to the sender and used exclusively for key transport. Not shown is the encapsulation of the receiver's public key in a certificate. As discussed in Section 2.2, "Authentication," without the use of a digital certificate, the key transport is also vulnerable to a MITM attack, as shown in Figure 2.16. The presumption is the sender erroneously uses the interloper's public key instead of the receiver's public key.

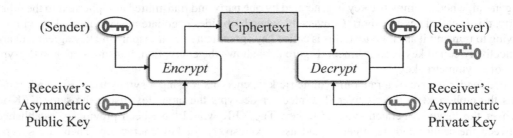

FIGURE 2.15   Asymmetric key transport.

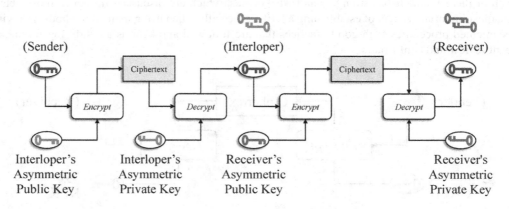

FIGURE 2.16   Asymmetric man-in-the-middle (MITM) key transport.

The sender generates a random symmetric key, encrypts it using the interloper's public key believing it was the receiver's public key, and transmits the ciphertext to the receiver. The ciphertext is intercepted and decrypted using the interloper's private key. At this point, the interloper now has a copy of the symmetric key. Using the receiver's public key, the interloper might re-encrypt the symmetric key or generate and encrypt another symmetric key, and then forward the ciphertext onto the receiver. Regardless, the receiver decrypts the ciphertext using its private key to recover the symmetric key. The sender and the receiver are under the false impression that they have securely exchanged a symmetric key without realizing the interloper is in the middle eavesdropping on any and all encrypted communications.

Figure 2.17 depicts a simplistic view of establishing a symmetric key without using key transport. Each party has its own asymmetric private key and public key certificate. The two parties must also exchange certificates. In general, each party using their own asymmetric key pair, and the public key of the other party, can mathematically compute a common shared secret from which a symmetric key is derived. The shared secret cannot be computed without access to one of the private keys. Thus, the symmetric key is not actually exchanged between the two parties. Examples of key agreement methods include Diffie–Hellman [B.1.5] based on the original paper "New Directions in Cryptography" [B.7.6], published in 1976, and elliptic curve cryptography (ECC) schemes [B.1.10] based on the papers "Uses of Elliptic Curves in Cryptography" [B.7.7] and "Elliptic Curve Cryptosystems" [B.7.8] independently authored two years apart.

The details of the key agreement process will vary depending on the algorithm employed. Some algorithms only require the private key of one and the public key of the other. Other algorithms use the key pair of one and the public key of the other. Yet others allow ephemeral key pairs, generated temporarily to increase the overall entropy of the symmetric key. In addition to the asymmetric keys, there are also domain parameters and other values that both parties need to agree upon for the crypto mathematics to operate successfully. These details are beyond the scope of this book but are available in various standards [B.1.5], [B.1.6], and [B.1.10] and specifications.

What we can say about symmetric and asymmetric keys is that there are security controls that must be in place in order for the overall system to be considered trustworthy. In general, we can treat symmetric keys and asymmetric private keys in a similar manner utilizing strong security controls around protecting the confidentiality of these keys. Note that asymmetric public keys have different requirements. We can summarize the primary key management controls: key confidentiality, key integrity, key authentication, and key authorization.

Key confidentiality: Symmetric and asymmetric private keys must be kept secret. Unlike data confidentiality where authorized entities are permitted to know the information, keys cannot be known by anyone. The primary key confidentiality control is the use of cryptographic hardware modules discussed in Section 2.5, "Cryptographic Modules." Some folks dispute this rule, claiming

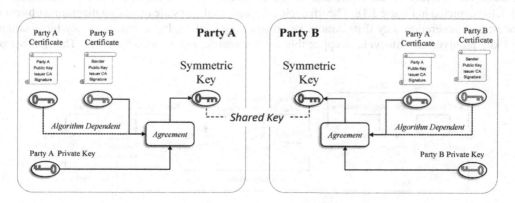

FIGURE 2.17 Asymmetric key agreement.

that key owners or system administrators are "authorized" to see or know keys; however, controls intended to prevent unauthorized access can fail, be circumvented, or individuals can be coerced. The better approach is to manage symmetric and asymmetric private keys such that they are never stored or displayed as cleartext. We summarize the key confidentiality controls as follows:

1. Symmetric keys and private asymmetric keys are used as cleartext inside cryptographic hardware modules but are not stored as cleartext outside the crypto module.
2. Symmetric keys and private asymmetric keys are stored as ciphertext outside cryptographic hardware modules.
3. Symmetric keys and private asymmetric keys are stored as key splits outside cryptographic hardware modules, managed using dual control and split knowledge. Each key split is managed by different individuals under supervision by a security officer to avoid collusion between the individuals.

It is important to recognize that key confidentiality does not apply to asymmetric public keys as knowledge of the public key does not reveal any information about the corresponding private key. Thus, the strength of PKI is that anyone can use the public key without endangering the security of the private key.

Key integrity: The integrity of any key must be maintained, including symmetric keys, asymmetric private keys, and asymmetric public keys. Controls must be in place to prevent the modification or substitution of any cryptographic key. More importantly, controls must also be in place to detect any adversarial or inadvertent modification or substitution. Any unintentional change must return an error and prevent the key from being used.

Key authentication: The authenticity of any key must be verified, including symmetric keys, asymmetric private keys, and public keys. Controls must be in place to prevent any illicit keys from entering the system. In addition, systems must have the capability to validate the key. Any failed validation must return an error and prevent the key from being used.

Key authorization: The use of symmetric and asymmetric private keys must be restricted to authorized entities. For example, individuals enter passwords to unlock keys, or applications are assigned processor identifiers with access to system files. Any unauthorized attempts must return an error and either trigger an alert for incident response or prevent the key from being used after some number of maximum attempts.

All four of these principal controls apply to the overall key management lifecycle. There are many key management models defined in many standards and specification, but for the purposes of this book, we refer to the American National Standard for PKI Asymmetric Key Management [B.1.14] depicted in Figure 2.18. The lifecycle is represented as a state transition diagram with seven nodes: key generation, key distribution, key usage, key backup, key revocation, key termination, and key archive. The lifecycle is applicable for symmetric and asymmetric keys. The number of

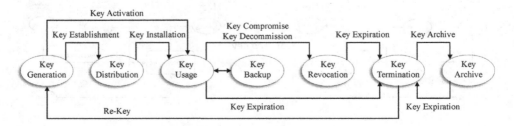

FIGURE 2.18 Key management lifecycle.

transition arrows has been simplified for our discussion. Depending on the application environment and events that drive the transitions, the cryptographic key state might not occur in every node.

Key Generation: This is the state when and where keys are generated for a specific purpose. Symmetric keys are basically random numbers, but asymmetric key pairs are more complex, incorporating random numbers and prime numbers in their creation. Keys might not be generated at the location or in the equipment they are to be used, and therefore might be distributed.

Key Distribution: This is the state when keys are transferred from where the keys were generated to the location or equipment where the keys are to be used. The distribution method might be accomplished using manual or automated processes, and depending on the method might occur in seconds, hours, or days.

Key Usage: This is the state when and where the keys are used for their intended purpose as an input into the cryptographic function. The key usage occurs within a cryptographic module that might be software or hardware, as discussed in Section 2.5, "Cryptographic Modules." In addition, the keys might be backed up and recovered to maintain system reliability.

Key Backup: This is the state when and where the keys are backed up for recovery purposes when the keys in use are inadvertently lost. When the keys are backed up they are often distributed from the usage to the backup locations, and when keys are recovered they are again distributed from the backup to the usage locations. Keys might also be backed up during distribution from generation to usage.

Key Revocation: This is the state where keys are removed from usage before their assigned expiration date due to operational or security issues. Operational issues include service cessation, merger, acquisition, or product end of life. Security issues include known or suspected system hacks, data breaches, or key compromises.

Key Termination: This is the state where keys are removed from usage or revocation when reaching their assigned expiration date. Essentially, every instance of the key is erased from all systems, including key backup, with the special exception of key archival. Termination might take seconds, hours, days, or longer to securely purge all key instances.

Key Archive: This is the state when and where keys are stored beyond their usage period for purposes of post-usage verification of information previously protected with the key. Archived keys are never reused in production systems but rather they are only utilized in archival systems.

Note that key escrow is not shown in Figure 2.18. Key escrow is a term borrowed from money escrow where funds are held by a third party for future dispersals such as mortgage insurance or property taxes and from software escrow where the source code is held by a third party in the event the provider goes bankrupt. Key escrow is the practice of storing keys for the explicit purpose of providing them to a third party. Third-party examples include government regulations, law enforcement in the event of a subpoena, or other legal obligations. In practice, key escrow is rarely used, and it would not be an independent key state, rather it would more likely be part of key backup or key archive to meet whatever escrow requirements might be imposed on the organization.

Now let's turn our attention to key management lifecycle controls. There are many standards and other resources that discuss key management controls in minute detail. It is not the intent of this book to reiterate what is already available. However, for continuity with later chapters, Table 2.3 provides a summary of controls. Each of the controls is discussed in more detail with references to relevant standards.

Crypto software: This control refers to cryptographic software modules that are basically software libraries that specialize in performing cryptographic functions that are accessible using cryptographic application programming interfaces (crypto API). Some operating systems provide native cryptographic capabilities, some programming languages provide additional cryptographic libraries,

TABLE 2.3
Key Management Lifecycle Controls

	Cryptographic Key Management Controls			
Key Lifecycle	Key Confidentiality	Key Integrity	Key Authentication	Key Authorization
Key Generation	Crypto software Crypto hardware	Key fingerprint Certificate	Originator ID	Access controls
Key Distribution	Key encryption Crypto hardware Key splits	Key fingerprint Certificate	Originator ID	Access controls Dual control Split knowledge
Key Usage	Key encryption Crypto software Crypto hardware	Key fingerprint Certificate	Source ID Requestor ID	Access controls
Key Backup	Key encryption Crypto hardware Key splits	Key fingerprint Certificate	Source ID	Access controls Dual control Split knowledge
Key Recovery	Key encryption Crypto hardware Key splits	Key fingerprint Certificate	Requestor ID	Access controls Dual control Split knowledge
Key Revocation	Key encryption Crypto software Crypto hardware Key splits	Key fingerprint Certificate	Source ID	Access controls Dual control
Key Termination	Key encryption Crypto software Crypto hardware Key splits	Key fingerprint Certificate	Source ID	Access controls Dual control
Key Archive	Key encryption Crypto hardware Key splits	Key fingerprint Certificate	Source ID	Access controls Dual control

and some systems need to incorporate third-party cryptographic toolkits. Cryptographic software modules are discussed in Section 2.5, "Cryptographic Modules."

Key encryption: This control refers to the storage or transmission of cryptographic keys as ciphertext. The cryptographic keys are encrypted using a key encryption key (KEK). KEKs are used solely to encrypt other keys; they are never used for any data functions such as data encryption, MAC, HMAC, or digital signatures. Key encryption is used for storage or transmission of other keys as ciphertext that provides key confidentiality.

Crypto hardware: This control refers to cryptographic hardware modules that consist of software, firmware, and hardware components that specialize in performing cryptographic functions accessible via API calls. Application developers incorporate cryptographic hardware modules, commonly called hardware security modules (HSMs), from vendors who manufacture cryptographic devices. Note that HSM vendors undergo mergers and acquisitions just like any other technology industries with products that suffer end-of-life time frames. Cryptographic hardware modules are discussed in Section 2.5, "Cryptographic Modules."

Key splits: This control refers to various techniques for dividing up keys into multiple parts. One common method is key components, and another is key shares. We use the term "splits" to refer to either method. Key splits provide key confidentiality.

Key components: This method uses the binary operator "exclusive or" often denoted by the abbreviation XOR or the $\oplus$ symbol. In general, 2 bits are combined such that if they are the same, the result is a binary 0; otherwise, if they are different, the result is a binary 1, that is: $0 \oplus 0 = 0$, $0 \oplus 1 = 1$, $1 \oplus 0 = 1$, and $1 \oplus 1 = 0$. For example, two individuals can each have a key component that is a binary string such that neither knows the other's key component, but when the two strings are combined using XOR, a key is formed. Knowing a bit in one string but not knowing the corresponding bit in the other string does not reveal any information about the bit in the key.

Key components can support any number of strings but to recover the key, all of them must be available. For instance, if the key is split into five key components where each is assigned to different individuals, then all five key component holders are needed to recover the key.

In practice, key components are typically written on paper and kept locked up by the key component holder (also called a key component custodian). Unlike passwords, key components are too long for an average person to remember. For example, using hexadecimal notation an AES-128 key component might be:

c7e2 f303 878a5 22d7 ef46 4ab0 317b dbe9

where each "hex" digit represents 4 bits. The key component is entered manually by each component holder, outside the view of the others, until all of the components have been entered. The key components are then locked up securely. This key management process is often supervised by a security officer and sometimes observed by an auditor [B.1.2].

Key shares: This method uses an algebraic equation, such as Shamir's Secret Sharing [B.7.9] such that the key is divided into M parts but only N parts are needed to recover the key. This is called an N of M scheme, where N < M. For example, 3 of 7 might be chosen where the key is divided into M = 7 parts and assigned to seven individuals, where only N = 3 individuals are needed to recover the key. The formula to calculate N possible combinations from M available individuals is M!/N! (M − N)! where "!" is the factorial function. So, for N = 3 and M = 7, we have $7! = 7 \times 6 \times 5 \times 4 \times 3 \times 2 \times 1 = 5040$ and $3! = 3 \times 2 \times 1 = 6$ so $(7 − 3)! = 4 \times 3 \times 2 \times 1 = 24$ such that 5040/(6 × 24) or 5040/144 = 35 possible combinations. Thus, there are 35 ways for 3 of 7 key shares to recover the key. Unlike key components, key shares are large numbers that are too big to use paper, so it is a common practice for the key shares to be written to removable media where each device is assigned to a key share holder. The devices are often PIN activated such that mere possession is insufficient to enter the key share. Each device is inserted into a device reader that uses the key shares to solve the equation and recover the key.

Key fingerprint: This control is a generic term that refers to a cryptographically derived checksum that provides a relatively unique reference value per key. Fingerprints provide key integrity and a means to verify a key value without having to display the actual key.

- For symmetric keys, the historical method is a key check value (KCV) that is created by encrypting a string of binary zeroes and commonly using the leftmost six digits as the KCV [B.1.2].
- For asymmetric keys, the common method is a hash of each key, one for the public key and another for the private key. Note that the key fingerprint algorithm may differ per vendor or crypto product but SHA1 is commonly used. Regardless of the algorithm, the key fingerprint can be used to verify the key stored in an HSM or when using key splits. The recovered key might have a fingerprint as well as each key split.

Certificate: This control refers to digital certificates introduced in Section 2.2, "Authentication." As discussed earlier, the certificate signature is over all of the certificate fields, which provides cryptographic bindings between the sender's name, public key, and the CA name. The certificate provides integrity of the public key. Certificates can also have a fingerprint, called a thumbprint, which is a hash of the whole certificate, including its digital signature.

Originator ID: This control refers to the key generation system. Tracking the origin of the key helps to maintain the overall system authentication.

Source ID: This control refers to the key usage system. Tracking the source of the cryptographic function and the associated key helps to maintain the overall system authentication.

Requestor ID: This control refers to the application accessing the cryptographic function. Tracking which requestor accessed the cryptographic function and the associated key helps to maintain the overall system integrity.

Access controls: These controls refer to the permissions granted to the originator, source, and requestors. Requestors include applications, end users, and system administrators. Access controls restrict who can perform key establishment, key installation, key activation, key backup and recovery, key revocation, key expiration, rekey, key archive, and other cryptographic functions.

Dual control with split knowledge: This control refers to the use of key splits for key distribution or key backup and recovery. Assigning different splits to different individuals is the essence of split knowledge, as no one person knows the value of the actual key. Requiring more than one person for a cryptographic function is the basis for dual control.

Certificate management is a subset of key management and follows the same patterns shown in Figure 2.18. The certificate contains information about the public key and indicates information about the corresponding private key. In addition to the certificate fields listed in Table 2.2, there are other basic certificate fields and certificate extensions. Another important certificate field is the validity element, which contains the start "not before" and end "not after" dates. Figure 2.10 shows how to walk up the chain and verify each certificate coming down the chain, but in addition, the validity dates of each certificate must also be checked. If the current date is not between the start and end dates, then the validation fails. Thus, the application performing the validation must be cognizant of the current date and time with an accurate clock.

The certificate extensions are related to X.509 v3 format. Each extension has an object identifier (OID), which asserts its presence, and the corresponding content. Other essential fields are the certificate revocation list (CRL) distribution points and authority information access extensions. The CRL extension provides a link to the CRL, and the authority extension provides a link to the Online Certificate Status Protocol (OCSP) service. If a certificate is revoked prior to its expiration not after date, the CRL or an OCSP responder provides a mechanism to check the certificate status. If any of the certificates within the chain have been revoked, then the validation fails.

2.5 CRYPTOGRAPHIC MODULES

The concept of a cryptographic module was introduced in Section 2.2, "Authentication," and Section 2.4, "Key Management," where differences between software and hardware modules were identified. NIST operates the Cryptographic Module Validation Program (CMVP) based on the Federal Information Processing Standard (FIPS) 140 revisions (140, 140–1, 140–2, and 140–3), which 140–2 [B.5.3] provides the current definitions:

- Cryptographic module: The set of hardware, software, and/or firmware that implements approved security functions (including cryptographic algorithms and key generation) and is contained within the cryptographic boundary.
- Cryptographic boundary: An explicitly defined continuous perimeter that establishes the physical bounds of a cryptographic module and contains all the hardware, software, and/or firmware components of a cryptographic module.

FIPS 140 was redesignated in April 1982 from Federal Standard 1027 General Security Requirements for Equipment Using the Data Encryption Standard. This standard specified the minimum general security requirements for implementing the Data Encryption Standard (DES) algorithm [B.5.1] in a telecommunications environment.

FIPS 140–1 was revised in January 1994 and renamed Security Requirements for Cryptographic Modules. This standard introduced four security levels from lowest to highest: level 1, level 2, level 3, and level 4. This version became effective six months later, in June 1994, and the previous version was deprecated three years afterward, in June 1997.

FIPS 140–2 [B.5.3] was revised in May 2011, which became effective six months later, in October 2011, and the previous version was deprecated six months afterward, in March 2012. Products certified per FIPS 140–1 were moved to a historical list.

FIPS 14–3 [B.5.36] was revised in March 2019, which became effective six months later, in August 2020, and the previous version was deprecated six months afterward, in January 2021. This version refers to ISO/IEC 19790 [B.4.12] and ISO/IEC 24759 [B.4.13]. Products certified per FIPS 140–2 were moved to a historical list.

While there are international and country-specific standards and validation programs, for the purposes of this book, we refer to FIPS 140–3 as the de facto standard. This is a common approach supported by many others. Another recognized standard is the Common Criteria transformed into ISO/IEC 15408 Information Technology – Security Techniques – Evaluation Criteria for IT Security [B.4.7], but this standard provides a security language to develop either security targets or protection profiles (PPs) for laboratory evaluations. Examples include the German cryptographic modules, security level "enhanced" [B.7.10], and the European Union cryptographic module for CSP signing operations [B.7.11]. For the financial services industry, there is also ISO 13491 Banking – Secure Cryptographic Devices (Retail), but unlike the CMVP, there is no corresponding validation program. Regardless, FIPS 140–3 defines four security levels (level 1 is the lowest) with 11 distinct security areas.

SPECIAL NOTE 2-2 SECURITY LEVELS

It is a common misconception that cryptographic hardware modules are automatically rated at higher levels 4 or 3, as many hardware modules are actually rated at software levels 2 or 1.

For example, the August 2015 CMVP list has over 2,200 product certificates issued by NIST to more than 400 manufacturers. FIPS 140–2 Security Levels 1 and 2 were designed for software modules, whereas levels 3 and 4 were designed for hardware modules. Roughly 67% of the products are listed as hardware, 29% as software, and 3% as firmware. However, only 1% of the hardware modules are rated at level 4 and 26% are rated level 3; 61% are rated at level 2 and 12% are rated at level 1. Thus, the majority 73% of cryptographic hardware modules are rated at a security level typical of a cryptographic software module. The reader should always check the security level of the FIPS certification.

The previous edition of this book discussed the FIPS 140–2 security areas, and while this edition discusses the FIPS 140–3 security areas, the ISO/IEC 19790 international standard has reorganized the security areas. Table 2.4 provides a summary comparison between the FIPS 140–2 versus the FIPS 140–3 security areas.

The following chapters provide a summary for the 11 FIPS 140–3 security areas.

2.5.1 CRYPTOGRAPHIC MODULE SPECIFICATION

Most HSMs have different operating modes, and how they are operated determines the actual FIPS 140–2 security level at which they are certified. Each cryptographic module certification includes a vendor-provided security policy that defines the configuration and the operating mode. Note that using a

TABLE 2.4
Summary Comparison

FIPS 140–2	FIPS 140–3
Cryptographic Module Specification	Cryptographic Module Specification
Cryptographic Module Ports and Interfaces	Cryptographic Module Ports and Interfaces
Roles, Services, and Authentication	Roles, Services, and Authentication
Finite State Model	Finite State Model is included in Life Cycle Assurance
Physical Security	Physical Security
Operational Environment	Operational Environment
Cryptographic Key Management	Sensitive Security Parameter Management
EMI/EMC	Federal Communications Commission (FCC) Code of Federal Regulations (CFR), Title 47, Part 15 regarding unlicensed transmissions is out of scope.
Self-Tests	Self-Tests
Design Assurance	Design Assurance is included in Life Cycle Assurance
Mitigation of Other Attacks	Mitigation of Other Attacks
Software/Firmware Security is addressed in Design Assurance	Software/Firmware Security
Telecommunications Electronics Materials Protected from Emanating Spurious Transmissions (TEMPEST) is addressed in Mitigation of Other Attacks	Non-Invasive Security
Software development practices addressed in Appendix B	Life-Cycle Assurance

TABLE 2.5
Cryptographic Module Specification

	Security Level 1	Security Level 2	Security Level 3	Security Level 4
FIPS 140–2	Specification of cryptographic module, cryptographic boundary, approved algorithms, and approved modes of operation; description of cryptographic module, including all hardware, software, and firmware components; includes statement of module security policy.			
FIPS 140–3	Specification of cryptographic module, cryptographic boundary, approved security functions, and normal and degraded modes of operation. Description of cryptographic module, including all hardware, software, and firmware components. All services provide status information to indicate when the service utilizes an approved cryptographic algorithm, security function, or process in an approved manner.			

cryptographic module outside the parameters of the security policy invalidates the FIPS operating mode. For example, if a cryptographic hardware module has a Security Level 3 certification but is operated in a different mode, the device is not magically a level 2, and it is simply no longer a level 3. Regardless, we now take a look at the security areas for each of the FIPS 140–2 and FIPS 140–3 security areas.

Requirements are summarized for both FIPS 140–2 and FIPS 140–3 in Table 2.5.

A cryptographic module must implement at least one approved security function used in an approved mode of operation. Unapproved security functions and modes may also be included; however, the operator shall be able to determine the difference. The NIST standard provides the following definitions for approved functions and approved modes of operation:

- Approved security function: For this standard, a security function (e.g., cryptographic algorithm, cryptographic key management technique, or authentication technique) that is either specified or adopted in an approved standard.
- Approved mode of operation: A mode of the cryptographic module that employs only approved security functions (not to be confused with a specific mode of an approved security function, e.g., Data Encryption Standard (DES) CBC mode).

For Security Levels 1 and 2, the cryptographic module security policy may specify when a cryptographic module is performing in an approved mode of operation; however, for Security Levels 3 and 4, the cryptographic module shall indicate when an approved mode of operation is selected. Furthermore, for any security level, the manufacturer must provide documentation as to which hardware, software, and firmware components reside within the security boundary, along with input and output ports, including the associated data paths.

Approved algorithm in FIPS 140–2 has been expanded to approved security functions.

Approved modes of operation in FIPS 140–2 has been expanded to normal and degraded modes of operation.

Statement of module security policy in FIPS 140–2 has been expanded to all services providing status information for services utilizing algorithms, security functions, or processes.

2.5.2 CRYPTOGRAPHIC MODULE INTERFACES

The cryptographic modules must have four logical application programming interfaces (API) for data input, data output, control input, and status output. External electrical power sources need a power port but not internal sources such as batteries. Furthermore, the data output path shall be logically disabled while performing key generation, manual key entry, or key zeroization.

Requirements are summarized for FIPS 140–2 and FIPS 140–3 in Table 2.6.

For Security Levels 1 and 2, the physical ports and logical API can be shared for any data and cryptographic keys. For levels 3 and 4, the physical ports or logical API for cryptographic keys shall be physically separated from all other data ports and be directly entered into the module, such as using a trusted path or directly attached cable.

Requirements for Security Level 1 and Security Level 2 are the same.

Requirements for Security Level 3 and Security Level 4 in FIPS 140–2 have been redefined using the term "trusted channel." A trusted channel is a link established between the cryptographic module and a sender or receiver to securely communicate unprotected plaintext CSPs, key components, and authentication data. A trusted channel protects against eavesdropping, as well as physical or logical tampering by unwanted operators/entities, processes, or other devices, between the module's defined input or output ports and along the communication link with the intended sender or receiver endpoint.

2.5.3 ROLES, SERVICES, AND AUTHENTICATION

Cryptographic modules must support a minimum of three authorized roles, but others are allowed. An operator may assume multiple roles. If a cryptographic module supports concurrent operators, then it shall separate and maintain roles and the corresponding services:

- User role: The role assumed to perform general security services, including cryptographic operations and other approved security functions.

TABLE 2.6
Cryptographic Module Ports and Interfaces

	Security Level 1	Security Level 2	Security Level 3	Security Level 4
FIPS 140–2	Required and optional interfaces. Specification of all interfaces and of all input and output data paths.		Data ports for unprotected critical security parameters logically or physically separated from other data ports.	
FIPS 140–3	Required and optional interfaces. Specification of all interfaces and of all input and output data paths.		Trusted channel.	

- Crypto officer role: The role assumed to perform cryptographic initialization or management functions (e.g., module initialization, input/output of cryptographic keys and critical security parameter [CSP], and audit functions).
- Maintenance role: The role assumed to perform physical maintenance and/or logical maintenance services (e.g., hardware/software diagnostics). All plaintext secret and private keys and unprotected CSP shall be zeroized when entering or exiting the maintenance role.

An operator is not required to assume an authorized role to perform services where cryptographic keys or CSP are not modified, disclosed, or substituted (e.g., show status, self-tests, or other services that do not affect the security of the module). In addition to the roles, services include all operations, functions, and features that can be performed by cryptographic modules. All cryptographic modules must support a minimum of three services:

- Show status: Output the current status of the cryptographic module.
- Perform self-tests: Initiate and run self-tests.
- Perform approved security function: Perform at least one approved security function used in an approved mode of operation.

Cryptographic modules may provide other services including unapproved functions, and specific services may be provided in more than one role (e.g., key entry services may be provided in the user role and the crypto officer role). Documentation must include all services performed by the cryptographic module, the service inputs and outputs, the roles allowed to access the services, and which services require an authorized role versus an unauthorized role. Depending on the security level, the cryptographic module must support either role-based or identity-based authentication mechanisms:

- Role-based authentication: The module requires that one or more roles be either implicitly or explicitly selected by the operator and the module authenticates the role (or set of roles). The individual identity of the operator need not be authenticated, and the role is implicitly authorized. If an operator is permitted to change roles, then the next role must be authenticated if the previous role was not.
- Identity-based authentication: The module requires that the operator be individually identified, that one or more roles be either implicitly or explicitly selected by the operator, and authenticated, and that the module authorizes the operator. Roles may be combined for each individual. If an operator is permitted to change roles, then the individual must be authenticated in the new role if the previous role was not.

Requirements are summarized for FIPS 140–2 and FIPS 140–3 in Table 2.7.

TABLE 2.7

Roles, Services, and Authentication

	Security Level 1	Security Level 2	Security Level 3	Security Level 4
FIPS 140–2	Logical separation of required and optional roles and services	Role-based or identity-based operator authentication	Identity-based operator authentication	
FIPS 140–3	Logical separation of required and optional roles and services	Role-based or identity-based operator authentication	Identity-based operator authentication	Multifactor authentication

Authentication methods for individuals include knowledge factors, possession factors, and biometrics. This book recognizes control factors (e.g., cryptographic key) in Chapter 1, "Introduction," as a separate method, but FIPS 140–2 includes keys as a knowledge factor. Individual authentication is not required, but role-based service separation is needed. For Security Level 2, role-based authentication is required. For Security Levels 3 and 4, identity-based authentication is required. Documentation must specify the authentication mechanisms, the types of authentication data, the initial and subsequent authentication methods, and the relative authentication strengths.

Authentication for Security Level 1, Security Level 2, and Security Level 3 are the same.

Authentication for Security Level 4 in FIPS 140–2 has been increased in FIPS 140–3 from identity-based to multifactor authentication (MFA) using any two or more single-factor authentication.

2.5.4 Software and Firmware Security

While a cryptographic module is defined as a hardware, software, firmware, or hybrid module, this section defines requirements that apply to the software and firmware components of a cryptographic module. One of the main requirements is the use of approved integrity techniques applied to all software and firmware components within the module's defined cryptographic boundary. The integrity techniques are automatically used during self-testing or manually initiated on command by an authorized operator.

Requirements are summarized for FIPS 140–3 in Table 2.8.

FIPS 140–2 includes software and firmware security within its Operating System Requirements section, while FIPS 140–3 addresses this area in a separate section. This is one of several areas where FIPS 140–2 and FIPS 140–3 have restructured the requirements. For the purposes of this book, the FIPS 140–3 structure is followed with cross-references to FIPS 140–2. Hopefully, this approach is useful to the reader, as the industry migrates from FIPS 140–2 to FIPS 140–3.

Software or Firmware Module Interface (SFMI): The total set of interfaces used to request the services of the software or the firmware module, including parameters that enter or leave the module's cryptographic boundary as part of the requested service.

Hybrid Software or Hybrid Firmware Module Interface (HSMI or HFMI): The total set of interfaces used to request the services of the hybrid software or hybrid firmware module, including parameters that enter or leave the module's cryptographic boundary as part of the requested service.

2.5.5 Operational Environment

The operational environment of a cryptographic module refers to the management of the software, firmware, or hardware components required for the module to operate. An operating system is an important component of the operating environment of a cryptographic module.

TABLE 2.8
Software and Firmware Security

	Security Level 1	Security Level 2	Security Level 3	Security Level 4
FIPS 140–2		No specific requirements.		
FIPS 140–3	Approved integrity technique, defined SFMI, HFMI, and HSMI	Approved digital signature or keyed message authentication code-based integrity test	Approved digital signature-based integrity test	

Requirements are summarized for FIPS 140–2 and FIPS 140–3 in Table 2.9.

- A non-modifiable operational environment is designed or configured in a manner to prevent modification by an operator or process to the module components, the computing platform, or the operating system. This environment may consist of a firmware module operating in a non-programmable computing platform or a hardware module, which prevents the loading of any additional software or firmware.
- A limited operational environment is designed or configured in a manner to allow controlled modification by an operator or process to the module components, the computing platform, or the operating system. This environment may be firmware operating in a programmable hardware module where the loading of additional firmware meets the firmware loading requirements specified for firmware or software loading (see Section 2.5.4 Software and Firmware Security).
- A modifiable operational environment refers to an operating environment that may be reconfigured to add/delete/modify functionality, and/or may include general-purpose operating system capabilities (e.g., use of a computer operating system, configurable smartcard operating system, or programmable software). Operating systems are considered to be modifiable operational environments if software components can be modified by an operator or process and/or an operator or process can load and execute software (e.g., a word processor) that is not part of the defined software, firmware, or hybrid module.

For Security Level 1, the cryptographic software and firmware shall be installed such that the software and firmware source and executable code are protected from unauthorized disclosure and modification. In addition, a cryptographic mechanism (e.g., message authentication or digital signature algorithm) must be used for cryptographic software and firmware to ensure its integrity. Single operator mode and restricted access to keys and CSP to prevent use by any other processes are additional requirements for Security Level 1 only.

For Security Level 2, in addition to the applicable requirements for Security Level 1, all cryptographic software and firmware, cryptographic keys and CSPs, and control and status information shall be under the control of a trusted operating system (e.g., a PP for Evaluation Assurance Level 3 per the Common Criteria).

Originally published as the Common Criteria for Information Technology (IT) Security Evaluation but later transformed as ISO/IEC 15408, this international standard is the basis for evaluation of security properties of IT products and systems. While still referred to as the *Common Criteria*, this standard is sometimes used as an alternative method to FIPS 140–2 for evaluating cryptographic modules, although FIPS 140–2 does refer to Evaluation Assurance Levels in several areas, so it can

TABLE 2.9
Operational Environment

	Security Level 1	Security Level 2	Security Level 3	Security Level 4
FIPS 140–2	Single operator. Executable code. Approved integrity technique.	Referenced PPs evaluated at EAL2 with specified discretionary access control mechanisms and auditing.	Referenced PPs plus trusted path evaluated at EAL3 plus security policy modeling.	Referenced PPs plus trusted path evaluated at EAL4.
FIPS 140–3	Non-Modifiable, Limited or Modifiable. Control of SSPs.	Modifiable. Role-based or discretionary access control. Audit mechanism.	No additional requirements.	

get rather confusing. ISO/IEC 15408 consists of the following parts, under the general title Evaluation Criteria for Information Technology Security.

- Part 1: Introduction and general model
- Part 2: Security functional requirements
- Part 3: Security assurance requirements

The Evaluation Assurance Levels (EALs) defined in Part 3 provide an increasing scale that balances the level of assurance obtained with the cost and feasibility of acquiring the assurance. The EALs are defined in either industry Protection Profiles (PP) or manufacturer Security Target (ST).

- Evaluation Assurance Level 1 (EAL1): Functionally tested
- Evaluation Assurance Level 2 (EAL2): Structurally tested
- Evaluation Assurance Level 3 (EAL3): Methodically tested and checked
- Evaluation Assurance Level 4 (EAL4): Methodically designed, tested, and reviewed
- Evaluation Assurance Level 5 (EAL5): Semiformally designed and tested
- Evaluation Assurance Level 6 (EAL6): Semiformally verified design and tested
- Evaluation Assurance Level 7 (EAL7): Formally verified design and tested

While EALs are required with Security Levels 2, 3, and 4 for FIPS 140–2, there are no additional security requirements with Security Levels 3 and 4 for FIPS 140–3. Further, FIPS 140–3 does not refer to Evaluation Assurance Levels or Common Criteria.

2.5.6 Physical Security

Cryptographic module shall employ physical security mechanisms to restrict unauthorized physical access to the contents of the module and to deter unauthorized use, modification, or substitution of the module when installed.

Requirements are summarized for FIPS 140–2 and FIPS 140–3 in Table 2.10.

All hardware, software, firmware, and data components within the cryptographic boundary shall be protected. FIPS 140–2 and FIPS 140–3 recognize three physical embodiments of a cryptographic module:

- Single-chip cryptographic modules are physical embodiments in which a single integrated circuit (IC) chip may be used as a stand-alone device or may be embedded within an enclosure or a product that may not be physically protected. Examples include single IC chips or smart cards with a single IC chip.

TABLE 2.10
Physical Security

	Security Level 1	Security Level 2	Security Level 3	Security Level 4
FIPS 140–2	Production grade equipment.	Locks or tamper evidence.	Tamper detection and response for covers and doors.	Tamper detection and response envelope. EFP or EFT.
FIPS 140–3	Production-grade components.	Tamper evidence. Opaque covering or enclosure.	Tamper detection and response for covers and doors. Strong enclosure or coating. Protection from direct probing. EFP or EFT.	Tamper detection and response envelope. EFP. Fault injection mitigation.

- Multiple-chip-embedded cryptographic modules are physical embodiments in which two or more IC chips are interconnected and are embedded within an enclosure or a product that may not be physically protected. Examples include adapters and expansion boards.
- Multiple-chip stand-alone cryptographic modules are physical embodiments in which two or more IC chips are interconnected and the entire enclosure is physically protected. Examples include encrypting routers or secure radios.

Another example of multiple-chip stand-alone cryptographic modules is an HSM used by a CA to protect the asymmetric private keys for signing certificates and status information. The physical security requirements for the security levels are summarized as follows. Note that these requirements apply to hardware only and not software or firmware modules. Further, when a cryptographic module is implemented solely in software, its physical security is wholly dependent on the host platform on which it operates.

Security Level 1 requires minimal physical protection.

Security Level 2 requires the addition of tamper-evident mechanisms. Tamper evidence is expanded to include opaque covering or enclosure for FIPS 140–3.

Security Level 3 adds requirements for the use of strong enclosures with tamper detection and response mechanisms for removable covers and doors. Environmental failure protection (EFP) or environmental failure testing (EFT) is also required for FIPS 140–3.

Security Level 4 adds requirements for the use of strong enclosures with tamper detection and response mechanisms for the overall enclosure. EPP and fault injection mitigation are also required for FIPS 140–3.

FIPS 140–3 notes that tamper detection and tamper response are not substitutes for tamper evidence. All three are needed for Security Level 3 and Security Level 4.

2.5.7 Non-Invasive Security

Non-invasive attacks attempt to compromise a cryptographic module by acquiring knowledge of the module's CSPs without physically modifying or invading the module. Modules may implement various techniques to mitigate these types of attacks.

Requirements are summarized for FIPS 140–3 in Table 2.11.

Security Levels 1 and 2 require that documentation specify all of the mitigation techniques employed to protect the module's CSPs from non-invasive attacks, including the effectiveness for each mitigation technique referenced in Annex F.

Security Levels 3 and 4 require that the cryptographic module be tested to meet the approved non-invasive attack mitigation test metrics referenced in Annex F.

However, no approved non-invasive attack mitigation test metrics are defined in Annex F.

2.5.8 Sensitive Security Parameter Management

FIPS 140–3 refers to Sensitive Security Parameters (SSPs), which consist of Critical Security Parameters (CSPs) and Public Security Parameters (PSPs). The security requirements for SSP

TABLE 2.11

Non-Invasive Security

	Security Level 1	Security Level 2	Security Level 3	Security Level 4
FIPS 140–2	No specific requirements.			
FIPS 140–3	Module is designed to mitigate against non-invasive attacks specified in Annex F: Approved Non-Invasive Attack Mitigation Test Metrics.			

management encompass the entire lifecycle of SSPs employed by the module. SSP management includes random bit generators (RBGs), SSP generation, SSP establishment, SSP entry/output, SSP storage, and unprotected SSP zeroization.

Requirements are summarized for FIPS 140–2 and FIPS 140–3 in Table 2.12.

Security Level 1 and Security Level 2 allow plaintext CSPs, key components, and authentication data to be entered and output via physical port(s) and logical interface(s) shared with other physical ports and logical interfaces of the cryptographic module.

For software modules or the software components of a hybrid software module, CSPs, key components, and authentication data may be entered into or output in either encrypted or plaintext form provided that the CSPs, key components, and authentication data are maintained within the operational environment (see Section 2.5.5 "Operational Environment").

Security Level 3 further requires that CSPs, key components, and authentication data be entered into or output from the module either encrypted or by a trusted channel (see Section 2.5.2 "Cryptographic Module Interfaces").

Security Level 4 also requires that the module employ multifactor separate identity-based operator authentication for entering or outputting each key component (see Section 2.5.3 "Roles, Services, and Authentication").

Cryptographic key management in FIPS 140–2 is renamed in FIPS 140–3 to Sensitive Security Parameter Management.

Cryptographic keys in FIPS 140–2 are expanded in FIPS 140–3 to include Sensitive Security Parameters, which include Critical Security Parameters and Public Security Parameters.

Key generation in FIPS 140–2 is redefined in FIPS 140–3 as random bit generators for SSP generation.

Automated SSP transport and agreement methods in FIPS 140–3 are separated from other SSP establishment methods.

2.5.9 SELF-TESTS

Cryptographic module self-tests provide assurance that faults have not been introduced that prevent the module's correct operation. Pre-operational self-tests are successfully performed prior to the module providing any data output via the data output interface. Conditional self-tests are performed when an applicable security function or process is invoked.

Requirements are summarized for FIPS 140–2 and FIPS 140–3 in Table 2.13.

TABLE 2.12
Sensitive Security Parameter Management

	Security Level 1	Security Level 2	Security Level 3	Security Level 4
FIPS 140–2	Key management mechanisms: random number and key generation, key establishment, key distribution, key entry/output, key storage, and key zeroization.			
	Secret and private keys established using manual methods may be entered or output in plaintext form.		Secret and private keys established using manual methods shall be entered or output encrypted or with split knowledge procedures.	
FIPS 140–3	Random bit generators, SSP generation, establishment, entry and output, storage and zeroization.			
	Automated SSP transport or SSP agreement using approved methods.			
	Manually established SSPs may be entered or output in plaintext form.		Manually established SSPs may be entered or output in either encrypted form, via a trusted channel or using split knowledge procedures.	

If a cryptographic module fails a self-test, the module enters an error state, outputs an error indicator, and the module cannot perform any cryptographic operations or output control and data via the control and data output interface while in an error state.

Self-tests in FIPS 140–2 are organized into pre-operational and conditional tests.

2.5.10 LIFE CYCLE ASSURANCE

Life-cycle assurance addresses requirements for configuration management, design, finite state model, development, testing, delivery and operation, and guidance documentation. The vendor documentation provides *best practices* for development, deployment, operations, and eventual end-of-life disposal processes.

Finite State Model, Design Assurance, and Appendix B: Software Development Practices in FIPS 140–2 is mapped to the Life Cycle Assurance security topic in FIPS 140–3, including Configuration Management, Design, Development, Delivery and Operation, and Guidance.

The *configuration management* topic provides assurance that the integrity of the cryptographic module is maintained during refinement and modification of the cryptographic module and related documentation. Controls prevent accidental or unauthorized modifications, and controls provide change traceability for the cryptographic module and related documentation. See Table 2.14.

The *design* topic addresses the functional specifications for a cryptographic module. The specifications provide assurance that the cryptographic module functionality complies with the corresponding security policy. See Table 2.15.

TABLE 2.13
Self-Tests

	Security Level 1	Security Level 2	Security Level 3	Security Level 4
FIPS 140–2	Power-up tests: cryptographic algorithm tests, software/firmware integrity tests, critical functions tests. Conditional tests.			
FIPS 140–3	Pre-operational: software/firmware integrity, bypass, and critical functions test. Conditional: cryptographic algorithm, pair-wise consistency, software/firmware loading, manual entry, conditional bypass, and critical functions test.			

TABLE 2.14
Configuration Management

	Security Level 1	Security Level 2	Security Level 3	Security Level 4
FIPS 140–2	Configuration management (CM).	CM system.	No additional requirements.	
FIPS 140–3	Configuration management system for cryptographic module, components, and documentation – each uniquely identified and tracked throughout lifecycle.		Automated configuration management system.	

TABLE 2.15
Design

	Security Level 1	Security Level 2	Security Level 3	Security Level 4
FIPS 140–2	Design and policy correspondence.	Functional specification.	High-level language implementation.	Formal model. Detailed explanations (informal proofs).
FIPS 140–3	Module designed to allow testing of all provided security-related services.			

The *finite state model* topic addresses the cryptographic module state transitions, including power on and power off, initialization, administrative states, operational states, self-tests, and error states. Each state is fully documented. See Table 2.16.

Finite State Model in FIPS 140–2 is mapped to Finite State Model (FSM) in FIPS 140–3.

The *development* topic addresses implementation of the functional specifications, security policy compliance, maintainability, and consistently reproducible. Level 1 requirements address source code, development tools, and hardware documentation. Levels 2 and 3 include industry non-proprietary development tools and avoidance of unnecessary code. Level 4 includes fully documented hardware, firmware, and software components. See Table 2.17.

The *testing* topic addresses vendor testing of the security functionality providing assurance that the cryptographic module behaves in accordance with the module security policy and functional specifications. Levels 1 and 2 specify the functional tests. Levels 3 and 4 include test procedures and results. See Table 2.18.

FIPS 140–2 includes Environmental Failure Protection (EFP): The use of features to protect against a compromise of the security of a cryptographic module due to environmental conditions or fluctuations outside of the module's normal operating range.

FIPS 140–2 includes Environmental Failure Testing (EFT): The use of testing to provide a reasonable assurance that the security of a cryptographic module will not be compromised by environmental conditions or fluctuations outside of the module's normal operating range.

TABLE 2.16
Finite State Model (FSM)

	Security Level 1	Security Level 2	Security Level 3	Security Level 4
FIPS 140–2	Specification of finite state model. Required states and optional states. State transition diagram and specification of state transitions.			
FIPS 140–3	Finite state model.			

TABLE 2.17
Development

	Security Level 1	Security Level 2	Security Level 3	Security Level 4
FIPS 140–2	No specific requirements.			Preconditions and postconditions.
FIPS 140–3	Annotated source code, schematics, or Hardware Description Language (HDL).	Software high-level language. Hardware high-level descriptive language.		Documentation annotated with pre-conditions upon entry into module components and postconditions expected to be true when components have completed.

TABLE 2.18
Testing

	Security Level 1	Security Level 2	Security Level 3	Security Level 4
FIPS 140–2	No specific requirements.			EFP/EFT
FIPS 140–3	Functional Testing.		Low-level Testing.	

TABLE 2.19

Delivery and Operation

	Security Level 1	Security Level 2	Security Level 3	Security Level 4
FIPS 140–2	Secure installation and generation.	Secure distribution.	No additional requirements.	
FIPS 140–3	Initialization procedures.	Delivery Procedures.		Operator authentication using vendor-provided authentication information.

TABLE 2.20

End of Life

	Security Level 1	Security Level 2	Security Level 3	Security Level 4
FIPS 140–2		No specific requirements.		
FIPS 140–3		Secure Sanitization.		Secure Destruction.

TABLE 2.21

Guidance

	Security Level 1	Security Level 2	Security Level 3	Security Level 4
FIPS 140–2		Guidance documents.		
FIPS 140–3		Administrator and non-administrator guidance.		

The *delivery and operation* topic addresses the secure delivery, installation, and startup of a cryptographic module. These controls provide assurance that the module is delivered, installed, and initialized securely. See Table 2.19.

The *end-of-life* topic addresses security requirements when a cryptographic module is no longer deployed or intended for further use by the operator. Levels 1 and 2 require secure sanitization. Levels 3 and 4 require secure destruction. See Table 2.20.

FIPS 140–3 describes *sanitization* as the process of removing sensitive information (i.e., SSPs, user data) from the cryptographic module, so that it may either be distributed to other operators or be disposed.

FIPS 140–3 defines *zeroization* as the method of destruction of stored data and unprotected SSPs to prevent retrieval and reuse.

FIPS 140–3 does not provide any details regarding destruction of a cryptographic module.

The *guidance* topic addresses guidance and procedures to administer and use the module in an approved mode of operation. All security levels need administrative and non-administrative guidelines. See Table 2.21.

Design assurance in FIPS 140–2 refers to a separate Implementation Guidance document, but for FIPS 140–3 the administrator and non-administrator guidance can be found in ISO/IEC 19790.

2.5.11 Mitigation of Other Attacks

The *mitigation of other attacks* topic allows other attack countermeasures not defined in FIPS 140–3 to be addressed. Levels 1, 2, and 3 require that the attacks are documented. Level 4 requires that the mitigation methods are also documented. See Table 2.22.

TABLE 2.22
Mitigation of Other Attacks

	Security Level 1	Security Level 2	Security Level 3	Security Level 4
FIPS 140–2	Specification of mitigation of attacks for which no testable requirements are currently available.			
FIPS 140–3	Specification of mitigation of attacks for which no testable requirements are currently available.			Specification of mitigation of attacks with testable requirements.

Mitigation of Other Attacks in FIPS 140–2 has the same requirements for all four levels.

Mitigation of Other Attacks in FIPS 140–3 has the same requirements for levels 1, 2, and 3 but requires the mitigation methods and tests are fully documented.

NOTES

1. Merriam-Webster, www.merriam-webster.com/dictionary/cryptography
2. www.ponemon.org
3. www.cert.org/insider-threat

3 PKI Building Blocks

This chapter builds on the general security and cryptography basics presented in the previous chapters. The public key infrastructure (PKI) building blocks include details of related standards, descriptions of selected protocols, and various architectural components. These PKI building blocks provide a foundational knowledge base for the remainder of the book and more generally for the reader's continuing education.

As noted in Chapter 1, "Introduction," Crypto-Agility is defined as the capability of a PKI to easily switch between cryptographic algorithms, encryption key strengths, and certificate contents in response to changing system and enterprise needs. See Section 7.7, "Crypto-Agility," for details.

Any PKI participant including managers, administrators, auditors, security professionals, subscribers, and even relying parties benefit from a better understanding of PKI technology and cryptography. Technology is usually based on industry standards or specifications and implemented by product manufacturers and service providers. Cryptography is based on mathematical research leading to standards and implemented in crypto hardware, firmware, or software products typically embedded in the same technology products and services.

- Chapter 1, "Introduction," discussed security basics and standards organizations. Security basics included confidentiality, integrity, authentication, authorization, accountability, and nonrepudiation. Standards organizations included Accredited Standards Committee (ASC) X9, Internet Engineering Task Force (IETF), International Telecommunication Union's Telecommunication Standardization Sector (ITU-T), National Institute of Standards and Technology (NIST), and RSA Labs.
- Chapter 2, "Cryptography Basics," connected the dots between security basics and cryptographic solutions, including symmetric and asymmetric cryptography, discussed the importance of key management, and introduced cryptographic modules.

Table 3.1 provides an overview of a typical X.509 certificate. All of the fields from the Version to the Subject Public Key Info, and all of the V3 Extensions, are hashed and signed to create the Certificate Signature, the last certificate field. Some certificates have fewer extensions, while others have proprietary extensions. This book refers to many of these fields and extensions.

Each of these certificate fields and extensions is well-defined in the ITU-T X.509 standard and related IETF specifications. There are other extensions defined in X.509, but these are typically unused. Further, any industry standard can define extensions and any organization can define proprietary extensions. Extensions are composed of three elements: (1) an object identifier (OID) naming the extension, (2) critical flag indicating the importance of the extension, and (3) the information content of the extension. The critical flag rules are as follows [X.509].

- *If an extension is flagged as critical and a relying party does not recognize the extension type or does not implement the semantics of the extension, then that relying party shall consider the public-key certificate as invalid.*
- *If an extension is flagged as non-critical, a relying party that does not recognize or implement that extension type may process the remainder of the public-key certificate ignoring the extension.*
- *If an extension is flagged as non-critical, a relying party that does recognize the extension shall process the extension.*

DOI: 10.1201/9781003425298-3

TABLE 3.1

Basic X.509 Certificate

X.509 Certificate

- Version
- Serial Number
- Signature Algorithm Identifier
- Issuer Name
- Validity Dates
    - Not Before Date and Time
    - Not After Date and Time
- Subject Name
- Subject Public Key Info
    - Public Key Algorithm Identifier
    - Public Key
- V3 Extensions
    - Authority Key Identifier (AKI) Extension
    - Subject Key Identifier (SKI) Extension
    - Key Usage BIT STRING Extension
        - Digital Signature (0)
        - Content Commitment (1) formerly called non-Repudiation
        - Key Encipherment (2)
        - Data Encipherment (3)
        - Key Agreement (4)
        - Key CertSign (5)
        - CRL Sign (6)
        - Encipher Only (7)
        - Decipher Only (8)
    - Extended Key Usage (EKU) Extension
    - Certificate Policies Extension
    - Subject Alternate Name (SAN) Extension
    - Basic Constraints Extension
    - CRL Distribution Points
    - Authority Info Access (AIA)[1]
- Certificate Signature

In this chapter, we look at standards, protocols, and various architectural components used for not only the registration authority (RA), the certificate authority (CA), and cryptographic modules but also PKI-enabled applications and other network components. The PKI building blocks presented in this chapter provide a foundational knowledge base for the remainder of the other chapters and for general use beyond the reading of this book.

3.1 PKI STANDARDS ORGANIZATIONS

While the politics between competing standards organizations and the disparate viewpoints of groups and individuals is a fascinating topic all by itself, it is not necessarily an ingredient to understand the underlying PKI standards and technologies. At the same time, an appreciation for the overall history of where things originated and their evolution to current status is valuable, especially when considering things continue to change. Figure 3.1 provides a timeline among various standards.

The ITU-T developed X.509 certificates to facilitate the interconnection of information processing systems for directory-based authentication services. Version 1 was published in 1988, version 2

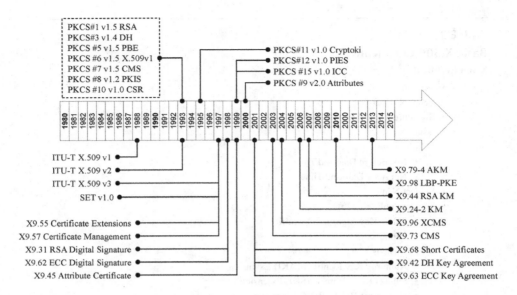

FIGURE 3.1   Abridged history of ITU-T, PKCS, and X9 Standards.

was published in 1993 with the addition of issuer and subject identifiers, and version 3 was published in 1997 with the addition of extensions. Extensions allow extra information to be added to an X.509 certificate in a consistent manner, and common extension fields defined in the standard provide continuity between PKI systems. An update was published in 2019 with the addition of three alternative cryptographic algorithms and digital signature extensions. These extensions provide capabilities for easy migration within a PKI from one set of cryptographic algorithms to another set of cryptographic algorithms, such as post-quantum cryptography (PQC). The following cryptographic algorithm and digital signature extensions are defined for that purpose:

- Subject alternative public key information extension
- Alternative digital signature algorithm extension
- Alternative signature value extension

Meanwhile, in the early 1990s, the adoption of asymmetric "public key" cryptography was slow due primarily to a lack of comprehensive standards. At the time, the Data Encryption Standard (DES) algorithm was used within the financial services industry for personal identification number (PIN) encryption at automated teller machine (ATM) and point of sale (POS) terminals, PIN verification, card authentication codes, and key management. RSA Data Security Incorporated (RSA DSI) proposed that Accredited Standards Committee X9 (ASC X9) develop any new PKI standards. However, the prevailing attitude at that time was that the industry was not ready for PKI. Consequently, RSA led by Burt Kaliski decided to develop its own standards called Public Key Cryptography Standards (PKCS) as shown in Table 3.2, which established the initial PKI building blocks.

In the mid-1990s, Visa and MasterCard began developing the Secure Electronic Transaction (SET) protocol that was published in 1997. By 2000, it was realized that SET had stagnated as some of the large processors felt SET did not match their business model and implemented alternate schemes such as Secure Socket Layer (SSL). By 2001, SET had failed to gain sufficient traction in the United States, and so in the spring of 2002, the SET PKI was decommissioned. SET had accomplished its goal of securing transactions and mitigating fraudulent merchant activity where it had been implemented, but global implementation was on the decline.

TABLE 3.2

Public Key Cryptography Standards

Public Key Cryptography Standards (PKCS)

PKCS #1 Recommendations for the RSA Algorithm
 • Describes the RSA algorithm and includes the RSA digital signature (PKCS#2) and RSA key syntax (PKCS#4). Maintenance has since been transferred to the IETF.

PKCS #2 Encryption of Message Digests
 • Note that PKCS #2 was incorporated into PKCS #1.

PKCS #3 Diffie–Hellman Key-Agreement Standard
 • Describes a method for implementing Diffie–Hellman key agreement.

PKCS #4 RSA Key Syntax
 • Note that PKCS #4 was incorporated into PKCS #1.

PKCS #5 Password-Based Encryption Standard
 • Describes a method for encrypting an octet string with a secret key derived from a password and is used in conjunction with PKCS #12. Maintenance has since been transferred to the IETF.

PKCS #6 Extended-Certificate Syntax Standard
 • Describes a syntax for extended certificates, consisting of an X.509 public key certificate and a set of attributes.

PKCS #7 Cryptographic Message Syntax (CMS) Standard
 • Describes a general recursive syntax for data that may have cryptography applied to it, such as digital signatures and digital envelopes. Maintenance has since been transferred to the IETF.

PKCS #8 Private Key Information Syntax Standard
 • Describes a syntax for private key information, including a private key for some public key algorithm and a set of attributes. Maintenance has since been transferred to the IETF.

PKCS #9 Selected Object Classes and Attribute Types
 • Defines new auxiliary object classes for use in conjunction with PKCS #7, PKCS #10, PKCS #12, and PKCS #15. Maintenance has since been transferred to the IETF.

PKCS #10 Certification Request Syntax Standard
 • Describes a syntax for certification signing requests (CSR). Maintenance has since been transferred to the IETF.

PKCS #11 Cryptographic Token Interface Standard
 • Specifies an application programming interface, originally called "Cryptoki," to devices that hold cryptographic information and perform cryptographic functions. Maintenance has since been transferred to OASIS.

PKCS #12 Personal Information Exchange Syntax
 • Describes a transfer syntax for personal identity information, including private keys, certificates, miscellaneous secrets, and extensions. Maintenance has since been transferred to the IETF.

PKCS #13 Elliptic Curve Cryptography Standard
 • Defines the elliptic curve cryptography (ECC) algorithms.

PKCS #14 Pseudo-Random Number Generation
 • Defines pseudorandom number generation algorithms.

PKCS #15 Cryptographic Token Information Syntax Standard
 • Complement to PKCS #11, defines the format of cryptographic credentials stored on cryptographic tokens such as smart card.

Beginning in the late 1990s, a new workgroup within ASC X9 was established to develop PKI standards for the financial services industry. The original work focused on defining digital signatures including the Digital Signature Algorithm (DSA) developed by NIST and the Rivest–Shamir–Adleman (RSA) algorithm developed by RSA DSI. The X9.30 DSA work was canceled since the DSA was already defined in Federal Information Processing Standards (FIPS) 186, and X9 standards are copyrighted – federal standards cannot be copyrighted and resold. The X9.31 RSA work was put on hold for several years due to ongoing patent infringement lawsuits, so consequently the first standard was X9.57 Certificate Management. Eventually, X9.62 ECDSA, an elliptic curve cryptography (ECC) version of the DSA, was also published. FIPS 186 was ultimately updated to include X9.31 and X9.62. Today, ASC X9 continues to maintain and develop numerous PKI-related standards.

The security area of the Internet Engineering Task Force (IETF) consists of workgroups that develop security mechanisms and security protocols or address the appropriate application of security mechanisms in protocols developed by working groups in other IETF areas. IETF specifications are numbered sequentially as Request for Comments (RFC) but also use best current practices (BCP) nomenclature. There have been more than three dozen security area workgroups that are now concluded and a dozen or more active workgroups. One such concluded workgroup was PKIX.

The PKIX Workgroup was established in the fall of 1995 with the goal of developing Internet standards to support X.509-based public key infrastructures (PKIs). Initially, PKIX pursued this goal by profiling X.509 standards developed by the Comité Consultatif International Téléphonique et Télégraphique (CCITT renamed as the ITU-T). Later, PKIX initiated the development of standards that are not profiles of ITU-T work but rather are independent initiatives designed to address X.509-based PKI needs in the Internet. Over time, this latter category of work has become the major focus of PKIX work, that is, most PKIX-generated RFCs are no longer profiles of ITU-T X.509 documents. Figure 3.2 continues the comparison of various standards and specifications.

RFC 1422 Privacy-Enhanced Electronic Mail: Part II: Certificate-Based Key Management published in 1993 was compatible with X.509 v1 framework and extended its key management procedures and conventions for use with Privacy-Enhanced Electronic Mail (PEM) and other protocols. RFC 2459 Internet X.509 Public Key Infrastructure Certificate and CRL Profile published in 1999 replicated and enhanced the X.509 v3 standard. The IETF has continued to revise its enhancements of the X.509 v3 framework in subsequent publications including RFC 3280 in 2002, RFC 4630 in 2006, and RFC 5280 in 2008. The IETF has also continued to revise its PKCS improvements with RFC 2985 for PKCS#9 in 2000, RFC 3447 for PKCS#1 in 2003, RFC 5208 for PKCS#8 in 2008, RFC 5967 for PKCS#10 in 2010, RFC 6070 for PKCS#5 in 2011, and RFC 7292 for PKCS#12 in 2014.

As one can surmise from Figures 3.1 and 3.2 timelines, PKI-related standards are numerous, varied, and constantly changing. Consequently, research is difficult, information is widely disseminated, and the standards are rather diverse. From the mid-1990s to the present, three organizations

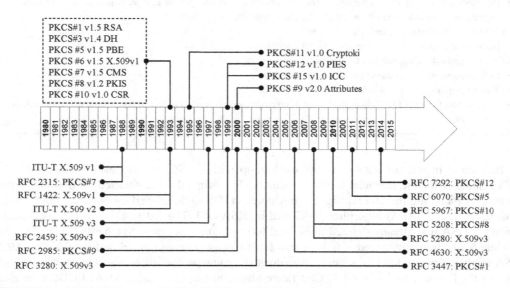

FIGURE 3.2   Abridged history of ITU-T, PKCS, and IETF Standards.

have continued to develop PKI-related standards and specifications: ASC X9, IETF, and ISO/IEC JTC1. However, the focus and purpose for each group are slightly different:

- The Accredited Standards Committee X9 (ASC X9) has the mission to develop, establish, maintain, and promote standards for the financial services industry in order to facilitate delivery of financial services and products.[2]
- The mission of the IETF is to make the Internet work better by producing high-quality, relevant technical documents that influence the way people design, use, and manage the Internet.[3]
- JTC1 is the standards development environment where experts come together to develop worldwide information and communications technology standards for business and consumer applications.[4]

PKI technologies and solutions that meet Internet needs do not necessarily align with general telecommunication needs and neither fully satisfy financial services. Other industries such as healthcare, manufacturing, and entertainment obviously have their own unique authentication and authorization needs, but in general these industries tend to follow the financial, Internet, or telecommunications security domains. The good news is that the standards are not developed in a vacuum, for example, the ASC X9, IETF, and JTC1 organizations are aware of each other, often the same individuals participate in their various workgroups, and the standards typically refer to each other where applicable. As one might suspect, the standards development world is relatively small, and many of the participants know and respect each other.

Table 3.3 lists selected groups that have developed numerous PKI standards and specifications that can serve as an index for further reading and reference. Technical standards and specifications are often developed in more than one group at the same time and tend to move around a bit, and, as they mature, they are adopted by larger and larger groups. Consequently, this can lead to multiple versions of similar standards. For example, several of the RSA Laboratories' PKCS series standards have been adopted by the IETF and the Organization for the Advancement of Structured Information Standards[5] (OASIS). Regardless, these organizations and their websites are excellent sources for PKI standards and specifications.

Table 3.4 is a selected list of IETF specifications that relate to X.509-based PKI systems. The Public-Key Infrastructure X.509 (PKIX) workgroup was established in 1995 and concluded in 2013, but the Limited Additional Mechanisms for PKIX and SMIME (LAMPS) was established in 2016 to continue the PKI work. These specifications provide a great number of details associated

TABLE 3.3
PKI-Related Standards Organizations

Organization	Websites
ASC X9	www.x9.org
ETSI	http://portal.etsi.org/esi/el-sign.asp
Federal PKI	http://csrc.nist.gov/archive/pki-twg/welcome.html
IEEE PKI	http://grouper.ieee.org/groups/1363/index.html
IETF Active Workgroups	http://datatracker.ietf.org/wg/
IETF Concluded Workgroups	www.ietf.org/wg/concluded/
IETF PKIX	www.ietf.org/wg/concluded/pkix.html
IETF Security Area	http://tools.ietf.org/area/sec/trac/wiki#
NIST PKI	http://csrc.nist.gov/groups/ST/crypto_apps_infra/pki/pkiresearch.html
OASIS PKI	www.oasis-pki.org/resources/techstandards/
RSA PKCS	www.emc.com/emc-plus/rsa-labs/standardsinitiatives/public-key-cryptography-standards.htm

TABLE 3.4
IETF Specifications

Internet Engineering Task Force (IETF)

RFC 2459 Internet X.509 Public Key Infrastructure Certificate and CRL Profile
- Note that this specification and its successors RFC 3280 and RFC 5280 are X.509 profiles adapted for the Internet and were never intended to replace the X.509 standard for general use or adoption within other industry segments.
- www.ietf.org/rfc/rfc2459.txt

RFC 2510 Internet X.509 Public Key Infrastructure Certificate Management Protocols
- www.ietf.org/rfc/rfc2510.txt

RFC 2511 Internet X.509 Certificate Request Message Format
- www.ietf.org/rfc/rfc2511.txt

RFC 2527 Internet X.509 Public Key Infrastructure Certificate Policy and Certification Practices Framework – Predecessor of RFC 3647
- www.ietf.org/rfc/rfc2527.txt

RFC 2528 Internet X.509 Public Key Infrastructure Representation of Key Exchange Algorithm (KEA) Keys in Internet X.509 Certificates
- www.ietf.org/rfc/rfc2528.txt

RFC 2559 Internet X.509 Public Key Infrastructure Operational Protocols – LDAPv2
- www.ietf.org/rfc/rfc2559.txt

RFC 2585 Internet X.509 Public Key Infrastructure Operational Protocols: FTP and HTTP
- www.ietf.org/rfc/rfc2585.txt

RFC 2587 Internet X.509 Public Key Infrastructure LDAPv2 Schema
- www.ietf.org/rfc/rfc2587.txt

RFC 3029 Internet X.509 Public Key Infrastructure Data Validation and Certification Server Protocols
- www.ietf.org/rfc/rfc3029.txt

RFC 3039 Internet X.509 Public Key Infrastructure Qualified Certificates Profile
- www.ietf.org/rfc/rfc3039.txt

RFC 3161 Internet X.509 Public Key Infrastructure Time Stamp Protocol (TSP)
- www.ietf.org/rfc/rfc3161.txt

RFC 3279 Algorithms and Identifiers for the Internet X.509 Public Key Infrastructure Certificate and Certificate Revocation List (CRL) Profile
- www.ietf.org/rfc/rfc3279.txt

RFC 3280 Internet X.509 Public Key Infrastructure Certificate and Certificate Revocation List (CRL) Profile
- www.ietf.org/rfc/rfc3280.txt

RFC 3647 Internet X.509 Public Key Infrastructure Certificate Policy and Certification Practices Framework – Replaces RFC 2527
- www.ietf.org/rfc/rfc3647.txt

RFC 3709 Internet X.509 Public Key Infrastructure: Logotypes in X.509 Certificates
- www.ietf.org/rfc/rfc3709.txt

RFC 3739 Internet X.509 Public Key Infrastructure: Qualified Certificates Profile
- www.ietf.org/rfc/rfc3739.txt

RFC 3779 X.509 Extensions for IP Addresses and AS Identifiers
- www.ietf.org/rfc/rfc3779.txt

RFC 3820 Internet X.509 Public Key Infrastructure Certificate Profile
- www.ietf.org/rfc/rfc3820.txt

RFC 5280 Internet X.509 Public Key Infrastructure Certificate and Certificate Revocation List Profile
- www.ietf.org/rfc/rfc5280.txt

with certificate policy, practices, and management messages and protocols. Readers interested in building a PKI library can use this list as a starting point. Many of these are referenced throughout the book. Any of the RFC specifications can be searched at the general IETF website www.ietf.org, or the particular document can be found on its individual web page.

Note that IETF documents are often found posted on other websites, so it is important to recognize that the RFC number reflects its version and publication date. Unlike many other standards that have a version or publication date separate from its designated number and title, the current RFC will indicate which previous versions it is intended to deprecate. Thus, the reader should always reference the most current RFC unless a previous version was implemented.

Table 3.5 is another selected list of IETF specifications that relate to PKCS-based PKI systems. These specifications extended the longevity of the original PKCS and expanded the developer participation to a larger group of engineers. Some PKCS have been transferred to other standards groups such as PKCS #11 to OASIS.[6]

Table 3.6 is one more list of relevant IETF specifications that address various other PKI algorithms and protocols. Readers should familiarize themselves with these specifications and include them in their PKI library, including elliptic curve cryptography (ECC). As Moore's law[7] continues to erode cryptographic strengths and so, in response, keys keep getting larger, there will be an inevitable shift away from RSA larger keys to ECC shorter keys that have equivalent cryptographic strengths; see NIST 800-57-1 [B.5.19].

TABLE 3.5
PKCS-Related IETF

Internet Engineering Task Force

RFC 2313 PKCS #1: RSA Encryption
- www.ietf.org/rfc/rfc2313.txt

RFC 2314 PKCS #10: Certification Request Syntax
- www.ietf.org/rfc/rfc2314.txt

RFC 2437 PKCS #1: RSA Cryptography Specifications
- www.ietf.org/rfc/rfc2437.txt

RFC 2898 PKCS #5: Password-Based Cryptography Specification Version 2.0
- www.ietf.org/rfc/rfc2898.txt

RFC 2986 PKCS #10: Certification Request Syntax Specification Version 1.7
- www.ietf.org/rfc/rfc2986.txt

RFC 3447 PKCS #1: RSA Cryptography Specifications Version 2.1
- www.ietf.org/rfc/rfc3447.txt

TABLE 3.6
PKI-Related IETF

Internet Engineering Task Force (IETF)

RFC 3278 Use of Elliptic Curve Cryptography (ECC) Algorithms in Cryptographic Message Syntax (CMS)
- www.ietf.org/rfc/rfc3278.txt

RFC 3281 An Internet Attribute Certificate Profile for Authorization
- www.ietf.org/rfc/rfc3281.txt

RFC 3379 Delegated Path Validation and Delegated Path Discovery Protocol Requirements
- www.ietf.org/rfc/rfc3379.txt

RFC 3628 Policy Requirements for Time Stamping Authorities (TSAs)
- www.ietf.org/rfc/rfc3628.txt

RFC 3766 BCP0086 Determining Strengths for Public Keys Used for Exchanging Symmetric Keys
- www.ietf.org/rfc/rfc3766.txt

RFC 4210 Internet X.509 Public Key Infrastructure Certificate Management Protocol (CMP)
- www.ietf.org/rfc/rfc4210.txt

RFC 5272 Certificate Management Messages over CMS (CMC)
- www.ietf.org/rfc/rfc5272.txt

NIST plays a leading role in the deployment of the Federal PKI, serving as an advisor for architectural issues and leading the development, evaluation, and maintenance of certificate policies for the Federal PKI. The Federal PKI architecture features the Federal Bridge Certification Authority (FBCA), which supports interoperability among PKI domains with disparate policies in a peer-to-peer fashion, and the Common Policy Root CA, which manages a hierarchical PKI.

The FBCA operates under the FBCA certificate policy, which specifies five levels of assurance. The FBCA issues certificates to the principal CA of a PKI domain after the Federal PKI Policy Authority (1) determines which FBCA levels of assurance are satisfied by the policies supported in that PKI domain, (2) determines that the PKI domain fulfills its responsibilities under those policies, and (3) establishes a legal agreement between the FBCA and the PKI domain. The NIST-managed Federal Certificate Policy Working Group (CPWG) leads (1) and (2). For an overview of the operations of the Federal PKI Policy Authority (FPKI PA), see the Criteria and Methodology for Cross-Certification with the U.S. Federal Bridge Certification Authority[8] (FBCA) or Citizen and Commerce Class Common Certification Authority (C4CA).

The Common Policy Root CA operates under the Common Policy Framework, which specifies three policies with a relatively uniform level of assurance. The Common Policy Root CA will issue a certificate to a subordinate CA operated by or on behalf of a federal agency after determining that the CA's operations satisfy the requirements of the Common Policy. The FPKI PA has delegated this responsibility to the CPWG and the Shared Service Provider (SSP) Subcommittee. The CPWG evaluates CAs operated by an agency for internal operations; the SSP Subcommittee evaluates CAs that offer PKI services to federal agencies based on the Common Policy.

Table 3.7 is a list of applicable NIST cryptographic programs to evaluate compliance to various Federal Information Processing Standards Publications (FIPS PUB) for algorithms and cryptographic modules. NIST does not actually perform the evaluations; rather it accredits laboratories to execute the derived test criteria: the National Voluntary Laboratory Accreditation Program is used to accredit laboratories, and the laboratories use Cryptographic Algorithm Validation Program or Cryptographic Module Validation Program for product certifications.

Table 3.8 is a list of applicable cryptographic Federal Information Processing Standards Publications (FIPS PUB) used by accredited laboratories. Document versions are denoted by hyphenated digits such as FIPS 46, 46–1, 46–2, and 46–3 numbering scheme. Each publication includes an effective date for the new version and a sunset date for the previous version. NIST uses a rigid review process to approve FIPS.

NIST follows rule-making procedures modeled after those established by the Administrative Procedures Act.[9] The proposed FIPS is announced in the Federal Register[10] for a 30- to 90-day public review and comment, additionally on NIST's electronic pages,[11] and to encourage review by senior information technology officials, the proposed FIPS is announced on the Chief Information Officers Council[12] site. Comments are reviewed by NIST to determine if changes are needed to the proposed FIPS, and a justification document is provided analyzing the comments and explaining what modifications were made or not. The recommended FIPS and the justification document are

---

TABLE 3.7

PKI-Related NIST Programs

National Institute of Standards and Technology

CAVP Cryptographic Algorithm Validation Program
- http://csrc.nist.gov/groups/STM/cavp/index.html

CMVP Cryptographic Module Validation Program
- http://csrc.nist.gov/groups/STM/cmvp/index.html

NVLAP National Voluntary Laboratory Accreditation Program
- http://csrc.nist.gov/groups/STM/testing_labs/index.html

TABLE 3.8

PKI-Related NIST Standards

National Institute of Standards and Technology

FIPS 140–2 Security Requirements for Cryptographic Modules
  • https://nvlpubs.nist.gov/nistpubs/FIPS/NIST.FIPS.140-2.pdf

FIPS 140–3 Security Requirements for Cryptographic Modules
  • https://nvlpubs.nist.gov/nistpubs/FIPS/NIST.FIPS.140-3.pdf

FIPS 180–4 Secure Hash Standard (SHS)
  • http://csrc.nist.gov/publications/fips/fips180-4/fips-180-4.pdf

FIPS 186–4 Digital Signature Standard (DSS)
  • http://nvlpubs.nist.gov/nistpubs/FIPS/NIST.FIPS.186-4.pdf

FIPS 196 Entity Authentication Using Public Key Cryptography – withdrawn October 2015
  • http://csrc.nist.gov/publications/fips/fips196/fips196.pdf

FIPS 197 Advanced Encryption Standard (AES)
  • http://csrc.nist.gov/publications/fips/fips197/fips-197.pdf

FIPS 198–1 Keyed-Hash Message Authentication Code (HMAC)
  • http://csrc.nist.gov/publications/fips/fips198-1/FIPS-198-1_final.pdf

---

submitted to the Secretary of Commerce for approval. The final FIPS is announced in the Federal Register and on NIST's electronic pages. A copy of the justification document is filed at NIST and available for public review.

Table 3.9 is a list of applicable NIST special publications (SP). Special publications are more informative in nature but similar to standards can include both requirements and recommendations. Whereas FIPS undergoes more rigid reviews, the process for special pubs is less intense, for example, its development is not posted in the Federal Registry, and the Secretary of Commerce does not need to approve the publication.

Any discussion of accreditation and certification programs would not be complete without at least mentioning the Common Criteria[13] and the National Information Assurance Partnership (NIAP) Common Criteria Evaluation and Validation Scheme (CCEVS).[14] Historically, the Information Technology Security Evaluation Criteria originally published in 1990 was used in Europe as an organized set of criteria for evaluating computer security within products and systems. In the United States, the Department of Defense used the Trusted Computer System Evaluation Criteria (TCSEC) also known as the Orange Book[15] part of the Department of Defense's (DoD's) Rainbow Series.[16] These and other standards were converted to the Common Criteria and adopted by European and North American countries. Eventually, the Common Criteria was internationalized as ISO/IEC 15408. Table 3.10 provides a list of the Common Criteria standards and supporting technical reports (TRs).

To help put the Common Criteria into perspective, FIPS 140–1 required evaluated operating systems and referenced the TCSEC classes C2, B1, and B2. However, TCSEC was replaced by the Common Criteria and FIPS 140–2 references the ISO/IEC 15408 Evaluation Assurance Levels EAL2, EAL3, and EAL4. Each Evaluation Assurance Level increases the reliability of products and systems by requiring additional design and testing criteria:

- EAL1 requires that products are functionally tested.
- EAL2 requires that products are structurally tested.
- EAL3 requires that products are methodically tested and checked.
- EAL4 requires that products are methodically designed, tested, and reviewed.
- EAL5 requires that products are semiformally designed and tested.
- EAL6 requires that products are semiformally verified, designed, and tested.
- EAL7 requires that products are formally verified, designed, and tested.

TABLE 3.9
PKI-Related NIST Special Publications
National Institute of Standards and Technology

NIST SP 800–29A Comparison of the Security Requirements for Cryptographic Modules in FIPS 140–1 and FIPS 140–2
- http://csrc.nist.gov/publications/nistpubs/800-29/sp800-29.pdf

NIST SP 800–32 Introduction to Public Key Technology and the Federal PKI Infrastructure
- http://csrc.nist.gov/publications/nistpubs/800-32/sp800-32.pdf

NIST SP 800–38A Recommendation for Block Cipher Modes of Operation: Three Variants of Ciphertext Stealing for CBC Mode
- http://csrc.nist.gov/publications/nistpubs/800-38a/addendum-to-nist_sp800-38A.pdf

NIST SP 800–38B Recommendation for Block Cipher Modes of Operation: The CMAC Mode for Authentication
- http://csrc.nist.gov/publications/nistpubs/800-38B/SP_800-38B.pdf

NIST SP 800–38C Recommendation for Block Cipher Modes of Operation: The CCM Mode for Authentication and Confidentiality
- http://csrc.nist.gov/publications/nistpubs/800-38C/SP800-38C_updated-July20_2007.pdf

NIST SP 800–38D Recommendation for Block Cipher Modes of Operation: Galois/Counter Mode (GCM) and GMAC
- http://csrc.nist.gov/publications/nistpubs/800-38D/SP-800-38D.pdf

NIST SP 800–38E Recommendation for Block Cipher Modes of Operation: The XTS-AES Mode for Confidentiality on Storage Devices
- http://csrc.nist.gov/publications/nistpubs/800-38E/nist-sp-800-38E.pdf

NIST SP 800–38F Recommendation for Block Cipher Modes of Operation: Methods for Key Wrapping
- http://nvlpubs.nist.gov/nistpubs/SpecialPublications/NIST.SP.800-38F.pdf

NIST SP 800–38G Recommendation for Block Cipher Modes of Operation: Methods for Format-Preserving Encryption –
- https://nvlpubs.nist.gov/nistpubs/SpecialPublications/NIST.SP.800-38G.pdf

NIST SP 800–52 Revision 2 Guidelines for the Selection, Configuration, and Use of Transport Layer Security (TLS) Implementations
- https://nvlpubs.nist.gov/nistpubs/SpecialPublications/NIST.SP.800-52r2.pdf

NIST SP 800–56A Recommendation for Pair-Wise Key-Establishment Schemes Using Discrete Logarithm Cryptography
- http://nvlpubs.nist.gov/nistpubs/SpecialPublications/NIST.SP.800-56Ar2.pdf

NIST SP 800–56B Recommendation for Pair-Wise Key-Establishment Schemes Using Integer Factorization Cryptography
- http://nvlpubs.nist.gov/nistpubs/SpecialPublications/NIST.SP.800-56Br1.pdf

NIST SP 800–56C Recommendation for Key Derivation through Extraction-Then-Expansion
- http://csrc.nist.gov/publications/nistpubs/800-56C/SP-800-56C.pdf

NIST SP 800–57 Part 1 Recommendation for Key Management – Part 1: General
- https://nvlpubs.nist.gov/nistpubs/SpecialPublications/NIST.SP.800-57pt1r5.pdf

NIST SP 800–57 Part 2 Recommendation for Key Management – Part 2: Best Practices for Key Management Organization
- https://nvlpubs.nist.gov/nistpubs/SpecialPublications/NIST.SP.800-57pt2r1.pdf

NIST SP 800–57 Part 3 Recommendation for Key Management – Part 3: Application-Specific Key Management Guidance
- https://nvlpubs.nist.gov/nistpubs/SpecialPublications/NIST.SP.800-57Pt3r1.pdf

NIST SP 800–63–3 Digital Identity Guidelines
- https://nvlpubs.nist.gov/nistpubs/SpecialPublications/NIST.SP.800-63-3.pdf

NIST SP 800–67 Recommendation for the Triple Data Encryption Algorithm (TDEA) Block Cipher
- http://csrc.nist.gov/publications/nistpubs/800-67-Rev1/SP-800-67-Rev1.pdf

NIST SP 800–77 Revision 1 Guide to IPsec VPNs
- https://nvlpubs.nist.gov/nistpubs/SpecialPublications/NIST.SP.800-77r1.pdf

NIST SP 800–92 Guide to Computer Security Log Management
- http://csrc.nist.gov/publications/nistpubs/800-92/SP800-92.pdf

NIST SP 800–102 Recommendation for Digital Signature Timeliness
- http://csrc.nist.gov/publications/nistpubs/800-102/sp800-102.pdf

NIST SP 800–107 Revision 1 Recommendation for Applications Using Approved Hash Algorithms
- http://csrc.nist.gov/publications/nistpubs/800-107-rev1/sp800-107-rev1.pdf

NIST SP 800–113 Guide to SSL VPNs
- http://csrc.nist.gov/publications/nistpubs/800-113/SP800-113.pdf

TABLE 3.10

Common Criteria Standards

ISO/IEC Standards

ISO/IEC 15408–1 Information Technology – Security Techniques – Evaluation Criteria for IT Security – Part 1: Introduction and General Model
- www.iso.org/standard/50341.html

ISO/IEC 15408–2 Information Technology – Security Techniques – Evaluation Criteria for IT Security – Part 2: Security Functional Components
- www.iso.org/standard/46414.html

ISO/IEC 15408–3 Information Technology – Security Techniques – Evaluation Criteria for IT Security – Part 3: Security Assurance Components
- www.iso.org/standard/46413.html

ISO/IEC TR 15446 Information Technology – Security Techniques – Guide for the Production of Protection Profiles and Security Targets
- www.iso.org/standard/68904.html

ISO/IEC 18045 Information Technology – Security Techniques – Methodology for IT Security Evaluation
- www.iso.org/standard/46412.html

ISO/IEC TR 19791 Information Technology – Security Techniques – Security Assessment of Operational Systems
- www.iso.org/standard/52905.html

ISO/IEC TR 20004 Information Technology – Security Techniques – Refining Software Vulnerability Analysis under ISO/IEC 15408 and ISO/IEC 18045
- www.iso.org/standard/68837.html

ISO/IEC 29128 Information Technology – Security Techniques – Verification of Cryptographic Protocols
- www.iso.org/standard/45151.html

While the IETF develops technical specifications for use on the Internet and NIST develops standards and special publications for U.S. government agencies, ASC X9 develops standards for the financial services industry. X9 standards address payments, corporate banking, securities, and information security including PKI-related topics. Note that the X9 standards are copyrighted, so unfortunately if you want any of these, you must purchase them from the X9 Standards Store or the American National Standards Institute (ANSI) Web Store.[17] Table 3.11 provides a list of American National Standards.

Several of the X9 standards were submitted to ISO TC68 as a U.S. submission for international standardization and transformed into ISO standards. For example, X9.55 became ISO 15782 Part 2 and X9.57 became ISO 15782 Part 1. As another example, X9.79 Part 1 became ISO 21188. Sometimes an ISO standard is adopted by X9 when no ANSI standard exists, and other times, the original X9 standard is retired in favor of the ISO standard. Sometimes the X9 standard is the ISO standard with embedded ANSI notes. It is important to recognize that PKI can be used for other industries than just financial services, for example, the healthcare industry. Similar to X9, the ISO standards are also copyrighted. Copies can be purchased from the ISO Store.[18] Table 3.12 provides a list of relevant TC68 standards.

Smart cards, plastic cards with an embedded integrated circuit chip, are often used within PKI systems to protect asymmetric private keys. For example, CA private keys can be managed using an N of M key management scheme, where each key share is stored separately on a passcode-activated smart card. As another example, end users might store their private signature keys on passcode-activated smart cards as removable media. Table 3.13 provides a brief list of contact and contactless smart cards.

Additional smart card resources include the NIST Smartcard Research & Development[19] efforts, the Smart Card Alliance,[20] and EMVCo[21] for credit cards. Other form factors such as the Universal Serial Bus might also be used. Mobile phones are a common form factor for end-user applications

TABLE 3.11
PKI-Related X9 Financial Industry
Accredited Standards Committee X9 Standards

X9.24–2 Retail Financial Services Symmetric Key Management Part 2: Using Asymmetric Techniques for the Distribution of Symmetric Keys
- https://webstore.ansi.org/Standards/ASCX9/ANSIX9242017-1665702

X9.30–1 Public Key Cryptography Using Irreversible Algorithm for the Financial Services Industry – Part 1: Digital Signature Algorithm (DSA)
- https://csrc.nist.gov/publications/detail/fips/186/4/final
- https://csrc.nist.gov/publications/detail/fips/186/5/draft

Standard X9.30 withdrawn by X9 in 2011, see FIPS 186 Digital Signature Standard (DSS).

X9.30–2 Public Key Cryptography Using Irreversible Algorithms for the Financial Services Industry – Part 2: The Secure Hash Algorithm
- https://csrc.nist.gov/publications/detail/fips/180/4/final

Standard X9.30 withdrawn by X9 in 2011, see FIPS 180 Secure Hash Standard (SHS)

X9.31 Digital Signatures Using Reversible Public Key Cryptography for the Financial Services Industry (rDSA)
- https://csrc.nist.gov/publications/detail/fips/186/4/final
- https://csrc.nist.gov/publications/detail/fips/186/5/draft

Standard X9.31 administratively withdrawn by ANSI in 2008. FIPS 186–4 referred to X9.31 but the RSA Digital Signature Algorithm was added to FIPS 186–5 draft.

X9.42 Public Key Cryptography for Financial Services Industry: Agreement of Symmetric Keys Using Discrete Logarithm Cryptography
- https://webstore.ansi.org/Standards/ASCX9/ANSIX9422003R2013

X9.44 Public Key Cryptography for the Financial Services Industry: Key Establishment Using Integer Factorization Cryptography
- https://webstore.ansi.org/Standards/ASCX9/ANSIX9442007R2017

X9.45 Enhanced Management Controls Using Digital Signatures and Attribute Certificates
- www.itu.int/itu-t/recommendations/rec.aspx?rec=14033

Standard X9.45 withdrawn by X9 in 2011, see X.509 Information technology – Open Systems Interconnection – The Directory: Public-key and attribute certificate frameworks.

X9.55 Certificate Extensions for Multi-Domain Operations
- www.iso.org/standard/63134.html

Standard X9.55 withdrawn by X9 in 2011, after transformed into ISO 15782–2 and note this standard was merged with ISO 21188 and subsequently withdrawn.

X9.57 Public Key Cryptography for the Financial Services Industry: Certificate Management
- www.iso.org/standard/63134.html

Standard X9.57 withdrawn by X9 in 2011, after transformed in ISO 15782–1 and note this standard was merged with ISO 21188 and subsequently withdrawn.

X9.62 Public Key Cryptography: The Elliptic Curve Digital Signature Algorithm (ECDSA)
- https://csrc.nist.gov/publications/detail/fips/186/4/final
- https://csrc.nist.gov/publications/detail/fips/186/5/draft

Standard X9.62 administratively withdrawn by ANSI in 2016. FIPS 186–4 referred to X9.62 but the Elliptic Curve Digital Signature Algorithm (ECDSA) was added to FIPS 186–5 draft.

X9.63 Key Agreement and Key Management Using Elliptic Curve-Based Cryptography
- https://webstore.ansi.org/Search/Find?in=1&st=x9.63

X9.68 Part 2 Digital Certificates for High Transaction Volume Financial Systems
- www.iso.org/standard/56427.html

Standard X9.68–2 withdrawn by X9 in 2011 as larger bandwidth and cheaper memory eliminated the original need for short certificates. The Internet of Things (IoT) began lightweight cryptography including ISO/IEC 29192–4 Information Technology –Security Techniques – Lightweight Cryptography – Part 4: Mechanisms Using Asymmetric Techniques

X9.69 Framework for Key Management Extensions
- https://webstore.ansi.org/Standards/ASCX9/ANSIX9692017

X9.73 Cryptographic Message Syntax
- https://webstore.ansi.org/Standards/ASCX9/ANSIX9732017

TABLE 3.11 (*Continued*)
Accredited Standards Committee X9 Standards

X9.79–1 Public Key Infrastructure – Part 1: Practices and Policy Framework for the Financial Services Industry
- www.iso.org/standard/63134.html

This is an important document that provided the basis for the WebTrust for CA auditing standard and translated into ISO 21188.

X9.79–4 Public Key Infrastructure – Part 4: Asymmetric Key Management for the Financial Services Industry
- https://webstore.ansi.org/Standards/ASCX9/ANSIX9792013

TABLE 3.12
PKI-Related International Standards

International Standards

ISO 11568–1 Banking – Key Management (Retail) – Part 1: Principles
- Developed per ISO TC68 Financial Services
- www.iso.org/standard/34937.html

ISO 11568–2 Financial Services – Key Management (Retail) – Part 2: Symmetric Ciphers, Key Management and Life cycle
- Developed per ISO TC68 Financial Services
- www.iso.org/standard/53568.html

ISO 11568–4 Banking – Key Management (Retail) – Part 4: Asymmetric Cryptosystems – Key Management and Life cycle
- Developed per ISO TC68 Financial Services
- www.iso.org/standard/39666.html

ISO 13491–1 Banking – Secure Cryptographic Devices (Retail) – Part 1: Concepts, Requirements and Evaluation Methods
- Developed per ISO TC68 Financial Services
- www.iso.org/standard/61137.html

ISO 13491–2 Banking – Secure Cryptographic Devices (Retail) – Part 2: Security Compliance Checklists for Devices Used in Financial Transactions
- Developed per ISO TC68 Financial Services
- www.iso.org/standard/72178.html

ISO 15782–1 Certificate Management for Financial Services – Part 1: Public Key Certificates
- Developed per ISO TC68 Financial Services
- www.iso.org/standard/46547.html

Note that this standard was merged with ISO 21188 and was subsequently withdrawn.

ISO 15782–2 Banking – Certificate Management – Part 2: Certificate Extensions
- Developed per ISO TC68 Financial Services
- www.iso.org/standard/30969.html

Note that this standard was merged with ISO 21188 and was subsequently withdrawn.

ISO 21188 Public Key Infrastructure for Financial Services – Practices and Policy Framework
- Developed per ISO TC68 Financial Services
- www.iso.org/standard/63134.html

This is an important document that provided the basis for the ISO/IEC 27099 PKI developed by ISO/IEC JTC1/SC27

ISO 17090–1 Health Informatics – Public Key Infrastructure – Part 1: Overview of Digital Certificate Services
- Developed per ISO TC215 Health Informatics
- www.iso.org/standard/63019.html

ISO 17090–2 Health Informatics – Public Key Infrastructure – Part 2: Certificate Profile
- Developed per ISO TC215 Health Informatics
- www.iso.org/standard/63020.html

ISO 17090–3 Health Informatics – Public Key Infrastructure – Part 3: Policy Management of Certification Authority
- Developed per ISO TC215 Health Informatics
- www.iso.org/standard/39847.html

ISO 17090–4 Health Informatics – Public Key Infrastructure – Part 4: Digital Signatures for Healthcare Documents
- Developed per ISO TC215 Health Informatics
- www.iso.org/standard/74357.html

TABLE 3.13

Smart Card-Related International Standards

International Standards

ISO/IEC 7810 Identification cards – Physical characteristics
* www.iso.org/standard/70483.html

ISO/IEC 7816–1 Identification cards – Integrated circuit cards – Part 1: Cards with contacts – Physical characteristics
* www.iso.org/standard/54089.html

ISO/IEC 7816–15 Identification cards – Integrated circuit cards – Part 15: Cryptographic information application
* www.iso.org/standard/65250.html
* www.iso.org/standard/74199.html *Amendment 1*

ISO/IEC 14443–1 Cards and security devices for personal identification – Contactless proximity objects – Part 1: Physical characteristics
* www.iso.org/standard/73596.html

ISO/IEC 14443–4 Identification cards – Contactless integrated circuit cards – Proximity cards – Part 4: Transmission protocol
* www.iso.org/standard/73599.html
* www.iso.org/standard/76927.html *Amendment 2*

such as payments or person-to-person money transfers; however, mobile devices are not yet being used for key management.

Another usage of asymmetric cryptography is secure e-mail. Senders can sign e-mails using their private key or encrypt e-mails using the receiver's public key, and receivers can verify signed e-mails using the sender's public key and decrypt e-mails using their private keys. Secure e-mail might use Privacy-Enhanced Electronic Mail (PEM) or Secure/Multipurpose Internet Mail Extensions (S/MIMEs), and either can incorporate Pretty Good Privacy (PGP). Table 3.14 provides references to various specifications.

The original OpenPGP standard was derived from Pretty Good Privacy (PGP) e-mail encryption software package first created by Phil Zimmermann in 1991. Despite the U.S. government's three-year investigation of the encryption program known as Pretty Good Privacy being posting to Usenet in June 1991, the case was declined in 1996.[22] Further information can be found at the OpenPGP Alliance[23] or at the Symantec[24] website as the Symantec Corporation acquired the PGP Corporation in June 2010.

3.2 PKI PROTOCOLS: SSL AND TLS

After discussing the various PKI standards, we now turn our attention to several of the associated PKI protocols. For the purposes of this book, we have selected three common PKI protocols that operate at different layers of the ISO Open Systems Interconnection (OSI) model, as shown in Figure 3.3. The Secure/Multipurpose Internet Mail Extensions (S/MIME) operate at the Application layer – basically e-mail applications. Transport Layer Security (TLS) can operate at either the Session or Transport layers. Internet Protocol Security (IPsec) can operate at the Network or Data Link layers. Let's begin our PKI protocol discussion at the Session and Transport layers using TLS.

Secure Socket Layer (SSL) and Transport Layer Security (TLS) are cryptographic protocols designed to provide secure communications on the Internet. These protocols provided endpoint authentication and communications privacy over the Internet using cryptography. Both SSL and TLS provide server-side and client-side authentication capabilities. However, in typical use, usually just the server is authenticated (i.e., its identity is ensured), while the client remains unauthenticated. To provide mutual authentication requires a PKI deployment of certificates to the clients. The protocols allow client/server applications to communicate in a way designed to prevent eavesdropping, message tampering, and message forgery. See Table 3.15 for a brief history of the SSL and TLS protocols.

TABLE 3.14

E-mail-Related IETF Specifications

Internet Engineering Task Force

RFC 1421 Privacy-Enhanced Electronic Mail (PEM) – Part I: Message Encryption and Authentication Procedures
- http://ietf.org/rfc/rfc1421.txt

This document defines message encryption and authentication procedures, in order to provide Privacy-Enhanced Electronic Mail (PEM) services for electronic mail transfer on the Internet.

RFC 1422 Privacy-Enhanced Electronic Mail (PEM) – Part II: Certificate-Based Key Management
- http://ietf.org/rfc/rfc1422.txt

This document defines a supporting key management architecture and infrastructure, based on public key certificate techniques, to provide keying information to message originators and recipients – RFC 1424 provides additional specifications for services in conjunction with the key management infrastructure described herein.

RFC 1423 Privacy-Enhanced Electronic Mail (PEM) – Part III: Algorithms, Modes, and Identifiers
- http://ietf.org/rfc/rfc1423.txt

This document provides definitions, formats, references, and citations for cryptographic algorithms, usage modes, and associated identifiers and parameters used in support of Privacy-Enhanced Electronic Mail in the Internet community.

RFC 1424 Privacy-Enhanced Electronic Mail – Part IV: Key Certification and Related Services
- http://ietf.org/rfc/rfc1424.txt

This document describes three types of service in support of Internet Privacy-Enhanced Electronic Mail: (1) key certification, (2) certificate revocation list (CRL) storage, and (3) CRL retrieval – such services are among those required of an RFC 1422 certification authority.

RFC 3156 MIME Security with OpenPGP
- www.ietf.org/rfc/rfc3156.txt

This document describes the Internet standards track protocol for the Internet community, with discussion and suggestions for improvements.

RFC 4134 Examples of S/MIME Messages
- www.ietf.org/rfc/rfc4134.txt

RFC 5750 Secure/Multipurpose Internet Mail Extensions (S/MIME) Version 3.2 Certificate Handling
- www.ietf.org/rfc/rfc5750.txt

RFC 5751 Secure/Multipurpose Internet Mail Extensions (S/MIME) Version 3.2 Message Specification
- www.ietf.org/rfc/rfc5751.txt

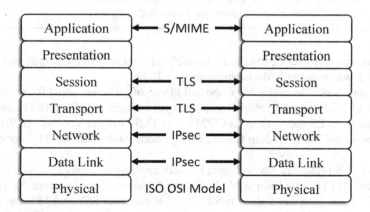

FIGURE 3.3 ISO Open Systems Interconnection (OSI) Model.

During the same time when Taher Elgamal was designing SSL, Netscape was also collaborating with MasterCard to develop a new payment protocol. Initially, MasterCard and Visa competed for a new protocol, but, eventually, MasterCard and Visa cooperated with Microsoft, IBM, Netscape, GTE, and others published the Secure Electronic Transaction (SET) in 1995. SET was deployed

TABLE 3.15

History of SSL and TLS Protocols

Version	Internet Engineering Task Force
SSL v1.0	SSL v1.0 was developed in 1994 by Taher Elgamal, known as the "Father of SSL" when at Netscape. But this version of SSL was never released publicly and was quickly replaced with SSL v2.0 in 1995.
SSL v2.0	SSL v2.0 was released in 1995 but was quickly replaced with v3.0 to correct several problems. However, this version was not officially deprecated until 2011 per RFC 6176 Prohibiting Secure Sockets Layer (SSL) Version 2.0 • https://tools.ietf.org/html/rfc6176
SSL v3.0	SSL v3.0 was released in 1996 and publicly documented in 2011 per RFC 6101 The Secure Sockets Layer (SSL) Protocol Version 3.0 • https://tools.ietf.org/html/rfc6101 This version was officially deprecated in 2015 per RFC 7568 Deprecating Secure Sockets Layer Version 3.0 • https://tools.ietf.org/html/rfc7568
TLS v1.0	TLS v1.0 was published in 1999 per RFC 2246 The TLS Protocol Version 1.0 • https://tools.ietf.org/html/rfc2246 While based on SSL v3.0, this protocol is not backward compatible but many browsers continued to support SSL and TLS.
TLS v1.1	TLS v1.1 was published in 2006 per RFC 4346 The Transport Layer Security (TLS) Protocol Version 1.1 • https://tools.ietf.org/html/rfc4346 This version contains some small security improvements, clarifications, and editorial improvements, including an explicit initialization vector (IV) and cleartext padding to protect against cipher block chaining (CBC) attacks.
TLS v1.2	TLS v1.2 was published in 2008 per RFC 5246 The Transport Layer Security (TLS) Protocol Version 1.2 • https://tools.ietf.org/html/rfc5246 This version contains improved flexibility, particularly for negotiation of cryptographic algorithms; including replacement of the MD5/SHA1 combination in the pseudorandom function (PRF) with SHA-256, merged AES from other RFC with TLS_RSA_WITH_AES_128_CBC_SHA being mandatory, added HMAC-SHA256, removed IDEA and DES, and changed SSL backward compatibility from *should* to *may*.
TLS v1.3	TLS v1.3 was published in 2018 per RFC 8446 The Transport Layer Security (TLS) Protocol Version 1.3 • https://tools.ietf.org/html/rfc8446 This version contains major and minor changes, including deletion of all legacy symmetric algorithms, addition of a zero round-trip time (0-RTT) mode, removal of static asymmetric cipher suites, mandate ephemeral keys, deprecation of RSA key transport, encryption of all messages following the Client Hello and Server Hello messages, updated key derivation functions with HMAC-based Extract-and-Expand Key Derivation Function (HKDF), and expansion of elliptic curve cryptographic (ECC) algorithms.

over the next six years. However, SSL and ultimately TLS were easier, cheaper, and available in all browsers, so SET was eventually decommissioned in 2002.

Meanwhile, jointly developed by Netscape and Microsoft, SSL version 3.0 was released in 1996, which later served as a basis to develop Transport Layer Security (TLS), an IETF standard protocol. The first definition of TLS appeared in RFC 2246: The TLS Protocol Version 1.0. Visa, MasterCard, American Express, and many leading financial institutions have endorsed TLS for commerce over the Internet.

The SSL and TLS protocols run on layers beneath application protocols, such as the Hypertext Transfer Protocol (HTTP), the Simple Mail Transfer Protocol or the Network News Transfer Protocol, and the Transmission Control Protocol (TCP). While both SSL and TLS can add security to any protocol that uses TCP, they occur and are most commonly used in HTTP Secure (HTTPS) implementations. HTTPS serves primarily to secure World Wide Web pages for applications such as electronic commerce. Both the SSL and the TLS protocols use public key cryptography and public key certificates to verify the identity of endpoints (servers and clients). Like SSL (which provided its base), the TLS protocol operates in modular fashion.

SPECIAL NOTE 3-1 SSL DEPRECATED

Neither SSL v2.0 nor SSL v3.0 should be used as a standard practice. Vulnerabilities revealed in 2014 make the use of SSL a poor system management practice. TLS should always be used as the replacement for SSL, and the later versions have fewer known vulnerabilities.

The TLS standard is closely related to SSL 3.0 and has been sometimes referred to as "SSL 3.1." TLS supersedes SSL 2.0 and should be used in all new development efforts and implementations. Because of the similarities between these two protocols, SSL details are not included in this book. The following is from RFC 2246:

> The differences between this protocol and SSL 3.0 are not dramatic, but they are significant enough that TLS 1.0 and SSL 3.0 do not interoperate (although TLS 1.0 does incorporate a mechanism by which a TLS implementation can back down to SSL 3.0).

Many people refer to both protocols as SSL, mostly because the term SSL was in use for such a long period of time, but also because TLS Version 1.0 is actually denoted as *ProtocolVersion* 3.1, which was done for historical purposes. However, calling the protocols SSL or SSL/TLS is incorrect as the two are not equivalent and therefore not interchangeable. Accordingly, TLS v1.1 is *ProtocolVersion* 3.2 and TLS v1.2 is *ProtocolVersion* 3.3 but TLS v1.3 added a Supported Version extension using 3.4 with Legacy Version 3.3. TLS specifications are available at the Transport Security Layer workgroup,[25] and a *Comparison of TLS Implementations* is at the Wikipedia[26] page.

One of the advantages of TLS is that it is a protocol that requires very little action from the end user to establish a secure session. In most common web browsers, users can tell their session is protected when the browser displays a padlock or, in the case of Extended Validation Certificates used with TLS, when the address bar displays both a padlock and a green bar. Usability is one of the primary reasons that TLS/SSL is in such widespread use today.

3.2.1 TLS v1.2 Overview

While TLS v1.0, v1.1, and v1.2 are very similar, this discussion focuses on TLS v1.2 but refers to just TLS as an all-inclusive term. TLS relies on a connection-oriented transport protocol, usually TCP or User Datagram Protocol (UDP). The TLS protocol allows client/server applications to detect the following types of security risks:

- Message tampering
- Message interception
- Message forgery

Figure 3.4 provides a summary of the scheme. TLS relies on a network connection such as TCP/IP to send messages backward and forward. Data flows from the application to the TLS record protocol, where it gets encrypted and compressed before being sent to the other application. The appearance is that information flows between applications.

The TLS handshake protocol also uses the TLS record protocol to send its messages during the handshake phase. The handshake protocol is used to negotiate the parameters of the record protocol that TLS is communicating. The record protocol layer operates according to a group of settings or parameters called a "connection state." The record protocol layer can store four connection

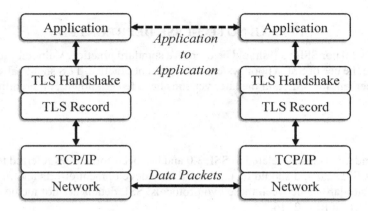

FIGURE 3.4   Transport Layer Security (TLS) protocol overview.

states: two connection states for each direction of communication. Two of the states are current and two are pending, as follows:

- Current transmit connection state
- Pending transmit connection state
- Current receive connection state
- Pending receive connection state

Current refers to the settings that are in effect now. Pending is a group of settings that are being prepared for use next. When a connection state change occurs, the pending state becomes the current state, and a new empty pending set is created. When the connection is first initialized, the current state is null; everything just passes through. There are no keys, no encryption method, and no compression. During this time, the handshake protocol can operate and build up the security parameters in the pending states. When everything is ready, the pending states become the current states and the security goes into effect.

TLS uses certificates for authentication. A certificate is delivered by the server for the client to verify. In the optional second part of the protocol, the server may request a certificate from the client. Client certificates are typically used when there is a need to verify the clients that are accessing the server.

The certificates that TLS uses are generally issued by public certification authorities (CAs) that are already recognized in most client browsers. The nature of asymmetric public key cryptography means that there is a greater overhead to encrypt and decrypt messages than for symmetric key operations. So, TLS does not use public key encryption for bulk data transfers; instead, it uses symmetric keys that are agreed upon between the parties during the TLS handshake phase.

The TLS handshake uses the certificates installed in the server and the client to perform public key cryptography during the authentication process. It also uses public key cryptography to exchange session keys that can be used to encrypt data during the session. Initial communication is established between a client and a server in TLS by using a handshake exchange as shown in Figure 3.5. This involves a series of messages sent between the client and server in a specific order.

At the start of the handshake, the client and server exchange hello messages. This is the start of the identification phase of the TLS protocol. TLS is not a symmetrical protocol; there will always be a client and server even if both computers are servers. One computer must take the role of the server and the other the client. The client sends its hello message first.

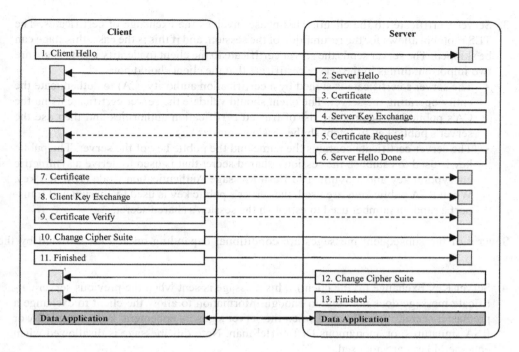

FIGURE 3.5 Transport Layer Security (TLS) handshake.

1. Client Hello (to the server): The *ClientHello* message initiates the TLS communication. It contains a list of the cipher suites, the highest TLS version the client supports, and any optional compression methods that the client can support. A cipher suite is a combination of cryptographic algorithms that the client can understand for protecting the communications to the server. In TLS, the cipher suite defines the type of certificates, the encryption method, and the integrity-checking method. The TLS RFC 2246 defines some standard combinations, and the client indicates which ones it supports, in order of preference. The *ClientHello* also carries a random number called *ClientHello.random*, which can be any value but should be completely unpredictable to everyone (except the client).

2. Server Hello (to the client): When the server receives the *ClientHello* message, it must check that it is able to support one of the cipher suites that the client presented and any optional compression methods. The server then replies with a *ServerHello* message. The *ServerHello* message contains another random number, called *ServerHello.random*, which is different from the client's random number. It also contains the cipher suite, the compression method chosen from the choices offered by the client and a session ID that the client and server use to refer to the session from then on. At this stage, the client and server have exchanged hello messages with the result:
   • The client and server have synchronized their states.
   • The client and server have agreed on a session ID.
   • The client and server have agreed on a cipher suite.
   • The client and server have exchanged two random numbers (nonces).

Synchronizing their states means that the client and the server have established communications and are in sync about the next steps. In the next part of the handshake, both the client and the server must track all the messages they have sent or received. At the end of the handshake, the messages can be used to prove that no intruder has altered or inserted any messages.

3. Server Certificate (to the client): This phase involves the exchange of certificates. The TLS protocol allows for the resumption of the session, and if this is the case, this stage can be skipped. The server sends the server certificate to the client to identify itself. There are two important things in the server certificate that the client should note:
   - The server's certificate is signed by a certification authority (CA) to authenticate the entity operating the server. The client should validate the server certificate using the CA's public key against the list of trusted certification authorities and then use the server's public key to establish the session's master key.
   - The server certificate contains the name and the public key of the server. The public key is used to establish the session's shared secret that is used to derive a symmetric encryption key and a Symmetric Hash Message Authentication Code (HMAC) key. When RSA public keys are used, the server's public key is used to encrypt and transport a random number used to establish the session's shared secret.

Several of the subsequent messages are conditional depending on actions initiated by the server.

4. Server Key Exchange (to the client): This message is sent when the previous server certificate message does not contain enough information to allow the client to exchange a premaster secret, typically used when the server signs its ephemeral keys using DSA or RSA signatures, or anonymous Diffie–Hellman. Note this message is disallowed when ephemeral keys are not used.
5. Client Certificate Request (to the client): As an optional part of the TLS protocol, the server may require the client to identify itself by sending a certificate. For most web-based applications, this is uncommon because many clients do not have a certificate. It is more common for server-to-server TLS sessions for both servers, the server acting as the client and the server acting as the server to have certificates.

A financial institution using TLS for internal network security might choose to give out certificates to all of its employees issued by its own certification authority. If this approach is taken, the server can be configured to request a certificate from the client for client-side identification.

6. Server Hello Done (to the client): At this point, the client and the server have exchanged hello messages. The server has sent its certificate and may have requested the client to send the client's certificate. At this point, the server sends a *ServerHelloDone* message and waits for the client to take the next step.
7. Client Certificate (to the server): The client sends the client's certificate to the server to identify itself only in response to the server's request for the client's certificate. Otherwise, the client does not offer its certificate.
8. Client Key Exchange (to the server): The *ClientKeyExchange* message is to create a master key between the client and the server. This key combines the random numbers that were exchanged in the hello message with a secret value that is created dynamically by the two parties (the client and the server).

The random numbers (nonces) sent during the hello phase could have been eavesdropped on by anybody monitoring the network because they were exchanged in the clear and not encrypted. There are two steps to this phase. First, a random value is created known as the premaster secret, which will be used to generate the master key. The client then generates a random number (48 bytes), encrypts it using the server's public key, and sends it to the server using a *ClientKeyExchange* message. The server decrypts it with the server's private key so that both sides have the premaster secret.

9. Certificate Verify (to the server): At this point, the client certificate is verified. The client does this by hashing together all the messages up to this point, including both the messages sent and the messages received. The client sends the result in a Certificate Verify message to the server and digitally signs the message with the private key of the client's certificate. The server receives the digitally signed message and checks the digital signature using the client's public key from the client's certificate. If the signature verifies, the server then computes the hash of messages and checks that the hash matches what the client sent. If the signature or the hash check fails, the server should drop the connection unless there is a technical or business justification to proceed. Otherwise, if all of the checks are successful, the server can proceed to the next step.

    The client and the server are now in a position to compute the master secret. Both the client and the server have the following information:
    - Premaster secret
    - Client random number (nonce)
    - Server random number (nonce)

Now both the server and the client can hash these values to produce a master secret (key). Because of the two random numbers shared between the server and the client, no one eavesdropping on the session can use a recording of the communication to generate the same value.

10. Change Cipher Spec (to the server): The client now sends a *ChangeCipherSpec* record, indicating to the server that all future communications will be authenticated and encrypted to the server with the new master key.
11. Finished (to the server): The last step for the client is to send an encrypted *Finished* message to the server. The finished message contains a hash of the new master secret and all the handshake messages that have been exchanged from the hello message up to (but not including) the finished message. The server will attempt to decrypt the client's finished message and verify the HMAC. If the decryption or verification fails, the handshake has failed and the connection should be torn down.
12. Change Cipher Spec (to the client): Now the server sends a *ChangeCipherSpec* message to the client indicating to the client that all future communications will be authenticated and encrypted to the client with the newly established session master keys.
13. Finished (to the client): The last step for the server is to send an encrypted *Finished* message to the client. The client then performs the same decryption and verification that the server just completed. At this point, the TLS handshake is completed and the application protocol is enabled for use between the client and the server. As you can see, the certificates of the server and optionally the client play a major role in the authentication and encryption of the TLS session. Without a trusted PKI to issue the certificates, the TLS protocol cannot function effectively. We now move down the OSI stack to the Network and Data Link layers using IPsec.

SPECIAL NOTE 3-2 EARLY TLS DEPRECATION

Neither TLS v1.0 nor TLS v1.1 should be used as a standard practice. Additionally, TLS v1.2 weaker cipher suites should not be used. Further, migration to TLS v1.3 should be paramount.

Functionally, all TLS protocol versions negotiate session keys, which are subsequently used to protect data packets during transmission. However, TLS v1.3 has significantly restricted its key negotiation and further changed its data structure using various extensions.

3.2.2 TLS v1.3 Overview

TLS v.1.3 includes major and minor changes. One of the major changes for TLS v1.3 is the cipher suite mandate for ephemeral keys. When a TLS server has a public key certificate, its public and private keys are considered static, meaning the static key pair is reused for many sessions. But when a TLS server dynamically generates a key pair per session, the key pair is ephemeral. Since the ephemeral key pair has such a short life span, literally a few seconds, there is insufficient time for the TLS server to get an ephemeral public key certificate. Mandating ephemeral keys impacts both key agreement and key transport methods.

1) The Diffie–Hellman (DH) key agreement protocol must be used with ephemeral (DHE) keys. However, there are differences between the IETF specifications and the X9.42 standard for how DHE can be processed.
2) The Elliptic Curve Diffie–Hellman (ECDH) key agreement protocol must be used with ephemeral (ECDHE) keys. However, there are differences between the IETF specifications and the X9.63 standard for how ECDHE can be processed.
3) The RSA key transport is deprecated because this algorithm cannot support ephemeral keys. Note that RSA digital signatures are still supported for signing certificates, signing ephemeral keys, and mutual authentication.

The security concept behind ephemeral keys is forward secrecy, sometimes called perfect forward secrecy (PFC), which is a countermeasure to static key compromise. Static key compromise is a situation where the TLS server's private key has been disclosed to an unauthorized entity, enabling an attacker to replay the TLS handshake, reestablish the session keys, and decrypt the transmitted data that was previously thought secure. Consider the following two conditions:

A. The complete TLS session, from the initial *ClientHello* message to the final *Close_Notify* alert message indicating the session has been terminated, has been recorded.
B. The server's static private key is made available to an authorized entity.

The handshake protocol from the *ClientHello* to the *Finished* messages can be replayed such that with the exchange of the server's static public key certificate and access to the server's static private key, the session keys can be reestablished. Thus, the encrypted data packets can be decrypted and the data can be disclosed any time after the actual TLS session. However, consider a third condition:

C. The server's static private key is compromised and available to an unauthorized entity.

When the recording is done by an unauthorized entity and the server's static private key is compromised, the session might be decrypted at any time in the future. The complete handshake protocol can be replayed, and the session keys can be reestablished. This is often called the "Harvest Now and Decrypt Later," attack but there are similar names. Even if the server static keys are changed, any previously recorded session can still be decrypted.

The inclusion of an ephemeral key pair and its immediate destruction following the establishment of the TLS session keys disable the replay capability. While the exchange of the ephemeral public key is recorded as part of the handshake protocol, the destruction of the ephemeral key prevents session keys from being reestablished. Thus, even if the server's static private key was ever compromised, an attacker still cannot replay the handshake protocol without access to the ephemeral private key. However, the IETF chose ephemeral-only keys.

Table 3.16 shows the static keys and ephemeral keys options included in the X9.42 and X9.63 financial services industry standards. Alice and Bob exchange public keys so they can each compute a shared secret using cryptographic key agreement. They might exchange static public certificates, ephemeral public keys, or both. The static keys use the same domain parameters and the ephemeral keys use the same domain parameters, but the domain parameters can be different for the static and ephemeral keys. Another option is for Alice to use both static and ephemeral keys, but Bob only uses a static key, and the reverse.

Regarding SSL and TLS, Diffie–Hellman ephemeral keys were supported as early as SSL v3.0, where the server ephemeral public key is signed using its RSA or DSA certificate. Thus, the server still has a static key and provides its RSA or DSA public key certificate for verification of the signed ephemeral public key. But the server static keys are only for signing and verifying its ephemeral public key and are not Diffie–Hellman static keys. Likewise, the client provides its ephemeral public key, but it is unsigned. Hence, SSL only supported the X9 option #6, where both parties, the TLS client and server, only used ephemeral keys. As noted in the RFC 6101 specification on cipher suites:

> DHE denotes ephemeral Diffie-Hellman, where the Diffie-Hellman parameters are signed by a DSS or RSA certificate, which has been signed by the CA. The signing algorithm used is specified after the DH or DHE parameter. In all cases, the client must have the same type of certificate, and must use the Diffie-Hellman parameters chosen by the server.

Elliptic Curve Cryptography (ECC) cipher suites for TLS v1.1 were introduced per RFC 4492 in 2006, which included Elliptic Curve Diffie–Hellman (ECDH) without ephemeral keys, ECDHE with ephemeral keys, and Elliptic Curve Digital Signature Algorithm (ECDSA). ECDH and ECDHE are used for key agreement, and ECDSA is used to sign static public key certificates or ephemeral public keys. All versions of TLS support the X9 second option, where the TLS client and server only use ephemeral keys for key agreement. See Table 3.17 for TLS v1.3 cipher suites.

TABLE 3.16
X9 Static and Ephemeral Keys

#	Alice		Bob	
1	Static Keys	-	-	Static Keys
2	-	Ephemeral Keys	Ephemeral Keys	-
3	Static Keys	Ephemeral Keys	Ephemeral Keys	Static Keys
4	Static Keys	Ephemeral Keys	-	Static Keys
5	Static Keys	-	Ephemeral Keys	Static Keys

TABLE 3.17
TLS v1.3 Cipher Suites

Description	Value	IETF
TLS_AES_128_GCM_SHA256	{0x13, 0x01}	RFC 8446
TLS_AES_256_GCM_SHA384	{0x13, 0x02}	RFC 8446
TLS_CHACHA20_POLY1305_SHA256	{0x13, 0x03}	RFC 8446
TLS_AES_128_CCM_SHA256	{0x13, 0x04}	RFC 8446
TLS_AES_128_CCM_8_SHA256	{0x13, 0x05}	RFC 8446

Another major change is the general use of extensions, added to many of the handshake messages including *ClientHello* (CH), *ServerHello* (SH), *EncryptedExtensions* (EE), *CertificateRequest* (CR), Certificate (CT), *NewSessionTicket* (NS), and *HelloRetryRequest* (HR). Other messages are not afforded extensions. See Table 3.18 for the list of extensions and messages.

Similar to previous versions of TLS, the Client Hello and Server Hello messages are exchanged unprotected across the network. However, unlike previous versions, the subsequent handshake messages are encrypted. The client and server exchange their Diffie–Hellman or Elliptic Curve Diffie–Hellman ephemeral public keys in the Client Hello and Server Hello messages using the key share (51) extension. This allows both sides to compute a shared secret, from which the session keys are derived. Alternatively, Pre-Shared Key (PSK) might also be used. Regardless, all Data Application messages are protected, as that is the point of using any version of TLS. See Figure 3.6 for an overview of the TLS v1.3 protocol.

At the start of the TLS v1.3 handshake, similar to previous TLS versions, the client and server exchange hello messages. However, the *ClientHello* and *ServerHello* messages contain a variety of extensions that replace several of the previous TLS version messages.

1. Client Hello (to the server): The *ClientHello* message initiates the TLS communication. It contains the same information as did previous TLS versions with extensions.
2. Server Hello (to the client): When the server receives the *ClientHello* message, it must check that it is able to support one of the cipher suites that the client presented, and then replies with a *ServerHello* message, which contains the same information as did previous TLS versions with extensions.

TABLE 3.18

TLS Extensions

Tag	Identifier	CH	SH	EE	CR	CT	HR	NS
(0)	server_name	CH	-	EE	-	-	-	-
(1)	max_fragment_length	CH	-	EE	-	-	-	-
(5)	status_request	CH	-	-	CR	CT	-	-
(10)	supported_groups	CH	-	EE	-	-	-	-
(13)	signature_algorithms	CH	-	-	CR	-	-	-
(14)	use_srtp	CH	-	EE	-	-	-	-
(15)	heartbeat	CH	-	EE	-	-	-	-
(16)	application_layer_protocol_negotiation	CH	-	EE	-	-	-	-
(18)	signed_certificate_timestamp	CH	-	-	CR	CT	-	-
(19)	client_certificate_type	CH	-	EE	-	-	-	-
(20)	server_certificate_type	CH	-	EE	-	-	-	-
(21)	padding	CH	-	-	-	-	-	-
(41)	pre_shared_key	CH	SH	-	-	-	-	-
(42)	early_data	CH	-	EE	-	-	-	NS
(43)	supported_versions	CH	SH	-	-	-	HR	-
(44)	cookie	CH	-	-	-	-	HR	-
(45)	psk_key_exchange_modes	CH	-	-	-	-	-	-
(47)	certificate_authorities	CH	-	-	CR	-	-	-
(48)	oid_filters	-	-	-	CR	-	-	-
(49)	post_handshake_auth	CH	-	-	-	-	-	-
(50)	signature_algorithms_cert	CH	-	-	CR	-	-	-
(51)	key_share	CH	SH	-	-	-	HR	-

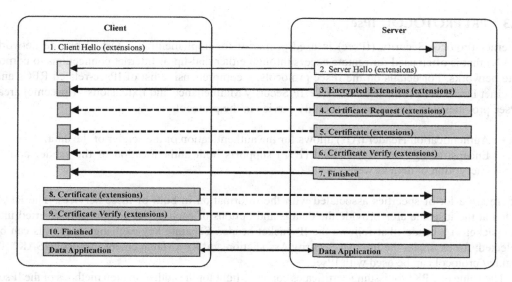

FIGURE 3.6   TLS v1.3 handshake.

The *ClientHello* and *ServerHello* messages with extensions exchange sufficient information such that the session keys are established and subsequent messages are encrypted.

3. Encrypted Extensions (to the client): In addition to the *ServerHello* message, when the server receives the *ClientHello* message, it must send an *EncryptedExtension* message immediately after the *ServerHello* message.
4. Certificate Request (to the client): An optional message requesting a client certificate for client authentication, sometimes called mutual authentication.
5. Server Certificate (to the client): The server optionally provides its certificate so the client can verify the server's signature on the server's ephemeral public key or a *CertificateVerify* message.
6. Certificate Verify (to the client): The server optionally provides a digital signature over the entire handshake using its private key corresponding to its public key in the previous *ServerCertificate* message.
7. Finished (to the client): The server provides a Message Authentication Code (MAC) over the entire handshake.
8. Client Certificate (to the server): The client sends the client's certificate to the server to identify itself only in response to the server request for the client's certificate.
9. Certificate Verify (to the server): The client provides a digital signature over the entire handshake using its private key corresponding to its public key in the previous Certificate message.
10. Finished (to the server): The client provides a Message Authentication Code (MAC) over the entire handshake.

Other changes include a new zero round-trip time (0-RTT) mode, saving a round trip at connection setup for some application data, at the cost of some security properties. The key derivation functions (KDF) have been redesigned using HMAC-based Extract-and-Expand Key Derivation Function (HKDF). Extensions have been provided for numerous messages, including the Client Hello, Server Hello, Encrypted Extensions, Certificate, Certificate Request, New Session Ticket, and Hello Retry Request.

3.3   PKI PROTOCOL: IPsec

Internet Protocol Security (IPsec) is used primarily for implementing a virtual private network (VPN) that is often used for remote access through either dial-up or Internet connections to corporate networks. For details on the IPsec protocols, a comprehensive list of IPsec-related RFCs and Internet Drafts are available at the IETF IP Security Maintenance and Extensions[27] (ipsecme) area. IPsec provides two choices of the security service in the protocol:

- Authentication Header (AH) allows for the authentication of the sender of the data.
- Encapsulating Security Payload (ESP) supports both authentication of the sender and encryption of data as well.

There are a lot of specifics associated with the information in both of these services. The RFCs listed at the ipsecme area provide the details and options of each of the components inserted into the packet in a header that follows the IP packet header. Separate key exchange protocols can be selected; for example, the Internet Security Association and Key Management Protocol (ISAKMP) Oakley protocol can be used with IPsec.

The value of a PKI for issuing certificates comes to light for the authentication methods of the IPsec protocol. Windows-based IPsec implementations allow you to use Kerberos, certificate-based authentication, or a pre-shared key (PSK) for authentication. Each of these approaches has its advantages and disadvantages, but certificate-based authentication is the most flexible and easiest to manage.

- Kerberos is the default authentication technology on Windows. This method can be used for any clients running Kerberos that are members of the same or trusted domains.
- Certificate-based authentication should be used across the Internet, for remote access to corporate resources and business-to-business (B2B) external business partner communications or for computers that do not support Kerberos. The certificates should be issued from a mutually trusted certification authority, preferably a commercial CA that both parties trust in the case of business-to-business (B2B) IPsec communications.
- The use of PSK carries with it the challenge of protecting the keys from generation to destruction and their management. The PSK must be transmitted to all parties involved in the IPsec communications and rotated at the same time for all of the parties involved.

Using certificates for IPsec-enabled devices such as routers means that certificates are issued to devices rather than people. The device name within the certificate needs to be meaningful within the domain of the VPN. The IPsec asymmetric private and public key pair needs to be generated, the public key certificate needs to be issued, and the various certificates need to be distributed to the other devices. Now let's move up the OSI stack to the Application layer and consider securing e-mail.

3.4   PKI PROTOCOL: S/MIME

Secure/Multipurpose Internet Mail Extensions (S/MIME) is a widely accepted protocol for sending digitally signed and encrypted messages. A comprehensive list of related RFCs and Internet Drafts is available at the S/MIME Mail Security[28] (SMIME) area. S/MIME provides cryptographic security services such as authentication message integrity and nonrepudiation of the sender using digital signatures and confidentiality using encryption. The sender signs the e-mail using its private key, and the receiver verifies the signature using the sender's certificate. The sender encrypts the e-mail using the receiver's certificate, and the receiver decrypts the e-mail using its private key.

S/MIME provides the option of using a single certificate for both encrypting messages and digital signing or using two certificates, one for signing and one for encrypting e-mails. Thus, the receiver might use the sender's certificate to validate the sender's signature and likewise the same sender's certificate to encrypt messages. Alternatively, the receiver might use one certificate to validate the sender's signature and another certificate to encrypt messages.

For S/MIME to verify the authentication of the sender, it is important to verify the validity of the certificates associated with the incoming signed messages by (1) validating the certificate authority trust chain for the certificate (the process of validating the CA trust chain involves traversing the chain of trust on certificates until a root CA is reached), (2) verifying that the certificate has not expired, and (3) verifying that the CA has not revoked the certificate used to sign or encrypt the message. To do this, you must either download the certificate revocation list (CRL) from the CA or send an Online Certificate Status Protocol (OCSP) query about the status of the certificate to the CA's OCSP responder.

The decision to use a single S/MIME certificate for both signing and encryption or use one certificate for signing and one certificate for encryption can be tied to the policies that the company is looking to implement. While a single S/MIME certificate for both signing and encryption can be easier for small companies to implement due to fewer certificates to issue and manage, combining the two functions into a single certificate can present a problem if the company intends to escrow the encryption keys. In the situation where the encryption private key and the digital signing private key are one and the same, when you escrow the encryption private key for the company to recover encrypted e-mails at a later date, you are also escrowing the private digital signing key. Larger companies may want to split the functions of signing and encryption into two certificates so that the encryption private keys can be escrowed, but the digital signing private key will not, so that there is only a single copy of the digital signing private key for non-reputation aspects.

3.5 PKI METHODS: LEGAL SIGNATURES

Above and beyond using S/MIME to exchange signed e-mail messages, let's consider using digital signatures for signing legal documents. The purpose of a signed legal document is to demonstrate authorization or agreement on the document's content. Because this is a business process, it does not reside within the Open Systems Interconnection (OSI) Application layer; rather, it sits above the OSI 7-layer model using the signer's private key to generate the digital signature. Figure 3.7 shows one possible scenario for signing legal documents.

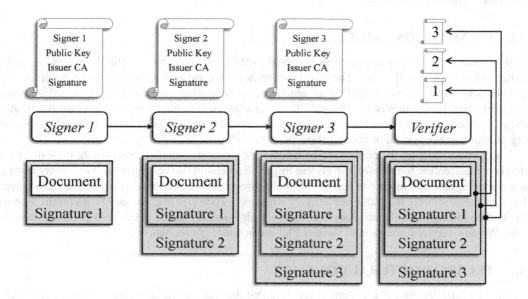

FIGURE 3.7 Example of a legal signature.

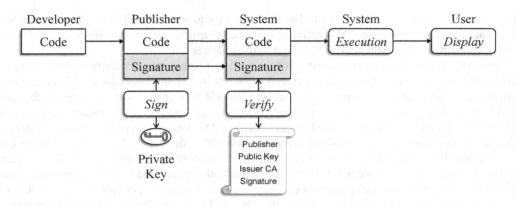

FIGURE 3.8   Example code signing.

In this scenario, we use three signers and one verifier. Signer 1 generates a digital signature over the document indicating agreement and then forwards the signed document to Signer 2. Signer 2 should validate Signer 1's certificate and signature before adding its signature to the document. Signer 2 generates a digital signature over the signed document indicating agreement and then forwards the double-signed document to Signer 3. Likewise, Signer 3 should validate both previous signers' certificates and signatures before adding its signature. Signer 3 generates a digital signature over the double-signed document indicating agreement and then forwards the triple-signed document to the verifier. The verifier then validates each of the signer's certificates and signatures to assure that each signer has provided agreement to the document.

In the legal signature scenario, the signers are actively engaged using a PKI-enabled application to generate signatures with their private keys and verify signatures with the other signers' certificates. The verifier is actively engaged using a PKI-enabled application to verify signatures with the signers' certificates. Another example of a technology process that relies on signatures and certificates without active user participation is code signing. Figure 3.8 shows a typical scenario for software authentication and integrity.

3.6   PKI METHODS: CODE SIGN

In this scenario, we show four entities involved in the code sign process: the developer, the publisher, the system, and the user. The developer writes the code and submits it to the publisher for distribution; the developer might be an employee or contractor of the publisher or a third-party provider hired by the publisher. The publisher signs the code using its private key and distributes the signed code to the system for verification and execution; the publisher might belong to the same organization as the system or another third-party provider.

The system validates the publisher's certificate and signature and then executes the code that then displays information to the user; the system might be a network server, a personal computer getting a software update or running an applet within a browser, or a mobile device running a mobile app. For this scenario, only the publisher actively engages in code signing; the user relies on the system to validate the signed code and does not verify the signature using the publisher's code sign certificate. We now turn our attention to various PKI architecture components.

3.7   PKI ARCHITECTURAL CONCEPTS

Public key infrastructure is a system of services that provide for the lifecycle management of public key certificates. This system has multiple operational components implemented in a legal and technical framework that can provide several security services. A PKI can provide the following services:

- Confidentiality: Assurance that the receiving entity is the intended recipient (encrypt/decrypt)
- Authentication: Proof that the entity is who they claim to be (public/private key)
- Integrity: Verification that no unauthorized modification of data has occurred (digital signature)
- Non-repudiation: Assurance that the entity sending information cannot deny participation (digital signature)

PKI is more than just a single technology or single process. Fundamentally PKI can be considered as an authentication technology. Using a combination of asymmetric key cryptography, a PKI enables several other security technologies including nonrepudiation, data integrity, data confidentiality, and key management. We will start with definitions of the key components in the PKI and then explore each of them in some depth. We will start with the certificates and the operation of the CA that issues them. The CA is the very foundation of the PKI since it is the only component that can issue public key certificates. Public key certificates are digitally signed by the issuing CA, which effectively binds the subject name to the public key.

Public key (digital) certificate: A certificate is a computer-generated object that ties the subscriber's identification with the subscriber's public key in a trusted relationship. This trust is based on the registration and identification policies and procedures in the trusted third party that the certification authority goes through each time it issues a certificate. The certificate contains several data elements including important identification information: the name of the certification authority issuing the certificate, the name of the subscriber, and the subscriber's public key. The CA digitally signs all of the data elements in the certificate to bind the information to the subscriber in a form that can be verified by any third (relying) parties that want to make use of the information in the certificate. We will explore more details of certificates later in the chapter.

Certification authority (CA): The CA is a trusted entity responsible for identifying and authenticating entities and creating the digital certificates that bind the entities to the public key presented to the CA. The CA is the issuer of certificates and provides status (valid, invalid, or unknown) on those certificates in the form of a certificate revocation list (CRL) or a real-time response via an Online Certificate Status Protocol (OCSP). It may also support a variety of administrative functions, although some of these can be delegated to one or more registration authorities (RAs). Operating a CA is much more than just running an application that can generate digital certificates; many open-source software programs can generate certificates with ease.

Operating a trusted CA is the core of a PKI. Consider the example of a driver's license issued by a department of motor vehicles of a state government. Compare that identity with a driver's license prepared on a copy machine by an individual. Both are working credentials vouching for someone's identity, but the two documents have vastly different strengths due to the trust placed in the issuer of the credentials. The process of identification and authentication that the driver's license bureau goes through prior to issuing a driver's license is what provides the strength of the credential. The driver's license bureau can even be consulted like a CA to determine if the license that it issued is still valid or not.

The CA implements processes and procedures that verify the identity of the subscriber to the PKI. The resulting digital certificate is the proof of that identity according to the CA. Certificates are issued for a specific time period, and the CA has the ability to revoke the certificate and inform relying parties of the PKI that the certificate has been revoked.

Registration authority (RA): The RA is a functional component of a PKI that can assume some of the administrative functions from the CA. The RA is normally associated with the subscriber registration process but can assist in other areas as well. This would include the identification and authentication of the identity of the subscriber registering with the PKI. However, the RA can perform several other functions, including the following:
- Validating the attributes of the entity who is requesting the certificate,
- Conducting interactions with the CA (or several CAs) as an intermediary of the subscriber, and
- Interacting with subscribers for certificate requests, certificate revocation requests, key compromise notifications, and key recovery requests.

Note that although the RA can off-load many functions from the CA, the RA can never be the issuer of a public key certificate. The use of RAs can provide multiple advantages to a PKI. RAs can spread the overall costs of operating a PKI to multiple locations and entities. This is especially true in large, geographically distributed organizations that require their users to be physically present for identification and authentication procedures. An example might be subscriber registration, but other PKI-related functions such as subscriber-initiated requests for certificate revocation or key pair recovery might also apply. There may also be other operational issues to consider, such as when an organization elects to outsource the operations of their CA but retains control over the registration processes of the end entities.

Repository: A repository is a generic term used to describe a method for storing certificates and revocation information (CRLs) so that they can be retrieved by subscribers or other relying parties. The term "repository" is often associated with a directory, for example, an X.500-based directory with client access via the Lightweight Directory Access Protocol (LDAP), or it may be something much simpler such as retrieval of a flat file on a remote server via the File Transfer Protocol (FTP or SFTP) or the Hypertext Transfer Protocol (HTTP or HTTPS).

Certificate chain: The certification path can also be referred to as the chain of certificates between a given certificate and its trust anchor (root CA certificate). Each certificate in the chain must be verified in order to validate the certificate at the end of the chain. This is a critical component of a PKI: the ability to check all aspects of a certificate's validity. Each CA of the PKI hierarchy is issued a certificate, and that certificate can be revoked just like an end entity certificate. A relying party can only be assured of the validity of the end entity certificate by validating each part of the certificate chain on which it is relying. Best practice is to validate the entire certificate chain prior to relying upon the end entity certificate.

Subscriber: Also called subject, is a generic term used to denote end users, devices (e.g., servers, routers), or any other entity that can be identified in the subject field of a public key certificate. Subscribers typically consume services from a PKI.

End entities: End entities can be thought of as the end users of the PKI. The term "end entity" is meant to be very generic in describing the consumer of the certificates produced by the CA. An end entity can be an end user, a device such as a router, firewall or a server, a software program or application, or anything that can be identified in the subject name of a public key certificate. An end entity can even be a part of the PKI. For example, an RA could be an end entity within a PKI because it is issued a certificate with the RA's information in the subject name of a certificate.

Relying Parties are people, devices, or organizations that rely on certificates and the PKI that issued the certificate to make decisions, make resources available to the users, or accept instructions from the users. Best practices for relying parties include the following:

- Verify that the certificate they are about to rely upon has not been revoked by checking either the CRL or OCSP status of the certificate.
- Verify that the certificate they are about to rely upon is within its valid usage period, has not expired, and is after the valid from date.
- Verify the certificate chain that all certificates issued to CAs within the certificate chain are valid.
- Only use the certificate for its intended use as described by policy, the Certificate Practice Statements of the PKI.

Chapter 4, "PKI Management and Security," uses definitions from the PKI Assurance Guideline (PAG) and ISO 21188 for the CA, the RA, the relying party, and the subscriber. See Table 4.9 for a comparison between the two sets of definitions.

Certificate validity checking: Part of the CA's responsibility is to issue digital certificates to individuals, computers, and applications. Once those certificates are issued, the CA also has the responsibility to provide a mechanism to determine if a certificate is valid or has been revoked by the PKI. The certificate revocation status information must be made available to individuals, computers, and applications attempting to verify the validity of certificates that the PKI has issued. Certificates are issued with a specific lifetime (one hour, one year, and five years) indicated by the difference between the valid to and valid from dates within the certificate. Once issued, a certificate becomes valid once its validity time has been reached as indicated in the valid from field within the certificate, and it is considered valid until its expiration date (valid to date). The circumstances that existed when the certificate was issued can change before the certificate might expire. Reasons for revocation of a certificate include the following:

- Suspected or actual private key compromise
- Change in affiliation (e.g., when an employee terminates employment with an organization)
- Change of the employee's name

Therefore, it is sometimes necessary to revoke a certificate before its expiration date. The revocation request allows an end entity (or RA) to request revocation of a given certificate. Under such circumstances, the CA needs to revoke the certificate and use one of the methods outlined as follows to make the revocation information available to relying parties.

Certificate Revocation List (CRL): A certificate revocation list (RFC 2459) is exactly that: a list of certificates that the CA has revoked and placed on a digitally signed revocation list. A CRL is a time-stamped list of revoked certificates, which is signed by a CA and made available to all subscribers of the PKI (all relying parties within the PKI). The CRL is a file that contains serial numbers of the certificates that have been revoked and are invalid. Relying parties should check the CRL for the certificate's serial number that they are about to rely upon, and if the certificate is on the CRL, the relying party should not trust the certificate and should abort the transaction.

There are several types of CRLs: full CRLs, delta CRLs (changes in the CRL from the last full CRL), and CRL distribution points (CDPs). Full CRLs contain the status of all certificates. Delta CRLs contain only the status of all certificates that have changed status between the issuance of the last full CRL and the current full CRL. CRL distribution points are used to indicate a location for full and delta CRLs.

Online Certificate Status Protocol (OCSP): OCSP is an Internet-based protocol used for obtaining the revocation status of an X.509 digital certificate. The OCSP is described in RFC 2560 and updated in RFC 6960. OCSP was created as a real-time way to check the status of a certificate in addition to checking the certificate revocation lists (CRLs). In a large PKI, the size and processing of very large CRLs can slow down and hamper many applications from checking the status of the certificates that a relying party is about to rely upon. Responses can be obtained on individual certificates via OCSP instead of downloading the entire CRL list or a portion of the CRL list. The "request then response" nature of OCSP queries led to OCSP servers being called OCSP responders.

An OCSP responder is typically a server or group of servers, run by the CA or outsourced to a third party to return a signed OCSP response indicating if a certificate specified in the request is "good," "revoked," or "unknown." If an OCSP responder cannot process a request, it may return an error code. If the OCSP server cannot respond, the client may time out. If the OCSP server cannot be reached, the client may incur a network error.

Certificate Transparency: is another Internet-based protocol (RFC 6962) used for publicly logging Transport Layer Security (TLS) certificates. The logging structure uses Merkle Hash Trees. When a certificate is submitted to a logging system, a Signed Certificate Timestamp (SCT) is returned, which might be included as an extension in the actual X.509 certificate. Conceptually the relying party or any auditor can verify the SCT within the certificate and corresponding log.

OCSP Stapling: is a host-based alternative (RFC 6961) to client-based SCT verification. Instead of the client checking the OCSP based on the SCT contained in the TLS certificate, the host can cache the OCSP response and provide it to the client as part of the TLS handshake. Thus, instead of each client checking the OCSP per TLS connection, the host checks the OCSP for many clients, reducing the number of OCSP checks possibly from hundreds of clients per minute to one host per minute. This technique is often used for performance improvement.

Certificate Pinning: is another relying party trust model (RFC 7469) using a whitelist. When a CA certificate is pinned, any end-entity certificate issued by that CA is implicitly trusted. When an entity-entity certificate is pinned only that specific certificate is trusted. Regardless, the certificate must still be validated, including its expiration date and revocation status. Some implementations might "pin" only the certificate public key or its corresponding Subject Key Identification (SKI), which is a hash of the actual public key.

Certificate Uniqueness: is the concept that each certificate has a unique name and unique public key. While an end-entity certificate with the same public key and name might be inadvertently issued by the same CA, the certificate will at least have a different serial number and therefore a different certificate signature. Thus, the relying party can still validate the certificates. Refer to Section 2.2, "Authentication," and Figure 2.10 for certificate validation. However, what if one of the CA certificates were not unique? Consider Figure 3.9 with two Root CA Certificates.

To construct the certificate chain, the relying party gets the issuing CA name from the subject certificate and gets the root CA name from the issuing CA certificate but discovers there are two different root CA certificates with the same name and public key. Assuming they are both valid,

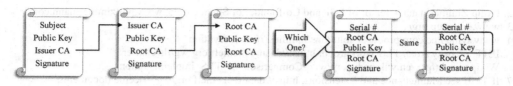

FIGURE 3.9 Certificate uniqueness.

either will work, but which one? Likely the relying party only has one root CA installed in its trust store, but then another relying party might have installed the other. Thus, two different relying parties might validate the same subject certificate but using different certificate chains from the same public PKI. Essentially, each certificate should be unique.

SPECIAL NOTE 3-3 CERTIFICATE UNIQUENESS

Every certificate in a PKI, especially CA certificates, needs to be relatively unique with different names, different public keys, and different serial numbers.

Now that we have discussed the various PKI building blocks including standards, protocols, and architectural components, we turn our attention toward managing PKI systems. Management aspects need to incorporate policies, practices, procedures, roles, responsibilities, and other considerations including security, operations, incidents, and overall governance. We begin with the next chapter on how to develop PKI policies and practices.

NOTES

1. AIA is an IETF extension, www.rfc-editor.org/rfc/rfc5280
2. ASC X9, http://x9.org/about/missions-and-objectives/
3. IETF, www.ietf.org/about/mission.html
4. ISO, www.iso.org/iso/jtc1_home.html
5. OASIS, www.oasis-open.org/
6. OASIS PKCS 11 Technical Committee, www.oasis-open.org/committees/tc_home.php?wg_abbrev=pkcs11
7. Moore's Law and Intel Innovation, www.intel.com/content/www/us/en/history/museum-gordon-moore-law.html
8. Entities Cross-Certified with the Federal Bridge, www.idmanagement.gov/entitiescross-certified-federal-bridge
9. Federal Information Processing Standards (FIPS) General Information, www.nist.gov/itl/fipsinfo.cfm
10. Federal Register, The Daily Journal of the United States Government, www.federalregister.gov
11. Federal Information Processing Standards Publications (FIPS PUBS), www.nist.gov/itl/fips.cfm
12. Chief Information Officer for the United States Government, http://cio.gov
13. Common Criteria v3.1. Release 4, www.commoncriteriaportal.org/cc/
14. National Information Assurance Partnership (NIAP), Common Criteria Evaluation and Validation Scheme (CCEVS), www.niap-ccevs.org/
15. Department of Defense, Rainbow Series Standards, http://csrc.nist.gov/publications/secpubs/#rainbow
16. National Security Agency, Computer Security Center (NCSC) Rainbow Series, http://fas.org/irp/nsa/rainbow.htm
17. American National Standards Institute, Standards Store, http://webstore.ansi.org
18. ISO Standards Store, www.iso.org/iso/home/store.htm
19. NIST Computer Security Division, Computer Security Resource Center, Smartcard Research & Development, http://csrc.nist.gov/groups/SNS/smartcard/
20. Smart Card Alliance (SCA), www.smartcardalliance.org/
21. Europay-MasterCard-Visa EMVCo., www.emvco.com/

22. Philip Zimmermann, Creator of PGP and Co-founder of Silent Circle, www.philzimmermann.com
23. www.openpgp.org/
24. www.symantec.com/products-solutions/families/?fid=encryption
25. IETF Security Area, TLS Workgroup, https://datatracker.ietf.org/wg/tls/charter/
26. Wikipedia, https://en.wikipedia.org/wiki/Comparison_of_TLS_implementations
27. IETF IPsec Maintenance and Extensions, https://datatracker.ietf.org/wg/ipsecme/documents/
28. IETF Security Area, Secure/Multipurpose Internet Mail Extensions (SMIME) Workgroup, www.ietf.org/
    mailman/listinfo/smim/

4 PKI Management and Security

This chapter builds on the security fundamentals, cryptography basics, and PKI building blocks presented in the previous three chapters. Further, in the first chapter, we mentioned that this book addresses public key infrastructure (PKI) policies, standards, practices, and procedures. We also discussed industry standards organizations, including ANSI, IETF, ISO, NIST, RSA Labs, W3C, and X9, which have all published PKI-related standards. While some businesses rely entirely on industry standards, others feel compelled to develop and maintain their own internal standards. Regardless, whether a business depends on external standards, internal standards, or both, standards play a special role between policies and practices.

Policy statements are basically high-level requirements, essentially goals that define "what" needs to be achieved. Practices are fundamentally statements of fact that identify "how" the goals are met. However, in order for the practices to be effective, detailed requirements are typically needed, which can be addressed by standards. Standards can fill the middle ground between policy and practices. For example, a policy statement might be the following:

- Example policy statement: *Cryptographic keys shall be managed in a secure manner.*

Attempting to write a corresponding practice statement from such a high-level, rather generic policy statement gives a relatively meaningless, unsubstantiated claim:

- Example practice statement: *Cryptographic keys are managed in a secure manner.*

Another approach might be to write practice statements at a more detailed level using the key life-cycle introduced in Chapter 2, "Cryptography Basics":

- Example 1: Keys are generated in compliance with approved methods.
- Example 2: Keys are distributed in compliance with approved methods.
- Example 3: Keys are used in compliance with approved methods.
- Example 4: Keys are backed up in compliance with approved methods.
- Example 5: Keys are revoked in compliance with approved methods.
- Example 6: Keys are terminated in compliance with approved methods.
- Example 7: Keys are archived in compliance with approved methods.

However, even these practice statements are still too high level to be meaningful as the "approved methods" remain undefined. Attempting to write more detailed practice statements would rapidly become tedious and difficult to manage. Consider the first example of key generation methods:

- Example A: Key generation methods include approved random number generation (RNG) algorithms.
- Example B: Key generation methods include approved pseudorandom number generation (PRNG) algorithms.
- Example C: Key generation methods include approved prime number generation (PNG) algorithms.
- Example D: Key generation methods include approved domain parameter generation (DPG) algorithms.

DOI: 10.1201/9781003425298-4

- Example F: Key generation methods include approved key derivation function (KDF) algorithms.

Clearly, this approach is rather unwieldy as it still contains somewhat vague claims about algorithms and approvals. If the seven high-level practice statements listed earlier are expanded into several detailed practice statements such as the five listed, then the single example policy statement might have 35 or more practice statements. Furthermore, if the overall policy has dozens of high-level statements, then there might be thousands of detailed practice statements. Obviously, developing and maintaining such documentation would be complicated and costly, and likely apathy would allow staleness and its eventual demise.

A more succinct approach might be for the policy statements to reference industry standards whose requirements ("shall") and recommendations ("should") can consequently be referenced in the practice statements, which subsequently provide the basis for procedures. Conversely, the procedures support the practices, which in turn are based on standards, which provide a foundation for the policies. Figure 4.1 shows the relationships between policy, standards, practices, and procedures. However, there is often a standard gap between what standards require or recommend, what the vendor product offers, and what the product deployment provides, such that the management of the system frequently needs to compensate by means of the procedures.

Product gaps might occur when an implementation ignores the relevant standard recommendations or misinterprets the requirements such that the product lacks complete capabilities. Deployment gaps can occur when the product implementation does not conform to the guidelines resulting in misconfigurations, inadequate controls, or inappropriate use. Management gaps may occur when applications are improperly operated, including insufficient staffing, inadequate monitoring, and/or lack of maintenance. Adequate policies, relevant standards, good practices, and appropriate procedures can overcome various security gaps. For the purposes of this book, we focus on the policy, practices, and procedures for operating a public key infrastructure, and for this chapter, we refer to standards for X.509 v3 certificates, certificate revocation list (CRL), Online Certificate Status Protocol (OCSP), certificate policy (CP), and certificate practice statement (CPS).

In Chapter 3, "PKI Building Blocks," we discussed various PKI-related standards defining X.509 certificates, certificate revocation lists, and Online Certificate Status Protocol, including ITU-T standards X.509, international standards ISO/IEC 9594, and IETF specifications RFC 2560, RFC 3280, RFC 5280, and RFC 6960. In addition, the IETF specifications define the certificate policy and certificate practice statement in the original RFC 2527 and the revision RFC 3647. In this chapter, we focus on developing the CP and provide CPS examples for small, medium, and large organizations.

It is important for the reader to recognize that industry standards for security procedures do not exist. Security procedures are specific to the application architectures, information technologies, and cryptographic products such that it is not practicable to develop a generic procedure. It is likewise not feasible to develop customized procedures for hundreds, thousands, or perhaps millions of possible combinations for vendors, products, releases, technologies, architectures, and business

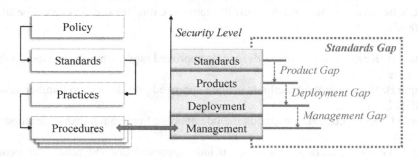

FIGURE 4.1   Standards gaps.

services. Certification programs have similar problems in that an evaluation can only address the specific hardware, firmware, and software components. Consequently, procedures need to be tailored to each particular instance. Furthermore, it is difficult to discuss policies or practices in a vacuum, so for the purposes of this book, we offer a series of scenarios, which begin with Figure 4.2.

In our example, the ABC Corporation campus consists of two facilities: an office building and a separate data center, surrounded by a perimeter fence with access from a public road. Access to the campus is from a public road to a private road with a gated entrance. The building entrances are located opposite to each other; the office building entrance is on the west side, and the data center building is on the east side. There are "invisible" barriers in front of each entrance and between the two buildings consisting of mounds populated with trees and large rocks. Along the sides of both buildings are employee and guest parking. The gate has one "in" lane and one "out" lane. The "in" gate is badge activated for employees and has a guard available during working hours for visitors. The "out" gate automatically opens for any departing vehicle. Next, let's zoom in to the office building shown in Figure 4.3.

As mentioned earlier, there is an invisible barrier in front of the entrance doors, which are badge-activated after hours but unlocked during working hours. The internal doors to the office area are badge activated 24×7, but the front desk is attended during working hours. Visitors are required to have employee escorts. The office area is separated from the eastern adjacent area by another set of doors that are kept unlocked during working hours but badge activated after hours. The restrooms, conference rooms, executive offices, and special rooms are located in the adjacent office space. One of the special rooms is the PKI room. There are also two emergency exits located in the eastern adjacent area. Now let's zoom into the data center building shown in Figure 4.4.

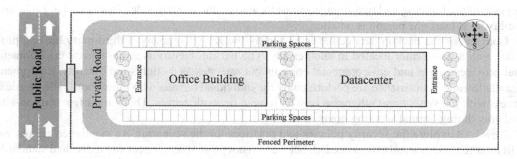

FIGURE 4.2   Example of a public key infrastructure campus.

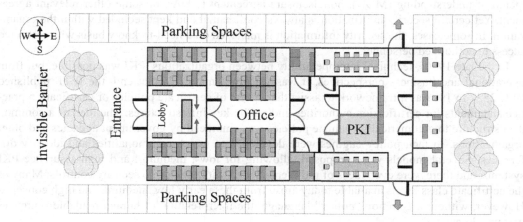

FIGURE 4.3   Example of public key infrastructure offices.

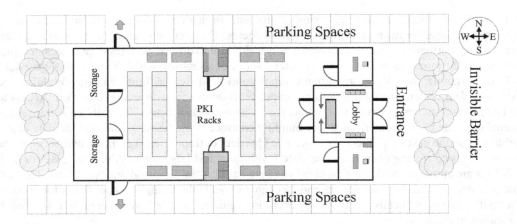

FIGURE 4.4 Example of public key infrastructure data center.

The primary data center is the building located east of the office building. It has the same invisible barriers, front entrance, guard desk, restrooms, and emergency exits. Unlike the office building, however, the front door is badge-activated 24 × 7, but the guard is only present during working hours. The data center is a typical open area with equipment racks lined up in the middle of the room for optimal air circulation and HVA units along the outer walls. The PKI racks are individually locked cabinets containing dedicated PKI cryptographic modules, servers, databases, switches, uninterrupted power supplies (UPS), and other equipment. There are two offices located on the eastern side of the building and two storage rooms located on the western side. This is a 24 × 7 manned facility so at least one person is on-site.

Conversely, the backup data center is hosted by the XYZ Company, a third-party hosting provider with a data center located in another city. The backup facility is a multitenant environment that provides power and environmental controls but operates as a "lights-out" facility. Equipment installation and maintenance are performed by the individual tenants who must coordinate physical access with the vendor and otherwise rely on remote network access. There are a few staff on-site and only during normal working hours.

Now let's explore the security policies and practices for the scenarios. As mentioned earlier, we will refer to various standards as needed, but we will not present nor dissect any individual standards within this chapter. Some security information might be intended for public consumption. Other security information might be proprietary and limited to controlled distributions such as under a memo of understanding (MOU), nondisclosure agreement (NDA), or some other relevant agreement. Yet certain security information is always confidential and kept secluded within the organization. In some cases, the security information is managed on a need-to-know basis with restricted access to authorized personnel.

In the late 1990s, technical interoperability between organizations' PKI was possible, but from operational and business perspectives, it was yet problematic. To that end, the IETF published RFC 2527 in 1999 as a framework to assist the writers of certificate policies or certification practice statements for certification authorities and public key infrastructures. The idea of a common data structure to automatically evaluate policies was embraced by government agencies and other organizations. In fact, policy engines were developed to match commonalities and identify differences. Several models were proposed, allowing for low-, medium-, and high-assurance PKI systems, and there were even ideas of rudimentary PKI with little or no security controls. Many of the certificate class levels available today arose from these early low, medium, and high concepts. However, without a common "policy" language, the interpretation of human-readable sentences was problematic.

Regardless, the concept was for two previously unknown PKI systems to exchange policies with the intent to determine their respective levels of trust before accepting certificates. At the onset, when a sender and receiver exchange digital certificates, the respective PKI systems would also inspect each other's policies. For example, if the PKI systems operate at significantly different assurance levels, then the higher-assurance PKI might reject the lower one. Alternatively, the higher assurance PKI might accept the lower-assurance PKI but limit the certificate use to low-risk transactions. For this level of sophistication, the policies would need to be unambiguous, contain sufficient information for automation, and use consistent terminology.

The IETF specification was updated as RFC 3647 in 2002 in coordination with the American Bar Association (ABA) Information Security Committee (ISC) within the Section of Science and Technology Law. See Table 4.1 for a comparison between the scopes of the earlier (RFC 2527) and latter (EFC 3647) revisions. The ISC wrote the PKI Assessment Guidelines [B.7.14] that embodies a great deal of technical, business, and legal experience in PKI operations. Some of the sections were restructured; however, many of the sections remained unchanged, with the significant addition of Section 4.9, "Other Business and Legal Matters," which contains business and legal topics including fees, financial responsibility, confidentiality, intellectual property, and privacy. Meanwhile, we make an important observation between the RFC 2527 and RFC 3647 abstract statements:

Notice that RFC 2527 includes CA and PKI within its scope, but RFC 3647 refers to PKI with the CA as an example. This is a significant focus change in that a CP (or CPS) is not just for an operational CA that issues certificates but necessary for a more general PKI-enabled application that might use its own certificates, certificates issued from another PKI, or assist in the certificate issue process such as a registration authority (RA). RFC 3647 rapidly became the PKI de facto standard across numerous industries. Security professionals and auditors alike depend on CA policies and practices written in this format:

§1. Introduction
§2. Publication and Repository Responsibilities
§3. Identification and Authentication
§4. Certificate Lifecycle Operational Requirements
  • 4.1 Certificate Application
  • 4.2 Certificate Application Processing
  • 4.3 Certificate Issuance
  • 4.4 Certificate Acceptance
  • 4.5 Key Pair and Certificate Usage
  • 4.6 Certificate Renewal
  • 4.7 Certificate Rekey
  • 4.8 Certificate Modification

§5. Facility, Management, and Operational Controls
§6. Technical Security Controls
§7. Certificate, CRL, and OCSP Profiles
§8. Compliance Audit and Other Assessment
§9. Other Business and Legal Matters

TABLE 4.1

Certificate Policy and Certification Practices

RFC 2527 (1999)	RFC 3647 (2003)
This document presents a framework to assist the writers of certificate policies or certification practice statements for certification authorities and public key infrastructures.	This document presents a framework to assist the writers of certificate policies or certification practice statements for participants within public key infrastructures, such as certification authorities, policy authorities, and communities of interest that wish to rely on certificates.

Each section addresses a specific set of topics that are numbered as subsections. If the topic is not relevant, then the expected statement is "no stipulation" rather than deleting the subsection to avoid renumbering, which would affect the document's overall structure. Additional topics can be added as new subsections, but care must be taken to avoid renumbering. Again, the idea is to keep the document format consistent for readability and comparison with other policies. Some organizations insist on restructuring the certificate policy according to corporate standards; however, this is a bad practice. The numbering scheme and content must be kept consistent in order for security assessments and audits to be performed.

SPECIAL NOTE 4-1 CP/CPS FORMAT

Renumbering or changing the certificate policy structure adversely affects its usefulness; consistency is mandatory for security assessments and audits.

According to RFC 2527, the concept of separate documents for the certificate policy versus the practice statement was never intended. In fact, the original concept was a single document that contained both policy and practice statements. However, experience has shown that publicly available practice statements, if too detailed, can inadvertently reveal too much information about the organization's security processes. Yet today, many certificate authorities only publish a CPS, many with combined policy and practice statements. Conversely, insufficient details in a general CPS are not very useful during an audit. Some organizations have developed two CPSs: one for public consumption and another for internal use. In any case, the organization will still need to have detailed operational procedures. Table 4.2 shows the recommendations advocated by this book.

The X.509 v3 structure includes the certificate policy extension. This extension allows the CP or CPS to be uniquely labeled using an object identifier (OID) and possibly a web page link to download the document. The RFC specification recommends for interoperability purposes that the extension only contains a standard OID as defined in the specification. However, it is more common to see a proprietary OID and a uniform resource identifier (URI) in this extension, which allows the CP or CPS to be uniquely identified and discoverable. It is important to recognize that providing a URI in this extension implicitly makes the document publicly available. Interestingly, the extension is named "certificate policies" and not "certificate practice statements," so pointing to a CPS is inconsistent with the extension's purpose. Furthermore, the RFC specification does not recognize an extension for CPS.

TABLE 4.2
Publication Management

Document Type	Publication	Intended Audience
Certificate Policy (CP)	Public	General public: Document is posted on publicly available website with no authentication, but the organization might require requestor registration to help track the number of downloads.
Certificate Practice Statement (CPS)	Proprietary	Limited access: Document is made available to authenticated individuals, such as employees, regulators, assessors, and auditors.
PKI Execution Procedures (PXP)	Confidential	Restricted access: Document is made available to authenticated individuals per need-to-know basis under adequate controls, such as security officers, key managers, assessors, and auditors.

```
┌─────────────────────────────┐
│      Certificate Policy      │
│             for              │
│       ABC Corporation        │
│                              │
│             Date             │
│           Version            │
│                              │
│      Public Information      │
└─────────────────────────────┘
```

FIGURE 4.5 Example of a certificate policy cover sheet.

Regardless, whether a CP or CPS is made public, an obvious but necessary item is a cover sheet with a meaningful title. At a minimum, the title should contain the document purpose, organization name, date, and version number. The cover sheet should also include the data classification and any other pertinent information such as the company logo, copyright date, corporation division name, or application name. For a graphic depiction, see Figure 4.5.

4.1 RFC 2527 INTRODUCTION

The RFC 3647 "Introduction" section is structured with the following subsections.

§1 Introduction
- Overview
- Document Name and Identification
- PKI Participants
- Certificate Usage
- Policy Administration
- Definitions and Acronyms

The first section RFC 3647 §1 Introduction is a typical composition for any technical specification that sets the stage for the remainder of the document. The CP is no different, and its first segment is §1 "Introduction" composed of six subsections. Depending on the chosen format style, the RFC 3647 §1 might contain introductory text or exist as only a placeholder for the subsections. For example, the ISO style does not permit text between two subsequent headings. Organizations can write the CP in almost any style as long as the section numbering and content remain consistent with the RFC 3647 specification as provided in its §6, "Technical Security Controls."

4.1.1 RFC 3647 OVERVIEW

The RFC 3647 §1.1 "Overview" subsection is intended to provide general information about the PKI such as a graphical representation of the PKI components or certificate assurance levels. The PKI elements for our hypothetical ABC Corporation are shown in Figure 4.6. There are two separate hierarchies: one for internal use and the other for external entities. The diagram shows the various hierarchical levels of each CA structure. The highest level is called a root CA and is operated in an offline mode, physically isolated from any network connection. The lower levels are called subordinate or intermediary CA and are operated in an online mode, connected to the organization's

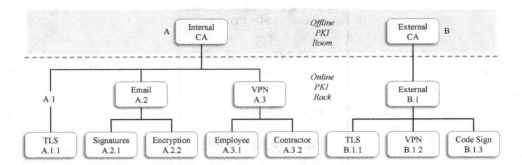

FIGURE 4.6   Example of a public key infrastructure hierarchy.

network. In our example, the internal CA uses an "A" numbering scheme, and the external CA uses a "B" number scheme:

- **Internal CA**: The internal root CA is denoted "A" with the next level consisting of A.2 for e-mail certificates and A.3 for VPN certificates. In this example, there is no A.1 per se but merely a placeholder to keep the numbering scheme consistent. The lowest online level consists of A.1.1 for TLS certificates, A.2.1 and A.2.2 for e-mail certificates, and A.3.1 and A.3.2 for VPN certificates. The e-mail certificates are further divided into those for verifying signed e-mails and those for encrypting e-mails. The VPN certificates, which are used for remote access into the network, are separated into those issued to employees and contractors. The TLS certificates are used for internal application communications.

- **External CA**: The external root CA is denoted "B," with the next level consisting of a B.1 external CA. The lowest online level consists of B.1.1 for TLS certificates, B.1.2 for VPN certificates, and B.1.3 for code sign certificates. The code sign certificates are used to verify executable code that has been digitally signed. The VPN certificates are used for remote access into the network. The TLS certificates are used for external application communications.

Note that the number scheme could have been anything, such as A1, A2, A11, A21, and so on. The important aspect is that each CA needs a unique identification. This is needed not only for the certificate chain validation but also for accuracy in the CP and CPS. The CA certificates must be clearly referenced in the policy such that no ambiguity exists. If the CA names in the certificates do not match the names in the policy, then there is uncertainty about which controls apply to which CA system. Exactness in the language is paramount for clarity and consistency. A well-articulated CA hierarchy diagram adds tremendous value to the certificate policy document.

Certificate assurance levels reflect the original aforementioned low-assurance, medium-assurance, and high-assurance PKI models. The assurance level conveys the overall trustworthiness of the certificate to the relying party or any other third party. Each assurance level indicates that certain conditions are or were true. To explore this further, let's reexamine the key management lifecycle introduced in Section 2.4, "Key Management," from the perspective of an asymmetric key pair as shown in Figure 4.7. All the state nodes and transitions occur but not always by the same party. The key owner actions are represented in the upper light-gray zone, and the relying party actions are shown in the lower dark-gray zone.

The key owner (Party A) is the legitimate proprietor of the asymmetric key pair and whose name is represented in the public key (digital) certificate. Systematically the key owner holds the private key and basically "advertises" the use of the public key by means of the digital

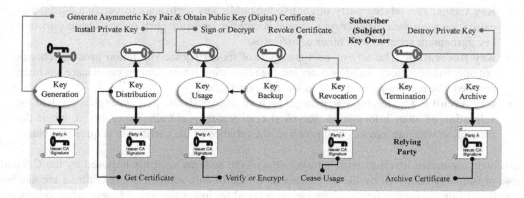

FIGURE 4.7   Asymmetric key lifecycle.

certificate. In general, the key owner takes the following key management actions regarding the key lifecycle:

- **Key Generation**: The key owner generates the asymmetric key pair, or a trusted third party generates the key pair and obtains the corresponding digital certificate from a CA.
- **Key Distribution**: The key owner installs the private key on the system that houses the application, which will use the private key. Note that the system used to generate the key pair might very well be the same system to use the private key.
- **Key Usage**: The key owner might use the private key to generate digital signatures on messages or data, decrypt data that were encrypted using the public key, or establish a symmetric key.
- **Key Backup**: The key owner might backup the private key for recovery purposes if the private key is lost due to system failure or might simply generate a new key pair.
- **Key Revocation**: The key owner might need to revoke the certificate before its valid expiration for a variety of reasons, including a private key compromise, cessation of operations (the key owner goes out of business), or due to a merger or acquisition that renders the certificate information invalid.

The relying party "borrows" the key owner's certificate and, therefore, depends on the certificate assurance level as indicated by the CA. Thus, the relying party is an end user of the certificate with certain expectations that the key owner is managing the corresponding private key over the key lifecycle using adequate controls and that the certificate has been issued with respect to the conditions laid out in the CPS. However, the relying party is involved in the key lifecycle and takes the following actions:

- **Key Distribution**: The relying party gets a copy of the digital certificate. Depending on the application environment and the certificate scheme, how the relying party obtains the certificate will vary. For example, if the relying party is using a browser to connect to an application server that supports TLS, the key owner's TLS certificate is exchanged during the protocol handshake, but the CA certificates are preinstalled by the browser manufacturer. As another example, if the relying party is also using a client server to connect to the application server, the application server's TLS certificate is likely exchanged between the two organization's engineering staff and preinstalled on the client server. For e-mail certificates, the sender might attach their certificate to the e-mail. For VPN certificates, the registration process might automatically collect and publish the certificate to a corporate repository.

- **Key Usage**: The relying party might use the public key certificate to verify a digital signature, encrypt data, or encrypt a shared secret for key transport, or be used as part of a key agreement scheme with other certificates.
- **Key Revocation**: The relying party, as part of its certificate validation process, checks not only the certificate validity dates but the revocation status. Once a certificate has been revoked, the relying party ceases to use the certificate.
- **Key Archive**: The relying party might archive the certificate past its expiration date for validation of older information. Revoked certificates might also be archived, but if the revocation was due to a key compromise, the reliance of the certificate is questionable.

Certificate assurance levels provide an overview of the security controls imposed by the CA and those presumably followed by the key owner as the certificate subject. Some controls are needed regardless of the assurance levels, some can be relaxed for lower assurance levels, while others are only required for higher levels.

Key Generation: The key owner needs to use certified or at least recognized random numbers, prime numbers, and key generation algorithms. Predictable numbers or non–prime numbers can affect the key generation process, as can invalid procedures. If a key pair can be duplicated by another party other than the key owner, then the private key has become unknowingly compromised. The cryptographic module used to generate the key pair is an important aspect of the overall assurance levels. Refer to Table 4.3 for control illustrations.

Once the asymmetric key pair has been properly generated, the key owner can then begin the process of obtaining a digital certificate for the public key. The key owner submits a certificate signing request (CSR) to a CA by signing the public key with the private key to demonstrate ownership. The signature does not authenticate the key owner; rather it only provides cryptographic proof that the requestor had access to the corresponding private key. The CA authenticates the requestor to the extent that the name in the certificate represents the key owner or the key owner's agent. Refer to Table 4.4 for control illustrations.

TABLE 4.3
Examples of Key Generation Assurance Levels

Assurance Level	Example Key Generation Controls
High Assurance	The asymmetric key pair is generated inside a cryptographic hardware module certified at FIPS 140–3 levels 3 or 4.
Medium Assurance	The asymmetric key pair is generated using a cryptographic hardware or software module certified at FIPS 140–3 levels 1 or 2.
Low Assurance	The asymmetric key pair is generated using a cryptographic software library or other unevaluated module.

TABLE 4.4
Examples of Certificate Authority Authentication Assurance Levels

Assurance Level	Example CA Authentication Controls
High Assurance	The CA validates the requestor using identification information and strong multifactor authentication methods.
Medium Assurance	The CA validates the requestor using identification information and a reasonable single-factor authentication method.
Low Assurance	The CA validates the requestor using multisource identification information such as e-mail address and phone number.

For the high- and medium-assurance levels, if the CA has never established authentication credentials with the requestor, then the CA must conduct an initial authentication to confirm the requestor's identity and authority to request the certificate. The initial authentication process will vary depending on the certificate type and the CA responsibilities. For example, a commercial CA that issues Extended Validation (EV) certificates for TLS or code signing must follow the WebTrust for EV audit guidelines [B.7.15] now managed by the CA Browser Forum.

Key Distribution: The key owner must install the private key for usage. If the key pair is generated by a different system than the usage system, then the key owner must ensure the confidentiality, integrity, and authenticity during its distribution to avoid a compromised key or a man-in-the-middle (MITM) attack as discussed in Chapter 2, "Cryptography Basics." Refer to Table 4.5 for control illustrations.

For the high- and medium-assurance levels, the key owner also enlists the aid of an independent auditor to oversee that the key transport was accomplished per documented procedures. Without documented procedures or an audited ceremony, the assurance level is basically an unsubstantiated claim with no material evidence as reasonable proof.

Key Usage: The key owner must use the private key only for its intended purpose, protect it from disclosure, maintain access control to prevent unauthorized access, and monitor its usage for availability and accountability purposes. Refer to Table 4.6 for control illustrations.

For the high-assurance level, the private key never appears as cleartext outside the cryptographic hardware model. For the medium- and low-assurance levels, the private key is stored locally on the application system either as an encrypted (ciphertext) key or as a cleartext object using system access controls. If the private key is stored as ciphertext, then a key encryption key (KEK) must

---

TABLE 4.5

Examples of Key Distribution Assurance Levels

Assurance Level	Example Key Distribution Controls
High Assurance	The asymmetric private key is transported using a key loading device (KLD) certified at FIPS 140–3 levels 3 or 4.
Medium Assurance	The asymmetric private key is transported using a key loading device (KLD) certified at FIPS 140–3 levels 1 or 2.
Low Assurance	The asymmetric private key is transported using a USB device with symmetric encryption key derived from a password.

TABLE 4.6

Examples of Key Usage Assurance Levels

Assurance Level	Example Key Usage Controls
High Assurance	The asymmetric key pair is generated inside a cryptographic hardware module certified at FIPS 140–3 level 3 or 4.
Medium Assurance	The asymmetric key pair is generated using a cryptographic hardware or software module certified at FIPS 140–3 level 1 or 2.
Low Assurance	The asymmetric key pair is generated using a cryptographic software library or other unevaluated module.

TABLE 4.7

Examples of Key Recovery Assurance Levels

Assurance Level	Example Key Recovery Controls
High Assurance	The asymmetric private key is recovered using an N of M split knowledge method with a PIN-activated cryptographic hardware module certified at FIPS 140–3 levels 2 or 3.
Medium Assurance	The asymmetric private key is recovered using split knowledge methods with dual control procedures and cryptographic hardware or software module certified at FIPS 140–3 level 1.
Low Assurance	The asymmetric private key is recovered using split knowledge methods with dual control procedures.

exist. The KEK is then either stored as a cleartext object using system access controls or dynamically recreated based on an end user entering a key encryption password.

> **Key Backup**: The key owner might maintain a copy of the private key for recovery purposes in the event that an application component has a malfunction, which causes a key erasure. Recovery is only viable when the private key has not been compromised and the failure can be attributed to a benign event. Refer to Table 4.7 for control illustrations.

Key recovery using split knowledge methods discussed in Section 2.4, "Key Management," is similar to key distribution methods mentioned earlier. The private key can be stored as M key shares on various form factors such as smart cards or USB devices that must be PIN activated but only requires N participants to recover the private key. Alternatively, a lost private key can be replaced with a new key pair and certificate; however, this depends on the nature of the application and the ease of distributing the certificate to relying parties.

> **Key Termination**: At the end of the key lifecycle, the key owner must destroy all instances of the private key, including any recovery copies. This is a common control as any remaining copies might be misused in an unauthorized manner. There are no control differences for any of the assurance levels, so the key destruction is equally applicable to each of the assurance levels.

Another valuable topic not mentioned in the RFC 3647 specification is a scoping statement. For example, the ABC Corporation might have a separate CP for its internal CA and another for its external CA. In this scenario, the CP would identify the existence of both CAs but clearly indicate its scope was limited to the internal CA and explicitly state that the external CA was out of scope. Also, the title of the coversheet might be revised to reflect the narrower scope – for example, Certificate Policy of the Internal CA for the ABC Corporation.

4.1.2 RFC 3647 Document Name and Identification

The RFC 3647 §1.2 "Document Name and Identification" subsection is meant to provide pertinent names and relevant identifiers. An important piece of information would be the complete names of each PKI component within the scope of the CP. Names occurring within certificates are based on the X.500 attribute types:

- CN is the common name.
- L is the locality name.
- ST is the state or province name.
- O is the organization name.

TABLE 4.8

Examples of Certificate Authority Names

Common Name (CN)	Organization (O)	Domain Component (DC)
CN = internal CA	O = ABC Corporation	DC = A
CN = TLS CA	O = ABC Corporation	DC = A.1.1
CN = e-mail CA	O = ABC Corporation	DC = A.2
CN = e-mail signatures	O = ABC Corporation	DC = A.2.1
CN = e-mail encryption CA	O = ABC Corporation	DC = A.2.2
CN = VPN internal CA	O = ABC Corporation	DC = A.3
CN = VPN employee CA	O = ABC Corporation	DC = A.3.1
CN = VPN contractor CA	O = ABC Corporation	DC = A.3.2

- OU is the organization unit name.
- C is the country name.
- STREET is the street address.
- DC is the domain component.
- UID is the user identifier.

For example, if the CP scope was the internal CA depicted in Figure 4.6, then the names of each CA can be listed. Table 4.8 shows the eight CA systems and their common names, organizational names, and domain component names.

Another important bit of information is the organization's object identifier arc registered with the Internet Assigned Numbers Authority (IANA). For example, the ABC Corporation might have the following OID arc: joint ISO ITU (2), country (16), United States (840), organization (1), and ABC Corporation (nnnnnn), which is often written as the following:

2.16.840.1.nnnnnn

Note that since the ABC Corporation is hypothetical, no actual organization OID has been registered with the IANA. The CP might be assigned an OID for the policy identifier, which is contained in the certificates issued by the internal CA. However, the policy identifier is often assigned to the certificate practice statement (CPS) and not the CP. If assigned, the CP should also include its policy identifier. Other OID arcs or identifiers that are important to the organization and its PKI can also be listed.

4.1.3 RFC 3647 PKI Participants

The RFC 3647 §1.3 "PKI Participants" subsection is expected to describe the various roles and responsibilities that occur within the PKI, including at a minimum the certification authorities, the registration authorities, subscribers, and relying parties. Each participant should be defined because, although these four entities are well known by PKI enthusiasts, the reader might not be so knowledgeable. Table 4.9 provides the PAG [B.7.14] and ISO 21188 [B.4.11] definitions for each entity. Additionally, if other PKI participants do not fall clearly into one of these four categories, then they need to be identified and articulated.

In addition to the list of general participants and definitions, RFC 3647 §1.3 should also identify specifics for each category. For example, the CA components previously identified in §1.2, "Document Name and Identification," subsection can be expanded upon in §1.3 to include any local, remote, or third-party RA instances. A more detailed list of subscribers reflects the types of certificates, such as what entities are issued TLS certificates, who gets e-mail certificates, and

TABLE 4.9

Definitions of Public Key Infrastructure Standards

Term	PAG Definition	ISO 21188 Definition
CA system or Certification Authority (CA)	The collection of the information technology components (including one or more trustworthy systems), along with the procedures and operations of the CA System, as specified in the CPS.	Entity trusted by one or more entities to create, assign, and revoke or hold public key certificates.
Registration Authority (RA)	An entity that is responsible for validating the identity (or other attributes) of certificate applicants but does not issue or manage certificates (i.e., an RA is delegated to perform certain tasks on behalf of a CA, such as approving certificate applications). The extent to which an RA is (exclusively) responsible for its acts depends on the applicable CP and agreements.	Entity that is responsible for identification and authentication of subjects of certificates but is not a CA and hence does not sign or issue certificates. Note: An RA may assist in the certificate application process or revocation process or both. The RA does not need to be a separate body but can be part of the CA.
Relying Party (RP)	The recipient of a certificate containing the public key of a certificate's subject who is in a position to rely, or otherwise relies, on the binding in a certificate between the public key appearing in it and the identity (and/or other attributes) of the person named in the certificate.	Recipient of a certificate who acts in reliance on that certificate, digital signatures verified using that certificate, or both.
Subscriber (Subject)	A person who (1) is the subject named or identified in a certificate issued to such person and (2) holds a private key that corresponds to a public key listed in that certificate.	Entity subscribing with a certification authority on behalf of one or more subjects (entity whose public key is certified in a public key certificate).

who gets VPN certificates, from the internal CA. If possible, the various types of relying parties should also be identified, if known. The mappings between participants, types of certificates, and actual certificate usage for subscribers and relying parties are defined in the next Section 4.1.4, "Certificate Usage."

4.1.4 RFC 3647 Certificate Usage

The RFC 3647 §1.4 "Certificate Usage" subsection is intended to provide descriptions of the applications in scope and the relevant certificate assurance levels. Certificates might be issued to individuals, devices, or applications; however, regardless of the owner's name, certificates are processed by PKI-enabled applications. For the CP, it is sufficient to identify the types of applications, the certificate types, and the relative certificate usage. As an example, the internal CA components from Figure 4.6 are mapped to the application and certificate types in Table 4.10.

In our example, the TLS CA designated A.1.1 issues TLS certificates to web application servers and firewalls located in a network demilitarized zone (DMZ). Certificates are issued to e-mail clients by the e-mail CA identified as A.2.1 for encryption certificates and by other e-mail CA tagged A.2.2 for signature certificates. VPN certificates are issued to VPN client and server applications by the VPN employee CA marked A.3.1 and the VPN contractor CA labeled A.3.2 for VPN certificates. This level of detail reduces ambiguity and enhances the CP usefulness.

TABLE 4.10

Examples of Certificate Usage

Application Type	Certificate Type	CA System	Certificate Usage
Web application servers	TLS certificate	A.1.1	Secure connections
DMZ firewalls	TLS certificate	A.1.1	Secure connections
E-mail client applications	Signature certificate	A.2.1	E-mail signing
E-mail client applications	Encryption certificate	A.2.2	E-mail encryption
VPN client applications	VPN certificate	A.3.1 A.3.2	Secure connections
VPN server applications	VPN certificate	A.3.1 A.3.2	Secure connections

TABLE 4.11

Example PA Information

Name	Address	Contact
PKI Policy Authority	One Private Road	800-ABC-nnnn phone
ABC Corporation	City, State, ZIP code	pki-pa@ABCcorp.tld[1]

4.1.5   RFC 3647 POLICY ADMINISTRATION

The RFC 3647 §1.5 "Policy Administration" subsection is meant to provide contact information and the policy administrative processes. The CP captures information at a point in time such that it needs periodic reviews and occasional updates. The various PKI entities that depend on the CP need the ability to contact the policy authority (PA) management team for a variety of reasons including queries, feedback, or disputes. Dispute resolution is discussed in RFC 3647 §9 "Other Business and Legal Matters." As shown in Table 4.11, the contact information should include all the relevant communication channels such as mailing address, phone number, and e-mail address. Note that no individual's name is provided since the membership changes over time.

As discussed in Chapter 1, "Introduction," of this book, the PKI complexity includes cryptography, information technology, information security, business, and legal. The CP reviews and updates are not trivial and need to be conducted in a formalized manner. A policy authority management team that represents all four areas needs to be established to maintain the CP. At a minimum, knowledgeable individuals representing cryptography, information technology, business groups, and legal counsel need to be members of the policy authority (PA) management team:

- **Cryptography**: Representation from the organization's cryptography group is critical to address key management lifecycle controls. The PKI team might be part of the crypto group or function as a separate operational division.
- **Information Technology** (IT): Representation from the organization's IT group is important to address system and network capacity and planning. In our examples for the internal CA, the IT department supports the e-mail and VPN systems.
- **Information Security** (IS): Representatives from the organization's security professionals are important to address cybersecurity operational controls, including application security, information security, network security, disaster recovery plan, and operational and end user security.
- **Business**: Representation from the organization's various lines of business (LOBs) is important to address different application needs. In our examples for the internal CA, the LOB would include the applications running on the web application servers.

- **Legal**: Representation from the organization's legal group is essential to the success of the PKI systems. Legal can address privacy, intellectual property, representations, warranties, disclaimers, liabilities, indemnities, terms, termination, notices, dispute resolution, national and international governing law, and compliance issues.

In addition to scheduled periodic reviews by the PA team, ad hoc updates might be necessary when there are significant changes. Technology changes can originate internally from IT or business issues or externally due to new vulnerabilities or market influence. Operational changes can originate internally due to cryptography, business, or legal issues or externally due to law, regulatory, or contractual requirements. Therefore, the CP needs to provide contact information for receiving comments and communicating to other groups within the organization. The PA processes need to be described in the CP and should include the following:

- **PA Management**: This includes the makeup of the PA membership, how members are added or rotated, roles and responsibilities, and review schedules.
- **CP Management**: This includes the review, editing, voting, and dispute resolution processes, including publication and notification processes for the CP.
- **CPS Management**: This includes the review, editing, voting, and dispute resolution processes, including publication and notification processes for the CPS.
- **PKI Management**: This includes supervising legal compliance with laws, regulations, and contractual obligations, along with monitoring internal organizational standards, external industry standards, security vulnerabilities, and technology trends.

Depending on the organization's size and structure, risk and compliance managers might also be part of the PA if business or legal members do not address those areas. Furthermore, business application owners or system managers might be included as part of the CP review process but not necessarily the CPS review or be regular members of the PA. The PA membership also needs to be consistent for continuity.

For small and medium organizations, the PA membership can be problematic as staff might not be available or insufficiently aware of PKI technology. For staffing, some roles might be outsourced; for example, PKI expertise or legal counsel can be hired. For awareness, smaller organizations should consider continual PKI training to build and maintain knowledge.

4.1.6   RFC 3647 Definitions and Acronyms

The RFC 3647 §1.6 "Definitions and Acronyms" subsection is expected to provide definitions of terms, abbreviations, and acronyms used within the policy. Terms can include individual words or phrases. Abbreviations used within the CP should be defined. And of course, acronyms are pronounceable abbreviations so the phonetic transcription [tran'skripSHən] might also be included. When providing definitions, care must be taken to avoid contradicting common industry terms unless absolutely necessary.

Another consideration for RFC 3647 §1.6 is ambiguous jargon. Manufacturers often use terms that differ from industry standards to help distinguish their products. Industry standards from dissimilar market segments, such as financial services versus telecommunications, often use different terminology. Various terms might mean the same thing to some, whereas the same term might mean something different to others. Note that national standards and international standards might use different terms, abbreviations, or acronyms. The same word or sound might mean or imply something different in various languages. Third-party service providers including cloud providers often use terminology that differs from industry standards or manufacturers. The rules "buyer beware" (*caveat emptor*) and "reader beware" (*cave videntiu*) are both good advice. It's a good idea to avoid reusing marketing literature.

4.2 RFC 2527 PUBLICATION AND REPOSITORY RESPONSIBILITIES

The RFC 3647 "Publication and Repository Responsibilities" section is structured with the following subsections.

§2. Publication and Repository Responsibilities
- 2.1 Repositories
- 2.2 Publication of Certification Information
- 2.3 Time or Frequency of Publication
- 2.4 Access Controls on Repositories

The second section RFC 3647 §2 "Publication and Repository Responsibilities" is intended to address roles and responsibilities, publication frequency, and access controls for various entities that manage information repositories.

4.2.1 RFC 3647 REPOSITORIES

The RFC 3647 §2.1 "Repositories" subsection identifies the various repositories and corresponding entities that own the content or operate the repositories within the PKI systems. Table 4.12 provides a summary of repositories. While some of the content is owned by different groups, ultimately the repositories are operated by PKI Operations running the CA or its associated RA subsidiary. Audit logs are typically not included within the repository scope.

The CP might provide a general declaration that the repositories are made available online, whereas the CPS would provide specific uniform resource locator (URL). For example, the ABC Corporation's repository might be accessed at either site:

- www.ABCcorp.TLD/pki
- https://pki.ABCcorp.TLD

Notice in our examples, the Hypertext Transfer Protocol Secure (HTTPS) is used to authenticate the website. HTTPS is running HTTP through a TLS tunnel whereby the server TLS certificate authenticates the website. Typically, publicly accessible sites such as Repositories do not implement TLS

TABLE 4.12

Examples of Repository Responsibilities

Information	Owner	Repository
Certificate Policy (CP)	Policy Authority	PKI Operations
Certificate Practice Statement (CPS)	Policy Authority	PKI Operations
Relying Party Agreement (RPA)	Legal	PKI Operations
Subscriber Agreement	Legal	PKI Operations
Subordinate CA Agreement	Legal	PKI Operations
Registration Authority (RA) Agreement	Legal	PKI Operations
PKI Procedures	PKI Operations	PKI Operations
Certificate Authority (CA) Certificates	PKI Operations	PKI Operations
End Entity (EE) Certificates	PKI Operations	PKI Operations
Certificate Revocation List (CRL)	PKI Operations	PKI Operations
Online Certificate Status Protocol (OCSP)	PKI Operations	PKI Operations
Audit Logs	PKI Operations	Information Technology

Client Authentication. In addition, the site might be operated by the ABC Corporation or hosted by a third party.

4.2.2 RFC 3647 PUBLICATION OF CERTIFICATION INFORMATION

The RFC 3647 §2.2 "Publication of Certification Information" subsection addresses the various PKI participants and their corresponding responsibilities. Table 4.13 provides a summary of possible information, entities, and access controls. The certificate policy and certificate practice statement are managed by the policy authority. As discussed in Table 4.2, the CP might be public, the CPS is proprietary, and procedures (PXP) are confidential. The access controls correspond to the same distribution model. The CP requires PA-authorized write access but has public read access. The various agreements, such as subscriber and relying party agreements, are typically managed by a legal group with authorized write access but equivalent CP public read controls. The CPS requires PA-authorized write access but has limited read access. The security procedures have restricted read access on a need-to-know basis but are managed by a security group with authorized write access.

4.2.3 RFC 3647 TIME OR FREQUENCY OF PUBLICATION

The RFC 3647 §2.3, "Time or Frequency of Publication," subsection addresses when information must be published and the frequency of publication. As an example of industry standards, consider the external CA depicted in Figure 4.6, which issues TLS and code sign certificates. The CA Browser Forum[2] created the Extended Validation (EV) guidelines to provide generally accepted authentication practices for issuing TLS and code sign certificates. The EV guideline requires that online CRL and OCSP services be available 24 × 7 and specific publication frequencies:

- For EV certificates, the CRL must be updated at least every seven days, the OCSP service at least every four days, and both can only be valid for a maximum of ten days.
- If the subordinate CA is not controlled by the same organization as the root CA, then the subordinate CA certificates are managed the same as the EV certificates, seven days for the CRL, four days for the OCSP service, and a maximum of ten days of expiration.
- Otherwise, if the subordinate CA is controlled by the same organization as the root CA, then for subordinate CA certificates that have not been revoked, the CRL and OCSP services must be updated at least every 12 months. Revocations must be published within 24 hours such that the 12-month clock begins anew.

As an example of the organization's practices, the CP and CPS might be reviewed and published annually by the policy authority (PA). Conversely, the various agreements might be reviewed and published by legal on an as-needed basis such that their publication frequency may be very different

---

TABLE 4.13

Examples of Repository Access

Information	Entity	Access	Availability
Policy	Policy authority	Publicly access	High availability
Practices	Policy authority	Limited access	High availability
Agreements	Legal	Publicly access	Medium availability
Procedures	PKI Operations	Restricted access	Medium availability
Certificates	PKI Operations	Publicly access	Medium availability
CRL updates	PKI Operations	Publicly access	High availability
OCSP updates	PKI Operations	Publicly access	High availability

from the policies and practices. Also, procedures managed by the security authority might only change when cryptographic equipment or products change.

4.2.4 RFC 3647 ACCESS CONTROLS ON REPOSITORIES

The RFC 3647 §2.4 "Access Controls on Repositories" subsection addresses access controls on the repositories. Some repositories are online and publicly available 24 × 7, such as CP and CRL postings or OCSP responders. Others are online but with limited external access such as CPS postings; however, since many organizations rely on a combined CP and CPS, where the X.509 certificate policy extension contains a uniform resource locator (URL) pointer, the CPS is by necessity publicly available. Other repositories might be online and publicly accessible but with lesser availability needs, such as agreements or certificates, since many relying parties get certificates directly from the certificate owners. Furthermore, some repositories might be online but restricted to internal network access such as key management procedures. Table 4.13 provides a summary of possible information, entities, access, and availability.

Since certificates, certificate revocation lists (CRLs), and Online Certificate Status Protocol (OCSP) responders need to be publicly available to any relying party, they all have public read access but require certification authority (CA) or registration authority (RA) authorized write access. Note that CRL or OCSP services might run on an online RA or CA system, but alternatively they might run on separate high-availability dedicated servers. The publication frequency for each information type is typically dependent on industry standards and the organization's policy and practices.

For smaller organizations with staffing limitations, managing publications and repositories can be problematic. Creating and managing content is difficult if legal, security, or PKI knowledge or experience is lacking. Maintaining publication dates and service level agreements (SLAs) is not easy with limited resources, as are access controls to maintain separation of duties.

4.3 RFC 2527 IDENTIFICATION AND AUTHENTICATION

The RFC 3647 "Identification and Authentication" section is structured with the following subsections:

§3. Identification and Authentication
- 3.1 Naming
- 3.2 Initial Identity Validation
- 3.3 Identification and Authentication for Rekey Requests
- 3.4 Identification and Authentication for Revocation Requests

The third section RFC 3647 §3 "Identification and Authentication" addresses subscriber's policies for keys and certificates. The RFC 3647 specification explicitly includes subsections for subscriber naming conventions, initial authentication for certificate requests, and subsequent authentication for rekey requests and revocation requests. As shown in Figure 4.7, the subscriber is also the asymmetric key pair owner that maps to the following topics:

- **Key Generation** includes the initial certificate request and subsequent certificate rekey requests. Initial authentication and authorization are important for initial certificate requests, and subsequent authentication and authorization are important for certificate rekey requests. Subscriber naming conventions are important for certificate requests and rekey requests.
- **Key Usage** includes the relying party use of the subscriber's certificate and the subscriber use of the corresponding private key. Subscriber naming conventions are important for certificate and key usage.

- **Key Revocation** includes subsequent certificate revocation requests. Authentication and authorization are important for subsequent certificate revocation requests. Subscriber naming conventions are also important for certificate revocation requests.

4.3.1 RFC 3647 Naming

The RFC 3647 §3.1 "Naming" subsection focuses on subscriber identity conventions, such as X.500 distinguished names or RFC 822 e-mail addresses. Note that the X.500 attribute names discussed for RFC 3647 "Document Name and Identification" subsection are for the PKI components and the corresponding CA certificates, whereas this subsection discusses names for the subscriber certificates. The RFC 3647 specification also refers to anonymity, name uniqueness, and trademarks:

- **Anonymity**: This is when the subject name in the certificate does not identify the subscriber by using a generic name (e.g., John Doe, Somebody, Anyone) or pseudonym. However, a PKI system issuing a certificate to an unconfirmed identity, pseudonyms notwithstanding, assumes unnecessary liability. Consider the man-in-the-middle attacks discussed in this book's Chapter 2, "Cryptography Basics." If the interloper can obtain a certificate in the sender's name, then an MITM signature attack is possible. If the interloper can obtain a certificate in the receiver's name, then a MITM key transport attack is possible. Note that a legal dispute might find the CA at fault for not verifying the certificate requestor's identity.
- **Name uniqueness**: This is when each certificate has a relatively unique name. Since one PKI system typically does not have access to the certificate repository of others, global uniqueness is not practical. However, a PKI system, which issues certificates with unique public keys but with duplicate names, also assumes unnecessary risk. Again, if a relying party accepts the wrong certificate due to a duplicate or similar name, a MITM attack and ensuing legal dispute are possible, affecting the CA.
- **Business names**: These include trademarked or registered names, so when a PKI system issues a certificate to an unconfirmed business identity, the CA assumes liability. For example, when the now-bankrupted Dutch CA DigiNotar was compromised in 2011, fraudulent certificates were issued for Google, Yahoo, Mozilla, and others. Issuing certificates to business names involves different authentication and authorization practices and methods than when issuing certificates to individuals.

However, there is also the aspect of issuing certificates to an individual when their name is associated with a business name. For example, issuing a certificate to "John Doe" and including a generic e-mail address (e.g., john.doe@e-mail.com), where "e-mail" is one of many service providers, is different than using john.doe@abccorp.com, which indicates employment. When dealing with business names, care must be taken to avoid unwanted implications of warranties, liabilities, or indemnifications. In addition to these topics, this book considers several relevant topics, which are not addressed by the RFC 3647 specification:

- **Device Names**: These include applications, servers, and network appliances. Similar to individual names being associated with a business name, devices are owned and operated by an organization. However, the organization might be external to the PKI system issuing the certificate, and the device ownership might be different than the management organization. Issuing certificates to devices involves different authentication practices and methods than when issuing certificates to individuals.
- **Public Key Verification**: This is the process of mathematically verifying the public key's syntax based on algorithm-specific attributes, including length, the number of bits, and structure. Note that this is not the same as certificate validation. An improperly constructed public key for some algorithms can enable certain cryptanalytic attacks. Consequently, a

PKI system issuing a certificate for a defective public key might put the subscriber or the relying party at risk, and in the case of a legal dispute, the CA may be found at fault for not verifying the subscriber's public key.

- **Public Key Uniqueness**: This is when the CA checks its certificate repository for a duplicate public key. Since the public and private keys are mathematically related, the same public key in a certificate request means that both key owners have generated the same key pair. However, this is a highly unlikely scenario. More likely, the subjects have used poor key generation tools, possibly with too low entropy for generating random numbers or random primes. The CA cannot notify the new requestor as that would compromise the existing key owner. However, the CA can refuse to issue a new certificate with the same public key as an existing certificate.

Certificate uniqueness was discussed in Section 3.7, "PKI Architectural Concepts," with Special Note 3-3 that every certificate in a PKI, especially CA certificates, needs to be relatively unique. While the same subject might submit a CSR with the same public key, each request will result in a different certificate with a unique serial number. However, to avoid ambiguity, the PKI should never issue more than one CA certificate for each public key.

4.3.2 RFC 3647 INITIAL IDENTITY VALIDATION

The RFC 3647 §3.2 "Initial Identity Validation" subsection considers initial authentication methods for each participant identified in the RFC 3647 "PKI Participants" subsection. Topics include why the various PKI participants are authenticated and authorized, what information is verified, and who performs the verification, authentication, and authorization processes. As discussed in RFC 3647, "Introduction," if certificate assurance levels are supported, then they also need to be addressed in this subsection. Table 4.14 provides CP and CPS examples for the internal CA shown in Figure 4.6.

Once the initial authentication has been accomplished and authentication credentials have been established, subsequent authentication can be relied upon. While the RFC 3647 "Initial Identity Validation" subsection focuses on initial authentication, subsequent authentication needs to be likewise addressed. Table 4.15 provides CP and CPS examples for the internal CA. The RFC 3647 "Identification and Authentication for Rekey Requests" and "Identification and Authentication for Revocation Requests" subsections only address subscriber interactions for rekey and revocation, but other entities (e.g., CA, RA, or relying parties) and other communications (e.g., CRL updates, CRL downloads, OCSP updates, OCSP responses, RA certificate requests) also need to be authenticated. We recommend that additional subsections be added to the RFC 3647 segment §3 "Identification and Authentication" as needed.

TABLE 4.14
Examples of Initial Authentication

PKI Entity	CP or CPS	Example Statement
CA	CP	Subordinate CA is issued certificates from its superior CA.
RA	CP	RA is issued certificates from its associated CA.
Subscribers	CP	Subscribers are issued system and network log-on identification and password credentials.
Employees	CP	Employees are initially identified and authenticated per the ABC Corporation's human resources (HR) hiring practices.
Vendors	CP	Vendors are initially identified and authenticated per the ABC Corporation's vendor relationship practices.
CA A	CPS	Internal CA A issues certificates to A.1.1 TLS, A.2 e-mail, and A.3 VPN.
CA A.2	CPS	Internal CA A.2 e-mail issues certificates to A.2.1 signatures and A.2.2 encryption.
CA A.3	CPS	Internal CA A.3 VPN issues certificates to A.3.1 employee and A.3.2 contractor.

TABLE 4.15

Examples of Subsequent Authentication

PKI Entity	CP or CPS	Example Statement
CA	CP	CA authenticates their CRL or OCSP updates to relying parties.
RA	CP	RA authenticates to its associate CA and is authorized to accept certificate requests from authenticated subscribers.
Subscribers	CP	Subscribers authenticate to the relative RA when submitting certificate requests.
TLS Certificates	CP	Employees authenticate to the TLS RA when submitting TLS certificate requests for internal applications or appliances.
E-mail Signature Certificates	CP	Employees authenticate to the e-mail signature RA when submitting e-mail signature certificate requests.
E-mail Encryption Certificates	CP	Employees authenticate to the e-mail encryption RA when submitting e-mail encryption certificate requests.
VPN Employee Certificates	CP	Employees authenticate to the VPN Employee RA when submitting VPN certificate requests for remote access.
VPN Vendor Certificates	CP	Vendors authenticate to the VPN vendor RA when submitting VPN certificate requests for remote access.
CA CRL	CPS	Each CA signs its associated CRL.
CA OCSP	CPS	Each OCSP responder signs its associated response.
TLS A.1.1 RA	CPS	RA signs each CSR message sent to the A.1.1 CA and is authorized to accept e-mail certificate requests from internal e-mail addresses.
E-mail signature A.2.1 RA	CPS	RA signs each CSR message sent to the A.2.1 CA and is authorized to accept e-mail certificate requests for internal e-mail addresses.
E-mail encryption A.2.2 RA	CPS	RA signs each CSR message sent to the A.2.2 CA and is authorized to accept e-mail certificate requests for internal e-mail addresses with special data confidentiality privileges.
VPN employee A.3.1 RA	CPS	RA signs each CSR message sent to the A.3.1 CA and is authorized to accept VPN certificate requests from employees for remote access to the ABC Corporation network.
VPN contractor A.3.2 RA	CPS	RA signs each CSR message sent to the A.3.2 CA and is authorized to accept VPN certificate requests from vendors with remote access privileges for remote access to the ABC Corporation network.

4.3.3   RFC 3647 IDENTIFICATION AND AUTHENTICATION FOR REKEY REQUESTS

The RFC 3647 §3.3 "Identification and Authentication for Rekey Requests" subsection considers subsequent authentication for rekey requests, both before and after revocation. Rekey requests can also be submitted before the current certificate expires and after the certificate expires.

Valid Certificate: If the current certificate is still valid, then the certificate rekey request for a new key pair might be authenticated via a digital signature per the key owner's current keys. Note that the certificate rekey request still needs to include a digital signature for the key owner's new key pair as evidence that the requestor is the owner of the new private key.

Note that the certification request as defined in RFC 2986 [B.6.8] only provides one digital signature field for the new keys and does not provide a digital signature field for the current keys. However, the Certificate Management Protocol (CMP) messages defined in RFC 4210 provide an optional PKI protection field, which can contain a digital signature for the current keys. In order for the current keys to provide authentication via a digital signature, the PKI system must support CMP.

Expired Certificate: If the current certificate is expired, then the certificate rekey request for a new key pair might need initial authentication if no other authentication credentials have been established. Note that the digital signature only provides evidence that the requestor is the owner of the new private key and does not authenticate the requestor.

Revoked Certificate: If the current certificate is revoked, then the certificate rekey request for a new key pair needs initial authentication. Revocation might occur for many reasons, including key compromise, cessation of operations, or an individual's demise. Most of the revocation reasons likely negate any other existing authentication credentials.

4.3.4 RFC 3647 Identification and Authentication for Revocation Requests

The RFC 3647 §3.4 "Identification and Authentication for Revocation Requests" subsection considers subsequent authentication for revocation requests. Certificates can be revoked for any entity and for a variety of reasons, and even be requested by various PKI participants, including the CA, the RA, the subscriber, or other parties. The RFC 5280 specification and X.509 standard provide numerous certificate revocation codes; see Table 4.16.

For any other revocation reason, the "unspecified (0)" code must be used. For example, in the infamous Comodo[3] compromise in 2011, an affiliate RA was compromised, resulting in the fraudulent

TABLE 4.16
Enumerated Revocation Reasons

RFC 5280	ITU-T X.509	Description
Used	unspecified (0)	*unspecified* can be used to revoke public key certificates for reasons other than the specific codes.
Used	keyCompromise (1)	*keyCompromise* is used in revoking an end-entity public key certificate; it indicates that it is known or suspected that the subject's private key or other aspects of the subject validated in the public key certificate have been compromised.
Used	cACompromise (2)	*cACompromise* is used in revoking a CA certificate; it indicates that it is known or suspected that the subject's private key or other aspects of the subject validated in the CA certificate have been compromised.
Used	affiliationChanged (3)	*affiliationChanged* indicates that the subject's name or other information in the certificate has been modified, but there is no cause to suspect that the private key has been compromised.
Used	superseded (4)	*superseded* indicates that the certificate has been superseded, but there is no cause to suspect that the private key has been compromised.
Used	cessationOfOperation (5)	*cessationOfOperation* indicates that the certificate is no longer needed for the purpose for which it was issued, but there is no cause to suspect that the private key has been compromised.
Used	certificateHold (6)	A public key certificate may be placed on hold by issuing a CRL entry with a reason code of *certificateHold*.
Used	privilegeWithdrawn (7)	*privilegeWithdrawn* indicates that the attribute certificate was revoked because a privilege contained within that attribute certificate has been withdrawn.
Used	removeFromCRL (8)	*removeFromCRL* reason code is for use with delta CRLs only and indicates that an existing CRL entry should now be removed owing to public key certificate expiration or hold release.
Used	privilegeWithdrawn (9)	*privilegeWithdrawn* indicates that a public key certificate was revoked because a privilege contained within that public key certificate has been withdrawn.
Used	aACompromise (10)	*aACompromise* is only relevant for ACRL entries.
Not Used	weakAlgorithmOrKey (11)	*weakAlgorithm* indicates that the public key certificate was revoked due to a weak cryptographic algorithm and/or key (e.g., due to short key length or unsafe key generation).

issuance of nine SSL certificates. The revocation reason might have been encoded as *rACompromise* but no such reason code is enumerated in the standards. Another revocation example might be a death certificate, where the individual is deceased. Alternatively, an employee might resign, retire, or get sacked, but arguably the *affiliationChanged* (3) code might be used. A more pragmatic example is when a licensed individual, such as a lawyer, accountant, broker, or investor, loses their license and their corresponding digital signature privileges, but *licenseRevoked* is not defined.

Revoking a certificate is serious business and should not be taken lightly. However, there are many other reasons a certificate might be revoked and who should be authenticated and authorized to request a revocation. And there are different types of certificates including CA certificates, RA certificates, and Subscriber certificates. The RFC §4.9 "Certificate Revocation and Suspension" subsection addresses these issues.

CA Certificates: The CA can revoke any of its own certificates; however, this will negate all of the downstream certificates during validation. Consider the scenarios in Figure 4.6. If the A.3.2 VPN contractor CA certificate is revoked by the A.3 VPN internal CA, then all contractor VPN certificates will fail validation, but the employee VPN certificates are still valid. Alternatively, if the A.3.1 VPN employee CA certificate is revoked, then all employee VPN certificates will fail, but the contractor VPN certificates are still good. Further, if the A.3 VPN internal CA certificate is revoked by the internal root CA, then all contractor and employee VPN certificates will fail validation. Due to the seriousness of revoking any CA certificate, the following controls are recommended for the CP:

- Review and approval by the policy authority (PA). The PA membership is the only group with sufficient understanding to evaluate the relative risks and impacts. Likely, senior management will also be engaged to confirm the PA recommendation; however, the CP needs to clearly articulate the importance of the PA role.
- Dual controls to prevent a single individual from revoking a CA certificate. Documented procedures will be needed to execute the revocation, but the CP only needs to stipulate the separation of duties. Audit logs will capture the event, along with a copy of the stepwise procedures, to fully document the event. Automatic alerts and announcements should be dispatched. Depending on the situation, a carefully crafted press release might be prudent.

RA Certificates: The RA might be intrinsic to the CA system, a stand-alone internal application that communicates to the CA, or an external service acting as an agent for the CA. In the event of key or system compromise, the RA can request that its own certificate be revoked and request a new certificate once the incident has been remediated. The RA should likewise request a revocation when it ceases operations. Conversely, the CA might revoke the RA certificate in the event of an agreement dispute. The revocation of an RA certificate does affect any previous subscriber certificates issued by the CA and only prevents any future requests from the RA:

- Revocation requests from the RA need to be authenticated by the CA; however, the RA is inherently authorized to revoke its own certificate. Ironically, in the event that the RA is compromised and an interloper submits a revocation request as a denial-of-service attack, the request is actually valid since the RA was compromised.
- Revocations initiated by the CA need to be authenticated and authorized to prevent RA services from being prematurely disabled. Note that unauthorized revocations are a denial-of-service attack.

Subscriber Certificates: Also called end-entity (EE) certificates, the subscriber can request that its own certificate be revoked for a variety of reasons including key compromise, system compromise, service termination, or certificate replacement. The CA might also revoke a subscriber certificate due to an agreement dispute. A family member, guardian, or legal representative might request revocation when the subscriber is debilitated, disabled, or deceased. An employer might request revocation in the event of job transfer, privilege withdrawal, or termination. Thus, a third party other than the subscriber or CA might have legitimate reasons for requesting a certification revocation. The CP needs to address all three scenarios:

- Revocation requests from the subscriber need to be authenticated by the RA or CA; however, the subscriber is inherently authorized to revoke its own certificate.
- Revocations initiated by the CA need to be authenticated and authorized to prevent subscriber services from being disrupted.
- Revocation requests from third parties need to be authenticated and authorized to prevent subscriber services from being disrupted.

It is important to recognize that it is not practical to identify every possible revocation scenario as the various types of certificates and variety of application environments would make for a very large list. Furthermore, as new applications and certificate usages are added to the CA capabilities, the legitimate revocation reasons will continue to grow. Also, since applications are divested or decommissioned, the revocation reasons will change. Therefore, the CP need only list the more significant revocation reasons, possibly list ones not supported, and provide the authentication, authorization, and accountability requirements for each PKI participant.

It is equally important to realize that revocation should not be the sole rejection control. For example, when a certificate is used for account authentication, access to the account is not blocked only per certificate revocation, rather access controls are also used. Analogously, when an employee is terminated, their badge access to the building is blocked and the badge itself is confiscated. This is unlike the movies where the stolen badge is used to access the building because nobody disabled the badge access.

4.4 RFC 2527 CERTIFICATE LIFECYCLE OPERATIONAL REQUIREMENTS

The RFC 3647 "Certificate Lifecycle Operational Requirements" section is structured with the following subsections.

§4. Certificate Lifecycle Operational Requirements
- 4.1 Certificate Application
- 4.2 Certificate Application Processing
- 4.3 Certificate Issuance
- 4.4 Certificate Acceptance
- 4.5 Key Pair and Certificate Usage
- 4.6 Certificate Renewal
- 4.7 Certificate Rekey
- 4.8 Certificate Modification
- 4.9 Certificate Revocation and Suspension
- 4.10 Certificate Status Services
- 4.11 End of Subscription
- 4.12 Key Escrow and Recovery

The fourth section RFC 3647 "Certificate Life Cycle Operational Requirements" addresses controls for the various PKI participants, including the CA, the RA, certificate subscribers, and relying parties, or others with regard to the key and certificate lifecycles. The RFC 3647 lifecycle terminology differs from the X9.79 key management lifecycle introduced in Chapter 2, "Cryptography Basics." Whereas X9.79 is a state transition diagram with nodes and transitions, the RFC 3647 specification uses a mixture of actions, processes, and protocols. Table 4.17 provides a comparison between the two lifecycles.

TABLE 4.17

Mapping X9.79 and RFC 3647 Lifecycles

RFC 3647 Lifecycle	X9.79 Key States	X9.79 Key Transitions
Certificate application	Key generation	–
Application processing	Key pair generation	–
Certificate issuance	Certificate generation	–
Key and certificate usage	Key usage	–
Certificate renewal	–	Rekey
Certificate rekey	–	Rekey
Certificate modification	–	Rekey
Certificate revocation	Key revocation	Key compromise
–	–	Key decommission
Certificate suspension	Key revocation	–
Not addressed	Certificate status	Key usage
Key revocation	Key termination	–
Key recovery	Key recovery	–
Key escrow	–	–

Key escrow is the practice of storing keys for the explicit purpose of providing them to a third party for the purpose of data recovery. Historically, key escrow was envisioned for law enforcement organizations, but today other implementations apply. In practice, however, key escrow is rarely used, as data recovery methods are much easier to manage.

4.4.1 RFC 3647 CERTIFICATE APPLICATION

The RFC 3647 §4.1 "Certificate Application" subsection deals with the PKI operational rules for generating key pairs, preparing the certificate signing request (CSR), and submitting the CSR application for a certificate to the RA for processing. Table 4.18 provides CP and CPS examples for the internal CA.

The RFC 2986 specification defines a certification request, commonly called the certificate signature request (CSR) originally defined in PKCS #10. The CSR includes four basic fields that provide sufficient information for the CA to generate a digital certificate:

- **Subject**: This is the name provided by the requestor that will typically appear in the certificate. The CA might enhance the subject name.
- **PKI Information**: This is the public key and associated algorithm information that will appear in the certificate. The algorithm information is replicated for the signature.
- **Attributes**: This includes additional information provided by the subject, some of which might appear in the certificate. The RFC 2985 specification provides a list of attributes for PKCS #10 originally defined in PKCS #9. Some attributes might be used for identification or authentication by the RA or CA, while others might not be supported and subsequently ignored.
- **Signature**: This is a digital signature generated by the requestor using the corresponding private as proof of ownership for the key pair. The signature is verified using the public key contained in the CSR.

The CSR syntax is defined in the various standards and should be supported by the RA and CA systems; however, the semantics supported by the RA and CA depends on the applications, the environments, and certificate types. Considering the internal CA in Figure 4.6, the applications include web servers using TLS certificates for internal connections, signature and encryption certificates for internal and external e-mails, and VPN certificates for remote access by employees and contractors.

TABLE 4.18

Examples of Certificate Application Rules

PKI Entity	CP/CPS	Policy or Practice Statement
CA	CP	Subordinate CA generates a key pair and CSR and submits the CSR to their superior CA to obtain a CA certificate for issuing certificates and signing CRL or OCSP updates.
RA	CP	RA generates a key pair and CSR and submits the CSR to their associated CA to obtain a certificate for signing certificate requests.
OCSP responders	CP	OCSP responders generate a key pair and CSR and submit the CSR to their associated CA to obtain a certificate for signing OCSP responses.
Subscribers	CP	Subscribers generate a key pair and CSR and submit the CSR to their associated RA to obtain TLS, e-mail, or VPN certificates.
TLS A.1.1 RA	CPS	RA generates a key pair and CSR and submits the CSR to the A.1.1 CA to obtain a certificate for signing certificate requests.
E-mail signature A.2.1 RA	CPS	RA generates a key pair and CSR and submits the CSR to the A.2.1 CA to obtain a certificate for signing certificate requests.
E-mail encryption A.2.2 RA	CPS	RA generates a key pair and CSR and submits the CSR to the A.2.2 CA to obtain a certificate for signing certificate requests.
VPN employee A.3.1 RA	CPS	RA generates a key pair and CSR and submits the CSR to the A.3.1 CA to obtain a certificate for signing certificate requests.
VPN contractor A.3.2 RA	CPS	RA generates a key pair and CSR and submits the CSR to the A.3.2 CA to obtain a certificate for signing certificate requests.

4.4.2 RFC 3647 CERTIFICATE APPLICATION PROCESSING

The RFC 3647 §4.2 "Certificate Application Processing" subsection describes the actions taken by the RA when a CSR is received from a requestor. The RA typically checks the syntax to ensure a well-formed request and the semantics to corroborate that the operating rules are being followed. In addition, the RA performs authentication and authorization of the requestor. This includes verification of the CSR signature to confirm that the requestor is the key owner. However, it is important to note that the CSR is a self-signed object and therefore vulnerable to a MITM attack. Figure 4.8 shows how an interloper might usurp a CSR application.

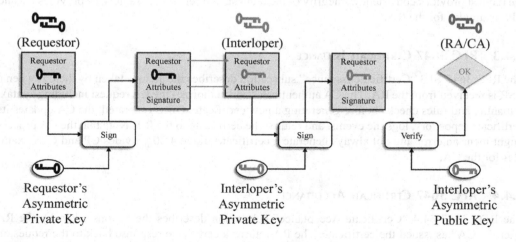

FIGURE 4.8 Certificate request man-in-the-middle (MITM) attack.

TABLE 4.19

Examples of Certificate Processing for the RA

PKI Entity	CP/CPS	Policy or Practice Statement
RA	CP	RA checks the CSR and authenticates to the associated CA.
RA	CPS	RA checks the CSR syntax to confirm it is a well-formed request.
RA	CPS	RA checks the CSR semantics to confirm it follows PKI operating rules.
RA	CPS	RA verifies the CSR signature to confirm the requestor is the key owner.
RA	CPS	RA signs the certificate request for submission to the CA.

The requestor constructs the certificate request (e.g., name, public key, and attributes), signs it with the corresponding private key, and submits it to the RA system. However, in this scenario, the interloper intercepts the CSR application, steals the requestor's name and attributes, and replaces the requestor's public with its own public key. When the RA system receives the modified CSR, it mistakenly uses the interloper's public key to verify the signature, presuming it is the requestor's public key, but because the signature verifies, the RA is spoofed into accepting the interloper as the requestor. Therefore, the CSR application process requires additional authentication of the requestor.

SPECIAL NOTE 4-2 RA AUTHENTICATION AND AUTHORIZATION

The RA authenticating and authorizing the requestor is a necessary control because the CSR is a self-signed object that only confirms the signer is the private key owner.

Furthermore, the CA needs to authenticate the RA. Since the RA sends unsolicited certificate requests to the CA for certificate issuance, the CA needs the ability to validate the requests received from any RA. The RA might be an embedded function within the CA system, it might be a separate internal application, or the RA might be an independent external service. For the latter two scenarios, having the RA sign the CSR with its own private key allows the CA to validate the RA request. For the former, the additional RA signature might not be explicitly needed as the combination RA/CA clearly trusts itself. However, from a continuity viewpoint, having the RA always sign the request provides consistency, integrity of the request, and reliability. Table 4.19 provides CP and CPS examples for the RA.

4.4.3   RFC 3647 CERTIFICATE ISSUANCE

The RFC 3647 §4.3 "Certificate Issuance" subsection describes the actions taken by the CA when a CSR is received from the RA. The CA authenticates and authorizes the RA request including syntax, semantic, and rules checks before generating a new certificate. Once generated, the CA updates its certificate repository, logs the events, and returns the certificate to the RA. Note that the CA process might incur an error and not always generate a certificate. Table 4.20 provides CP and CPS examples for the CA.

4.4.4   RFC 3647 CERTIFICATE ACCEPTANCE

The RFC 3647 §4.4 "Certificate Acceptance" subsection describes the actions taken by the RA after the CA has issued the certificate. The RA returns a certificate response back to the requestor, and depending on the nature of the interaction the subscriber might receive the certificate in the

TABLE 4.20

Examples of Certificate Issuance for the CA

PKI Entity	CP/CPS	Policy or Practice Statement
CA	CP	CA checks the CSR.
CA	CPS	CA authenticates the RA by validating the certificate request signature.
CA	CPS	CA authorizes the RA certificate request privileges.
CA	CPS	CA confirms the CSR is valid based on policy rules.
CA	CPS	CA generates the certificate.
CA	CPS	CA updates the certificate repository.
CA	CPS	CA returns a certificate response back to the RA.
CA	CPS	CA logs the certificate issuance event.

TABLE 4.21

Examples of Certificate Issuance for the RA

PKI Entity	CP/CPS	Policy or Practice Statement
RA	CP	RA returns a certificate response back to the requestor.
RA	CP	RA confirms acceptance by the requestor.
RA	CP	RA logs the subscriber acceptance.
TLS A.1.1 RA	CPS	RA returns the certificate via an e-mail response to the requestor.
E-mail signature A.2.1 RA	CPS	RA returns the certificate via an e-mail response to the requestor.
E-mail encryption A.2.2 RA	CPS	RA returns the certificate via an e-mail response to the requestor.
VPN employee A.3.1 RA	CPS	RA returns a unique certificate URL via an e-mail response to the requestor with a time to live (TTL) of 10 hours.
VPN contractor A.3.2 RA	CPS	RA returns a unique certificate URL via an e-mail response to the requestor with a time to live (TTL) of 10 hours.

response, a link to the posted certificate, or an indicator to check later on its status. Some certificate requests might be automatically approved based on operating rules, while others might require human intervention. Regardless, subscriber acceptance might vary by the certificate type, the RA, or the CA support infrastructure such as web or e-mail services. Table 4.21 provides CP and CPS examples for the RA.

Small organizations might issue certificates from a common RA system and therefore use a single certificate issuance method. Medium organizations might have multiple RA solutions and consequently use different issuance methods. Large organizations might need to support different issuance methods for various lines of business (LOBs) and accordingly need to operate multiple RA solutions. Furthermore, as any organization migrates from one RA solution to another, there is typically a migration period when multiple systems need to be operated.

4.4.5 RFC 3647 Key Pair and Certificate Usage

The RFC 3647 §4.5 "Key Pair and Certificate Usage" subsection refers to key usage for subscribers and relying parties; however, the CP should also include CA and RA. As discussed earlier in Section 3.7, "PKI Architectural Concepts," and Section 4.1, "RFC 2527 Introduction," subscribers use their private keys and relying parties use the subscriber's public keys, as shown in Figure 4.7. RFC 3647 §4.5 needs to include not only key usage but also key backup, key revocation, and key archive. Table 4.22 provides CP and CPS examples for subscribers and their private keys.

This is twice so far, when discussing RFC §3.4 and §4.5, we have made a forward reference to the RFC §4.9 "Certificate Revocation and Suspension" subsection, which raises an interesting topic. When writing a CP, there are two mutually exclusive approaches – either have information stated in one place using references throughout the document or duplicate the information in multiple places. The former approach makes for easier maintenance, but the reader often needs to flip back and forth. Conversely, the latter makes for easier reading but requires more work keeping the various parts of the document synchronized. This book recommends the former, having information only appearing once to avoid conflicting statements and using cross-references where needed.

SPECIAL NOTE 4-3 AVOID DUPLICATION

Information in the CP should only occur once to avoid conflicting statements, and other parts of the document should cross-reference to the appropriate place.

The relying party uses the subscriber's public key in the digital certificate. Table 4.23 provides CP and CPS examples for the relying party.

TABLE 4.22
Examples of Subscriber Private Keys and Certificates

PKI Entity	CP/CPS	Policy or Practice Statement
Subscriber key usage	CP	Subscribers agree to use their private keys only for their intended purpose and only by authorized personnel.
Subscriber key backup	CP	Subscribers agree to back up their private keys for maintaining business continuity and in the event of disaster recovery.
Subscriber key revocation	CP	Subscribers agree to revoke certificates per RFC §4.9 "Certificate Revocation and Suspension."
Subscriber TLS key usage	CPS	TLS private keys are only used for key establishment and client authentication.
Subscriber e-mail signature key usage	CPS	E-mail signature private keys are only used for signing e-mails.
Subscriber e-mail encryption key usage	CPS	E-mail encryption keys are only used for decrypting e-mails.
Subscriber VPN key usage	CPS	VPN private keys are only used for key establishment and peer authentication.

TABLE 4.23
Examples of Relying Party Public Keys and Certificates

PKI Entity	CP/CPS	Policy or Practice Statement
Relying Party key usage	CP	Relying parties agree to use the subscriber's public key only for their intended purpose and not misuse the subscriber's digital certificate.
Relying Party key revocation	CP	Relying parties agree as part of the certificate validation process to check the certificate validity dates and the revocation status.
Relying Party Key archive	CP	Relying parties agree that when they archive a subscriber's digital certificate past its expiration date, it is only for validation of older information created when the certificate was valid.
Relying Party CRL status	CPS	Relying parties agree to download and check the CRL for certificate status if an OCSP responder is not available.
Relying Party OCSP status	CPS	Relying parties agree to access and check the OCSP for certificate status if the CRL is not available.

Regarding RA and CA key usage, both entities are subscribers using their private keys, and with respect to the RA, the CA is also a relying party using the RA's certificate. Table 4.24 provides CP examples for the RA and CA.

4.4.6 RFC 3647 CERTIFICATE RENEWAL

The RFC 3647 §4.6 "Certificate Renewal" subsection describes circumstances under which renewal takes place, entities who can request a certificate renewal, and the related RA and CA actions including application, issuance, and acceptance processes. RFC 3647 describes renewal as the issuance of a new certificate without changing the public key or other information. For example, renewal is a method for extending the lifetime of a key pair by updating the certificate validity period. However, there are no industry standards or common practices defining which X.509 fields are permitted for renewal and which ones are not. Therefore, the PKI operational rules need to address renewal conditions and options. Table 4.25 provides CP examples for various PKI entities.

However, validity dates reflect the allocated lifecycle for a specific key pair and arbitrarily extending the operational period for a given key pair increases the likelihood of a key or system breach. As discussed in Chapter 2, "Cryptography Basics," cryptographic keys do not last forever and need to be changed periodically based on their operational periods. Lengthening the key lifecycle affects the RA, the CA, the subscriber, and the relying party. The RA needs to enforce the PKI operation rules for renewal, and the CA needs to support the various certificate fields that are updated. Analogous to reusing the same password for too long, renewing the certificate increases the probability of the subscriber's private key being compromised. A renewed certificate has a new

TABLE 4.24
Examples of RA and CA Keys and Certificates

PKI Entity	CP/CPS	Policy or Practice Statement
RA and CA Key usage	CP	RA and CA use their private keys only for their intended purpose and only by authorized personnel.
CA Key usage	CP	CA uses the RA's public key only for its intended purpose and does not misuse the RA's digital certificate.
RA and CA Key backup	CP	RA and CA back up their privates for maintaining business continuity and in the event of disaster recovery.
CA Key revocation	CP	CA as part of the certificate validation process to check the RA's certificate validity dates and the revocation status.
RA and CA Key revocation	CP	RA and CA revoke certificates per RFC §4.9, "Certificate Revocation and Suspension."

TABLE 4.25
Examples of Certificate Renewal Processing

PKI Entity	CP/CPS	Policy or Practice Statement
CA	CP	Subordinate CA generates and submits a CSR for certificate renewal to their superior CA to extend the validity period.
RA	CP	RA generates and submits the CSR for certificate renewal to their associated CA to extend the validity period.
OCSP responders	CP	OCSP responders generate and submit a CSR for certificate renewal to their associated CA to extend the validity period.
Subscribers	CP	Subscribers generate and submit a CSR for certificate renewal to their associated RA to extend the validity period.

serial number, but it contains the same subscriber name and public key, which might cause operational issues for the relying party. This book recommends that PKI systems do not support certificate renewal and always rekey new certificates.

SPECIAL NOTE 4-4 CERTIFICATE RENEWAL

Certificate renewal extends the key lifecycle beyond its original operational period, which is a risky practice; certificates should not be renewed; they should always be rekeyed.

Note that there is an interesting "gray area" between certificate renewal versus rekey. When a new CSR is submitted but with an old public key, a new certificate is generated with new validity dates and serial number. This replaces the old certificate but essentially extends the key lifecycle beyond its original operational period. Since a "new" certificate is issued with a different serial number, it is not renewal; however, neither is it rekey. *Public Key Uniqueness* is discussed in Section 4.3, "RFC 2527 Identification and Authentication."

4.4.7   RFC 3647 CERTIFICATE REKEY

The RFC 3647 §4.7 "Certificate Rekey" subsection describes circumstances under which rekey takes place, entities who can request a certificate rekey, and the related RA and CA actions including application, issuance, and acceptance processes. Rekey is described as the issuance of a new certificate for a new key pair when a previous certificate already exists. If the previous certificate is still valid, then it might be used for subsequent authentication; otherwise, initial authentication is needed as if it was the original certificate request. Table 4.26 provides CP examples for various PKI participants.

4.4.8   RFC 3647 CERTIFICATE MODIFICATION

The RFC 3647 §4.8 "Certificate Modification" subsection describes circumstances under which modification takes place, entities who can request a certificate modification, and the related RA and CA actions including application, issuance, and acceptance processes. RFC 3647 describes modification as the issuance of new certificate due to changes in the information in the certificate other than the subscriber public key. Unlike renewal, the validity dates remain unchanged, but again there are no industry standards or common practices defining which X.509 fields are permitted for modification and which ones are not. Therefore, the PKI operational rules need to address modification conditions and options. Table 4.27 provides CP examples for various PKI participants.

TABLE 4.26

Examples of Certificate Rekey Processing

PKI Entity	CP/CPS	Policy or Practice Statement
CA	CP	Subordinate CA generates a new key pair and CSR and submits the CSR for certificate rekey to their superior CA.
RA	CP	RA generates a new key pair and CSR and submits the CSR for certificate rekey to their associated CA.
OCSP responders	CP	OCSP responders generate a new key pair and CSR and submit the CSR for certificate rekey to their associated CA.
Subscribers	CP	Subscribers generate a new key pair and CSR and submit the CSR for certificate rekey to their associated RA.

However, a modified certificate has a new serial number with an existing public key but with newer information, which might cause operational issues for the relying party. Either the original validity dates remain unchanged in which case the lifecycle is shortened for the modified certificate or the validity dates are reset in which case the lifecycle is extended as for renewed certificate. Furthermore, the RA needs to enforce the PKI operation rules for modification, and the CA needs to support the various certificate fields that are updated. This book recommends that PKI systems do not support certificate modification and always rekey new certificates.

SPECIAL NOTE 4-5 CERTIFICATE MODIFICATION

Certificate modification changes the key lifecycle from its original operational period, which is a risky practice; certificates should not be modified; they should always be rekeyed.

There continues to be confusion between certificate renewal, rekey, and modification so for a quick reference guide, Table 4.28 compares critical certificate elements. Note that for any certificate change, the issuer signature is always updated. For certificate renewal, only the validity-to-date, sometimes called the certificate expiration date, is updated. For certificate rekey, the serial number, both validity dates, and the subject's public key are updated. For certificate modification, the serial number is always changed, while the validity-to-date or the subject name details might change.

For certificate renewal or modification, the validity-from-date should never be updated, as that implies the subject's key pair was newly generated, which is not the case. For certificate modification, some of the subject's name attributes might be updated, such as the organization name (O), the organization unit (OU), locality name (L), or country name (C), but the common name (CN) does

TABLE 4.27

Examples of Certificate Modification Processing

PKI Entity	CP/CPS	Policy or Practice Statement
CA	CP	Subordinate CA generates and submits a CSR for certificate modification to their superior CA to extend the validity period.
RA	CP	RA generates and submits the CSR for certificate modification to their associated CA to extend the validity period.
OCSP responders	CP	OCSP responders generate and submit a CSR for certificate modification to their associated CA to extend the validity period.
Subscribers	CP	Subscribers generate and submit a CSR for certificate modification to their associated RA to extend the validity period.

TABLE 4.28

Comparison Renewal versus Rekey versus Modification

Certificate Element	Renewal	Rekey	Modification
Serial number	Same	Updated	Updated
Issuer name	Same	Same	Same
Issuer signature	Updated	Updated	Updated
Valid from date	Same	Updated	Same
Valid to date	Updated	Updated	Maybe
Subject name	Same	Same	Maybe
Subject public key	Same	Updated	Same

not typically change. Not that changing any of the subject name attributes can lead to more confusion during certificate validation.

4.4.9   RFC 3647 CERTIFICATE REVOCATION AND SUSPENSION

The RFC 3647 §4.9 "Certificate Revocation and Suspension" subsection describes circumstances under which revocation or suspension takes place, entities who can request a certificate revocation or suspension, and the related RA and CA actions including application, issuance, and acceptance processes. Suspension occurs when a certificate is temporarily put on hold to prevent its use and eventually is either reinstated or revoked. Revocation occurs when a certificate is permanently canceled. Table 4.29 provides CP examples for various PKI entities.

Revocation and suspension are treated synonymously in RFC 3647; however, since suspension is reversible and revocation is irreversible, the circumstances are different. Table 4.30 provides a contrast between the two. Suspension might inadvertently leak sensitive information such as mergers or

---

TABLE 4.29

Examples of Certificate Revocation and Suspension Processing

PKI Entity	CP/CPS	Policy or Practice Statement
CA	CP	Subordinate CA submits a request to their superior CA to revoke or suspend its certificate.
RA	CP	RA submits a request to their associated CA to revoke or suspend its certificate.
OCSP responders	CP	OCSP responders submit a request to their associated CA to revoke or suspend its certificate.
Subscribers	CP	Subscribers submit a request to their associated RA to revoke or suspend its certificate.

TABLE 4.30

Comparison of Suspension and Revocation Circumstances

Circumstances	Certificate Suspension	Certificate Revocation
Key compromise	The organization might suspend its certificate during an investigation to determine key compromise.	The organization revokes its certificate if a key compromise is known or suspected.
CA compromise	The CA might suspend its certificate during an investigation to determine system compromise.	The CA revokes its certificate if a system compromise is known or suspected.
RA compromise	The CA might suspend an RA certificate during an investigation to determine system compromise.	The CA revokes an RA certificate if a system compromise is known or suspected.
Subscriber compromise	The CA might suspend a subscriber certificate during an investigation to determine end-entity compromise.	The CA revokes a subscriber certificate if an end-entity compromise is known or suspected.
Affiliation change	The organization might suspend its certificate during a merger or acquisition change.	The organization revokes its certificate when its affiliation changes.
Superseded by another certificate	The organization might suspend its certificate during application for a replacement certificate.	The organization revokes its certificate after it obtains a replacement certificate.
Cessation of operations	The organization might suspend its certificate for business cessation.	The organization revokes its certificate after business cessation.
Privilege withdrawal	An authority suspends a certificate during an investigation to determine privilege withdrawal.	An authority revokes a certificate to withdraw privileges.

acquisitions to third parties that could financially affect an organization. The complexities of managing suspension privileges between various authorized individuals possibly from different organizations far exceed the benefits of certificate suspension. For these reasons, this book recommends that certificate suspension not be supported and only offers certificate revocation.

Regarding any type of compromise, there are investigative stages when an organization escalates from an unknown "event" to a known "compromise" situation. For example, going from a "monitoring" stage to a "data breach" stage is outlined in X9.141 Data Protection and Breach Notification standard [B.1.21] in its Data Operations Framework. Table 4.31 provides an overview of the X9.141 Data Operations Framework.

When an organization monitoring (Stage 0) its information technology environment detects an anomaly, it investigates the event (Stage 1) to determine if things are normal or if an incident has occurred. If an incident has occurred (Stage 2), the organization further investigates to determine its severity, which might escalate (Stage 3) from a cybersecurity incident to a data security incident. When the data security incident results in a known data exfiltration, the organization shifts into data breach notification (Stage 4) including mitigation, remediation, and in some cases compensation. For the purposes of this book "Stage 4" is a compromise.

SPECIAL NOTE 4-6 CERTIFICATE SUSPENSION

Certificate suspension should not be supported due to the complexities and side effects of managing authorized individuals possibly from different organizations. Many CA software products do not support certificate suspension.

It is not feasible to list all possible revocation circumstances (or suspension if supported), but the CP should list at least the most critical revocation categories (e.g., key compromise, system compromise). The revocation circumstances in RFC 3647 §4.9 need to be synchronized with RFC 3647 §4.5 and with RFC 3647 §3.4; however, neither of the other two subsections includes suspension so the CP needs to be aligned with the relevant topics.

4.4.10   RFC 3647 Certificate Status Services

The RFC 3647 §4.10 "Certificate Status Services" subsection addresses the characteristics for the certificate revocation lists (CRLs) and Online Certificate Status Protocol (OCSP) services. As other

---

TABLE 4.31

X9.141 Data Operations Framework

Stage	Circumstances	Description
Stage 0: Normal	Monitoring	Applications and systems operate in a business as usual (BAU) mode with ongoing monitoring.
Stage 1: Event	Information Technology Event	One or more events are detected, such that further investigation either resolves the events as benign or elevates to an incident.
Stage 2: Incident	Cybersecurity Incident	One or more incidents are investigated, such that further examination either resolves the incidents per mitigation or elevates to a data security incident.
Stage 3: Incident	Data Security Incident	One or more incidents are examined to determine if a data breach is known or suspected, but if not then resolves the incidents per mitigation, otherwise elevates to a data breach.
Stage 4: Breach	Data Breach	One or more data records have been exfiltrated.

methods become available, they would be included in this subsection. Table 4.32 provides sample CRL and OCSP statements.

The certificate status rules need to be aligned with the RFC 3647 §2 "Publication and Repository Responsibilities" section. As mentioned in Chapter 4, "PKI Management and Security," the CRL and OCSP operations might be based on industry standards.

4.4.11   RFC 3647 End of Subscription

The RFC 3647 §4.11 "End of Subscription" subsection addresses subscribers terminating services with the PKI system. Certificate expiration or revocation does not necessarily terminate the subscriber's relationship but either is a necessary condition when terminating subscription services. Table 4.33 provides CP examples for subscriber termination.

Subscriber inactivity should not be ignored when all certificates have been either revoked or expired. Regular subscriber activity such as certificate rekey keeps the subscription active, such that any unexpected actions or inaction by the subscriber are an "event" that regular monitoring can detect. See Table 4.31 for an overview of a Data Operations Framework.

4.4.12   RFC 3647 Key Escrow and Recovery

The RFC 3647 §4.12 "Key Escrow and Recovery" subsection is intended to address asymmetric private key and symmetric key recovery processes. However, the RFC 3647 specification incorrectly regards key escrow as equivalent to key recovery. As discussed in Chapter 2, "Cryptography Basics," key escrow is the practice of storing keys for the explicit purpose of providing them to a third party. Regarding key recovery, Table 4.34 provides CP and CPS examples for various PKI entities.

The organization size tends to be proportional to the number of certificates. More employees, applications, network appliances, and vendors will need more certificates that must be issued, managed, renewed, and possibly revoked. More certificates typically require both additional staffing and more automated tools. More certificates also need better management tools. For a

---

TABLE 4.32
Examples of Certificate Status Processing

PKI Entity	Example Certificate Status Rules
Root CA	The CRL service is updated annually. Revocations of subordinate CA certificates are posted within 24 hours.
	The OCSP service is updated annually. Revocations of subordinate CA certificates are posted within 24 hours.
Subordinate CA	The CRL service is updated weekly. Revocations of any certificate are posted within 24 hours.
	The OCSP service is updated every 4 days. Revocations of any certificate are posted within 24 hours.

TABLE 4.33
Examples of End of Subscription Processing

PKI Entity	CP/CPS	Policy or Practice Statement
Subscribers	CP	Subscribers submit a termination request to their associated RA with an immediate revocation of all certificates.
Subscribers	CP	Subscribers submit a termination request to their associated RA with an eventual expiration of all certificates when renewal, rekey, or modification is not planned.

TABLE 4.34

Examples of Key Recovery Processing

PKI Entity	CP/CPS	Policy or Practice Statement
CA	CP	CA private keys are backed up solely for business continuity and disaster recovery.
Root CA	CPS	Root CA keys are backed up and recoverable within 72 hours.
Subordinate CA	CPS	Subordinate CA keys are backed up and recoverable within 24 hours.

small organization managing hundreds of certificates, manual processes are possible. For medium organizations that might manage thousands or tens of thousands of certificates, manual methods are no longer a viable option. Large organizations that manage hundreds of thousands or even millions of certificates need distributed management processes that provide reporting and constant monitoring tools.

RA and OCSP private keys might also be backed up; however, that is an operational risk decision for the organization as sometimes it is easier to rekey other PKI systems. Regarding third-party data escrow, if the topic needs to be included, it should be in its own subsection. Regarding key escrow, if the topic needs to be included, it will have many of the same characteristics as key backup and recovery.

4.5 RFC 3647 FACILITY, MANAGEMENT, AND OPERATIONAL AND PHYSICAL CONTROLS

The RFC 3647 "Facility, Management, and Operational and Physical Controls" section is structured with the following subsections:

§5. Facility, Management, and Operational Controls
- 5.1 Physical Security Controls
- 5.2 Procedural Controls
- 5.3 Personnel Controls
- 5.4 Audit Logging Procedures
- 5.5 Records Archival
- 5.6 Key Changeover
- 5.7 Compromise and Disaster Recovery
- 5.8 CA or RA Termination

The fifth section RFC 3647 §5 "Management, Operational, and Physical Controls" addresses what the specification calls nontechnical security controls for physical, procedural, and personnel areas. Note that this segment seems to have two dissimilar titles – the table of contents and the framework use facility, management, and operational controls, but the actual segment uses management, operational, and physical controls. Regardless, the subsections address physical security, procedures, personnel security, audit logging, records archival, key changeover, disaster recovery, and operational termination.

4.5.1 RFC 3647 PHYSICAL SECURITY CONTROLS

The RFC 3647 §5.1 "Physical Security Controls" subsection deals with campus and building security, including physical access controls. This subsection also deals with environmental controls including heating, ventilation, and air conditioning (HVAC), power, fire detection, alarms, suppression systems, waste disposal, and on-site and off-site storage. The purpose for declaring physical controls is to demonstrate reasonable operational processes. Refer back to Figures 4.2

through 4–4 for an overview of the ABC Corporation. Table 4.35 provides sample statements for various facility types.

Small organizations might only have a single server room that contains all computer and network equipment, including PKI systems. Alternatively, small organizations might outsource all of their IT to management services and use external hosting services, including cloud. A medium to large organization might use both internal and external IT services. Physical controls need to address both internal and external scenarios, internal controls managed directly by the organization, and external controls provided by the service providers.

Physical and technical controls for third-party service providers, including cloud providers, might be determined by independent third-party Service Organization Controls[4] (SOC) audits. Table 4.36 provides a summary of the three SOC reports (SOC 1, SOC 2, and SOC 3). The first two, SOC 1 and SOC 2 reports, are restricted to the management of the service organization, user entities, and user

TABLE 4.35
Examples of Physical Security Controls

Facility Type	Example Physical Security Rules
Campus	The ABC Corporation campus is a secured facility.
Buildings	The ABC Corporation buildings are individually secured.
Rooms	The root CA is located in a secured PKI room.
Racks	The subordinate CA is located in secured PKI racks.
Services	The HVAC, power, fire, and waste services have restricted access.
Storage	On-site storage is located in secured buildings.
Storage	Off-site storage is located at a secured third-party site.

TABLE 4.36
Audit SOC Reports

Audit	AICPA Description
SOC 1	*Report on Controls at a Service Organization Relevant to User Entities' Internal Control over Financial Reporting (ICFR)*[5] Reporting on an Examination of Controls at a Service Organization Relevant to User Entities' Internal Control Over Financial Reporting is specifically intended to meet the needs of entities that use service organizations (user entities) and the CPAs that audit the user entities' financial statements (user auditors), in evaluating the effect of the controls at the service organization on the user entities' financial statements. There are two types of reports for these engagements:
SOC 2	*Report on Controls at a Service Organization Relevant to Security, Availability, Processing Integrity, Confidentiality, or Privacy*[6] These reports are intended to meet the needs of a broad range of users that need detailed information and assurance about the controls at a service organization relevant to security, availability, and processing integrity of the systems the service organization uses to process users' data and the confidentiality and privacy of the information processed by these systems. These reports can play an important role in: • Oversight of the organization • Vendor management programs • Internal corporate governance and risk management processes • Regulatory oversight
SOC 3	*Service Organizations: Trust Services Criteria for General Use Report*[7] These reports are designed to meet the needs of users who need assurance about the controls at a service organization relevant to security, availability, processing integrity, confidentiality, or privacy, but do not have the need for or the knowledge necessary to make effective use of a SOC 2 Report.

auditors. Consequently, an "audit letter" is often provided, identifying the audit client, audit firm, auditor, nature of the audit, and general audit result. Note that there are no "bad" audit results provided in such letters; if the client did not pass the audit, no letter is provided. Alternatively, because SOC 3 are general user reports, they can be freely distributed.

All three SOC audits can be done at either a specific date (Type 1) or a specific period (Type 2); see Table 4.37 for a summary. Type 1 audits address the design of the controls, whereas Type 2 audits address the design and operating effectiveness of the controls. While either audit can take days, weeks, or months to complete, the scope of the audit is either a specific date (point in time) or specific period (period of time). For example, a Type 1 audit would limit its scope to relevant documentation (e.g., policy, practices, standards, procedures, reports, logs) relating to a specific date. Alternatively, a Type 2 audit would include any documentation correlating to the specific period, such as six months or a full year, including revisions, withdrawals, and changes in staff or management status.

In either case, the auditor cannot attest to the client's controls before or after the specific date or specific period. Audits consist of three basic steps: reading the client's documented controls, conducting interviews to verify that the documented controls are used, and observing operations to verify that the documented controls are effective. Type 1 audits are considered less accurate, as the auditor only has documentation, interviews, and logs to verify controls. Type 2 audits are more involved, executed over months, with many interviews and observations including testing. But again, the auditor can only attest to what was present during the audit.

4.5.2 RFC 3647 Procedural Controls

The RFC 3647 §5.2 "Procedural Controls" subsection deals with trusted PKI roles and separation of duties, including identification and authentication for each role. Based on the relative risks, each role might require different authentication levels using one, two, or three factors depending on the associated responsibility. Table 4.38 provides sample statements for various PKI roles and responsibilities.

4.5.3 RFC 3647 §5.3 Personnel Security Controls

The RFC 3647 §5.3 "Personnel Security Controls" subsection addresses hiring processes, additional background checks, education and training, and other considerations including similarities or differences between employees and contractors. An organization's human resources (HR) processes will establish an individual's identity and initial authentication. However, an organization's HR processes are for employees and not necessarily for contractors. The resource agency will have its own HR processes. The PKI roles might require additional background checks above and beyond the organization's HR processes or the agency's HR processes if contractors are permitted to fulfill PKI roles. For example, CA and RA operators need updated background checks every three years (triennially), whereas Security officers need annual background checks. Note that HR policy and

TABLE 4.37

Audit SOC Types

SOC	AICPA Description
Type 1	Report on the fairness of the presentation of management's description of the service organization's system and the suitability of the design of the controls to achieve the related control objectives included in the description as of a specified date.
Type 2	Report on the fairness of the presentation of management's description of the service organization's system and the suitability of the design and operating effectiveness of the controls to achieve the related control objectives included in the description throughout a specified period.

practices will vary among countries according to local laws and regulations. Table 4.39 provides sample additional authentication controls for various PKI roles.

Regarding education and training, academic degrees in technology might be helpful, industry security credentials are also useful, and either might be mandated by HR policy. However, academic and industry credentials tend to be generic. Specific training on the actual systems, applications, and cryptographic products in use is extremely beneficial. Initial training, refresher courses, and updates are important. Table 4.32 also provides sample education and training controls for various PKI roles. For example, CA operators, RA operators, and security officers need annual training.

4.5.4 RFC 3647 Audit Logging Procedures

The RFC 3647 §5.4 "Audit Logging Procedures" subsection addresses audit log management, which includes the events, access controls, confidentiality and integrity controls, and analysis. Minimally, sufficient information needs to be captured such that if a security incident occurs, there are adequate

TABLE 4.38
Examples of Procedural Controls

PKI Role	PKI Role Responsibility	Example Authentication Rules
Facility officers	The facility officers are responsible for campus and building security.	Two factors: (1) identification (ID) picture badge and (2) corresponding passcode
System admin	System administrators are responsible for managing hardware, system software, and network components.	Single factor: (1) log-on passcode
Application admin	Application administrators are responsible for managing application configurations, accounts, and logs.	Single factor: (1) log-on passcode
CA operators	Application operators are responsible for managing the CA systems.	Single factor: (1) log-on passcode
RA operators	Application operators are responsible for managing the RA systems.	Single factor: (1) log-on passcode
Security officers	Security officers are responsible for managing cryptographic materials and ensuring security policies are followed.	Two factors: (1) identification (ID) picture badge and (2) biometric verification

TABLE 4.39
Examples of Personnel Security Controls

PKI Role	Example Additional Authentication	Example Education and Training
Facility officers	Undergoes initial financial and criminal background checks	Completes initial and biannual physical security training
System admin	Undergoes initial financial and criminal background checks	Completes initial and biannual system admin training
Application admin	Undergoes initial financial and criminal background checks	Completes initial and biannual application admin training
CA operators	Undergoes triennial financial and criminal background checks	Completes initial and annual CA operations training
RA operators	Undergoes triennial financial and criminal background checks	Completes initial and annual RA operations training
Security officers	Undergoes annual financial and criminal background checks	Completes initial and annual security training

data to determine the sequence of events, identify the root cause, and determine an appropriate remediation. Ideally, information is captured and analyzed in a timely manner to detect and prevent a potential security incident. Table 4.40 provides CP and CPS examples for various PKI entities. Unfortunately, real-time log analysis is rare and as discussed with Table 4.31, logs are often used as latent "fingerprints" during cybersecurity (Stage 2) or data security (Stage 3) incident response.

A basic audit control is the comparison of two interrelated but independent events. Thus, the RA and CA can reconcile the certificate and revocation requests as a comparison check for system reliability. For audit logs to be available, they must be managed in an appropriate manner. Table 4.41 provides examples of audit log management control statements for various PKI entities.

Log reconciliation is like balancing a checkbook; begin with the current balance, add the deposits, subtract the withdrawals, and confirm the new balance. Analogously, begin with the number of certificates issued by the CA, add the newly issued certificates, subtract the revoked certificates, and confirm the new balance. The number of RA certificate requests should match the CA newly issued certificates. The number of RA revocation requests should match the CA updates to the CRL or the OCSP database. Simple reconciliation can often determine problems and pinpoint failures to a specific RA or CA service.

4.5.5   RFC 3647 Records Archival

The RFC 3647 §5.5 "Records Archival" subsection addresses general records and audit log archive processes including access controls, confidentiality and integrity controls, backup, and recovery. Audit logs are typically kept online for short-term access, perhaps months, and then transferred to a log repository for long-time archive. Since many root CA certificates are issued for 20 or more years, the log archive needs to avoid hardware deterioration or software obsolescence. Table 4.42 provides CP examples for various PKI entities.

General records include any publications such as dated versions of the CP or CPS, various legal or contractual agreements, third-party audit letters, and possibly certificates. Special consideration should be given to mergers, acquisitions, and divestitures. New owners (or new management) tend

TABLE 4.40
Examples of Audit Log Events

PKI Entity	CP/CPS	Policy or Practice Statement
CA	CP	CA generates logs for certificate issuance and CRL issuance.
CA	CP	CA generates logs for key changeover.
RA	CP	RA generates logs for key changeover.
RA	CP	RA generates logs for service requests.
RA	CPS	RA generates logs for certificate requests.
RA	CPS	RA generates logs for revocation requests.

TABLE 4.41
Examples of Audit Log Management Controls

PKI Entity	CP/CPS	Policy or Practice Statement
CA	CP	CA restricts access to its audit logs to authorized personnel.
CA	CP	CA digitally signs its audit logs.
CA and RA	CP	CA and RA audit logs are reconciled on a daily basis.
RA	CP	RA restricts access to its audit logs to authorized personnel.
RA	CP	RA digitally signs its audit logs.

to update publications as if existing certificates issued at a specific date per a particular CP/CPS somehow "magically" transform from old controls to new ones.

4.5.6   RFC 3647 KEY CHANGEOVER

The RFC 3647 §5.6 "Key Changeover" subsection deals with replacing the current CA public key with a new public key, essentially a CA rekey. Consider the internal CA in Figure 4.6 and all of the VPN employee certificates signed by the A.3.1 VPN employee CA private key. Operationally, the CA generates a new key pair and gets a new certificate from its superior A.3 VPN internal CA before its current certificate expires. The A.3.1 VPN employee CA begins issuing all new VPN employees using the new private key, which changes the CA certificate chain. As the current VPN employee certificates expire, they eventually get rekeyed using the newer CA certificate and alternate CA certificate chain. Table 4.43 demonstrates the current chain and the newer chain.

The current forward certificate chain consists of the certificates #22 ⇒ #12 ⇒ #15 and the newer chain consists of the certificates #22 ⇒ #12 ⇒ #16, but both chains represent the same CA hierarchy. The old A.3.1 VPN employee CA certificate #15 is rekeyed and replaced by the newer A.3.1 VPN employee CA certificate #16, where both are issued by the A.3 VPN internal CA. So, for example, the VPN certificate #1003 issued by the old A.3.1 CA has the backward chain #1003 ⇒ #15 ⇒ #12 ⇒ #22 and the VPN certificate #1006 issued by the newer A.3.1 CA has the chain #1005 ⇒ #16 ⇒ #12 ⇒ #22. Table 4.44 provides CP and CPS examples of rekey controls for various PKI entities.

TABLE 4.42
Examples of Audit Log Archive Controls

PKI Entity	CP/CPS	Policy or Practice Statement
CA	CP	CA retains its audit logs for the lifecycle of its asymmetric keys.
CA	CP	CA restricts access to its audit logs to authorized personnel.
RA	CP	RA retains its audit logs for the lifecycle of its asymmetric keys.
RA	CP	RA restricts access to its audit logs to authorized personnel.

TABLE 4.43
Examples of Certificate Changeover Chains

Old Certificate Chain	New Certificate Chain
A. Internal CA #22	A. Internal CA #22
↳ A.3 VPN internal CA #12	↳ A.3 VPN internal CA #12
↳ A.3.1 VPN employee CA #15	↳ A.3.1 VPN employee CA #16
↳ VPN employee certificates #1003	↳ VPN employee certificates #1005

TABLE 4.44
Examples of Rekey Controls

PKI Entity	CP/CPS	Policy or Practice Statement
CA	CP	Root CA rekeys six months prior to its certificate expiration.
CA	CP	Subordinate CA rekeys three months prior to its certificate expiration.
RA	CP	RA rekeys one month prior to its certificate expiration.
Subscribers	CP	Subscribers are expected to rekey one week prior to its certificate expiration.
Subscribers	CPS	Subscribers receive one month, one week, and then daily reminders to rekey certificates.
Subscribers	CPS	Subscribers can opt in or out to receive rekey reminders.

The validity dates for subscriber (end-entity) certificates may vary greatly depending on the application environment. For example, the CA Browser Forum [CABF Baseline] has been steadily reducing the operational period for all subscriber certificates, issued: between July 2016 and March 2018 maximum of 39 months (or 1,186 days), between March 2018 and September 2020 maximum of 825 days, and after September 2020 maximum of 397 days. Conversely, keys generated in telecommunications equipment (e.g., routers) or financial devices (e.g., ATM) have an operational life span of ten years (or 3,650 days). Therefore, the CPS will need to address rekey controls depending on the application software and hardware characteristics.

4.5.7 RFC 3647 COMPROMISE AND DISASTER RECOVERY

The RFC 3647 §5.7 "Compromise and Disaster Recovery" subsection addresses business continuity and disaster recovery including facility, application, system, and key compromise. Each PKI entity has different reliability requirements depending on its criticality. Some systems and keys are backed up with full redundancy, while others have lesser needs. Table 4.45 provides CP examples for various PKI entities.

Root CA systems, also called trust anchors, are typically operated in an "offline" mode, as the root CA is only used to issue or revoke subordinate CA certificates. Consequently, whenever a new subordinate CA is created, the root CA is brought "online" to generate the subordinate CA certificate. Likewise, whenever an existing subordinate CA certificate needs revoking, the root CA is brought "online" to revoke the subordinate CA certificate. There is some debate as to what constitutes an "offline" mode. For some, offline means the physical system is kept powered down and kept physically secured under lock and key. For others, offline means the physical system is isolated from the network, possibly its own private LAN, with physical and logical access limited to authorized personnel.

4.5.8 RFC 3647 CA OR RA TERMINATION

The RFC 3647 §5.8 "CA or RA Termination" subsection addresses the conditions and processes for decommissioning PKI systems or their components. Depending on the situation, a termination might be graceful or abrupt. A graceful termination is when the certificates expire with no rekey for conditions such as a minor security incident, decommissioning an application, ending a service, or ceasing operation due to a merger or acquisition. An abrupt termination is when the certificates are revoked with no rekey for circumstances such as a major security incident, court order for immediate cease and desist, lawsuit, or ceasing operation due to bankruptcy. Table 4.46 provides CP examples for various PKI entities.

For either scenario of an abrupt or graceful termination, the PKI entity should be prepared to notify its customers and business partners and possibly issue a press release. Whenever possible, contingency plans should be provided. Depending on the situation, the PKI entity might incur legal action, ranging from civil lawsuits to criminal proceedings. Further, when the PKI entity is a

---

TABLE 4.45

Examples of Recovery Controls

PKI Entity	CP/CPS	Policy or Practice Statement
CA	CP	Online CA systems operate 7 × 24 with full redundancy.
CA	CP	All CA keys are backed up with full recovery.
CA	CP	All CA keys are immediately revoked and replaced if compromised.
RA	CP	RA keys are immediately revoked and replaced if compromised.
Subscriber	CP	Subscriber keys are immediately revoked if compromised.

TABLE 4.46

Examples of Termination Controls

PKI Entity	CP/CPS	Policy or Practice Statement
RA	CP	For abrupt terminations, the RA submits a termination request to their associated CA with an immediate revocation of all certificates with no rekey.
RA	CP	For graceful terminations, the RA submits a termination request to their associated CA with an eventual expiration of all certificates that disallows rekey.
CA	CP	For abrupt terminations, the subordinate CA certificates are immediately revoked by their associated superior CA.
CA	CP	For graceful terminations, the subordinate CA certificates eventually expire with no rekey.
Root CA	CP	For abrupt terminations, the root CA certificates are immediately revoked.
Root CA	CP	For graceful terminations, the root CA certificates eventually expire with no rekey.

division or subsidiary of a larger organization, the holding company needs to be duly notified and correspondingly prepared. Section 4.9, "RFC 2527 Other Business and Legal Matters," deals with financial responsibility, governing law, and other legal matters.

4.6   RFC 2527 TECHNICAL SECURITY CONTROLS

The RFC 3647 "Technical Security Controls" section is structured with the following subsections.

§6. Technical Security Controls
- 6.1. Key Pair Generation and Installation
- 6.2. Private Key Protection and Cryptographic Module Engineering Controls
- 6.3. Other Aspects of Key Pair Management
- 6.4. Activation Data
- 6.5. Computer Security Controls
- 6.6. Life Cycle Security Controls
- 6.7. Network Security Controls
- 6.8. Timestamping

The sixth section RFC 3647 §6 "Technical Security Controls" addresses requirements and rules for protecting system and network components including hardware, software, applications, and information objects. Various aspects of key management not discussed in the fourth section "Certificate Life Cycle Operational Requirements" are included in this section:

- **Cryptographic keys** include asymmetric key pairs and any symmetric keys.
- **Hardware** includes servers, workstations, laptops, mobile devices, network appliances, wireless access points, and even cables and power cords.
- **Software** encompasses source code, firmware, executable code, scripts, data structures, message formats, protocols, and configuration data.
- **Applications** include access controls and audit logs for system administrators, application administrators, application managers, and application users.
- **Information** consists of data in any format or media that might be generated, distributed, transmitted, stored, printed, or processed.

Any size organization might use third-party services, including cloud services. Thus, since one or more of the PKI services might be hosted or provided by third parties, the technical security controls also need to address reviews of third-party controls. For an overview of security basics, refer

TABLE 4.47

Examples of Key Generation and Installation Controls

PKI Entity	CP/CPS	Policy or Practice Statement
CA	CP	All internal CA systems generate key pairs inside cryptographic hardware modules.
RA	CP	All internal RA systems generate key pairs inside cryptographic hardware modules.
Subscribers	CP	System owners are responsible for generating server key pairs within a secure environment.
Subscribers	CP	Employees and contractors are responsible for generating key pairs within a secure environment.
CA	CPS	Internal root CA systems generate key pairs inside FIPS 140–3 Security Level 3 cryptographic hardware modules within a physically secured isolated environment.
CA	CPS	Internal CA systems generate key pairs inside FIPS 140–3 Security Level 4 cryptographic hardware modules.
RA	CPS	All internal RA systems generate key pairs inside FIPS 140–3 Security Level 3 cryptographic hardware modules.
Subscribers	CPS	Subscribers are responsible for generating key pairs inside FIPS 140–3 Security Level 2 cryptographic hardware modules within a secure environment.

to Chapter 1, "Introduction," and for a discussion of key management and cryptographic basics, see Chapter 2, "Cryptography Basics."

4.6.1 RFC 3647 KEY PAIR GENERATION AND INSTALLATION

The RFC 3647 §6.1 "Key Pair Generation and Installation" subsection deals with the first two key lifecycle stages presented in Figure 4.7 key generation and key distribution. Each key pair might be generated by the key owner or another party, and if done by another party, then the keys need to be securely transferred to the owner. Each certificate needs to be generated by a CA such that the public key needs to be sent to the CA and the certificate needs to be sent to the key owner. If the keys or certificates are used in a different location than where they are generated, then they need to be distributed from the generation to the usage locations. Table 4.47 provides CP and CPS examples for various PKI entities.

We discussed the four increasing NIST FIPS 140–3 security levels in Section 2.5, "Cryptographic Modules." Conceptually an acceptable assurance level can be achieved when combining the appropriate security level with operational controls. Generally speaking, lower controls need higher security levels. For example, a Security Level 4 cryptographic module operating with "strong" controls might achieve the same assurance level as a level 3 module operating with "lower" controls. However, there is no universal equation to determine assurance levels. The security levels and operational controls can be managed for the PKI components within an organization and might be specified to third-party service providers but likely are at best recommendations to subscribers and relying parties per the CP and CPS agreements.

4.6.2 RFC 3647 PRIVATE KEY PROTECTION AND CRYPTOGRAPHIC MODULE CONTROLS

The RFC 3647 §6.2 "Private Key Protection and Cryptographic Module Engineering Controls" subsection deals with the third, fourth, and sixth key lifecycle stages presented in Figure 4.7 key usage, key backup, and key termination. As noted in §4 "Certificate Life Cycle Operational Requirements," the RFC 3647 specification incorrectly regards key escrow as equivalent to key recovery. Regardless, this subsection addresses key protection controls after keys have been generated and installed. Table 4.48 provides CP and CPS examples for various PKI entities.

Note the root CA systems might use a FIPS 140–3 level 3 module but other CA systems need a stronger FIPS 140–3 level 4 module. Note that the root CA systems operate within a physically secure isolated environment while the other CA systems, although running in a physically secured environment, are connected to the network.

4.6.3 RFC 3647 OTHER ASPECTS OF KEY PAIR MANAGEMENT

The RFC 3647 §6.3 "Other Aspects of Key Pair Management" subsection deals with the remaining fifth and seventh key lifecycle stages presented in Figure 4.7 key revocation and key archive. Another topic is the operational crypto period of the key pair; however, the RFC 3647 specification presumes that private and public keys have the same crypto periods. For example, if the private key is used to generate digital signatures up to the last minute of the certificate validity period, the relying party only has seconds to validate the digital signature. Table 4.49 provides CP examples for various PKI entities.

The key lifecycle stages are shown in Figure 4.7 and the RFC 3647 §6. Technical Security Controls mapping is summarized here for quick reference:

1) Key Generation: RFC §6.1 Key Pair Generation and Installation
2) Key Distribution: RFC §6.1 Key Pair Generation and Installation
3) Key Usage: RFC 3647 §6.2 Private Key Protection and Cryptographic Module Engineering Controls
4) Key Backup: RFC 3647 §6.2 Private Key Protection and Cryptographic Module Engineering Controls
5) Key Revocation: RFC 3647 §6.2 Private Key Protection and Cryptographic Module Engineering Controls
6) Key Termination: RFC 3647 §6.3 Other Aspects of Key Pair Management
7) Key Archive: RFC 3647 §6.3 Other Aspects of Key Pair Management

Including lifecycle cross-references for both symmetric and asymmetric cryptographic keys can help clarify the CP and CPS. Figure 2.18 provides a general key management lifecycle for both

---

TABLE 4.48

Examples of Key Protection Controls

PKI Entity	CP/CPS	Policy or Practice Statement
CA	CP	All internal CA systems use private keys only inside cryptographic hardware modules.
RA	CP	All internal RA systems use private keys only inside cryptographic hardware modules.
Subscribers	CP	All internal servers use private keys only inside cryptographic hardware modules.
Subscribers	CP	All employees and contractors use private keys only within a secure environment.
CA	CPS	Internal root CA systems use private keys inside FIPS 140–3 Security Level 3 cryptographic hardware modules within a physically secured isolated environment.
CA	CPS	Internal CA systems use private keys inside FIPS 140–3 Security Level 4 cryptographic hardware modules.

TABLE 4.49

Examples of Other Key Management Controls

PKI Entity	CP/CPS	Policy or Practice Statement
CA	CP	All internal CA systems only generate certificates for shorter validity periods than its CA public key.
RA	CP	All internal RA systems only process certificate requests for shorter lifetimes than its RA public key.

symmetric and asymmetric keys, and Figure 4.7 provides a key management lifecycle specific to asymmetric keys. PKI terminology is important and too often the term "certificate" becomes a misnomer when used interchangeably for symmetric, asymmetric private, and asymmetric public cryptographic keys.

4.6.4 RFC 3647 ACTIVATION DATA

The RFC 3647 §6.4 "Activation Data" subsection is actually about authentication data used to verify either a person or a nonperson entity using noncryptographic methods. For persons, this includes knowledge factors such as passwords, possession factors such as smart cards, and biometric factors such as fingerprints, voice prints, or facial images. For nonperson entities, this includes possession factors such as passphrases and device recognition methods. Another authentication method is one-time passcodes (OTP) valid for a temporary period of time. These authentication methods are typically used to enhance controls over asymmetric keys:

- CA might back up and recover its private keys using key shares stored on smart cards that are password activated.
- RA might send an OTP to a subscriber to download and activate a new certificate.
- Subscribers might activate their private keys using a password, smart card, or biometric.
- Subscribers might forward their certificates to relying parties using a password or another certificate.

In addition to protecting cryptographic keys, RA and CA have system administrators, application administrators, and application managers that likewise require authentication. Some functions might only require single-factor authentication such as password log-on, while others might need multifactor authentication. Table 4.50 provides CP and CPS examples for various PKI entities.

There are several ANSI standards on authentication methods. X9.8 Personal Identification Number (PIN) Management and Security [B.1.16] addresses financial PIN-based authentication. Passwords should be handled as securely as PIN, but often they are not. X9.117 "Mutual Authentication for Secure Remote Access" [B.1.19] includes all three authentication factors: knowledge (some you have), possession (something you know), and biometric (something you are) factors. This standard also addresses multifactor authentication (MFA) and mutual authentication. X9.122 "Secure Customer Authentication for Internet Payments" [B.1.20] includes PIN, static passwords, dynamic

TABLE 4.50

Examples of Activation Data Controls

PKI Entity	CP/CPS	Policy or Practice Statement
CA	CP	CA private keys are backed up using password-activated tokens.
RA	CP	RA issues OTP for subscriber downloads of new certificates.
Subscribers	CP	Subscribers are expected to protect private keys using appropriate access controls.
CA	CPS	CA private keys are backed up using password-activated USB tokens using three of the seven key sharing schemes.
CA	CPS	USB tokens and passwords are stored in different physical safes with separate access and dual controls.
Subscribers	CPS	Subscribers are expected to protect private keys using access controls such as strong passwords for local or smart card private key storage.
Subscribers	CPS	Subscribers are expected to protect private keys using access controls such as biometrics for local or smart card private key storage.

passwords, biometrics, physically unclonable functions (PUF), and cryptography-based authentication. X9.84 "Biometric Management and Security" [B.1.17] addresses biometric enrollment, biometric verification, and biometric identification. These ANSI standards define requirements and provide recommendations for financial services authentication.

4.6.5   RFC 3647 COMPUTER SECURITY CONTROLS

The RFC 3647 §6.5 "Computer Security Controls" subsection addresses system hardware and software management including access controls, application development and maintenance, product assurance, certifications, and evaluation programs. The CP needs to contain sufficient information to convince the reader that computer security controls are in place but not provide too many details valuable to an attacker. Table 4.51 provides CP examples for various PKI entities.

Notice that the policy statements provide assurance that computer security controls are in place without revealing too many details of the actual practices. Within a CPS, more details might be provided but care should be taken to avoid revealing too much information to an attacker who might be interested in how quickly systems are updated to patch vulnerabilities. Also notice that the policy statements do not distinguish between root CA, intermediate CA, and issuing CA, thus revealing very little on how offline root CA might be managed differently than online CA.

4.6.6   RFC 3647 LIFE CYCLE SECURITY CONTROLS

The RFC 3647 §6.6 "Life Cycle Security Controls" subsection addresses the software development lifecycle (SDLC) and corresponding security management controls. Functional requirements and designs need to incorporate security controls, development needs to include software assurance mechanisms, and test cases need to confirm security controls exist and are effective. Table 4.52 provides CP examples for various PKI entities.

When managing any information technology environment, there is always the basic "buy or build" question. The "buy" decision is when products fit the needs and can be used with no modifications beyond the usual configurations. Today, the "buy" decision has been augmented by the "rent" decision, where products or third-party services are leased, including the cloud. The "build" decision is when products (or services) need to be enhanced by the organization, the manufacturer, or some third party. However, there seems to be third "free" option for software.

TABLE 4.51

Examples of Computer Security Controls

PKI Entity	CP/CPS	Policy or Practice Statement
CA	CP	CA systems use identity-based access controls.
CA	CP	CA software is maintained to current releases and modifications.
CA	CP	CA applications are managed using quality controls (QC).
CA	CP	CA services experience annual external audits.

TABLE 4.52

Examples of Lifecycle Security Controls

PKI Entity	CP/CPS	Policy or Practice Statement
CA	CP	Design processes incorporate security controls.
CA	CP	Development processes include software assurance controls.
CA	CP	Testing processes confirm functionality and security controls.

Where software was once licensed per a "buy or lease" agreement, free software is "accept as-is" with zero liability to the manufacturer. Regardless, most organization do not "build" their own cryptography, rather they rely on cryptographic libraries that have been certified by the NIST Cryptographic Algorithm Validation Program (CAVP) or similar authoritative source. Otherwise, a badly implemented cryptographic algorithm or protocol might have bugs, weaken security, or non-interoperability issues. Similarly, when managing a PKI, the same "buy, rent, or build" issues apply.

4.6.7 RFC 3647 NETWORK SECURITY CONTROLS

The RFC 3647 §6.7 "Network Security Controls" subsection focuses on network components including firewalls, routers, switches, and other appliances. Configuration management is an important network security control that addresses specifications, review and approvals, and roles and responsibilities. Table 4.53 provides CP examples for various PKI entities.

There are two basic methods for ensuring that networks and systems are properly configured per an organization's standards. The first is vulnerability scanning and the second is penetration testing (commonly called a *pen test*). Vulnerability scans are performed frequently and widely against the organization's network and systems, both externally (e.g., from the Internet) and internally (within the organization's network). Pen tests can be external or internal but can be performed less often and focused on a specific target.

- **Vulnerability Scan** [B.1.18] *A vulnerability scan is a test process that attempts to identify the presence of potential vulnerabilities to known network based attacks. Automated scan tools are typically employed when conducting a vulnerability scan; however, manual methods can also be utilized.*
- **Penetration Test** [B.1.18] *Penetration tests attempt to exploit vulnerabilities to determine whether unauthorized access or other malicious activity is possible. Penetration testing includes network and application testing as well as controls and processes around the networks and applications, and can occur from both outside the network trying to come in (external testing) and from inside the network.*

For example, the PCI SSC manages the Approved Scanning Vendors[8] (ASV) program as part of its overall PCI Data Security Standard (DSS) program. As another example, the ANSI standard X9.111 [B.1.18] defines requirements and provides recommendations for conducting penetration testing with financial service organizations.

4.6.8 RFC 3647 TIME STAMPING

The RFC 3647 §6.8 "Time Stamping" subsection addresses time stamps for messages, transaction processing, and audit logs. The Network Time Protocol (NTP) supports local and regional time servers synchronized to a national time source such as the National Institute of Standards and Technology (NIST) or the United States Naval Observatory (USNO), which are calibrated to

---

TABLE 4.53

Examples of Network Security Controls

PKI Entity	CP/CPS	Policy or Practice Statement
CA	CP	Network components are configured to standard specifications.
CA	CP	Network specifications are managed by a standards committee.
CA	CP	Network component configurations are reviewed periodically.

TABLE 4.54

Examples of Time Stamping Controls

PKI Entity	CP/CPS	Policy or Practice Statement
CA	CP	CA systems employ a Network Time Protocol to synchronize clocks that are calibrated to a national time source.
CA	CPS	Root CA systems are manually synchronized to an external time source that is synchronized to the network time sources.
CA	CPS	Other CA systems are automatically synchronized using the Network Time Protocol (NTP v3).

the International Timing Authority (ITA). Table 4.54 provides CP and CPS examples for various PKI entities.

Local system clocks might not be synchronized, and so different systems will generate different timestamps. NTP allows systems to synchronize clocks to a consistent time. However, allowing clock synchronization means the clocks can be adjusted, which in turn means the clocks can be maliciously backdated (or predated) for fraudulent purposes. Alternatively, trusted time stamps [B9.1.15] use a Time Stamp Token (TST) generated by a Time Stamp Authority (TSA) whose clock is calibrated (vs. synchronized) to a national time source. The TSA clock cannot be adjusted, rather its clock is calibrated for the time difference. See Section 2.3, "Nonrepudiation," for details.

4.7 RFC 2527 CERTIFICATE, CRL, AND OCSP PROFILES

The RFC 3647 "Certificate, CRL, and OCSP Profiles" section is structured with the following subsections:

§7. Certificate, CRL, and OCSP Profiles
- 7.1 Certificate Profile
- 7.2 CRL Profile
- 7.3 OCSP Profile

The seventh section RFC 3647 §7 "Certificate and CRL Profiles" addresses data structure formats and field options for certificates, CRL, and OCSP profiles. The different formats are defined in various standards that have data elements that are expected to be supported and optional fields that might be supported by the PKI organization. The assorted protocols used to exchange the data structures are likewise defined in several standards. This segment allows a PKI organization to define its profile support, including messaging handling, error codes, and default values.

4.7.1 RFC 3647 CERTIFICATE PROFILE

The RFC 3647 §7.1 "Certificate Profile" subsection addresses digital certificates. Public keys can be encapsulated in a variety of data structures, which generally we call a PKI credential. The most recognizable PKI credential is an X.509 certificate, originally defined in the ITU-T X.509 standard and subsequently described in the RFC 5280 specification and the ISO/IEC 9594 – Part 8 [B.4.21] standard. The CP should identify at least the following information:

- List of supported PKI credentials, including at a minimum X.509 certificates
- List of relevant standards for the associated PKI credentials

Details regarding the individual data elements for each supported PKI credential do not belong in a CP but rather in a CPS for interoperability with subscribers and relying parties. Protocol specifications do not belong in a CP or CPS but rather fit and are more usable in procedures for developers and testing guidelines. Table 4.55 provides CP examples for various PKI entities.

Certificate-specific profiles such as those for Transport Layer Security (TLS), Code Sign, or Time Stamping might be stipulated in the CPS associated with an issuing CA, versus having a generic CPS that applies to the whole PKI hierarchy. Typically, the X.509 Extended Key Usage (EKU) extension contains the object identifier (OID) relative to the certificate profile. Several of the EKU OID are defined in the IETF RFC 5280 specification as referenced in Table 4.56.

The OID structure has the following descriptions: iso (1) identified-organization (3) dod (6) internet (1) security (5) mechanisms (5) pkix (7) kp (3) with the last digit defined in RFC 5280.

4.7.2 RFC 3647 CRL Profile

The RFC 3647 §7.2 "CRL Profile" subsection addresses certificate revocation list (CRL) for managing certificate status. The RFC 5280 specification explains a complete CRL contains all unexpired certificates that have been revoked within the CA scope. Thus, each CA maintains its own CRL such that a relying party needs to deal with more than one CRL. The various CRL are posted on an accessible site where relying parties can download the certificate status information. Table 4.57 provides CP examples for various PKI entities.

The intent behind expiration dates (Validity: *notAfter*) and the revocation is to help prevent relying parties from using invalid certificates. Therefore, once a revoked certificate has expired, it no

TABLE 4.55
Examples of Certificate Profile Controls

PKI Entity	CP/CPS	Policy or Practice Statement
CA	CP	CA supports X.509 v3 certificates.
RA	CP	RA supports X.509 v3 certificates.
Subscribers	CP	Subscribers are expected to support X.509 v3 certificates.
Relying parties	CP	Relying parties are expected to support X.509 v3 certificates.

TABLE 4.56
Example EKU Object Identifiers

EKU	Certificate Profile	OID
Server Authentication	TLS	1.3.6.1.5.5.7.3.1
Client Authentication	TLS	1.3.6.1.5.5.7.3.2
Code Signing	Code Sign	1.3.6.1.5.5.7.3.3
E-mail Protection	E-mail	1.3.6.1.5.5.7.3.4
Time Stamping	TST	1.3.6.1.5.5.7.3.8
OCSP Signing	OCSP	1.3.6.1.5.5.7.3.9

TABLE 4.57
Examples of CRL Profile Controls

PKI Entity	CP/CPS	Policy or Practice Statement
CA	CP	CA supports X.509 v2 CRL.
RA	CP	RA supports X.509 v2 CRL.
Subscribers	CP	Subscribers are expected to support X.509 v2 CRL.
Relying parties	CP	Relying parties are expected to support X.509 v2 CRL.

TABLE 4.58
Examples of OCSP Profile Controls

PKI Entity	CP/CPS	Policy or Practice Statement
CA	CP	CA supports OCSP v1.
RA	CP	RA supports OCSP v1.
Subscribers	CP	Subscribers are expected to support OCSP v1.
Relying parties	CP	Relying parties are expected to support OCSP v1.

longer needs to be retained on the CRL as that is redundant. While some argue that the purpose for revocation should be maintained using the CRL, the counter argument is that the Validity dates are checked first, and if expired the certificate is rejected, thus the revocation checking would never happen, negating the CRL Reason code altogether.

4.7.3 RFC 3647 OCSP Profile

The RFC 3647 §7.3 "OCSP Profile" subsection addresses the use of an Online Certificate Status Protocol (OCSP) responder. The RFC 6960 specification proposes that OCSP is useful in determining the current status of a digital certificate without requiring certificate revocation lists (CRLs). However, it is more likely that a PKI system needs to support both CRL and OCSP methods for backward compatibility. Furthermore, the certificate status for OCSP is typically based on the issuance of a CRL. Table 4.58 provides CP examples for various PKI entities.

Since the CRL is a "negative" file of revoked certificates, the original OCSP was envisioned to be a "positive" file of all certificates issued by a particular PKI. Essentially the OCSP would be a database of every certificate that was issued, revoked, suspended, etc. However, this would require an online interface with timely updates from each CA within the PKI hierarchy. Consequently, many OCSP are updated per the typical weekly CRL publication.

4.7.4 Other PKI-Related Profiles

RFC 3647 §7 "Certificate, CRL, and OCSP Profiles" does not address any other PKI-related profiles. As other IETF specifications or other industry standards evolve and are adopted, they should be included in the CP and CPS. Some examples of newer methods include the following.

- RFC 6962 Certificate Transparency
- RFC 8555 Automatic Certificate Management Environment (ACME)
- RFC 8894 Simple Certificate Enrolment Protocol (SCEP)
- NIST Post-Quantum Cryptography (PQC)

And as technologies are developed and adopted, such as blockchain, quantum computers, and post-quantum cryptography (PQC), they too should be included in the CP and CPS.

4.8 RFC 2527 COMPLIANCE AUDITS AND OTHER ASSESSMENTS

The RFC 3647 "Compliance Audits and Other Assessments" section is structured with the following subsections.

§8. Compliance Audit and Other Assessment
- 8.1 Frequency or Circumstances of Assessment
- 8.2 Identity/Qualifications of Assessor

- 8.3 Assessor's Relationship to Assessed Entity
- 8.4 Topics Covered by Assessment
- 8.5 Actions Taken as a Result of Deficiency
- 8.6 Communication of Results

The eighth section RFC 3647 §8 "Compliance Audit and Other Assessment" addresses internal and external security audits, assessments, and evaluations. External audits are performed by licensed professionals and depending on the jurisdiction might be governed by legal or regulatory rules. Internal audits, assessments, or evaluations are done by employees or outsourced to third-party service providers or private consultants. Evaluations target specific PKI components, products, or controls. Table 4.59 provides CP examples for various PKI entities.

In this book Chapter 9, "PKI Governance, Risk, and Compliance," discusses the management and security organizational hierarchies needed to support an independent audit capability for maintaining compliance. The chapter also addresses various audit standards and programs. A competent audit process needs to address internal and external audits, assessments, and evaluations. Qualified internal and external resources need to demonstrate knowledge, experience, and competence.

4.8.1 RFC 3647 Frequency or Circumstances

The RFC 3647 §8.1 "Frequency or Circumstances of Assessment" subsection addresses the frequency of assessments and other circumstances that might trigger an assessment. For example, in the United States, some state laws require commercial CAs to be licensed service providers and undergo annual audits. Private CAs do not operate under the same restrictions. Other countries and industries might have their own CA audit programs. Unscheduled assessment might occur when a security incident is detected, as part of an investigation or remediation.

4.8.2 RFC 3647 Identity/Qualifications of Assessor

The RFC 3647 §8.2 "Identity/Qualifications of Assessor" subsection addresses the qualifications of the assessors and the assessment program. External assessments or evaluations should be performed by security professionals with credentials and demonstrated experience. Internal audits, assessments, or evaluations done by employees or outsourced staffing need to have sufficient training and knowledge to be meaningful.

4.8.3 RFC 3647 Assessor's Relationship to Assessed Entity

The RFC 3647 §8.3 "Assessor's Relationship to Assessed Entity" subsection addresses the independence of the assessor. External assessments performed by security professionals or auditors are independent, despite being under contract with the organization. Internal assessments done by employees, contractors, or outsourced staffing are inherently influenced by the organization.

TABLE 4.59

Examples of Compliance Controls

PKI Entity	CP/CPS	Policy or Practice Statement
CA	CP	Internal CA undergoes internal audits annually.
CA	CP	Internal CA undergoes external audits triennially.
CA	CP	External CA undergoes external audits annually.
RA	CP	RA undergoes internal assessments annually.

4.8.4   RFC 3647 Topics Covered by Assessment

The RFC 3647 §8.4 "Topics Covered by Assessment" subsection addresses the scope of the assessment and the methodology employed. For example, our hypothetical ABC Corporation operates an internal CA and an external CA, so an assessment might be for either. In addition, each PKI system consists of multiple CA systems (root, intermediary, and issuing) so an assessment might be for one system. The methodology depends partially on the jurisdiction and the scope of the assessment, such as one CA hierarchy or another, or one CA system or another.

4.8.5   RFC 3647 Actions Taken as a Result of Deficiency

The RFC 3647 §8.5 "Actions Taken as a Result of Deficiency" subsection addresses appropriate remediation as a result of deficiencies or assessment gaps. Assessments might provide a rating similar to network vulnerability scans – low, medium, high, or critical issues. For example, critical problems would require a shorter remediation timeline than lesser problems.

4.8.6   RFC 3647 Communication of Results

The RFC 3647 §8.6 "Communication of Results" subsection addresses the distribution of the assessment report. Regardless of whether the assessment is external or internal, any censorship lessens the reliability of the report. An independent copy needs to be shared with the highest authority of the organization, such as the board of directors. Care must be taken when providing an executive summary to not alter the overall results of the assessment.

4.9   RFC 2527 OTHER BUSINESS AND LEGAL MATTERS

The RFC 3647 "Other Business and Legal Matters" section is structured with the following subsections.

§9. Other Business and Legal Matters
- 9.1 Fees
- 9.2 Financial Responsibility
- 9.3 Confidentiality of Business Information
- 9.4 Privacy of Personal Information
- 9.5 Intellectual Property Rights
- 9.6 Representations and Warranties
- 9.7 Disclaimers of Warranties
- 9.8 Limitations of Liability
- 9.9 Indemnities
- 9.10 Term and Termination
- 9.11 Individual Notices and Communications with Participants
- 9.12 Amendments
- 9.13 Dispute Resolution Procedures
- 9.14 Governing Law
- 9.15 Compliance with Applicable Law
- 9.16 Miscellaneous Provisions
- 9.17 Other Provisions

The ninth section RFC 3647 §9 "Other Business and Legal Matters" deals with financial and user agreements when operating a PKI as either a private or a commercial enterprise. The CA and RA are components of the PKI enterprise, although some RAs might be affiliated third parties, whereas the subscribers are customers and relying parties are indirect users. The CP and CPS might include contractual language or alternatively terms and conditions applicable to different parties might be in separate documents. Regardless, the organization needs to engage legal counsel for developing this segment of the CP.

4.9.1   RFC 3647 FEES

The RFC 3647 §9.1 "Fees" subsection is allocated for the discussion of applicable fees, such as issuing or renewing certificates, additional charges for revocation, or costs in relation to other services provided by the PKI system. Pricing schedules, when applicable, are often better managed as separate documents rather than having to update a CP or CPS when changing general fees or providing special arrangements or discounts. However, instead of defaulting to the "no stipulation" clause, providing a URL or contact information for pricing is more useful.

4.9.2   RFC 3647 FINANCIAL RESPONSIBILITY

The RFC 3647 §9.2 "Financial Responsibility" subsection is for the discussion of financial information such as the types of insurance and coverage. Actual listings of assets or other financial instruments are better managed in separate documents rather than having to update a CP or CPS annually to reflect current information. Again, instead of defaulting to the "no stipulation" clause, providing a URL or contact information for financial information is more useful.

4.9.3   RFC 3647 CONFIDENTIALITY OF BUSINESS INFORMATION

The RFC 3647 §9.3 "Confidentiality of Business Information" subsection contains provisions for data protection controls. Chapter 1, "Introduction," describes data confidentiality with a more detailed discussion in Chapter 9, "PKI Governance, Risk, and Compliance," on data classification. Any enterprise is expected to maintain a data classification policy as part of its overall security governance. Consequently, it is better to manage data classification definitions in a separate policy document, but the CP needs to be aligned with the confidential data definitions. One company's confidential data might not be another's, so any intercompany communications need to be coordinated for mutual data protection, such as a mutual nondisclosure agreement.

4.9.4   RFC 3647 PRIVACY OF PERSONAL INFORMATION

The RFC 3647 §9.4 "Privacy of Personal Information" subsection contains provisions for privacy controls. Privacy laws and data elements vary among jurisdictions so the CP needs to identify which laws are applicable. However, privacy is an important topic that is better managed in a separate policy document, but the CP needs to be aligned with the privacy data definitions and corresponding practices. Further privacy details might be provided in the CPS; however, again, privacy is better managed in a separate policy and practices document not linked specifically to the PKI policy and practices.

4.9.5   RFC 3647 INTELLECTUAL PROPERTY RIGHTS

The RFC 3647 §9.5 "Intellectual Property Rights" subsection deals with intellectual property (IP) including patents, copyrights, trademarks, or trade secrets. However, intellectual property rights are better managed in a separate policy document, but the CP needs to be aligned with the IP policy and corresponding practices. Per the IP policy, the CP needs to state its process for dealing with IP claimed by a subscriber for any certificate-related information.

4.9.6   RFC 3647 Representations and Warranties

The RFC 3647 §9.6 "Representations and Warranties" subsection deals with contractual issues relating to PKI entities. A representation is a statement made by one of two contracting parties to the other, before or at the time of making the contract, in regard to some fact, circumstance, or state of facts pertinent to the contract, which is influential in bringing about the agreement, whereas a warranty is the promise a company makes to ensure the conditions of a contract are fulfilled.[9] In some cases, the CP might be included as part of a contract or contain CA, RA, subscriber, or relying party agreements.

4.9.7   RFC 3647 Disclaimers of Warranties

The RFC 3647 §9.7 "Disclaimers of Warranties" subsection deals with limiting contractual conditions relating to PKI entities. A disclaimer might identify restrictions that may otherwise be presumed, restrictions from other agreements not applicable to PKI entities, or restrictions from applicable law. In some cases, the CP might be excluded from contracts with non-PKI participants involved with other parts of the organization.

4.9.8   RFC 3647 Limitations of Liability

The RFC 3647 §9.8 "Limitations of Liability" subsection deals with limiting contractual obligations within the CP relating to CA, RA, subscriber, or relying party agreements. Liability caps include limits on the types and amounts of recoverable damages. The CP might be included as part of a contract or contain CA, RA, subscriber, or relying party agreements.

4.9.9   RFC 3647 Indemnities

The RFC 3647 §9.9 "Indemnities" subsection deals with provisions by which one party (such as the PKI organization) makes a second party (such as a subscriber or relying party) whole for losses or damage incurred by the second party, typically arising out of the first party's conduct. Again, in some cases, the CP might be included as part of a contract or contain CA, RA, subscriber, or relying party agreements.

4.9.10   RFC 3647 Term and Termination

The RFC 3647 §9.10 "Term and Termination" subsection deals with the time period the CP or other agreements remain valid and subsequent termination conditions. Term includes when the document becomes effective and when it expires. Termination includes circumstances under which the document terminates earlier, and consequences of its termination. The CP might be included as part of a contract or contain CA, RA, subscriber, or relying party agreements.

4.9.11   RFC 3647 Individual Notices and Communications with Participants

The RFC 3647 §9.11 "Individual Notices and Communications with Participants" subsection deals with interactions between PKI participants. This subsection differs from the second segment RFC 3647 §2 "Publication and Repository Responsibilities," which addresses information to a wide audience. And while individual messages need to align with confidentiality considerations in the RFC 3647 §9.3 subsection and privacy considerations in the RFC 3647 §9.4 subsection, for some communications to be legally effective, they might need to employ an electronic signature. While many jurisdictions have various electronic signature laws, for the purposes of this discussion, we refer to the U.S. public law 106–229 Electronic Signatures in Global and National Commerce Act[10] (the ESIGN Act) for a definition of an electronic signature.

SPECIAL NOTE 4-7 ELECTRONIC SIGNATURE

The term "electronic signature" means an electronic sound, symbol, or process attached to or logically associated with a contract or other record and executed or adopted by a person with the intent to sign the record. Note that any of these methods might incorporate a digital signature.

Thus, while a digital signature is an electronic process that satisfies the definition of an electronic signature, there are many other techniques recognized by law. This is an important legal and technological concept since logically a relying party cannot validate a digital signature using the signer's certificate until after the subscriber has obtained the certificate in the first place. But the process for the subscriber to obtain the certificate might require the legal equivalent of an electronic signature, which includes many other methods such as clicking on a link to accept the newly generated certificate and thereby accepting the terms and conditions of the CP or CPS and subscriber agreement. Likewise, the relying party accessing the certificate chain, CRL, or OCSP responder during the certificate validation might also require an electronic signature signifying acceptance of the relying party agreement.

4.9.12 RFC 3647 Amendments

The RFC 3647 §9.12 "Amendments" subsection deals with substantive changes to the CP or other agreements that materially affect the acceptable use of certificates. As discussed earlier, the RFC 3647 §1.5 subsection provides guidance on the roles and responsibilities of the policy authority (PA), but this subsection addresses change control procedures for amending a document, notification procedures for alerting various PKI entities, and to some reasonable extent, the conditions that require an amendment. Consider the hypothetical situation for the A.2.1 e-mail signature CA in Figure 4.6.

In this scenario, previously issued certificates were used by employees to sign e-mails and software, and per the CA policy this was an acceptable practice. But the decision was made to stand up a new CA for issuing code signing certificates such that separate certificates were now needed, one for e-mail signing and another for code signing. An amended CP with a new version number might be published with the new rules, and the previous policy identifier in the certificates would likewise be updated to two different identifiers, one for e-mail signing and the other for code signing. Employees would be notified that effective per some future date, code signing required a different certificate, and per some later date, any signed code could no longer be validated using the old e-mail certificates. Eventually, all of the existing e-mail certificates with the old policy identifier would expire and be replaced with the newer identifier.

4.9.13 RFC 3647 Dispute Resolution Procedures

The RFC 3647 §9.13 "Dispute Resolution Procedures" subsection deals with processes for addressing disagreements and possibly challenges to the CP. Contact information for general queries and feedback was discussed in RFC 3647 §1 "Introduction." The same contact information might be used for dispute resolution. Regardless, the PKI system needs the ability to receive, review, process, and respond to a dispute. This is a consensual process in which the parties attempt to reach agreement. In the event the resolution is further disputed, then adjudicative processes, such as litigation or arbitration, might be necessary.

4.9.14 RFC 3647 Governing Law

The RFC 3647 §9.14 "Governing Law" subsection identifies the jurisdictions that govern the interpretation and enforcement of the subject CP or CPS or agreements. In our scenario, the applicable laws include the jurisdiction in which the ABC Corporation is incorporated. In the event of an adjudicative processes, as discussed in RFC 3647 §9.13, the legal jurisdiction would prevail over dispute resolution.

4.9.15   RFC 3647 COMPLIANCE WITH APPLICABLE LAW

The RFC 3647 §9.15 "Compliance with Applicable Law" subsection deals with legal, regulatory, and contractual requirements impacting the various PKI entities. For example, many jurisdictions or other organizations impose their own requirements when operating within their domains. These requirements might affect how each PKI entity manages its cryptographic keys. Examples of legal and contractual requirements include the following:

- Many U.S. states require that commercial CA be licensed and undergo a Statement on Standards for Attestation Engagements (SSAE) No. 16 Reporting on Controls at a Service Organization audit.
- Browser manufacturers require that a PKI system undergo a Trust Service Principles and Criteria for Certification Authorities (WebTrust for CA) audit in order to have their root CA certificate included within the product.
- Payment card brands require that smart cards be compliant to the EMV Integrated Circuit Card Specification for Payment Systems and mobile payment be compliant to the EMV Payment Tokenization Specification.

Each PKI system needs to determine which legal, regulatory, and contractual requirements are applicable to its operations and include them in its CP and relevant documents.

4.9.16   RFC 3647 MISCELLANEOUS PROVISIONS

The RFC 3647 §9.16 "Miscellaneous Provisions" subsection deals with common provisions typically found in contract law. The CP might include various clauses that would be aligned with various agreements or other contracts with vendors and other suppliers.

4.9.17   RFC 3647 OTHER PROVISIONS

The RFC 3647 §9.17 "Other Provisions" subsection is for any other legal statements addressing roles and responsibilities not covered in the other "Business and Legal Matters" subsections.

NOTES

1. TLD is a placeholder for the top-level-domain name as defined in the Internet Assigned Numbers Authority (IANA) Root Zone Database at www.iana.org/domains/root/db
2. CA Browser Forum, https://cabforum.org/
3. Comodo Blog, https://blog.comodo.com/other/the-recent-ra-compromise/
4. AIPCA, https://us.aicpa.org/interestareas/frc/assuranceadvisoryservices/sorhome.html
5. AICPA, https://us.aicpa.org/interestareas/frc/assuranceadvisoryservices/aicpasoc1report.html
6. AICPA, https://us.aicpa.org/interestareas/frc/assuranceadvisoryservices/aicpasoc2report.html
7. AICPA, https://us.aicpa.org/interestareas/frc/assuranceadvisoryservices/aicpasoc3report.html
8. www.pcisecuritystandards.org/assessors_and_solutions/approved_scanning_vendors
9. Black's Law Free Online Legal Dictionary 2nd ed., http://thelawdictionary.org/
10. ESIGN, www.gpo.gov/fdsys/pkg/PLAW-106publ229/html/PLAW-106publ229.htm

5 PKI Roles and Responsibilities

As discussed in Chapter 4, "PKI Management and Security," the certificate policy (CP) and the certificate practice statement (CPS) address controls for the public key infrastructure (PKI) participants – the certificate authority (CA), the registration authority (RA), the relying party, and the subscriber. We also introduced the policy authority (PA). This chapter continues the discussion of the various PKI roles and responsibilities. We first consider Table 5.1, which provides a high-level description of responsibilities for each primary role.

Chapter 10, "PKI Industry," addresses the audit process for the annual or ad hoc security and risk assessments of any or all PKI components. The remainder of this chapter maps the primary roles to the various PKI components, namely, the certificate authority, registration authority, policy authority, subscriber, and relying party. Additional roles are introduced as needed per each PKI component and italicized to indicate their specialty. We also will discuss the issues for managing a PKI for small, medium, and large organizations.

TABLE 5.1

Public Key Infrastructure Primary Roles and Responsibilities

Primary Role	Responsibilities
PKI technicians	Technicians are individuals who configure and operate PKI components, which include RA, CA, CRL, and OCSP services.
PKI administrators	Administrators are individuals who configure and manage PKI-associated network and system components, which include hardware, firmware, and software elements such as routers, firewalls, workstations, and servers.
PKI custodians	Custodians are individuals who are not key owners but handle cryptographic material for PKI services, which includes keys for RA, CA, OCSP, and other cryptographic-enabled services.
Security officers	Security officers are individuals who are neither key owners nor handle cryptographic material but oversee the management of cryptographic material to ensure security policies, practices, and procedures are followed. Security officers observe regular CA events.
Subscribers	Subscribers are key owners who request public key certificates and use their asymmetric private keys. Subscribers might be individuals or might be application, system, or network components.
Relying parties	Relying parties are not key owners but use certificates, which contain the subscriber public keys. Relying parties might be individuals or might be applications, systems, or network components.
Security managers	Security managers are individuals who oversee physical security controls for the campus, data center, office, and server rooms where PKI services and other application, system, or network components are deployed.
Auditors	Auditors observe significant CA events to ensure each participant follows documented procedures. Auditors also perform annual or ad hoc security and risk assessments of any or all PKI components.
Attorneys	Attorneys represent the organization's legal group to address liability, warranty, intellectual property, privacy, and other business matters.
Business managers	Business managers represent the organization's various lines of business (LOBs) to address different application needs and risks associated with the use and reliance upon PKI and certificates.
Application and network managers	Application and network managers install, upgrade, and decommission PKI-enabled applications or PKI-capable network devices.

DOI: 10.1201/9781003425298-5

5.1   CERTIFICATE AUTHORITY

The primary role of any certificate authority (CA) is to sign digital objects using its private key, which includes signing certificates and certificate revocation list (CRL). Root CA systems sign certificates and CRL for itself since it is the apex authority within a given PKI system, and for its subordinate CA. Subordinate CA only signs certificates and CRL for its subordinate CA. In addition to publishing CRL for public access by validation processes, the CRL might be used as status information for Online Certificate Status Protocol (OCSP) services. Therefore, OCSP services are included in our discussion on CA.

The terms "offline" versus "online" is a common PKI concept but as mentioned in Section 4.5.7, "RFC 3647 Certificate Rekey," when discussing RFC 3647 Compromise and Disaster Recovery, there is some debate as to what constitutes an "offline" mode. Essentially an "offline" system has no communications to any "online" systems, including the organization's network, wired or wireless, and especially no Internet connectivity of any kind. However, the "offline" systems might operate on their own isolated network segment. Ideally, the isolation control is a physical air-gap network.

5.1.1   Root CA

Initially, the root CA system is installed by administrators and subsequently updated as needed for new hardware or software. Since the root CA system is offline, updates are performed manually. Software upgrades are carried into the PKI room using portable media in cooperation with technicians for physical access. Installations and upgrades do not require the presence of any cryptographic keys so custodians are not involved. As newer equipment replaces older equipment, the older hardware can be decommissioned after PKI custodians ensure that all cryptographic materials have been properly terminated. First, we look at Table 5.2 for examples.

Preceding any root CA operations, security managers ensure that all physical security controls are in place and effective. Any incidents are immediately reported to the technicians since a security breach might indicate a key compromise. Likewise, any abnormalities with the root CA physical security controls are immediately reported to the security managers. Otherwise, no news is often assumed to be good news; however, the two primary roles need to periodically synchronize information and status of the overall physical security controls.

Before the root CA event begins, auditors are present to ensure technicians and custodians follow documented procedures. Each procedure is a custom set of stepwise processes with assignments

---

TABLE 5.2
Public Key PKI Offline CA Roles and Responsibilities

Primary Role	Root CA Responsibilities
PKI technicians	Technicians operate and manage the offline CA systems, including generating root CA keys, root CA certificates, CRL updates, and OCSP updates; revoking CA certificates; and configuring offline CA functions and application features.
PKI administrators	Administrators install, upgrade, and decommission software or hardware offline CA system components for use by PKI technicians.
PKI custodians	Custodians enable CA keys for use by PKI technicians and provide backup and recovery services, using dual controls with split knowledge.
Security officers	Security officers observe regular offline CA events to ensure each participant follows documented procedures.
Security managers	Security managers oversee campus and building controls that house the offline CA systems and provide physical security.
Auditors	Auditors observe significant offline CA events to ensure each participant follows documented procedures.

allocated per role and responsibility. The security officer or auditor follows the procedures, checking that each step is correctly performed by the appropriate role, is initialed by each participant, with a final sign-off sheet. Root CA procedures include the following scenarios.

Significant CA events that should be observed by an auditor include the following events:

- Generation of root CA keys
- Generation of root CA certificates
- Generation of subordinate CA certificates by the root CA
- Signing CRL updates with revoked CA certificates
- Termination of root CA keys

SPECIAL NOTE 5-1 ROOT CA REVOCATION

Note that a compromised root CA revoking its own certificate is legitimate when an authorized officer performed the revocation, and ironically the revocation is still legitimate if an attacker revokes the certificates, as in both cases the root CA is compromised.

Regular CA events that need only be observed by a security officer and not necessarily by an auditor include the following events:

- Signing any empty CRL updates for any CA including the root CA
- Signing CRL updates with revoked subscriber certificates

Prior to any cryptographic operations being performed by technicians, the root CA private keys need to be enabled by the custodians. Offline root CA systems are typically powered down, such that when powered up, the root CA private keys remain unavailable. Depending on the system architecture, the private keys might be stored as N of M shares on separated smart cards, each activated by individual custodians. Alternatively, the private keys might be stored encrypted, and the decryption key might be stored as N of M shares on separated smart cards, each activated by individual custodians. There are many methods to securely manage the CA private keys including keeping them inside an HSM under dual custodian control. Regardless of the private key protection practices, once the root CA private keys are available, the procedures can be completed. Figure 5.1 shows the relationships between the various participants and the components.

The offline CA is an application running on a dedicated computer that interfaces to the offline HSM and neither has any network connection. PKI custodians import the CA private keys using smart cards with a smart card reader connected to the HSM. PKI technicians or administrators log on to the CA application using keyboard–video–mouse (KVM) local access. All three PKI participants follow the documented PKI procedures, and auditors or security officers observe the event to ensure the procedures are followed. At the completion of a PKI event, the CA private keys are returned to

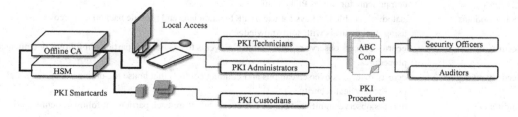

FIGURE 5.1 Example of offline certificate authority roles.

their original unavailable state and the CA application is powered off. As discussed for our ABC Corporation scenario, the offline CA and HSM reside in the PKI room in the office building.

Maintenance and reporting operations that are noncryptographic in nature such as configuring the root CA applications do not require access to the root CA private keys. Therefore, only technicians are needed for maintenance, so auditors and custodians are not involved. Reporting includes reviewing or pulling audit logs, checking ad hoc statistics, or running analytical reports.

Smaller organizations might find staffing a challenge. Maintaining proper separation of duties among a small group is problematic. For example, having a primary and backup PKI technician, a primary and backup PKI administrator, seven PKI custodians (assuming a key split three of seven schemes), at least one security officer, and an auditor as 13 separate roles might not be practical. In general, the main goal is to avoid any one person accessing the root CA private keys. Accordingly, the key split scheme provides dual control but only if properly implemented as neither the HSM nor the offline CA is omniscient and cannot recognize if the same person is using all three smart cards.

Consequently, the PKI technicians and the PKI administrators might also be PKI custodians; however, neither the technicians nor the administrators can be a security officer or an auditor as that would compromise the audit independence. The person checking the procedures cannot be the same person executing the procedures. Furthermore, the security officer might also be a PKI custodian; regardless, to maintain independence auditors must not be PKI custodians.

5.1.2 SUBORDINATE CA

We now turn our attention to the online CA systems. Obviously, the fundamental difference between the root CA and others is that the root CA is operated in an offline mode, while the others are available on a network. This affects the overall security controls and the related PKI procedures. Next, we look at Table 5.3 for examples.

Initially, the online CA systems are installed by administrators and subsequently updated as needed for new hardware or software. Unlike root CA systems, software upgrades are possible over the network using remote access controls, so technicians need not be involved. Similar to root CA systems, installations and upgrades do not require the presence of any cryptographic keys so custodians need not be involved. And like root CA systems, as newer equipment replaces older equipment, the older hardware can be decommissioned after technicians, custodians, and auditors ensure that all cryptographic materials have been properly terminated. Figure 5.2 shows the relationships between the participants and components.

TABLE 5.3

PKI Online CA Roles and Responsibilities

Primary Role	Online CA Responsibilities
PKI technicians	Technicians operate and manage the online CA systems, including generating CA keys, CA certificates, CRL updates, and OCSP updates; revoking CA certificates; and configuring online CA functions and application features.
PKI administrators	Administrators install, upgrade, and decommission software or hardware online CA system components for use by PKI technicians.
PKI custodians	Custodians enable CA keys for use by PKI technicians and provide backup and recovery services, using dual controls with split knowledge.
Security officers	Security officers observe regular online CA events to ensure each participant follows documented procedures.
Security managers	Security managers oversee campus and building controls that house the online CA systems and provide physical security.
Auditors	Auditors observe significant online CA events to ensure each participant follows documented procedures.

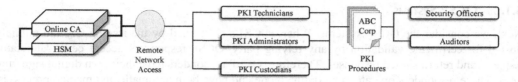

FIGURE 5.2 Example of online certificate authority roles.

The online CA is an application running on servers that interface to the online HSM and both have network access. Note that the online CA might also communicate to the HSM over the network through a secure connection. PKI custodians initially import the CA private keys remotely over the network through a secure connection, and once the CA private keys are installed, the keys remain active in the HSM. PKI technicians or administrators log on to the CA application or the HSM over the network per the documented PKI procedures, and auditors or security officers observe the event to ensure the procedures are followed. As discussed for our ABC Corporation scenario, the online CA and HSM reside in the PKI racks in the data center building.

Preceding any online CA operations, security managers ensure that all physical security controls are in place and effective. Any incidents are immediately reported to the technicians since a security breach might indicate a key compromise. Likewise, any abnormalities with the online CA physical security controls are immediately reported to the security managers. And similar to root CA systems, no news is good news, but periodically the two primary roles need to synchronize information and status of the overall physical security controls.

Before key generation begins, auditors are present to ensure technicians and custodians follow documented procedures and all documentation and video evidence are recorded of the proceedings. For online CA systems, technicians generate keys inside HSM and generate a CSR to obtain CA certificates from the superior CA (e.g., root CA). As part of the key generation procedures, technicians and custodians might back up keys for subsequent recovery in the event of an HSM failure or deployment of additional HSM. Otherwise, auditors need not be involved in normal automatic operations.

Significant CA events that should be observed by an auditor include the following events:

- Generation of subordinate CA keys
- Generation of subordinate CA certificates by a superior (non-root) CA
- Termination of subordinate CA keys

Regular CA events that need only be observed by a security officer and not necessarily by an auditor include the following events:

- Signing any empty CRL updates for any CA including the root CA
- Signing CRL updates with revoked subscriber certificates
- Manually installing CRL updates

Maintenance and reporting operations that are noncryptographic in nature such as configuring the CA applications do not require access to the CA private keys. Therefore, only technicians are needed for maintenance, so auditors and custodians need not be involved. Reporting includes reviewing or pulling audit logs, checking ad hoc statistics, or running analytical reports.

Similar to offline CA issues, smaller organizations might find staffing a challenge for managing online CA systems. Again, PKI technicians or PKI administrators might also be PKI custodians; however, it is easier to demonstrate dual controls if the roles are separate. Likewise, neither a technician nor the administrator can be a security officer or an auditor, but the security officer can be a PKI custodian. To maintain independence, auditors must not be PKI custodians.

5.1.3 OCSP Systems

Next, we consider the OCSP systems. Whereas CRLs are signed by the issuing CA and publicly posted for certificate validation by any relying party, OCSP responders accept certificate status requests and return signed responses. Therefore, OCSP responders have their own digital signature keys. These responders operate in an online mode and have both automatic and manual processes, which affect the overall security. Let's look at Table 5.4 for examples.

Initially, the OCSP systems are installed by administrators and subsequently updated as needed for new hardware or software. Similar to online CA systems, software upgrades are possible over the network using remote access controls, so technicians need not be involved. Installations and upgrades do not require the presence of any cryptographic keys so custodians are not involved. And like any CA system, as newer equipment replaces older equipment, the older hardware can be decommissioned after technicians, custodians, and auditors ensure that all cryptographic materials have been properly terminated.

Preceding any OCSP operations, security managers ensure that all physical security controls are in place and effective. Any incidents are immediately reported to the technicians in the event of a security breach that might indicate a key compromise. Likewise, any abnormalities with the OCSP physical security controls are immediately reported to the security managers. And similar to any CA system, no news is good news, but the two primary roles need to periodically synchronize information and status of the overall physical security controls. Before key generation begins, auditors are present to ensure technicians and custodians follow documented procedures. For OCSP systems, technicians generate keys inside HSM and generate a CSR to obtain CA certificates from an online CA. As part of the key generation procedures, technicians and custodians might back up keys for subsequent recovery in the event of an HSM failure or deployment of additional HSM. Otherwise, auditors are not involved in normal manual or automatic operations.

Significant OCSP events that should be observed by an auditor include the following events:

- Generate OCSP keys
- Obtain OCSP certificates

Regular OCSP events that need only be observed by a security officer and not necessarily by an auditor include the following events:

- Manual installation of OCSP updates
- Request OCSP certificate revocation

TABLE 5.4
PKI OCSP Responder Roles and Responsibilities

Primary Role	OCSP Responsibilities
PKI technicians	Technicians operate and manage the OCSP systems, including generating OCSP keys, requesting OCSP certificates, updating OCSP information, revoking OCSP certificates, and configuring online OCSP functions and application features.
PKI administrators	Administrators install, upgrade, and decommission software or hardware online OCSP system components for use by PKI technicians.
PKI custodians	Custodians enable OCPS keys for use by PKI technicians and provide backup and recovery services, using dual controls with split knowledge.
Security officers	Security officers observe regular OCSP events to ensure each participant follows documented procedures.
Security managers	Security managers oversee campus and building controls that house the online OCSP systems and provide physical security.
Auditors	Auditors observe significant OCSP events to ensure each participant follows documented procedures.

Maintenance and reporting operations that are noncryptographic in nature such as configuring the OCSP applications do not require access to the OCSP private keys. Therefore, only technicians are needed for maintenance, so auditors and custodians need not be involved. Reporting includes reviewing or pulling audit logs, checking ad hoc statistics, or running analytical reports.

5.2 REGISTRATION AUTHORITY

The primary role of a registration authority (RA) is to be the front end to the CA services. The RA provides requestor authentication and authorization such that the CA can reliably perform its functions. Requests include certificates and revocations along with status information. The RA might also support CRL and OCSP services. Furthermore, the RA might be anything from a simple web interface dependent on network authentication to a stand-alone affiliated application. Consider Table 5.5 for examples.

Initially, the online RA systems are installed by administrators and subsequently updated as needed for new hardware or software. Like any online system, software upgrades are possible over the network using remote access controls, so technicians need not be involved. Installations and upgrades do not require the presence of any cryptographic keys so custodians need not be involved. And similar to any CA systems, as newer equipment replaces older equipment, the older hardware can be decommissioned after technicians, custodians, and auditors ensure that all cryptographic materials have been properly terminated.

Preceding any online RA operations, security managers ensure that all physical security controls are in place and effective. Any incidents are immediately reported to the technicians since a security breach might indicate a key compromise. Likewise, any abnormalities with the online RA physical security controls are immediately reported to the security managers. And similar to any CA systems, no news is good news, but the two primary roles need to periodically synchronize information and status of the overall physical security controls.

Before key generation begins, auditors are present to ensure technicians and custodians follow documented procedures. For online RA systems, technicians generate keys inside HSM and generate a CSR to obtain RA certificates from the corresponding CA. As part of the key generation procedures, technicians and custodians might back up keys for subsequent recovery in the event of an HSM failure or deployment of additional HSM. Otherwise, auditors need not be involved in normal automatic operations.

TABLE 5.5
PKI Online Registration Authority

Primary Role	RA Responsibilities
PKI technicians	Technicians operate and manage the RA systems, including generating RA keys, requesting RA certificates, updating RA information, revoking RA certificates, and configuring RA functions and application features.
PKI administrators	Administrators install, upgrade, and decommission software or hardware online RA system components for use by PKI technicians.
PKI custodians	Custodians enable RA keys for use by PKI technicians and provide backup and recovery services, using dual controls with split knowledge.
Security officers	Security officers observe regular RA events to ensure each participant follows documented procedures.
Security managers	Security managers oversee campus and building controls that house the online RA systems and provide physical security.
Auditors	Auditors observe significant RA events to ensure each participant follows documented procedures.

Significant RA events that should be observed by an auditor include the following events:

- Generate online RA keys
- Obtain RA certificates

Regular RA events that need only be observed by a security officer and not necessarily by an auditor include the following events:

- Manual authentication and authorization of subscriber certificate request
- Request RA certificate revocation

Maintenance and reporting operations that are noncryptographic in nature such as configuring the RA applications do not require access to the RA private keys. Therefore, only technicians are needed for maintenance, so auditors and custodians need not be involved. Reporting includes reviewing or pulling audit logs, checking ad hoc statistics, or running analytical reports. Reports might be automatic or manually run by technicians and provided to auditors or PKI administrators.

5.3 POLICY AUTHORITY

The primary role of the policy authority (PA) is the management of the certificate policy (CP) and certificate practice statement (CPS) for the CA. Each CA instance might have its own CP and CPS, or the organization might combine all CA instances into a single CP and CPS. Other CP and CPS separation might be by root CA hierarchies. For example, with our hypothetical ABC Corporation, there might be a CP and CPS for the internal CA and another for the external CA, and consequently, there might be a separate PA for each. However, as we will discuss, there must be common practices and participants for consistency and continuity of the overall PKI systems.

As discussed in Chapter 4, "PKI Management and Security," the CP and CPS reserve a section for the policy authority to provide contact information and the administrative processes. In this section, we discussed the various roles for the PA and their respective responsibilities. For the PA, we add two special roles, attorneys to represent the legal group and business managers to represent the organization's lines of business (LOBs), as shown in Table 5.6 for example.

The PA is a committee of individuals representing different areas of the organization. As introduced in Chapter 1, "Introduction," the concept is to include critical support areas such as cryptography, information technology, business, and legal. Depending on the organization's structure, risk and

---

TABLE 5.6
PKI Policy Authority Roles and Responsibilities

Primary	Role Responsibilities
PKI technicians	Technicians represent the organization's cryptography group to address key management lifecycle controls.
PKI administrators	Administrators represent the organization's IT group to address system and network capacity and planning.
Attorneys	Attorneys represent the organization's legal group to address liability, warranty, intellectual property, privacy, and other business matters. Attorneys are also a necessary part of the CP and CPS creation with respect to the legal, regulatory, and jurisdictional aspects of operating the PKI.
Business managers	Business managers represent the organization's various lines of business (LOBs) to address different application needs and risks associated with the use and reliance upon PKI and certificates.

compliance managers might also be part of the PA if the business or legal members cannot address these areas. For the purposes of this book, we assume attorneys and business managers can speak to risk and compliance issues.

Technicians operate and manage various PKI systems and therefore provide a viewpoint with experience and knowledge. An understanding of the assorted CA, RA, and OCSP applications, features, functions, limits, and bugs is invaluable. In addition, having a basic comprehension of cryptography and key management is likewise important. Technicians also are responsible for following the CP, CPS, and associate procedures.

Administrators install, maintain, and decommission hardware and software elements for network and system components. An understanding of general information technology, infrastructure, and network architectures provides another experienced viewpoint. Administrators are also responsible for reliability, capacity planning, and software vulnerability management lifecycle.

Attorneys provide a legal perspective of liabilities, warranties, and interpret law, regulatory, and contractual obligations that affect the PKI systems. Other business matters include fees, privacy issues, and intellectual property concerns such as patents, trademarks, and copyrights. Outside counsel might be needed specializing in PKI technology and cryptographic jurisdictions.

Business managers are responsible for managing business applications, dealing with vendors and third-party service providers, and confirming functional requirements. Managers provide a business and risk viewpoint of PKI-enabled applications, security needs, and information flows. Other areas include business continuity and disaster recovery issues.

There also needs to be a committee chair to facilitate the meetings, provide meeting minutes, track issues, and manage assignments. The committee mixture might need to be refreshed from time to time, and ad hoc participation might be needed for specific topics. However, for consistency and continuity, the chair is typically held by senior management in the PKI team.

5.4 SUBSCRIBERS

The primary role of the subscriber is to use its private key for cryptographic operations, including digital signatures, encryption, and key management. The subscriber might be an individual using a PKI-enabled application, a network device with an embedded cryptographic module, or an application using a cryptographic module. The subscriber's identity and corresponding public key are encapsulated within the subscriber's digital certificate. Subscribers can also be relying parties when using other subscribers' certificates. But subscribers do not operate in isolation; consider Table 5.7 for examples.

Initially, applications and network devices are installed by application or network managers and subsequently updated as needed for new software or hardware. Software upgrades are possible over

TABLE 5.7

PKI Subscriber Roles and Responsibilities

Primary Role	Responsibilities
Subscribers	Subscribers operate and manage PKI-enabled applications, including generating end-user keys, requesting end-user certificates, certificate revocation, and protecting end-user private keys.
PKI custodians	Custodians enable RA keys for use by PKI technicians and provide backup and recovery services, using dual controls with split knowledge.
Security managers	Security managers oversee campus and building controls that house many PKI-enabled application systems and provide physical security.
Application and network managers	Application and network managers install, upgrade, and decommission PKI-enabled applications or PKI-capable network devices.

the network using remote access controls. Installations and upgrades do not require the presence of any cryptographic keys, so the PKI custodians are not involved. As newer equipment replaces older equipment, the older hardware can be decommissioned after PKI custodians ensure all cryptographic materials have been properly terminated.

Preceding any subscriber operations, security managers ensure that all physical security controls are in place and effective. Any incidents are immediately reported to the subscriber or security manager since a security breach might indicate a key compromise. Likewise, any abnormalities with the subscriber's physical security controls are immediately reported to the security managers.

Subscribers generate keys using cryptographic hardware or software modules and might back up keys for subsequent recovery. For PKI-enabled applications and PKI-capable network devices, custodians might be involved in the key generation, key backup, certificate request, or revocation request processes. Otherwise, PKI custodians are not involved in the normal automatic cryptographic operations, including the following:

- Generate subscriber keys
- Obtain subscriber certificates
- Digitally sign data or messages
- Authenticate via digital signatures
- Establish data encryption keys
- Request subscriber certificate revocation

Maintenance and reporting operations that are noncryptographic in nature such as configuring PKI-enabled applications do not require access to the subscriber private keys. Therefore, only application or network managers are needed for maintenance. Reporting includes reviewing or pulling audit logs, checking ad hoc statistics, or running analytical reports. Reports might be automatically or manually run by technicians and then provided to auditors or PKI administrators.

5.5 RELYING PARTY

The primary role of the relying party is to use subscriber's certificates for cryptographic operations, including signature verification and key management. The relying party might be an individual using a PKI-enabled application, a network device with an embedded cryptographic module, or an application using a cryptographic module. But relying parties do not operate in isolation; consider Table 5.8 for examples.

Preceding any relying party operations, security managers ensure that all physical security controls are in place and effective. All incidents are immediately reported to the relying party, since an incident might be escalated to a security breach, and a security breach might indicate a system compromise. Likewise, any abnormalities with physical security controls are immediately reported to the security managers.

TABLE 5.8

PKI Relying Party Roles and Responsibilities

Primary Role	Responsibilities
Relying parties	Relying parties operate and manage PKI-enabled applications, including validating subscriber certificates.
Security managers	Security managers oversee campus and building controls that house many PKI-enabled application systems and provide physical security.
Application and network managers	Application and network managers install, upgrade, and decommission PKI-enabled applications or PKI-capable network devices.

From a cryptography viewpoint, relying parties work in concert with subscribers to implement security controls. Relying parties employ applications for normal automatic operations:

- Validate certificate chains
- Verify signed data or signed messages
- Authenticate subscribers via signature verification
- Establish data encryption keys

Maintenance and reporting operations that are noncryptographic in nature such as configuring PKI-enabled applications do not require access to the subscriber private keys. Therefore, only application or network managers are needed for maintenance. Reporting includes reviewing or pulling audit logs, checking ad hoc statistics, or running analytical reports. Reports might be automatic or manually run by technicians and provided to auditors or PKI administrators.

5.6   AGREEMENTS

An agreement is essentially an understanding between two or more parties with respect to their relative rights and duties. In Chapter 4, "PKI Management and Security," we discussed certificate policy (CP) and practices (CPS) and introduced the concept of agreements between the CA and the various PKI participants. From a CA perspective, agreements are primarily for entities that are involved in certificate request processes (subscribers and RA) or certificate validation processes (relying parties). Another agreement area is cross-certification with another CA.

Agreements might be incorporated into the CP or CPS; however, it is a common practice to maintain separate documents. In this manner, warranties and liabilities can be managed without having to constantly update and republish the policy and practices. This allows legal, regulatory, and contractual issues to be addressed in a timely manner as changes occur within different industries that affect the PKI operations, warranties, or liabilities.

SPECIAL NOTE 5-2 DOCUMENT SEPARATION

It is a good practice to maintain agreements as separate documents to remain flexible and minimize the publication impacts on the CP and the CPS.

In addition to managing the CP and CPS, the policy authority (PA) is also responsible for reviewing and approving agreements. Since agreements contain mostly business and legal considerations, attorneys and business managers are the primary authors. Attorneys address warranty and liability constraints, and business managers address the various application needs and restrictions. The PA needs to synchronize the agreements with the CP and CPS to ensure there are no contradictions and that they share common language for ease of reading.

5.6.1   CERTIFICATE AUTHORITY AGREEMENTS

From a technical perspective, the CA is responsible for managing its private keys and corresponding certificates. From a functional viewpoint, the CA exists to generate other CA certificates or, depending on the CA hierarchy, subscriber certificates. Within the same PKI hierarchy, CA agreements are not normally needed as the business, information technology, legal, and cryptography have shared infrastructures.

Conversely, when different PKI hierarchies interact, the relationships and certificate chains can become rather complex, making the CA agreement an essential component. Let's consider several

CA interactions beginning with Figure 5.3, which shows three separate organizations (A, B, and C), each with its own PKI hierarchy. Each hierarchy consists of a root CA and two subordinate CA. The subordinate CA issues subscriber certificates, but for the purposes of this discussion, we need only to consider the CA certificates. Furthermore, each PKI system is independent of each other with separate certificate chains:

- Root A, subordinates A1 and A2, so we have chains A ⇒ A1 and A ⇒ A2
- Root B, subordinates B1 and B2, so we have chains B ⇒ B1 and B ⇒ B2
- Root C, subordinates C1 and C2, so we have chains C ⇒ C1 and C ⇒ C2

Now let's look at two very different PKI intersections: root certification and subordinate (sub) certification. For either of these two scenarios, there are many legitimate business reasons to interconnect two PKI hierarchies. As examples, perhaps one organization has acquired another, maybe one organization is outsourcing its services to another, or possibly two different applications need to interoperate. Regardless of the business reason, let's first consider the root certification scenario, where organization A needs to merge its PKI with organization B.

Figure 5.3 shows a root certification where root A is issued a certificate from root B, essentially making root A subordinate to root B. However, root A now has two certificates, its own self-signed certificate and another signed by root B. So, for subordinates A1 and A2, we have created two new possible certificate chains:

- Root B, subordinate root A, so we have chains B ⇒ A ⇒ A1 and B ⇒ A ⇒ A2

Depending on how organization A configures its browsers, applications, servers, routers, and whatever other components rely on certificates, both sets of certificate chains are valid and can interoperate. However, misconfigurations might inadvertently force certificate validation resolving to the wrong root CA and organization. Thus, an application accepting and using a certificate validated to root B, which should have been validated to root A, might not be covered by organization B's warranties and consequently take on unacceptable liability and risk. The CA agreement might address such an issue and protect both organizations. Figure 5.3 also shows a subordinate (sub) certification where subordinate C1 is issued a certificate from root B, making C1 a subordinate of both root B and root C. Thus, C1 now has two certificates, creating two new possible certificate chains:

- Root C, subordinates C1, so we have chains C ⇒ C1
- Root B, subordinates C1, so we have chains B ⇒ C1

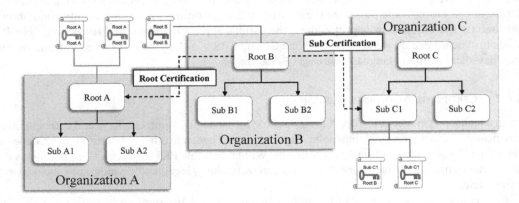

FIGURE 5.3   Examples of certificates.

Depending on how organization C configures its browsers, applications, servers, routers, and whatever other components rely on certificates, both sets of certificate chains are valid and can interoperate. Yet again, misconfigurations might inadvertently force certificate validation resolving to the wrong root CA and organization (i.e., root B instead of root C). And again, the CA agreement might address a similar issue and protect both organizations. Figure 5.4 shows the same three organizations, where organization A and organization C independently cross-certify with organization B. Root A issues a certificate for root B, and conversely root B issues a certificate for root A. Likewise, root B issues a certificate for root C, and equally root C issues a certificate for root B. Depending on how the business rules define interoperability for certificate validation between organizations and how each organization needs to configure its PKI-enabled applications, a CA agreement might define a bilateral arrangement.

Our last CA interaction example is shown in Figure 5.5, which is different than cross-certification. In this scenario, organization B acts as a PKI bridge between organization A and organization C. Unlike the previous diagrams, organization B only needs to operate a bridge CA with no internal subordinate CA. An example of a real-world bridge certification is the federal bridge CA,[1] which was established to facilitate trusted electronic business transactions for federal organizations. The functional purpose of a PKI bridge is to provide interoperability and functionality between disparate PKI hierarchies. Consequently, a CA agreement can enhance the bridge CA policy and practices by specifying business rules.

We conclude that when different PKI hierarchies interact, a CA agreement (CAA) might be beneficial to outline the differences, commonalities, and business rules. System configurations and

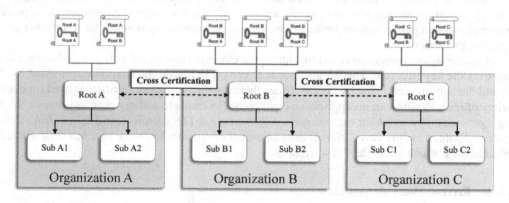

FIGURE 5.4 Examples of cross-certification.

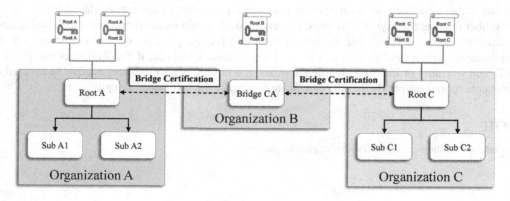

FIGURE 5.5 Examples of bridge certificate authority.

certificate validation processes might also be specified, along with warranties and other legal and pertinent business information.

5.6.2 Registration Authority Agreements

From a technical perspective, the RA is responsible for authenticating and authorizing subscriber requests. From a functional viewpoint, the RA processes various types of requests, acting as the CA portal. When the RA is part of the CA, an agreement is rarely needed. When the RA is a separate application that interfaces with the CA but part of the same organization, an RA agreement (RAA) is akin to a service level agreement that establishes RA responsibilities such as response times. An RAA can be beneficial for managing internal services when the RA application is operated as a separate application.

When the RA is an affiliate, a third-party service provider, to the CA and operates independently as a separate legal entity, an RAA is needed. The RAA provides the foundation of an affiliate contract, describing the RA role and responsibilities. The contract might contain the RAA in an appendix or exhibit or refer to it as a separate document. In addition, the same policy authority (PA) legal representative should be engaged in the RA contract negotiations.

5.6.3 Subscriber Agreements

From a technical perspective, the subscriber is responsible for managing its private keys and corresponding public key certificates. From a functional viewpoint, the subscriber might use its private key to sign messages, sign documents, authenticate itself via digital signatures, decrypt data encrypted with its public key, or for key management to establish symmetric keys for other cryptographic processes.

Subscriber agreements (SAs) need to address the CA expectations regarding the subscriber controls over the key lifecycle. The SA also needs to clearly delineate the warranties provided by the CA and the liabilities accepted by the CA. Since there are many types of certificates used for a wide variety of reasons with various applications, either the SA needs to address each use case or the PA might provide different SA for each scenario. For example, a TLS certificate is different from a code sign certificate, which is very different than an e-mail certificate. Each use case has different risks and liabilities, which affect the CA warranties.

5.6.4 Relying Party Agreements

From a technical perspective, the relying party is responsible for validating and properly using subscribers' public key certificates. From a functional viewpoint, the relying party simply utilizes the subscriber certificate according to the use case represented by the certificate. However, if the subscriber misuses the asymmetric keys, the relying party might inadvertently misuse the subscriber certificate. Thus, the subscriber agreement (SA) and relying party agreement (RPA) need to be synchronized in their definitions and terms. From a legal viewpoint if the RPA does not provide sufficient warranty or lacks acceptable liabilities, the relying party might not accept the subscriber certificate regardless of whether the certificate is valid or the subscriber is legitimate.

NOTE

1. Federal PKI, https://playbooks.idmanagement.gov/fpki/

6 Security Considerations

This chapter discusses security considerations that might affect the operational environments of the CA and the RA, and ultimately the subscriber or relying party. The security considerations in this chapter are organized into four control areas: physical controls, logical controls, audit logs, and cryptographic modules. Let the reader be forewarned that there is some overlap among these areas, so it is difficult when discussing one area to not mention another. We have attempted to separate these topics into discrete thoughts, but again these controls have interdependencies that reflect the real world. As we dig deeper into each area, the reader will discover that at some level, things tend to become uncertain and we are limited by those annoying laws of physics.

For example, when we place a valuable into a safe, we can check the contents of the safe to see if the valuable is still there. If a valuable jewel, say a diamond, is stolen by a master thief who bypasses all of the security controls, the theft is noticeable when the owner opens the safe – the diamond is missing. But, if a valuable piece of information, say a secret password written on a piece of paper, is "stolen" the original paper might still be in the safe but the information is gone unbeknownst to the owner. Likewise, if the information is electronic in nature, say a USB thumb drive, its contents can be copied but the original data bits are still in the USB stick. Conversely, if the master thief left a man-made carbon duplicate of the diamond in place of the real jewel, its theft might also go undetected for a very long time.

However, just because a professional thief can bypass a household security system and pick a lock to rob your home is not a justification to leave your backdoor unlocked. Reasonable security measures are exactly that – *reasonable*. Just because, with sufficient time and resources, a cryptographic key can be determined is not justification to leave cryptographic keys unprotected or data unencrypted. Security precautions address a range of threats with low threats at one end of the spectrum and high threats at the other. Some security controls might deter low to medium threats, while others are focused on higher threats. At the same time, other security controls might not be preventive measures; rather they might be detection methods to corroborate other controls.

SPECIAL NOTE 6-1 EIGHTY-TWENTY RULE

Regarding software, the 80/20 rule means that 20% of the code can address 80% of the scenarios, but the remaining 20% of scenarios take the other 80% of the code. Security is similar, where 20% of the controls can prevent 80% of the threats, but the remaining 20% of the threats, including zero-day attacks (previously unknown threats) need the other 80% of the controls.

In Chapter 4, "PKI Management and Security," we introduced a scenario for the ABC Corporation and provided a bird's-eye view of their campus consisting of two facilities: an office building and a data center separated by landscaping with large rocks and trees. The building entrances are located at the opposite ends of the two buildings; the office building entrance is on the West side, and the data center building entrance is on the East side. The two facilities are surrounded by parking lot areas that are in turn surrounded by a perimeter fence. Access to the campus is from a public road over a private drive through a gate that has 7 × 24 badge access for employees and a guard during working hours for visitors.

DOI: 10.1201/9781003425298-6

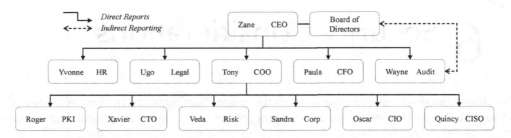

FIGURE 6.1   ABC Corporation organizational chart.

We also introduced the PKI elements for our hypothetical ABC Corporation. Recall that there are two separate CA hierarchies, one for internal use (denoted as "A" or PKI-A) and the other for external entities (denoted as "B" or PKI-B), each with its own root CA.

- The internal PKI-A consists of five online issuing CAs: The lowest online level consists of A.1.1 for SSL/TLS certificates, A.2.1 for e-mail signature, A.2.2 for e-mail encryption, A.3.1 for employees VPN access, and A.3.2 for contractor VPN access. There are two intermediate CAs consisting of A.2 for e-mail certificates and A.3 for VPN certificates; there is no A.1 for SSL/TLS certificates. The internal root CA is "A" sometimes called A.0 or A-zero. We intentionally introduced the ambiguity of having different names for the same root CA because in many organizations this is very typical.
- The external PKI-B consists of three online issuing CA: The lowest online level consists of B.1.1 for SSL/TLS certificates, B.1.2 for VPN certificates, and B.1.3 for code sign certificates. There is one intermediate CA, the B.1 external CA. The external root CA is "B" sometimes called B.0, B-zero, or the outer-CA. The latter term is unfortunate as it will turn out in our discussion that the name is a misnomer, which causes confusion.

In addition to the geography of the campus, the physical aspects of the facilities, and the logical structure of the PKI hierarchy, we also need to consider the management structure. Figure 6.1 provides a hypothetical organizational chart.

The topmost layer consists of the chief executive officer (CEO, Zane) and the board of directors (BoD). The CEO's direct reports are human resources (HR, Yvonne), legal (Ugo), the chief operating officer (COO, Tony), the chief financial officer (CFO, Paula), and audit (Wayne). The remaining groups report to the COO: public key infrastructure (PKI, Roger), the chief technology officer (CTO, Xavier), risk (Veda), corporate security (Corp, Sandra), the chief information officer (CIO, Oscar), and the chief information security officer (CISO, Quincy). Note that audit has an indirect reporting channel to the board of directors (BoD) supposedly independent of the CEO.

In the following sections, we revisit the ABC Corporation and its PKI operations for its security controls, weaknesses, successes, and failures. The security considerations are organized into four control areas: physical controls, logical controls, audit logs, and cryptographic modules.

6.1   PHYSICAL SECURITY

For large organizations, physical security is typically managed within its corporate security division, and the ABC Corporation is no different. Sandra's (Corp) responsibilities include maintenance and physical security controls, which are commonly referred to as guns, guards, and dogs. In our ongoing example, Sandra (Corp) reports to Tony (COO), who reports to Zane (CEO), who recently was appointed as Chairman of the board of directors (BoD). Any facility or building issues or repairs that might affect physical security are dutifully reported by Sandra to Tony. However, only high-risk issues or incidents are reported to Zane. Consequently, Zane is aware of some problems before the board of directors is informed, and often the BoD never hears about physical security issues. Wayne (audit) is responsible for bringing issues directly to the BoD, but Wayne reports to Zane, who can censor the audit reports, and Wayne is a peer to Tony, who might not share his information except with Zane.

Let's consider the existing physical security controls. The bird's-eye view of the ABC Corporation campus from Chapter 4, "PKI Management and Security," is revisited using side views for a different perspective. Figure 6.2 shows the public road, the guard shack, the perimeter fence, the private property signs, and the invisible barriers in front and between the buildings.

- The *guard shack* provides the sole entrance to the campus. The gated entrance has one "in" lane and one "out" lane per the private lane leading to the public road. The "in" gate is badge activated 7 × 24 hours for employees and has a guard available during working hours for visitors. The "out" gate automatically opens for any departing vehicle.
- The *perimeter fence* surrounds the campus on all four sides acting as a deterrent to trespassers. The 6-feet tall fence is basically a warning to the average thrill seeker to not enter the property. The fence has no other security features such as barbed or razor wire, electrification, or closed-circuit television (CCTV) monitoring.
- The *private property signs* are posted at regular intervals along the fence. The wording is compliant to local ordinances. The signs are a warning to would-be trespassers.
- *Invisible barriers* are landscaping berms with trees and large rocks designed to protect the building entrances from vehicular incidents. The intent is to prevent out-of-control or intentionally driven vehicles from driving into the building entrances. There are no other barriers along the side of the buildings.

The guard shack at the gate and the perimeter fences with its private property signs are the *outer defense ring*. Figure 6.3 shows the hypothetical gate. The entrance actually has two physical

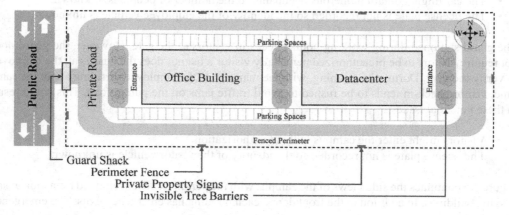

FIGURE 6.2 ABC Corporation campus security.

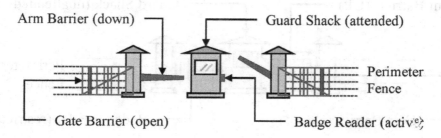

FIGURE 6.3 Guard shack work hours.

barriers, a gate barrier that is kept open during work hours and an arm barrier for ingress and egress. The ingress arm barrier rises when an employee swipes their badge and closes automatically triggered by a motion sensor. The guard can also open the arm barrier after checking in a visitor. Visitors are asked to show identification and the employee contact they are visiting, and the guard dutifully captures the visitor information. The egress arm barrier automatically opens to allow departures per another motion sensor when a vehicle pulls up and closes automatically when triggered by a third motion sensor.

Figure 6.4 shows the same gate during nonworking hours. The arm barrier is locked into an open position, and the gate barrier is closed. The guard shack is unattended so the only access is via the badge reader with restricted access. The ingress gate barrier opens when an employee swipes their badge and closes automatically when triggered by a motion sensor. The egress gate barrier automatically opens to allow departures per another motion sensor when a vehicle pulls up and closes automatically when triggered by a third motion sensor.

From a security perspective, the gate attempts to restrict traffic to a single control point; however, from a safety perspective, a vehicle accident might prevent other access. For example, it might interfere or obstruct:

- Employees from leaving the campus during a fire or other emergency.
- Rescue vehicles from entering the campus during a fire, heart attack, or other emergency.

However, the badge access at the gate, while convenient for employees during work hours and after hours, only scans the badge used at the gate by the driver of the car and does not record any additional information resulting in these potential issues:

- The badges might be borrowed or stolen such that the identity of the driver is unknown.
- The car might contain numerous occupants so the number of people is unknown.
- The license plate is not recorded so the identity of the employee vehicle is unknown.

The guard stationed during working hours checks in visitors at the gate. However, the guard does not require visitors to be preauthorized per a daily visitor's list nor does the guard call the employee to verify the visit. During the morning, with the majority of the employees arriving about the same time, visitor check-in tends to be rushed to avoid traffic jams on the public road. This could result in these potential issues:

- Visitors might enter the campus without authorization.
- The license plate is not recorded so the identity of the visitor vehicle is unknown.

Figure 6.5 continues the side views of the campus with the perimeter fence removed for a look at and into the buildings. In addition to the front doors, each building has emergency exits. The emergency

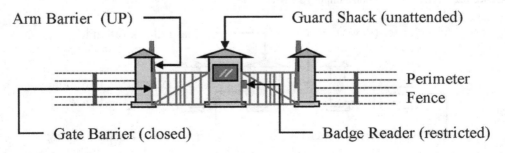

FIGURE 6.4 Guard shack after hours.

exit doors are designed for egress only, without exterior door handles, but their proximity is relatively close to the PKI room in the office building and the PKI racks in the data center. If an unauthorized visitor or a disgruntled employee is discovered pilfering either of the PKI areas, a quick escape via the emergency exit doors is possible.

In general, PKI systems notwithstanding, network equipment is susceptible to unauthorized physical access including routers, switches, firewalls, web servers, application servers, database servers, and cryptographic modules (HSM). This has consequences including the following:

- Equipment can be stolen.
- Equipment can be damaged.
- Equipment can be reconfigured.
- Equipment including network cables can be tapped.

As discussed earlier, since visitors can enter the campus without authorization, access to sensitive areas or equipment is restricted by the access controls of the buildings. The building exterior walls and building access is the second defense ring, which begins with the lobby areas. Figure 6.6 shows the interior of the lobby, which has the same configuration as the office building and the data center. The exterior doors are unlocked during work hours, and the guard desk is attended for visitor access; otherwise, the exterior doors are badge access during after hours, and the guard desk is unattended. Behind the guard desk and divider wall are the interior office doors to the other office areas, which are badge access 7 × 24.

Similar to the guard shack practices, the desk guards asked visitors to show identification and the employee contact they are visiting. As an additional step, the guard calls the employee to provide visitor escort along with a temporary one-day visitor sticky badge. However, once entering the office areas or the data center areas, visitors are no longer required to be escorted. Thus, visitors have unsupervised access to most areas of the buildings. Consequently:

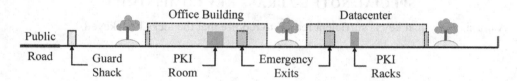

FIGURE 6.5   Zone security.

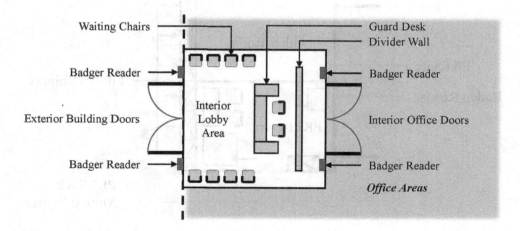

FIGURE 6.6   Lobby areas.

- Visitors might steal, copy, change, or insert sensitive information.
- Visitors might see and remember written passwords or combination codes.
- Visitors might steal or copy physical keys.
- Visitors might steal, damage, or reconfigure equipment.
- Visitors might install illicit equipment or insert electronic eavesdropping devices.

Regarding physical security for the PKI system, Figure 6.7 shows the third defense ring housing the offline CA components. Access to the room is restricted using a badge-access door that is locked 7 × 24. An internal motion sensor triggers an external flashing light when the room is occupied. The room contains a combination safe for storing cryptographic material, a filing cabinet, a powered rack for the offline root CA equipment, and workstation seating.

The PKI racks in the PKI room and the two PKI racks in the data center are individually locked cabinets using common physical keys. The locks used for the three PKI racks are different than any other equipment racks in the data center. The PKI team manages the locks and physical keys, sometimes called a brass key to distinguish physical keys from cryptographic keys. Despite these controls, the following weaknesses might remain:

- Lack of a brass key inventory affects the reliability of the locked cabinets.
- Never changing the safe combination lock also affects the reliability of the locked safe.
- The flashing motion sensor light cannot differentiate unauthorized room occupancy.

Allowing PKI team members to keep the physical cabinet keys on their personal key chains increases the likelihood that the keys might be stolen or copied. Without a current inventory, it is impossible to know if a key was ever lost or stolen. As a matter of practicality, if a physical key is missing, it must be presumed that the keys are compromised and the lock needs to be changed.

SPECIAL NOTE 6-2 BRASS KEY COMPROMISE

A missing physical key is sufficient reason to require that the locks be rekeyed.

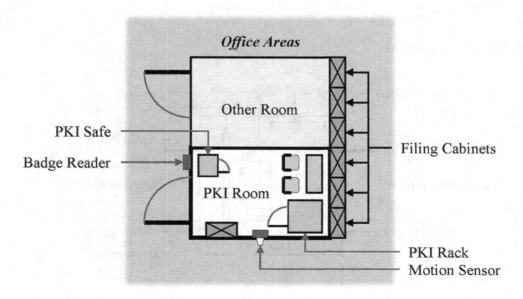

FIGURE 6.7   Public key infrastructure room.

In a similar manner, whenever a PKI team member leaves the group, quits the company, or is terminated, the safe lock should likewise be rekeyed. Further, even when the combination code is known to have never been shared, lost, or otherwise compromised, it should nonetheless be changed periodically.

SPECIAL NOTE 6-3 SAFE COMBINATION CODES

Similar to passwords, safe combination codes need to be protected and changed periodically.

While the motion sensor is a good countermeasure against unauthorized access, its inability to distinguish between legitimate and unauthorized is problematic. A better control would be to disable the alarm light during authorized use such that the flashing light only indicates a problem when the room should be unoccupied. However, forgetting to enable the alarm light is another risk. Figure 6.8 shows an alternative construction approach.

A better option would be to install a camera along with the motion sensor, but care must be taken to not view the keyboard to avoid inadvertently recording passwords. The door is replaced with a badge-activated mantrap such that each person is recorded as they enter the room. The rack is also accessed using a badge-activated lock. In this manner, the access controls are managed by security managers independently from the PKI staff. The motion sensor is linked to the badge readers such that it only triggers the flashing light if everyone has left the room. Furthermore, a camera positioned over the table monitors the room's comings and goings but does not have a view of the keyboard to avoid inadvertently capturing keystrokes. In summary, this section described three rings of physical defense:

- Ring 1: Guarded gate and perimeter defense
- Ring 2: Physical building and lobby access controls
- Ring 3: Locked PKI room and locked PKI cabinets

These three layers represent a form of defense in depth, where each layer has to be defeated before the next layer can be attacked. In this section, we discussed various physical security considerations for each defensive ring. We also noted that the management structure permits information to be repressed such that peers or superiors are not fully aware of physical security problems. Wayne (audit) needs to have (1) transparency to each group within Tony's (COO) division as an audit control and (2) a direct reporting channel to the board of directors independent of Zane (CEO). The remaining sections discuss the other three areas: logical controls, audit logs, and cryptographic modules.

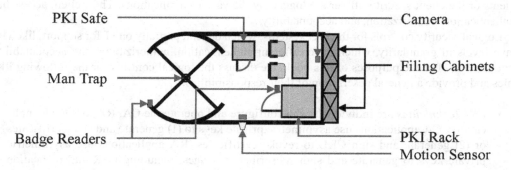

FIGURE 6.8 Enhanced public key infrastructure room.

6.2 LOGICAL SECURITY

For large organizations, logical security for network and system components is typically managed within its information technology (IT) team as part of its chief technology officer (CTO) group, and the ABC Corporation is no exception. Other logical controls relating to physical access such as badge readers are usually managed by corporate security, which was discussed in Section 6.1, "Physical Security." Physical security is managed by Sandra (Corp), whereas logical security is managed by Xavier (CTO), both of whom report to Tony (COO). However, overall security is the responsibility of Quincy (CISO), who is a peer to Xavier (CTO) and who also reports to Tony (COO). In addition, Wayne (audit) is responsible for bringing issues directly to the board of directors (BoD), but Wayne reports to Zane who can censor the audit reports, and Wayne is a peer to Tony who might not share his information except with Zane.

Regardless, logical security controls rest on three cornerstones – authentication, authorization, and accountability – that were defined in Chapter 1, "Introduction," as three of the six basic security areas including confidentiality, integrity, and nonrepudiation. Authentication provides a level of assurance as to the identity of the requestor, human or otherwise, whereas authorization defines what privileges are associated with the requestor. Accountability tracks who did what and when they did it, either as real-time monitoring to measure overall system and network reliability or latent analysis to determine what went wrong and who is responsible.

Privileges include access to systems or services and might have various levels of granularity, which may have lesser or stronger authentication requirements. For example, access to the ABC Corporation public website does not require an individual to identify themselves, but downloading a white paper requires the end user to provide their contact information. While the contact information is requested and the end user cannot proceed otherwise, the information is not verified as it is collected for use by the sales department and no authorization is required. Hence, there are no authentication or authorization processes for this particular application environment. Furthermore, as part of the web interface, the end user's browser is queried as the IT staff collects information on the types of systems accessing the web pages for optimization, but since the end user is not authenticated, there are no accountability processes. Web servers often tag a client computer using a cookie or equivalent technology, which allows the data to be collected locally on the client and recognized during a revisit to the same website.

As another example, business clients of ABC Corporation can log on to the private website to check on existing orders, place new orders, submit payments, interact with online sales staff, and manage access using various applications. Authentication is required for application log-ons using an identifier (ID) and password over a VPN channel. The ID is system allocated per the business account, but the password is individually client selected. Adding and deleting individual clients to a business account is separated by an assigned client security officer using a designated VPN certificate and whose ID and log-on only permit managing other clients. All client log-ons, log-offs, and session time-outs are logged by the system access controls. All activities performed by individual clients or the client security officer are logged by the various applications. Thus, client access has authentication, authorization, and accountability.

Logical security controls for the PKI systems, which depend partially on IT for support, likewise have levels of granularity, which have different authentication, authorization, and accountability requirements. For the purposes of this book, we discuss the logical controls for the following PKI roles and provide a general description of their responsibilities:

- *PKI Technicians* are individuals who configure and operate the CA, RA, or OCSP applications. CA applications use asymmetric private keys to (1) generate and sign certificates or (2) generate and sign CRL to revoke certificates. RA applications use asymmetric private keys to generate and sign subscriber messages, including CSR and revocation requests. OCSP applications use asymmetric private keys to generate and sign certificate status response messages.

- *PKI Administrators* are individuals who install and configure network or system components that support the CA or RA applications, including hardware or software components. For large organizations, the administrator role is typically separate from the technician role, but for smaller ones, the two roles are often the same group.
- *PKI Custodians* are individuals who manage cryptographic materials to generate, distribute, back up, recover, or terminate CA or RA asymmetric keys. Custodians manage keys using split knowledge with dual control. As discussed in Chapter 2, "Cryptography Basics," this essentially means no single individual has access to all of the cryptographic material at any given time.
- *Subscribers* are individuals or other nonperson entities such as applications, routers, or other network components that are key owners, which (1) initially use their asymmetric private keys to generate and sign the CSR to obtain the public key certificates and (2) subsequently use private keys to (a) generate digital signatures, (b) decrypt data that was encrypted using public keys, or (c) establish additional keys used to perform other cryptographic functions. Note that subscribers are also relying parties when accepting another subscriber's certificates.
- *Relying Parties* are individuals or other nonperson entities that use the subscribers' public key certificate to (a) verify digital signatures, (b) encrypt data, or (c) establish additional keys used to perform other cryptographic functions. Note that relying parties are often subscribers when owning private keys and public key certificates.

Table 6.1 provides an overview of divvying up responsibilities to avoid collusion among PKI staff, subscribers, and relying parties. Smaller organizations might have trouble separating duties due to insufficient resources. Although, as jobs change and positions are rotated, it might become problematic to maintain continual separation of duties. One logical security control is to change passwords and other access codes when a team member leaves the organization or group for another position.

TABLE 6.1
Public Key Infrastructure Separation of Duties

Role	Separation of Duties
PKI technicians	Technicians are employees and part of Roger's (PKI) team, and while they operate the CA, RA, and OCSP applications, they are not permitted to manage any of the network or system components. Modifications to any network or system components require a formal change control process. This prevents any ad hoc or rogue systems from being installed.
PKI administrators	Administrators are employees or contractors part of Xavier's (CTO) team, and while they manage network and system components, they are not permitted to operate any of the CA, RA, or OCSP applications. This prevents any unofficial PKI actions from being executed.
PKI custodians	Custodians are employees; however, the handling of cryptographic materials should not be allowed by a single person or group. For example, if a 3-of-5 key share was used to manage the CA private keys, then only a maximum of two custodial roles can be allocated to PKI technicians or PKI administrators. Consequently, at least a fifth custodian needs to be allocated to a third group, such as corporate security (Corp.). Thus, no one group can generate, distribute, back up, or recover cryptographic keys.
Subscribers	Subscribers might be employees, ABC systems, contractors, clients, or client systems that obtain certificates from the ABC Corporation's CA. The internal CA can provide SSL/TLS certificates to ABC systems, e-mail or VPN certificates to employees, or VPN certificates to contractors. The external CA can provide SSL/TLS certificates to client systems, and VPN or code sign certificates to clients.
Relying parties	Relying parties might be employees accepting ABC certificates for encrypted or signed e-mails, VPN servers enabling remote access, ABC systems using SSL/TLS connections to securely communicate with other ABC systems, or applications verifying signed code. Relying parties might also be employees, ABC systems, or applications accepting certificates from external non-employees or clients issued from another third-party certificate authority (TPCA).

Table 6.2 provides examples of relying parties, the subscribers providing the certificates, the types of certificates, and the CA that issued the certificates. Rows 1–8 show e-mail, VPN, TLS, and code sign certificates issued from the ABC internal or external CA, and rows 9–12 have e-mail, TLS, and code signing certificates issued from a third-party CA (TPCA).

- Row 1 shows employees using e-mail certificates with other employees issued by the ABC internal CA.
- Row 2 shows VPN servers accepting VPN certificates from employees also issued by the ABC internal CA.
- Row 3 shows VPN servers accepting VPN certificates from contractors also issued by the ABC internal CA.
- Row 4 has ABC servers sending SSL/TLS certificates issued by the ABC internal or external CA to employee–client browsers.
- Row 5 has ABC servers receiving SSL/TLS certificates issued by the ABC internal or external CA from employee–client browsers for mutual authentication.
- Row 6 has ABC servers exchanging SSL/TLS certificates issued by the ABC internal CA for mutual authentication.
- Row 7 shows ABC servers verifying code signed by application providers using code sign certificates issued by the ABC internal CA.
- Row 8 shows employees using browsers to verify and run code signed by application providers using code sign certificates issued by the ABC external CA.
- Row 9 shows employees receiving e-mail certificates issued by a TPCA from non-employees.
- Row 10 has XYZ servers sending SSL/TLS certificates issued by a TPCA to employee–client browsers.
- Row 11 has XYZ servers receiving SSL/TLS certificates issued by a TPCA from employee–client browsers for mutual authentication.
- Row 12 shows employees using a mobile device or computer to verify and run code signed by application providers using code sign certificates issued by a TPCA.

The arrows indicate the direction the certificate is sent – from the subscriber to the relying party – and for row 6 the arrow is bidirectional. Sometimes, the relying party is a person while others are non-persons such as a VPN or other application server. The issuing CA might be from the ABC

TABLE 6.2

Examples of Relying Parties

	Relying Party	Direction	Subscriber	Certificate	CA
1	Employee	$\Leftarrow$	Employee	E-mail	ABC
2	VPN Server	$\Leftarrow$	Employee	VPN	ABC
3	VPN Server	$\Leftarrow$	Contractors	VPN	ABC
4	Employee–client	$\Leftarrow$	ABC server	TLS	ABC
5	ABC server	$\Leftarrow$	Employee–client	TLS	ABC
6	ABC server	$\Leftrightarrow$	ABC server	TLS	ABC
7	ABC server	$\Leftarrow$	App signer	Code sign	ABC
8	Employee	$\Leftarrow$	App signer	Code sign	ABC
9	Employee	$\Leftarrow$	Nonemployees	E-mail	TPCA
10	Employee	$\Leftarrow$	XYZ server	TLS	TPCA
11	XYZ server	$\Leftarrow$	Employee–client	TLS	TPCA
12	Employee	$\Leftarrow$	App signer	Code sign	TPCA

Corporation or another TPCA. As more third-party CA certificates are deemed acceptable, the complexity of the overall PKI system increases along with related risks, for example, depending on outside organizations such as browser manufacturers to determine which CAs are trustworthy.

For example, probably the most famous CA compromise was DigiNotar, a Dutch company owned by VASCO Data Security International that issued certificates under their own name Digi-Notar and for the Dutch government's PKI program. According to DigiNotar's own investigation, they discovered the compromise in July 2011 where several rogue SSL certificates had been illicitly issued by an RA that had been compromised. Two months later, in September 2011, VASCO announced that its subsidiary DigiNotar declared voluntary bankruptcy filed at the Haarlem court. All of the legitimate and illegitimate certificates were revoked.[1]

For our hypothetical ABC Corporation, if any DigiNotar certificates had been accepted merely because of its availability in a browser's approved certificate list, the real-world CA compromise might have severely affected the company. There are dozens of commercial CAs issuing millions of certificates to individuals and servers, but relying solely on the CA without understanding its policy and practices is foolhardy. As discussed in Chapter 1, "Introduction," before any authentication credential is issued, there must be an initial authentication process to verify the entity's identity; otherwise, the credential is untrustworthy. Thus, for any ABC Corporation entity to accept a certificate issued by any third-party CA, there must be some level of assurance that the certificate belongs to the subscriber.

SPECIAL NOTE 6-4 TRUSTWORTHY CA

It is a bad practice to blindly trust an unknown certificate issued from an unknown CA. It is a good practice to only trust known certificates issued from a known CA. It is a best practice to only trust certificates issued from a CA that been audited using industry standards (e.g., WebTrust CA).

As introduced in Chapter 1, "Introduction," an initial authentication must be performed before the authentication credential can be established. And as discussed in Chapter 4, "PKI Management and Security," the certificate policy (CP) and certificate practice statement (CPS) "Initial Identity Validation" section address initial authentication methods for each PKI participate. Before the authentication credential, such as a digital certificate, can be issued, the entity must be initially authenticated to an appropriate assurance level. Identity verification can occur in many ways, and decisions must be weighed for feasibility and practicality. Here are some verification approaches and their limitations:

- Hiring practices for security personnel should incorporate background checks that may include fingerprints or other biometrics and criminal background checks against national or international databases. However, these are negative files and only provide identity verification if the individual has been arrested. Otherwise, no arrest, no verification. Some countries might maintain national biometric databases for identity verification, which are positive files.
- Some hiring practices, such as those for the financial services industry, typically include drug testing for illegal substances. Drug testing can be a sensitive subject, sometimes mandated by the organization's human resources (HR) policy, affected by federal or local jurisdictions, and may differ[2] internationally.
- Government-issued photo identification, such as a passport or driver's license, might be relied upon for identification verification. For example, the U.S. Citizen and Immigration Service Form I-9[3] is used for verifying the identity and employment authorization of

individuals hired for employment in the United States. However, this presumes the government agency has performed its due diligence, and the individual has not provided false information. This also presumes the individual has not illegally acquired counterfeit credentials from a criminal element.

- Face-to-face interviews might provide more reliable identity verification. However, this also presumes the individual has not provided false information or false credentials.
- Knowledge-based authentication might be used, assuming the organization has information about the individual. However, publicly available information can be gathered by fraudsters, and data breaches might reveal identity information.

Once initial authentication has been verified and an entity's identity (ID) can be trusted to some acceptable level of assurance, the ID can then be used for subsequent authentication. Table 6.3 provides a summary of authentication factors and describes verification versus identification methods. Authentication is typically categorized into three factors: something you know (knowledge), something you have (possession), and something you are (biometrics) – but as discussed in the previous book *Security Without Obscurity: A Guide to Confidentiality, Integrity, and Authentication*,[4] a fourth factor was added: something you control (cryptography). Verification is when an entity claims an identity, and based on that single profile, the entity can actively be verified to some assurance level – so because there is one entity and one profile, verification is often called one-to-one (1–1) authentication. Identification is when the entity is passively evaluated to determine an identity against a list of profiles to some assurance level – so because there is one entity but many profiles, identification is often called one-to-many (1–N) authentication. An entity's identity (ID) might be a username, account number, or other relatively unique value that allows the entity's profile to be determined.

However, once an entity is authenticated, its privileges can then be evaluated to determine if the entity is authorized to perform a particular function. In some cases, additional authentication is required. For example, some functions might only need single-factor authentication, whereas others might need two-factor authentication. And in some cases, dual control is also needed, where more than one individual must be involved. Table 6.4 provides a summary of authorization, authentication, and additional controls for our ongoing hypothetical ABC Corporation scenario.

Table 6.4 has four columns, the first column lists various PKI-related functions, the second column recognizes who is authorized to perform the function, the third column indicates the authentication level, and the fourth column identifies additional controls.

- The first two functions, (1) generate and (2) recover CA keys, require at least one PKI technician to log in and enter commands and at least three of five custodians to manage the CA keys. In this example, the PKI technician needs two-factor authentication for logging on to the CA system to access the key generation or key recovery services. In addition,

---

TABLE 6.3

Public Key Infrastructure Authentication

Factor	Verification	Identification
1. Knowledge	ID is used to fetch user profile, which provides sufficient information to verify password.	Not applicable.
2. Possession	ID is used to fetch user profile, which provides sufficient data to verify physical token.	Device data are captured to identify mobile communications device.
3. Biometric	ID is used to fetch user profile, which provides biometric template to verify biometric sample.	Biometric sample is used for comparing with multiple biometric templates to identify user profile.
4. Cryptography	ID is used to fetch user profile, which provides sufficient data to verify cryptographic value.	Not applicable.

TABLE 6.4

Public Key Infrastructure Authorization

Function	Authorization	Authentication	Additional Controls
(1) Generate CA keys	PKI technicians and PKI custodians	Two factor	Dual control with split knowledge
(2) Recover CA keys	PKI technicians and PKI custodians	Two factor	Dual control with split knowledge
(3) Generate CA certificates	PKI technicians	Two factor	Dual control
(4) Revoke CA certificates	PKI technicians	Two factor	Dual control
(5) Generate subscriber certificates	PKI technician or PKI application	Single factor	No additional controls
(6) Revoke subscriber certificates	PKI technician or PKI application	Single factor	No additional controls
(7) Generate and post CRL	PKI technician	Single factor	No additional controls
(8) Update OCSP service	PKI technician	Single factor	No additional controls
(9) Install PKI service	PKI administrators	Two factor	Change controls
(10) Update PKI service	PKI administrators	Two factor	Change controls

each of the custodians has a password-activated physical token that contains one of five key shares. The tokens provide the spilt knowledge since nobody has knowledge of the CA private keys, and the three custodians along with the technician provides the dual control.

- The next two functions, (3) generate and (4) revoke CA certificates, require two PKI technicians due to the operational risks. As discussed in Chapter 2, "Cryptography Basics," a man-in-the-middle (MITM) certificate would allow an alternate but seemingly legitimate certificate chain. Purposely or inadvertently revoking a CA certificate would disrupt service. Consequently, both technicians require two-factor authentication, and the presence of both technicians provides dual control.
- The two functions, (5) generate and (6) revoke subscriber certificates, only require one entity, a PKI technician for manual or a PKI application for automated processes. Either PKI entity only requires single-factor authentication due to the relatively low risks.
- The two functions, (7) generate and post CRL and (8) update OCSP server, only require one PKI technician for manual processes. The technician only needs single-factor authentication.
- The next function, (9) install PKI services, only requires one PKI administrator and due to the higher risk of corrupting the PKI service despite the additional change controls two-factor authentication is needed.
- The last function, (10) update PKI services, also only requires one PKI administrator, but due to the higher risk of disrupting any PKI service despite the additional change controls, two-factor authentication is required.

Now that we have reviewed the authentication and authorization controls, let's turn our attention toward accountability controls. Table 6.5 provides a summary of accountability and audit controls for our ongoing hypothetical ABC Corporation scenario.

Table 6.5 has three columns, the first column is a relisting of the various PKI-related functions from Table 6.4, the second column identifies which logs are collected, and the third column indicates when an audit event is performed. Logs are automatically generated by either system components or application services, and audit events are when the functions are observed by an independent observer.

- The first two functions, (1) generate and (2) recover CA keys, include system and application logs, and the event is audited.

TABLE 6.5
Public Key Infrastructure Accountability

Function	Accountability	Audit
(1) Generate CA keys	System and application logs	Audit event
(2) Recover CA keys	System and application logs	Audit event
(3) Generate CA certificates	Application logs	Audit event
(4) Revoke CA certificates	Application logs	Audit event
(5) Generate subscriber certificates	Application logs	No audit event
(6) Revoke subscriber certificates	Application logs	No audit event
(7) Generate and post CRL	Application logs	Audit event
(8) Update OCSP service	Application logs	Audit event
(9) Install PKI service	System logs	No audit event
(10) Update PKI service	System logs	No audit event

- The functions (3) generate CA certificates, (4) revoke CA certificates, (7) generate and post CRL, and (8) update OCSP services, only require application logs, and the events are audited.
- The functions (5) generate and (6) revoke subscriber certificates include application logs, but the events do not require a live audit.
- The functions (9) install and (10) update PKI services only have system logs, and the events do not require a live audit.

System logs are generated by either the platform operating system (OS), a system component that might have been bundled by the OS provider, or an add-on service component as part of a common server or workstation build provided by the information technology (IT). The system logs are typically captured in a local circular file that eventually gets overwritten so the logs are copied from the servers and captured within a log management system (LMS). For the online PKI systems, the logs are pushed to the LMS hourly and for the offline root CA systems, the logs are manually pulled and uploaded to the LMS per event.

Application logs are generated by the various PKI service components, which are also captured in a local circular file that sooner or later gets overwritten. For the online PKI systems, the logs are pushed in real time to the LMS, and for the offline root CA systems, the logs are manually pulled along with the system logs and uploaded to the LMS per event.

Audit events consist of an independent observer who confirms the documented procedures are properly followed. To maintain independence, the observer cannot be anyone reporting to Roger's (PKI) group. But since a knowledgeable individual is needed, typically someone from Quincy's (CISO) group performs the live audit. Each participant – PKI technician, custodian, or administrator – initials each step as it is completed, and on conclusion, the auditor and participants sign the completed procedures. Table 6.6 provides a simplistic three-page example of the initialed and signed procedures.

Live audits provide evidence that procedures exist, they are documented and that means they are repeatable, and ultimately they are followed. Unlike the simple example shown in Table 6.6, actual procedures are more detailed and include error conditions and recovery procedures. If the procedures are incomplete, inaccurate, or are not followed, the live audit fails. On the other hand, if the procedures do exist, are documented, and are followed successfully, this indicates an adequate set of controls.

- Page 1: PKI Participants provide a list of roles and individuals. The blank procedures list the roles, and the specific names are added at the time of the PKI event.

TABLE 6.6
Key Generation Procedures

PKI Participants List

Technician	Keith L. Massey	KLM
Custodian #1	Lisa S. Stevens	LLS
Custodian #2	Joe T. Waylon	JTW
Custodian #3	Thom C. Rice	TCR
Custodian #4	Sam B. Adams	SBA
Custodian #5	Nancy R. Lee	NRL
Auditor	Cathy C. Doyle	CCD

Page 1

Key Generation Procedures

Step 1: Log-on	**KLM**
Step 2: Generate keys	**KLM**
Step 3a: Set up token #1	**LLM**
Step 3a: Set up token #2	**JTW**
Step 3a: Set up token #3	**TCR**
Step 3a: Set up token #4	**SBA**
Step 3a: Set up token #5	**CCD**
Step 4: Log-off	**KLM**

Page 2

Procedures Sign-Off Sheet

Keith L. Massey	Keith Massey
Lisa S. Stevens	Lisa Stevens
Joe T. Waylon	Joe Waylon
Thom C. Rice	Thom Rice
Sam B. Adams	Sam Adams
Nancy R. Lee	Nancy Lee

Page 3

- Page 2: Key Generation Procedures provide a list of steps. The blank procedures list the steps, and as each step is executed, the participant initials the page. The auditor observes each step and the initialization.
- Page 3: Sign-Off Sheet provides the list of participants. The names from the first page are added to the blank procedures, and on completion, each participant signs the last page.

The success or failure of live audits is dutifully reported by Quincy's (CISO) group to Wayne's (audit) group. However, as noted in Section 6.1, "Physical Security," Wayne (audit) is responsible for bringing issues directly to the Board of Directors (BoD), but Wayne reports to Zane who can censor the audit reports, and Wayne is a peer to Tony who might not share his information except with Zane.

SPECIAL NOTE 6-5 AUDIT INDEPENDENCE

Auditors, both internal and external, should report directly to the Board of Directors to maintain independence and separation of duties.

In the previous section, we discussed physical security considerations that included three basic rings of defense: (1) campus perimeter, (2) building and lobby, and (3) PKI rooms and racks. In this section, we discussed logical security considerations that included four areas: (1) separation of duties, (2) authentication, (3) authorization, and (4) accountability. In the next section, we consider the importance of audit logs for both physical and logical security controls and their relationship to audit events.

6.3 AUDIT LOGS

Audit logs can originate from a variety of automated sources, including system logs and application logs as discussed in Section 6.2, "Logical Security." Automated system and application logs can also originate from access controls as discussed in Section 6.1, "Physical Security." Manual sources include sign-in sheets and signed audit procedures. Other security-related information sources might be incorporated into the audit process depending on its need. For example, phone records might be examined for inbound or outbound calls, or video recordings might be reviewed for individuals entering or departing building areas.

Physical security audit logs include the following log sources:

- Automated access control logs provide a history of employee traffic. The badge-activated front gate records which employees come onto the campus. The badge-activated lobby doors record which employees enter the buildings during after-hours. The badge-activated door records which employees enter the PKI room.
- Manual sign-in sheets provide a history of visitor traffic. The sign-in sheet at the front gate records which visitors come onto the campus. The sign-in sheet at the lobby desks records which visitors enter the building.

Logical security audit logs include the following log sources:

- Automated access control logs provide a history of employee and client access. Remote VPN access records which employees and clients access the network. Local network access records which employees access the network. Network monitoring records which applications employees and clients use for various services.
- Automated application logs provide a history of employee and client actions. Access to some applications records actions taken by employees and clients. Commands executed by PKI technicians or PKI administrators are recorded, as are various requests submitted by subscribers to generate or revoke certificates.
- Manual audit procedures provide a history of employee processes. As discussed for the example shown in Table 6.6, the PKI participants and their role are recorded as part of the procedures. Thus, the participants are known to be present in the PKI room during any event.

Other security information might include the following:

- Phone records provide a history of incoming and outgoing calls, including duration.
- E-mails provide a history of inbound and outbound electronic communications.
- Chat connections provide a history of internal electronic communications.
- Wireless access points provide a history of device access.
- Guard reports provide a history of incidents.

According to the Basic Accounting Principles and Guidelines,[5] the Matching Principle requires that expenses be matched with revenues. This provides reconciliation between incoming and outgoing amounts. Audit logs provide an analogous correlation. For every action, there should be at least one corresponding result in an audit log. The actions can be reconciled with the results in the audit logs.

For example, an employee who participates in a key generation ceremony should be traceable in a series of audit logs.

1. The employee's badge should have been registered at the front gate, depending on who was driving the vehicle.
2. The employee's badge should have been registered at the lobby door, assuming no one was tailgating through the door.
3. The employee's badge might be registered at the PKI room door, depending on who opened the door.
4. The employee's ID might be registered by the PKI application, depending on the individual's role and responsibility for the key generation ceremony.
5. The employee's initials and signature should be captured in the key generation procedures.

An auditor can reconcile the key generation procedures against the PKI application logs, the PKI room physical access logs, the lobby door access logs, and the front gate access logs. If the audit logs are inconsistent or irregularities are discovered, then many scenarios are possible – including logs being lost, overwritten, or tampered. As discussed earlier in Section 6.2, "Logical Security," the procedures need to be complete, accurate, and followed correctly. As an example, if the wrong date is captured on the procedures, then the corresponding logs would likely not reconcile, giving a false negative. On the other hand, if logs are unavailable and the procedures are assumed to be valid, this might give a false positive.

While discrepancies in logs might seem trivial, small irregularities can indicate big things. For example, in 1986, a former astronomy professor at Berkley was asked to reconcile a 75¢ error between two computer usage accounting systems. Clifford Stoll[6] uncovered a Soviet spy ring working with a group of German hackers who were using the university servers to attack U.S. government systems. Eventually, the search gained the attention of the Central Intelligence Agency (CIA) and ultimately trapped an international spy ring fueled by cash, cocaine, and the Russian Komitet Gosudarstvennoy Bezopasnosti (KGB). The 75¢ discrepancy was due to the hackers altering some of the accounting records and corresponding audit logs. The lesson here is that the integrity and authenticity of the audit logs need to be maintained over their lifetime, as shown in Figure 6.9.

Figure 6.9 depicts five stages of log management: generation, collection, retention, archive, and eventually termination. Analysis is shown as an intermittent stage that might occur during the log retention or log archive stages.

- **Log generation** occurs at the event source, including badge readers, remote access, network log-on, system log-on, application log-on, and application logs. Since logs originate at numerous sources, an accurate time source is needed to synchronize events across the various platforms. Each log source needs to provide data integrity controls on the local system to detect (1) unauthorized modification or substitution of an individual log record and (2) addition or deletion of log records within the whole log file.
- **Log collection** occurs when logs are either pushed or pulled from their generation source to one or more log management systems. Some sources might contain a log

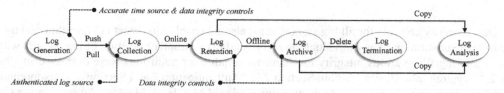

FIGURE 6.9   Log management lifecycle.

agent that periodically pushes individual logs or whole log files to a collection point. Other sources might post logs to files that are periodically pulled by the log manager. The collection points need to authenticate the generation sources to prevent unauthorized sources.

- **Log retention** occurs when logs are kept for short-term storage within an online environment such that logs can be reviewed or analyzed for predefined or ad hoc reporting. The retention period will vary depending on industry regulations, laws, or contractual requirements. For example, PCI DSS[7] Requirement 10: Track and monitor all access to network resources and cardholder data specifies in 10.7 a minimum of three months immediately available for analysis. The log retention environment needs to provide data integrity controls to detect (1) unauthorized modification or substitution of an individual log record and (2) addition or deletion of log records within the whole log file.

- **Log archive** occurs when logs are kept for long-term storage within an offline environment such that logs might be retrieved for later analysis. The archive period will vary depending on industry regulations, laws, or contractual requirements. For example, PCI DSS[8] Requirement 10: Track and monitor all access to network resources and cardholder data specifies in 10.7 a log storage for at least one year. The log archive environment needs to provide data integrity controls to detect (1) unauthorized modification or substitution of an individual log record and (2) addition or deletion of log records within the whole log file.

- **Log termination** occurs when archived logs are permanently deleted. Once deleted, the log details are no longer available for analysis, only summary information remains, often called metadata. The metadata might be converted into another type of log record that is retained or archived. Eventually, the log information ages until such time that the data are outdated and no longer of value.

- **Log analysis** is an intermediate state that occurs when logs are examined for specific log records or vulnerability patterns. Analysis can occur for retained logs, archived logs, or both. The logs might be processed within the short-term or long-term storage systems or copied to a third system dedicated to log analysis.

Access controls for all log systems must be enabled to prevent unauthorized modification or substitution of log records and log files. Individuals and applications must be authenticated and authorized before access to log systems is allowed. Furthermore, logs might contain confidential information such as Internet Protocol (IP) addresses, server names, account numbers, or other individual or system identifiers. If sensitive data are not filtered at the log source, then its transmission during collection needs to be considered. For example, cross-border transmission is affected by international laws. If sensitive data are not filtered within log retention, then data encryption or other protection methods need to be considered.

SPECIAL NOTE 6-6 LOG PROTECTION

Sensitive information should be filtered at the source during log generation.

Data integrity controls for all log storage must also be enabled to detect (1) unauthorized modification or substitution of an individual log record and (2) addition or deletion of log records within the whole log file. Various integrity mechanisms suitable for audit logs were discussed in Chapter 2, "Cryptography Basics," within Section 2.2, "Authentication," and Section 2.3, "Nonrepudiation." Methods include Message Authentication Code (MAC), Hash Message Authentication Code (HMAC), digital signature, and Time Stamp Token (TST).

In the first two sections, we discussed physical and logical security. Physical security considerations included three basic rings of defense: (1) campus perimeter, (2) building and lobby, and (3) PKI rooms and racks. Logical security considerations included (1) separation of duties, (2) authentication, (3) authorization, and (4) accountability. In this section, we discussed audit logs and the log management lifecycle. In the next section, we consider device and key management issues when employing cryptographic modules.

6.4 CRYPTOGRAPHIC MODULES

We introduced cryptographic modules in Chapter 2, "Cryptography Basics," provided definitions, identified ANSI and ISO standards, and discussed the NIST Cryptographic Module Validation Program (CMVP), along with the FIPS 140–2 and FIPS 140–3 security requirements. Cryptographic modules are developed by vendors from many countries, including Australia, Canada, Finland, France, Germany, Israel, Singapore, the United Kingdom, and the United States. Not all countries explicitly use NIST evaluations but prefer to use protection profiles per ISO/IEC 15408 and rely on Common Criteria–accredited laboratories. However, many protection profiles, although written in Common Criteria language, refer to NIST for its security requirements. Ironically, NIST refers to Common Criteria Evaluation Assurance Levels (EAL) for operating environments.

Like any other standard, the Security Requirements for Cryptographic Modules continue to evolve. The first version FIPS 140–1 was published in 1994, and its successor FIPS 140–2 was published in 2001. The latest version FIPS 140–3[9] was published in 2019 with references to ISO/IEC 19790 and ISO/IEC 24759 standards. Previously, FIPS 140–2 and its Derived Test Requirements (DTR) were submitted to Joint Technical Committee One (JTC1) Subcommittee 27 and the two international standards were developed, with updates since these publications.

- ISO/IEC 19790:2012 Information Technology – Security Techniques – Security Requirements for Cryptographic Modules[10]
- ISO/IEC 24759:2014 Information Technology – Security Techniques – Test Requirements for Cryptographic Modules[11]

The primary purpose of cryptographic modules is to provide an application programming interface (API) for applications to access various cryptographic functions. The concept of a cryptographic function having two basic inputs, parameters and a cryptographic key, and single output, the results, was introduced in Chapter 2, "Cryptography Basics." Figure 6.10 shows the API interface for a cryptographic software module. The module is depicted as a dotted line box indicating a software boundary. The input parameters include the function call, in this scenario Function 1, and the data to be affected. The corresponding key, shown as the Red Key, is the other input to the API. The API passes the inputs to the function that executes its programmed algorithm and returns the output results. The API then returns the results to the calling application. The overall security controls for the Red Key are minimal, it might be stored in a system file or an application

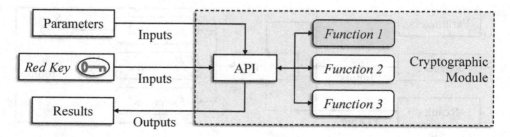

FIGURE 6.10 General purpose crypto module.

configuration file, and access controls might limit who or what can read or replace the key, but ultimately the key is vulnerable.

The secondary purpose for cryptographic hardware modules addresses the security controls over the cryptographic key. For cryptographic hardware modules, the cryptographic functions reside within the security boundary of the module, and since cryptographic functions require access to the associated cryptographic keys, the module needs access to the keys. Hardware security modules (HSM) are designed to prevent cryptographic keys from being exposed outside the module as cleartext. We now extend the concept to an API residing within an HSM shown in Figure 6.11. The solid box indicates that the cryptographic module is a hardware security module (HSM) with a well-defined security boundary.

In the first HSM example shown in Figure 6.11, the two API inputs are the parameters and the name of the cryptographic key, in this scenario Red Key. The parameters include which function to perform, in this scenario Function 1, and the data to be affected. The Red Key resides within the HSM, so Function 1 can process the input parameters. The output results are returned to the calling application through the API. In this scenario, the Red Key was generated inside the HSM and never leaves the HSM security boundary. An alternate key management scenario is shown in Figure 6.12.

In the second HSM example shown in Figure 6.12, the two API inputs are the parameters and the encrypted key; in this scenario, the *Red Key* is encrypted by the *Black Key*, a key encryption key (KEK). The parameters are the same as the first scenario. However, for this scenario, the *Black Key* resides within the HSM, and the application passes the encrypted *Red Key* to the API. The *Black Key* is a special KEK, commonly called a master file key (MFK), which is used to encrypt many other keys. Each application typically has its own keys, but all of which are stored outside the HSM encrypted by the MFK. The HSM uses the *Black Key* to decrypt the *Red Key*, which is then used by *Function 1* on the input data.

The tertiary purpose for using an HSM is its performance capability for cryptographic algorithms; however, this is not a be-all and end-all situation. Asymmetric cryptography requires costly mathematical functions such as exponentiation and modular arithmetic. Most general computers cannot perform complex mathematics efficiently such that asymmetric cryptography is better handled by an HSM. However, most symmetric cryptographic algorithms employ far similar functions such that general computers have near-performance equivalence to an HSM. The disadvantage of an HSM is that the data must be transferred from the calling application to the function within the cryptographic boundary. The data transfer rate is typically the limiting factor for symmetric cryptography. Small data sizes are easier to transfer and so are ideal for HSM use, such as PIN encryption, but large data sizes tend to be problematic, such as file encryption.

Some vendors use a hybrid approach for some solutions such as Transport Layer Security (TLS). The asymmetric private key is retained in the HSM, but during the TLS handshake, the shared secret, which is used to derive the various symmetric keys, is returned to the application for symmetric processing. The argument is that the application server has access to the decrypted data anyway,

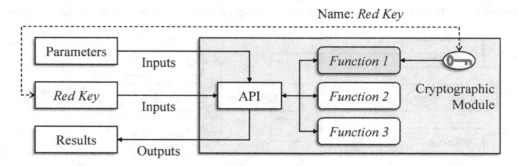

FIGURE 6.11   Hardware security module: Red Key.

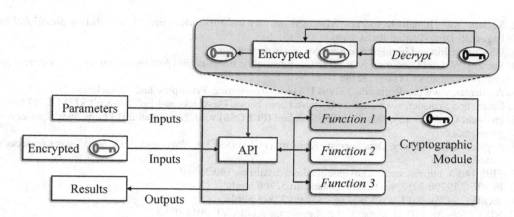

FIGURE 6.12   Hardware security module: Black Key (MFK).

so exposing the session keys within the server is an equivalent risk. However, while this claim might be valid for confidentiality, the same argument does not necessarily hold for integrity, as a dishonest application could alter the decrypted data and replace the legitimate hash with an illegitimate hash, for perpetrating fraud.

Other vendors might use an HSM in an inappropriate manner. For example, if keys are encrypted as data objects using a data encryption key, then the HSM unknowingly will return a decrypted key, which is a very poor key management practice. As described for Figure 6.12, the master file key is a key encryption key (KEK) that the HSM uses to decrypt keys within its security boundary. The MFK scheme uses the Black Key to protect the Red Key such that only the encrypted Red Key is stored outside the HSM as ciphertext, and the Black Key only resides inside the HSM and never appears outside the HSM as cleartext.

Regarding cryptographic models in general, certification provides assurance that the cryptographic algorithms are correctly implemented and produce accurate results. However, there are other considerations that might affect overall performance. For example, free open software is available but sometimes has undocumented or unresolved bugs. Furthermore, buggy software or firmware used within an HSM can affect reliability. Memory leaks, buffer overflows, and similar coding errors can cause cryptographic modules to fail or become unresponsive. The NIST validation programs for cryptographic algorithms (CAVP) and cryptographic modules (CMVP) are useful, but they do not check for general programming problems. For example, in April 2014, NIST released CVE-2014–0160[12] and CERT released VU#720951[13] identifying the HeartBleed bug. In a nutshell, up to 64k of residual buffer information can be disclosed due to a flaw in the OpenSSL TLS and DTLS protocols.

In general, when implementing cryptographic solutions, an organization needs to be aware of what cryptographic products it is considering. However, not every HSM supports all algorithms, functions, and protocols so the right HSM must be used for the right job. The HSM vendor can assist with aligning solutions with business and security requirements. The specifics of how the cryptographic module handles keys will vary between products so each implementation needs to be designed, configured, and tested. As discussed in Chapter 4, "PKI Management and Security," the appropriate policy, practices, and procedures are also needed.

NOTES

1. *VASCO Announces Bankruptcy Filing* by DigiNotar, B.V., September 20, 2011, www.vasco.com/company/ about_vasco/press_room/news_archive/2011/news_vasco_announces_bankruptcy_filing_by_diginotar_ bv.aspx (accessed October 1, 2015).

2. Society for Human Resources Management, www.shrm.org/ResourcesAndTools/hr-topics/global-hr/Pages/US-Drug-Testing-Rules.aspx
3. US Citizenship and Immigration Services, www.uscis.gov/i-9
4. Security Without Obscurity: A Guide to Confidentiality, Integrity, and Authentication, http://www.crcpress.com/product/isbn/9781466592148
5. Academia, www.academia.edu/37796431/Basic_Accounting_Principles_and_Guidelines
6. Simon and Schuster, www.simonandschuster.com/books/The-Cuckoos-Egg/Cliff-Stoll/9781416507789
7. Payment Card Industry, Data Security Standard (PCI DSS) v3.0, November 2013 https://www.pcisecurit-ystandards.org/
8. Payment Card Industry, Data Security Standard (PCI DSS) v3.0, November 2013, https://www.pcisecurit-ystandards.org/.
9. FIPS 140-3, https://csrc.nist.gov/publications/detail/fips/140/3/final
10. ISO/IEC 19790:2012, www.iso.org/standard/52906.html
11. ISO/IEC 24759:2017, www.iso.org/standard/72515.html
12. NIST CVE-2014-0160, https://nvd.nist.gov/vuln/detail/CVE-2014-0160
13. CERT VU#720951, www.kb.cert.org/vuls/id/720951/

7 Operational Considerations

This chapter addresses operational issues relating to public key infrastructure (PKI) architectures, business continuity, disaster recovery, and third-party service providers. The ability to quickly stand up a new certificate authority (CA) or decommission a CA within an existing hierarchy is as important as building a whole new CA hierarchy. Maintaining the existing CA infrastructure can also be a challenge. In the previous chapters, we discussed various topics that might enhance or influence PKI operations:

- Chapter 1, "Introduction," presented the convergence of legal matters, business rules, information technology (IT), and cryptography within PKI operations and the importance of standards. All four areas need representation and balanced participation.
- Chapter 2, "Cryptography Basics," talked about the problems of allowing self-signed certificates, the importance of key management, and the significance of cryptographic hardware modules. Bad key management practices can disrupt operations.
- Chapter 3, "PKI Building Blocks," reviewed various standards, security protocols, and architectural components. Standards define minimal security requirements, industry specifications define protocols, and architectures need interoperability.
- Chapter 4, "PKI Management and Security," provided sample controls for publication and document retention, authentication, certificate management, physical and logical security, audit, and business and legal issues. Good policy and practices together with well-documented procedures help keep consistent operations.
- Chapter 5, "PKI Roles and Responsibilities," looked at the elements of the CA, the registration authority (RA), and the policy authority (PA). Well-defined roles with separation of duties also help keep consistent operations.
- Chapter 6, "Security Considerations," examined physical, logical, audit, and cryptographic module issues. Bad security practices can also disrupt operations.

For the purposes of this chapter, the operational considerations are based on ABC Corporation's internal CA operations. The CA hierarchy discussions are first represented as certificate chains including Transport Layer Security (TLS) certificates for applications, e-mail certificates for individuals, and virtual private network (VPN) certificates for remote access by employees and contractors. The end-entity certificates are denoted in gray, the associated CA certificate chains are shown in white, and the root CA-A certificate is common to each chain.

Figure 7.1 shows the CA hierarchy from Chapter 4, "PKI Management and Security," consisting of the root CA certificate, an intermediate CA certificate, and the application certificate. Looking left-to-right, the root CA-A public key certificate is used to verify both its own certificate and the

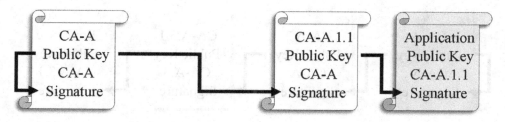

FIGURE 7.1 Transport Layer Security (TLS) certificate chain.

DOI: 10.1201/9781003425298-7

issuing CA-A.1.1 certificate. The issuing CA-A.1.1 public key certificate is used to verify the Application TLS certificate.

Figure 7.2 shows the CA hierarchy from Chapter 4, "PKI Management and Security," consisting of the root CA certificate, an e-mail intermediate CA certificate, the e-mail signature intermediate CA certificate, and the individual's e-mail certificate. Looking left-to-right, the root CA-A public key certificate is used to verify both its own certificate and the issuing CA-A.2 certificate. The intermediate CA-A.2 public key certificate is used to verify the issuing CA-A.2.1 certificate, and the issuing CA-A.2.1 public key certificate is used to verify the individual's certificate for signing e-mails.

Figure 7.3 shows the CA hierarchy from Chapter 4 consisting of the root CA certificate, an e-mail intermediate CA certificate, the e-mail encryption intermediate CA certificate, and the individual's e-mail certificate. Looking left-to-right, the root CA-A public key certificate is used to verify both its own certificate and the issuing CA-A.2 certificate. The intermediate CA-A.2 public key certificate is used to verify the issuing CA-A.2.2 certificate, and the issuing CA-A.2.2 public key certificate is used to verify the individual's certificate for encrypting e-mails.

Figure 7.4 shows the CA hierarchy from Chapter 4 consisting of the root CA certificate, a VPN intermediate CA certificate, the VPN employee CA certificate, and the employee's VPN certificate. Looking left-to-right, the root CA-A public key certificate is used to verify both its own certificate and the issuing CA-A.3 certificate. The intermediate CA-A.3 public key certificate is used to verify

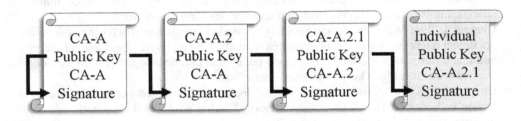

FIGURE 7.2 E-mail signature certificate chain.

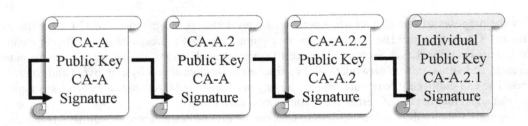

FIGURE 7.3 E-mail encryption certificate chain.

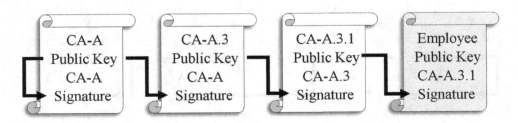

FIGURE 7.4 Virtual Private Network (VPN) employee certificate chain.

the issuing CA-A.3.1 certificate, and the issuing CA-A.3.1 public key certificate is used to verify the employee VPN certificate.

Figure 7.5 shows the CA hierarchy from Chapter 4 consisting of the root CA certificate, a VPN intermediate CA certificate, the VPN contractor CA certificate, and the contractor's VPN certificate. Looking left-to-right, the root CA-A public key certificate is used to verify both its own certificate and the issuing CA-A.3 certificate. The intermediate CA-A.3 public key certificate is used to verify the issuing CA-A.3.2 certificate, and the issuing CA-A.3.2 public key certificate is used to verify the contractor VPN certificate.

In general, the entire CA architecture is not readily apparent when only looking at individual certificate chains. Typically, any CA hierarchy is based on an initial design, but often many have evolved over time to support different certificate types. New applications or infrastructures often require new certificates, or older technologies are decommissioned, and the existing certificates are no longer needed. However, there is more than one way to design and operate a CA hierarchy, so in the next section, we discuss the benefits and constraints for different CA hierarchies.

7.1 CA ARCHITECTURES

A root CA is at the top of a PKI system and can have a self-signed CA certificate or could be signed by another trusted commercial certification authority. Larger organizations' Root CA generally have multiple levels of subordinate or intermediate CA to which the root CA has issued specialized CA certificates. These intermediate or subordinate CA then issues the subscriber certificates that are validated by relying parties all the way up to the root CA. We begin our discussion on CA hierarchies with a single CA. A single CA is the most basic of the PKI architectures. A small organization might build a PKI with just a single CA to provide for all of the certificates the organization needs as shown in Figure 7.6.

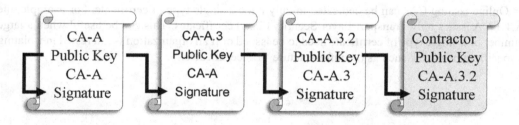

FIGURE 7.5 Virtual Private Network (VPN) contractor certificate chain.

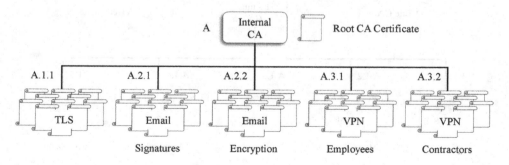

FIGURE 7.6 Single certificate authority hierarchy structure.

In a single CA hierarchy, all subscriber certificates will be issued by the root CA. In a single CA architecture, all certificate chains will be two certificates deep in length. The root certificate of the root CA will be the start of the chain, and the chain will end at the subscriber certificate. This most basic of configurations is presently in use in many small to medium enterprises and functions surprisingly well as long as nothing goes wrong. In the event of a compromise of the single root CA, the entire structure and all of its issued certificates must be revoked and a new CA structure put in place before any new subscriber certificates can be issued. Replacement of a whole PKI is a major undertaking for any-sized organization. A better design for a small company than the single CA is adding an offline root CA to the hierarchy so that the company's root CA is protected from any network-based attack. The root CA issues a single CA certificate to the online issuing CA, which is then able to issue all of the end-entity certificates that the company needs. This improved design for a small organization is shown in Figure 7.7.

The idea of an offline CA is to store the CA's key material, server, and all backups disconnected from the public Internet and the company's private network, so any network-based attacks cannot be launched against the CA. The offline location of the CA material must be stored in secure locations with tightly controlled and very limited access. Chapter 4, "PKI Management and Security," discusses the RFC 3647 specification relative to offline Cas. Chapter 5, "PKI Roles and Responsibilities," discusses the controls that should be in place for offline CAs. Chapter 6 discusses physical security relevant to offline CAs.

When a CA is operated in an offline mode, provisions for transporting certificates and certificate revocation lists (CRLs) issued by the offline CA to the online CAs must be made. Removable media such as USB drives, CDs, or DVDs can be used with the proper controls in place to transport certificates and CRLs issued by offline CAs to the needed locations online.

Many small to medium organizations will find that two-tier (two-level) hierarchies are sufficient for their needs. Larger organizations with more complex requirements for issuing certificates may find that two tiers are insufficient, and more specialized CAs are required. For these types of PKIs in a hierarchical CA structure, two or more CAs are organized in a structure with a single root CA with one or more subordinate CAs as shown in Figure 7.8.

Online issuing CAs can be dedicated to only issue a single type of certificate. For example, the A.1.1 CA issues only Transport Layer Security (TLS) certificates. This can be useful when a large number of a single type of certificate need to be issued or if an organization is interested in isolating a specific type of risk such as the infrastructure TLS certificates.

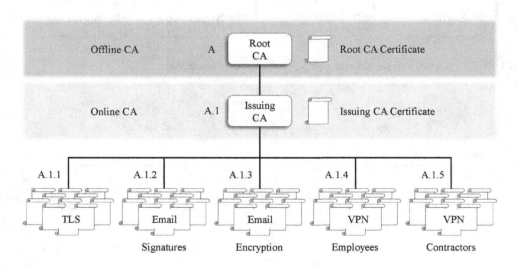

FIGURE 7.7   Single offline root and single online certificate authority hierarchy.

Further isolation can be obtained by creating two independent PKI hierarchies. For example, Figure 7.8 also shows the option of building a PKI hierarchy for issuing internal certificates that will only be recognized within the organization. Another PKI hierarchy can be built or purchased from a commercial CA to be used by customers coming in from an unsecured network like the Internet. The two different root Cas will not overlap and will separate out the risks associated with issuing and relying upon certificates for different internal and external purposes.

When two organizations need to communicate but have separate PKI hierarchies, there are various ways to interoperate. Cross-certification allows two organizations to establish a trust relationship between their PKI hierarchies. There are several different ways that organizations can cross-certify their PKI hierarchies. For example, Figure 7.9 shows cross-certification between two root CAs.

A cross-certificate is a special-purpose certificate that is issued by one peer CA to another peer CA, in this example between Company A root CA and Company B root CA. So, a cross-certificate is a certificate that contains the public key of a CA that has been digitally signed by another CA. Cross-certification can be bidirectional or unidirectional. Bidirectional cross-certification occurs between peer CAs. Unidirectional cross-certification typically occurs in a hierarchical trust model where superior CAs issue cross-certificates to subordinate CAs in a separate PKI, but the reverse is not true.

Alternatively, the cross-certification may take place between subordinate CAs, rather than between root CAs as shown in Figure 7.10. The actual design may vary depending on specific organizational or business requirements. For example, consider the cross-certification of VPN issuing subordinate CAs.

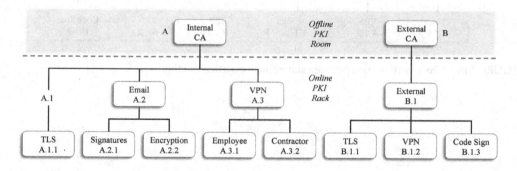

FIGURE 7.8 Multitiered hierarchical public key infrastructure structure.

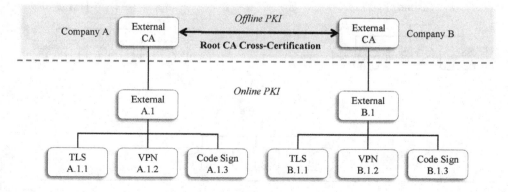

FIGURE 7.9 Cross-certification of public key infrastructure structures.

Another type of cross-certification is a bridge. A bridge CA takes the idea of cross-certification between two organizations and extends the model to allow multiple organizations to configure trust between their CA hierarchies. In a bridge CA, one CA becomes the hub or center bridge for trust between the other CA hierarchies. The other CAs are essentially the spokes of a theoretical wheel. Figure 7.11 shows a bridge CA that links three separate CA hierarchies.

Once the best-fit PKI hierarchy has been determined, whether it's a single CA, single offline/online CA, multitiered CA, cross-certified CA, or bridged CA, the operational cycles for each CA and validity periods for all CA certificates need to be planned.

If we look at the most complex model presented, a three-tier hierarchy as presented in Figure 7.8, this will meet most large organizations' needs in terms of both security and scalability. In building the lifetime of the CA certificates, we need to begin with the end-entity certificates and their lifetime. One-year and two-year certificates are pretty common from a compliance and manageability standpoint. However, the CA Browser Forum has changed its server certificate

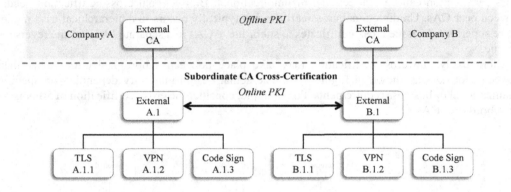

FIGURE 7.10   Cross-certification between subordinate certificate authorities.

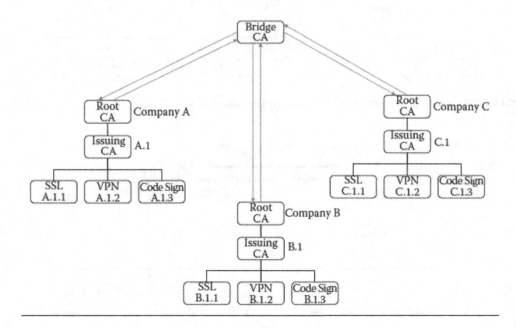

FIGURE 7.11   A bridge certificate authority hierarchy.

validity rules since the first edition of this PKI book. See Table 7.1 CA Browser Evolving Rules from 2015 through 2020.

The CA Browser Forum Business Requirements, Version 1.8.4 dated April 2022 includes the following scope statement and caveats:

> *These Requirements only address Certificates intended to be used for authenticating servers accessible through the Internet. Similar requirements for code signing, S/MIME, time-stamping, VoIP, IM, Web services, etc. may be covered in future versions.*
>
> *These Requirements do not address the issuance, or management of Certificates by enterprises that operate their own Public Key Infrastructure for internal purposes only, and for which the Root Certificate is not distributed by any Application Software Supplier.*

Much longer than two years and the system administrators will probably have moved on, and the certificates may be forgotten and expire unexpectedly causing an outage. You may have a need for shorter-duration certificates for a highly secure application like an Online Certificate Status Protocol (OCSP) responder, but the shorter-lived certificates can be issued from a CA within the overall hierarchy as presented in Figure 7.12.

When calculating the CA certificate lifetimes, you need to start with the lifetime of your certificates that you want to issue, most likely either one or two years. You will then want to have your issuing CA be valid for at least two or two and a half times the lifetime of your certificates. Therefore, if you are going to be issuing two-year certificates, a five-year lifetime for the issuing CA certificate makes sense. Keep in mind that an issuing CA cannot issue certificates that are valid for longer than its own lifetime. So, the issuing CA then has a five-year life span based on two and a half times the two-year certificate life span, and the intermediate CA has a ten-year life span based on two times the five-year issuing CA certificate life span. And finally, the root CA life span would be 20 years based on two times the intermediate CA life span. You can see that if you were only implementing a two-tier hierarchy, then you could use the same five-year life span for the issuing CA, but the root CA would only be ten years in duration.

TABLE 7.1

CA Browser Evolving Rules

Change Date	CA Browser Forum Business Requirements
2015-04-01	CAs SHALL NOT issue certificates with validity periods longer than 39 months, except under certain circumstances.
2016-06-30	CAs MUST NOT issue Subscriber Certificates with validity periods longer than 39 months, regardless of circumstance.
2018-03-01	Certificates issued MUST have a Validity Period no greater than 825 days and re-use of validation information limited to 825 days.
2020-09-01	Certificates issued SHOULD NOT have a Validity Period greater than 397 days and MUST NOT have a Validity Period greater than 398 days.

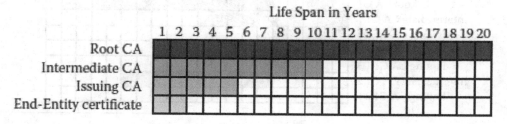

FIGURE 7.12   Three-tier certificate authority hierarchy life span.

To track the lifecycle of each of the different CAs within our three-tier hierarchy, we can assign them a numbering scheme that has the generation (G) and the first number being the instance of the root CA (G1) with the instance of the intermediate CA as the second digit (G1.1) and the issuing CA as the third digit (G1.1.1). With this hierarchy, three years into the issuing CA's lifetime, it will not be able to issue two-year end-entity certificates anymore, as you cannot issue an end-entity certificate that has a longer life span than the issuing CA. To plan for this eventuality, you need to bring on the next generation of the issuing CA G1.1.2 as indicated in Figure 7.13. In planning for the next generation of the issuing CA G1.1.2, it is important to plan to generate the new key pair for the new issuing CA G1.1.2 and have the intermediate CA G1.1 sign the issuing CA G1.1.2 certificate well in advance of when you plan on using it to issue end-entity certificates. Figure 7.13 shows the new issuing CA G1.1.2 coming online one year before the plan to issue end-entity certificates from the CA to provide for distribution of the new CA certificate to all of the endpoints that require its use.

SPECIAL NOTE 7-1 RUSHING CA CERTIFICATES

Plan on sufficient time to push new CA certificates out into your infrastructure and user base. Do not attempt to generate a new CA certificate, and plan to start using it to issue end-entity certificates on the same weekend! Last-minute changes can have disastrous results.

The issuing CA G1.1.2 certificate is pushed out to the PKI infrastructure in year 3 and begins issuing end-entity certificates in year 4 when the issuing CA G1.1.1 can no longer issue two-year certificates. Similarly in year 5, a new issuing CA G1.1.3 certificate is created and pushed out to the PKI. In year 6, a new intermediate CA G1.2 is created and pushed out for being able to continue to issue five-year issuing CA certificates. Note that issuing CA G1.2.1 is issued from intermediate CA G1.2 and not from the intermediate CA G1.1.

Planning for managing the lifecycle of all of the CAs within your PKI will require a solid plan upfront and regular yearly review to make sure that all of the end-entity certificates are being adequately supplied and that you allow time for each new CA certificate to be propagated throughout your PKI before subscribers need to validate certificates in the new CA chain.

In the past several years, a number of commercial CAs have come under attack, and there have been several very-high-profile breaches of commercial CA operations. The intermediary CA's infrastructure was not up to the task, leading to problems for their partners and, above all, for their customers. In one notorious incident, the CA itself was completely compromised, causing major browsers to revoke that CA's roots to render all certificates issued by that CA invalid and ultimately causing that CA to go out of business.

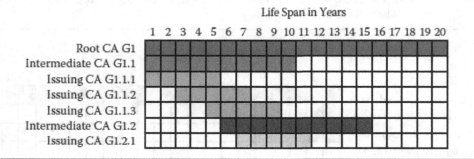

FIGURE 7.13 Multigenerational certificate authority hierarchy.

SPECIAL NOTE 7-2 TARGETING PKI

CAs and RAs have become targets for cyberattacks and cybercrime.

Several CAs have had to stop issuing certificates because their systems were successfully breached. CA-issued certificates could be blacklisted by browser manufacturers if the CA has been breached or if the CA does not offer strong enough encryption in its certificates. When evaluating a CA, it is worth considering the vendor's history of trust and security.[1]

Comodo was one of the first commercial CAs to suffer such a successful cyberattack. Comodo revealed that one of their registration authorities had been compromised by a March 15, 2011, attack. The attack resulted in the compromise of a username and a password of a Comodo Trusted Partner in southern Europe. At the time, Comodo did not require two or more factors in the authentication of the RA. The RA account was then fraudulently used to issue nine digital certificates across seven different domains, including login.yahoo.com, mail.google.com, login.skype.com, and addons.mozilla.org. All of these certificates were revoked immediately upon discovery but could have been used for phishing sites, malware delivery, or sending fraudulent e-mails before they were discovered. This event led to a significant reputation loss for Comodo in the commercial CA world.

In August of the same year, another commercial CA was successfully compromised by a cyberattack: the Dutch Certification Authority DigiNotar, owned by VASCO Data Security International. On September 3, 2011, after it was determined that a security breach had resulted in the fraudulent issuance of certificates, the Dutch government took over the operational management of DigiNotar's systems.

A few weeks later, the company was declared bankrupt and closed. Major browser manufacturers moved DigiNotar's root CA certificates into the untrusted root CA stores, and all of DigiNotar's customers had to go elsewhere to replace all of the certificates that DigiNotar issued. With commercial CAs coming under increasing attacks, it will not be long before corporate CAs receive more focused attention and a larger number of targeted attacks within the enterprise. Imagine what would happen if your internal CA were compromised by an outside attacker. As discussed in Chapter 6, "Security Considerations," insufficient CA security was to blame for allowing fraudulent certificates to be issued. In such cases, even genuine certificates had to be treated with suspicion, and in one case, this caused an entire CA to shut down.

SPECIAL NOTE 7-3 SECURITY VIGILANCE

Constantly check the security controls and physical security of your CA operations.

To keep your PKI operations as safe as possible, daily vulnerability scans and frequent infrastructure audits should be performed to ensure that adequate security measures are in place to protect the CAs, RAs, and any web-based enrollment servers. This constant checking of the infrastructure can prevent avoidable security breaches rather than waiting for them to happen. Ideally, these scans should be performed both internally and externally to the network. This gives you an overall security status of the PKI infrastructure. Any changes or findings can be used to trigger a security incident or alert you to a potential disaster from which you may need to recover. Regular penetration tests – a series of exercises performed from outside the system to determine if there are any exploitable openings or vulnerabilities in the PKI infrastructure – should be performed at regular intervals.

7.2 SECURITY ARCHITECTURES

The physical construction of an operations center is comparable to government-grade protection of military and intelligence services communications. Such operations often use a tiered approach to their physical environment with increasing levels of security. Individuals are granted selective access to tiers on only a "need to know" basis. The higher tiers require dual control with two or more authorized individuals to enter or remain within the physical location. Real-time video monitoring might be used for higher tiers and recordings often used for all tiers.

The security architecture of an operations center likewise has layers. Such architectures use a layered approach to their security design. The network perimeter is protected by a demilitarized zone (DMZ) isolated by firewalls, and internal zones might be further segmented by additional firewalls as shown in Figure 7.14. The Internet is depicted as the highest risk arrow, the DMZ as a lower risk arrow, the network zone as the next lowest risk arrow, and the enclave zone as the lowest risk arrow. Each zone is separated by a firewall denoted as Layers 1, 2, and 3.

The DMZ between the external firewall (Layer 1) and the internal firewall (Layer 2) contains web servers and primary mail servers. Web servers might include sales and marketing information, pricing, general information such as certificate policy and certificate practice statement (CPS) along with other legal documents such as relying party agreements (RPA), and other services. RA services include subscriber certificate and revocation requests and certificate status information including certificate revocation lists (CRLs) and Online Certificate Status Protocol (OCSP) responders. Mail, chat, and voice servers provide external communications to sales staff and technical support.

The network zone between the internal firewall (Layer 2) and the enclave firewall (Layer 3) contains database servers and secondary mail servers. Database servers include customer services such as billing and payments, certificate databases, and RA services such as subscriber certificate and revocation request queries and CRL and OCSP information. Mail, chat, and voice servers provide external communications to customers and internal communications among the employees.

The PKI enclave zone sits behind the enclave firewall (Layer 3) and contains RA servers that authenticate and authorize subscriber requests and CA servers that sign certificates and CRL updates. The CA servers use cryptographic hardware security modules (HSMs) to protect the CA private keys and generate digital signatures to sign certificates and CRL updates.

SPECIAL NOTE 7-4 EVENT LOGS

Logs are an important aspect of an overall network architecture's security defense in depth.

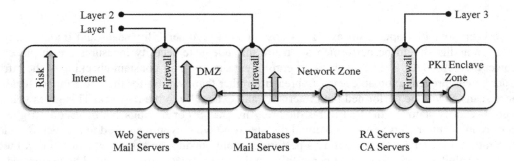

FIGURE 7.14 Network security architecture.

This architecture provides defense in depth, as an intruder must pass through or compromise at least two separate firewalls to breach the network zone and another firewall to reach the enclave zone. Another aspect of defense in depth are network and system logs:

- Each firewall logs events to disk.
- Log files are reviewed daily.
- Log files are retained for future forensic analysis.
- Firewall logs are regularly reviewed for any "unusual" events.

Beyond the firewalls, other systems are actively monitored for signs of intrusion. Each router, switch, web server, database, and application is monitored for known vulnerabilities, patch updates, compliant configurations, and unauthorized access attempts. In the event of a detected compromise, the monitoring applications notify the appropriate personnel. Notifications often use multiple delivery channels such as e-mail, text, phone call, or console alerts. At the same time, each notification is duplicated by system or application logs, including:

- Routers, firewalls, and network machines
- Database activities and events
- Transactions
- Operating systems
- Access control systems
- Mail servers

Logs can be collected, either pushed by a local agent or pulled remotely over the network, into a log management application that provides real-time monitoring and analytics. It is important that logs be archived in a secure location and kept, for example, a full year, to allow historical examination when a breach is suspected. Consequently, certain significant events need to be logged as noted by VeriSign's CPS:

- CA key lifecycle management events, including key generation, backup, storage, recovery, archival, and destruction
- Cryptographic device lifecycle management events, including configuration, initialization, access, errors, and decommission
- CA and subscriber certificate lifecycle management events, including certificate applications, renewal, rekey, and revocation
- Successful and unsuccessful processing of requests, including system, application, or cryptographic failures
- Generation and issuance of certificates and CRLs
- Security-related events, including successful and unsuccessful PKI system access attempts
- PKI and security system actions performed by the CA personnel
- Security-sensitive files or records read, written, or deleted
- Security profile changes, including adding, modifying, and deleting accounts
- System crashes, hardware failures, and other anomalies
- Firewall and router activity, including configuration changes, updates, access, and network errors
- CA facility visitor entry/exit

Other events should also be logged. The relative importance of what might be a significant event versus what could be considered trivial needs to be evaluated based on the CA architecture and the corresponding applications supported by the issuing CA systems. For example, critical applications or important management roles might need both successful and failed requests logged, whereas noncritical processes might only need failed requests logged.

7.3 CERTIFICATE MANAGEMENT

We have discussed several types of certificates earlier in this book. In Chapter 3, "PKI Building Blocks," we introduced several PKI protocols including Secure Socket Layer (SSL) and Transport Layer Security (TLS). In Chapter 4, "PKI Management and Security," we provided an example of the ABC Corporation's internal and external CA hierarchies. We will now look at managing SSL and TLS certificates. As discussed in Chapter 3, while TLS was originally based on SSL, the two protocols are different. However, the names are often used interchangeably; security professionals, marketing literature, product documentation, and public articles erroneously misname the protocols.

SPECIAL NOTE 7-5 SSL AND TLS CONFUSION

The two protocols SSL and TLS are different, but often the names are used interchangeably, sometimes as SSL/TLS, or just SSL when TLS is meant.

One of the major drivers for operating a PKI today is the need for TLS certificates for use within the enterprise's intranet. As companies grow and build more and more complex infrastructures, protecting server-to-server and employee-to-server communications becomes more and more important. Internet-facing websites will also be protected with TLS certificates, but these externally facing TLS certificates are usually sourced from commercial certification authorities. As the number of internal and external servers grows, this can lead to an environment that includes hundreds if not thousands of TLS certificates protecting everything from web servers, application servers, and network routers, to firewalls, and VPN concentrators. These TLS certificates may come from a variety of different CAs both internally and externally. As an example, you may have installed TLS certificates from a well-known, trusted certification authority on your company's website for name recognition and the trust seal on your customer-facing website, and you are deploying your own PKI's self-signed certificates on your intranet. Both the large number of TLS certificates and the number of associated CAs create a management problem for keeping track of all these certificates.

If you add different policies for different servers to the fact that you have multiple different CA's TLS certificates in your network, you add another tracking and reporting challenge to the uphill TLS management problem you have. Larger enterprises may have security policies that differ from one group to the next group and may have been commercially issued an extended validation certificate for your e-commerce site at RSA-2048 with SHA256 where your internal servers may be perfectly happy with an internally issued standard TLS certificate at RSA-2048 with SHA1 (for backward compatibility). With different policies, the reporting tools go from "nice to have" to "must have"; otherwise, you would not have a mechanism to find out if your organization follows your policies or not; however, SHA1 backward compatibility has its own issues.

- Microsoft deprecated SHA1 in July 2020 per its policy[2] such that older Windows devices that have not updated to SHA2 will no longer receive updates through Windows Update.
- NIST deprecated SHA1 in 2017 and disallowed it for signature generation in March 2019; however, NIST allows until December 31, 2030, to end its use per NIST 800–141Ar2.[3]
- PCI SSC disallows SHA1 in some of its standards[4] and disallowed it shortly after August 2016 per PQC FAQ[5] number 1435.

The TLS management problem grows even more complex for larger organizations that have multiple system administrators managing their own TLS certificates on their own servers. These system administrators probably have their own methods for installation and support of TLS certificates that vary from group to group. Furthermore, as you might have noticed in larger organizations, there is a significant turnover rate of the system administrators either changing groups within the organization or leaving to another company altogether. Those systems once protected by TLS certificates are now at risk of those same TLS certificates bringing the system down. New system administrators trying to learn their jobs only to have a TLS certificate expire on the new system that they just inherited poses a significant risk to the organization. Large organization IT teams are usually busy and frequently overworked. Having the PKI team provide some sort of tracking and reporting of TLS certificates can significantly reduce the risk to the organization of expired TLS certificates.

SPECIAL NOTE 7-6 EXPIRED TLS CERTIFICATE

An expired TLS certificate in your internal network can have very real negative consequences, as it takes just one expired TLS certificate to put your business at risk.

An expired TLS certificate can lead to lost business. When customers go to your website only to see security warnings pop up, there is an immediate perception of the lack of security related to your website and computer operations. Many customers will simply leave your site and purchase products and services elsewhere that do not have security warnings and are secured with unexpired TLS certificates. It is important to remember that most customers do not know how public key encryption works, but seeing a security warning that is intended to scare away the unwary very often will work with your customers. They may not come back. Remembering the time that your site had that security warning may be the last impression that your customers have.

SPECIAL NOTE 7-7 CUSTOMER TRUST

If your TLS certificates on your Internet external-facing e-commerce site expire, you will lose your customers' trust resulting in loss of business.

Another potential consequence of expired TLS certificates can be to provide attackers the opening to mount a phishing attack against your company. In a phishing attack, an attacker will assume the identity of your business by creating a fake website that looks just like your real site. The phishing site will have an unexpired TLS certificate on it. Your unsuspecting customers may then enter their confidential information, like credit card or social security numbers. The phished site feeds data directly to the attacker, who may in turn sell it to other criminals. If a phishing attack like this is successful, your company's reputation may suffer to the point that you may not be able to recover. Thanks to years of headlines about data breaches, the public is more aware and concerned about identity theft than ever before.

Failure to properly manage your TLS certificates will have an additional consequence on your customer support organization. If customers visit an Internet website and see a security warning because of an expired TLS certificate, they may have concerns about whether their private data are at risk. Either they will abandon the site, or they may pick up the phone and call your customer support line to ask about what caused the situation. A flood of customer support calls will fill up your customer support queue and cost a lot of time and money that could be better used elsewhere. In addition to a group of upset customers, you can add an upset call center manager to the list. Similar to customers who call your call center when they are uncertain about a website's security, employees who see warnings on internal websites that have expired TLS certificates will be calling in to the PKI group. Answering internal calls will divert PKI resources away from updating the TLS certificates to just answer the same question again and again.

The problem with not answering all these calls and explaining the situation and what to do about the warning messages is users may get the impression that ignoring these warnings is just fine and they can go about their business without paying attention to the warning message. This sets a negative precedent for security compliance by creating the impression that staff and customers may disregard security messages if they pop up.

Fortunately, there are services that make it easy to discover and manage TLS certificates across your enterprise. Almost all commercial CAs offer online tools to track and manage their brand of certificates. This can be challenging if you use more than one commercial CA for your external websites. Having more than one commercial CA provider can be a good decision to avoid vendor lock-in and provide a readily available alternative source of TLS certificates in the event a commercial CA is compromised. This decision can, however, make problems having to interface with multiple management consoles and having to track lots of different TLS certificates from all the CAs in your environment. How you monitor your TLS certificate inventory to get a comprehensive view can be a real reporting and monitoring challenge. Several commercial CAs at the time of writing offer free software tools to perform a network-based discovery of all the TLS certificates in your network. These tools or other public domain software products can help you get an up-to-date picture of all the TLS certificates within your network and the current certificate information, like expiration dates so you can track all the TLS certificates and their current locations. This is especially helpful in large diverse networks, with large numbers of TLS certificates from multiple CAs.

These monitoring tools usually provide the capability of alerting and reporting on certificate-based events as well: an expired TLS certificate puts your data at risk, so building a set of tools that will send you alerts before a certificate needs renewal is going to make your job much easier. Generating reports that are easy to read and understand is also very important as the number of TLS certificates that you must manage increases. Reporting capabilities will give you a comprehensive view of your TLS certificates in your network and allow you to provide those reports to other staff and system administrators who may be managing their own TLS certificates.

7.4   BUSINESS CONTINUITY

The most basic question anyone can ask is what business continuity (BC) and disaster recovery (DR) are. Business continuity and disaster recovery can mean different things to different people, but the core concepts are the same: build, deploy, and test policies, test procedures, and test technology. These concepts allow your PKI operations to continue to function in the event some type of disaster strikes. This can be something as easy as having full backups of your servers in the event of hardware failure to failing over from one data center to a geographically independent secondary data center. Generally speaking, DR is a series of policies, procedures, and technology that when implemented allow your organization to recover the PKI operations from a disaster. Key metrics of your DR plan will be RTO and RPO:

- Recovery time objectives (RTOs): how long will it take you to recover your PKI operations?
- Recovery point objectives (RPOs): what data are lost, if any, and how old the data will be once you are back online?

Disaster recovery is a subset of the overall practice of business continuity. Business continuity is not only the process of saving your PKI data for being able to recover it in the event of a disaster but also the people, processes, and overall business operations that allow your PKI to support your organization. Disasters from an IT perspective can range from minor to major: the minor loss of data from deleting a file or log to the major loss of an entire data center or an earthquake that can devastate an entire city. Your disaster recovery plan is to ensure you can recover your data in the event that they are lost, inaccessible, or compromised. A good disaster recovery plan should include everything required to get your PKI environment back up and operational, including (1) how and where backup files are stored, (2) how backups can be retrieved, (3) what hardware is needed to access them, (4) where to get the hardware if the primary systems are destroyed, and (5) where your operating system software and application software is stored and how to reinstall all of the pieces.

Business continuity (BC) is defined as the capability of the organization to continue delivery of products or services at acceptable predefined levels following a disruptive incident (Source: ISO 22301:2012). Business continuity starts before and picks up after the disaster recovery team has stabilized the environment from whatever event occurred. Business continuity plans for PKI often rely on high availability (HA) architectures with redundant systems operating in real time (hot–hot) and with a shared data cluster. These architectures are designed so that if one CA or database server fails, others can pick up the load without creating an outage. Having these HA architectures in place will not prevent disaster but should make the recovery after the disaster that much quicker and easier.

Business continuity ties together the availability goals of HA with the recoverability goals of disaster recovery.[6] A carefully planned and architected PKI design can allow you to recover from a full-blown disaster with limited downtime and very little data loss. Designing these highly redundant architectures with all the failover mechanisms is not for the faint of heart. They can be expensive to build and expensive to maintain, but with all that is dependent on the PKI infrastructure, it is a small price to pay for the business continuity aspects of PKI.

What both disaster recovery and business continuity have in common is the need for testing and verifying that the testing actually accomplishes the goals of DR or BC. A regular test plan must be performed and evaluated for both DR and BC. Without regular testing, you will never know that the data you thought were backed up can actually be restored or that your failover data center will come online when a disaster strikes. If you do not test your DR and BC plans, your PKI organization will fail when it is needed most. Backups can and do fail occasionally. If you do not test restoring your backups, you will never know if the data will be available in a crisis.

With cuts to IT organizations and stressed and overworked PKI engineers, it may sound like an area to take shortcuts in. The DR test worked the last time so it should work this time, so the results can just be penciled in without actually testing the plan. This line of thinking will get you into trouble in the next disaster faster than anything else. The effort put into performing the DR and BC test plans will pay off in streamlined processes to get your infrastructure backed up and running in the fastest, most efficient way possible. You can even incorporate some of the DR actions in day-to-day operations. Switching between data centers for backup windows or switching processing loads between data centers can test failover plans on a regular basis. Having confidence in your PKI DR capabilities will reduce some of the stress the next time you experience an outage.

SPECIAL NOTE 7-8 BC/DR PLANS

There is no one size fits all when it comes to BC and DR plans. The plans that work the best are the ones you write, test, and can rely upon. Many formats and specific tasks can be included, but only when the plans are regularly tested and updated can they save your PKI operations.

The National Institute of Standards and Technology (NIST) has produced a very comprehensive document on BC and DR planning in Special Publication 800–34 Contingency Planning Guide for Federal Information Systems.[7] The information presented in the NIST document is independent of hardware, operating systems, and applications. The major areas covered are as follows:

1. Develop the contingency planning policy.
2. Conduct the business impact analysis.
3. Identify preventive controls.
4. Create contingency strategies.
5. Develop an information system contingency plan.

6. Ensure plan testing, training, and exercises.
7. Ensure plan maintenance.

There are all sorts of good information in these documents to use in your BC and DR plans.[8] The document can assist you in understanding the purpose, process, and format of a variety of contingency plans and how they are developed. The document provides background information on the interrelationships between information system contingency planning and other types of security and emergency management-related contingency plans, including restoring an organization's mission essential functions (MEFs); see Table 7.2 Contingency Planning.

TABLE 7.2

NIST 800–34 Contingency Planning

Type of Plans	Purpose	Scope	Plan Relationship
Business continuity plan (BCP)	Provides procedures for sustaining mission/business operations while recovering from a significant disruption	Addresses mission/business processes at a lower or expanded level from COOP MEFs	Mission/business process-focused plan that may be activated in coordination with a COOP plan to sustain non-MEFs
Continuity of operations (COOP) plan	Provides procedures and guidance to sustain an organization's MEFs at an alternate site for up to 30 days; mandated by federal directives	Addresses MEFs at a facility; information systems are addressed based only on their support of the mission essential functions	MEF-focused plan that may also activate several business unit-level BCPs, ISCPs, or DRPs, as appropriate
Crisis communications plan	Provides procedures for disseminating internal and external communications; means to provide critical status information and control rumors	Addresses communications with personnel and the public; not information system focused	Incident-based plan often activated with a COOP or BCP, but may be used alone during a public exposure event
Critical infrastructure protection (CIP) plan	Provides policies and procedures for protection of national critical infrastructure components, as defined in the National Infrastructure Protection Plan	Addresses critical infrastructure components that are supported or operated by an agency or organization	Risk management plan that supports COOP plans for organizations with critical infrastructure and key resource assets
Cyber incident response plan	Provides procedures for mitigating and correcting a cyberattack, such as a virus, worm, or Trojan horse	Addresses mitigation and isolation of affected systems and cleanup and minimizes loss of information	Information system–focused plan that may activate an ISCP or DRP, depending on the extent of the attack
Disaster recovery plan (DRP)	Provides procedures for relocating information systems operations to an alternate location	Activated after major system disruptions with long-term effects	Information system–focused plan that activates one or more ISCPs for the recovery of individual systems
Information system contingency plan (ISCP)	Provides procedures and capabilities for recovering an information system	Addresses single information system recovery at the current or, if appropriate, alternate location	Information system–focused plan that may be activated independent from other plans or as part of a larger recovery effort coordinated with a DRP, COOP, and/or BCP
Occupant emergency plan (OEP)	Provides coordinated procedures for minimizing loss of life or injury and protecting property damage in response to a physical threat	Focuses on personnel and property particular to the specific facility, not mission/business process or information system based	Incident-based plan that is initiated immediately after an event, preceding a COOP or DRP activation

Business continuity is the big picture, and we will start there and then move to the more specific disaster recovery planning. Business continuity typically includes the management oversight and planning involved with ensuring the continuous operation of PKI functions in the case of system or enterprise disasters. Some of the elements necessary for successful business continuity planning include the data center and office space of the PKI staff, the actual staff themselves, and all the equipment needed for the PKI operations; this includes networks, servers, firewalls, HSMs, and web servers, as well as the actual data recovery procedures.

Business continuity plans differ from disaster recovery plans in several ways. First, business continuity is not so much focused on recovering the data as it is making sure the business process continues regardless of circumstance. "The whole point of business continuity is to continue to do business during a failure or disaster. In basic terms, it means that when a failure or disaster happens, that data is still accessible with little to no downtime"[9] and that all people and processes will continue to support the PKI infrastructure.

Business continuity has to be a combination of hardware and software to keep data in at least two different data centers at the same time. For example, if the production CA server in one building or data center goes down for some reason, the certificate data and the CA application are "failed over" to a second CA system that subscribers can then use. Usually, the CA application only pauses, and users do not even know there was a problem, if you have done your planning and testing correctly.

What this really means is that you must plan, purchase, and deploy the infrastructure to support business continuity. It does not get there by magic but only through hard work on the planning, lobbying of senior management for funds, and the installation of proper hardware will you be put in a solid position for your business continuity plans to work. One of the most common designs for high availability is clustering of servers. Clustering allows the replication of data or applications between multiple systems, enabling you to have that data accessible from a secondary source in the event of some failure. Active–active clustering between data centers is a great example. If your CA application goes down on the production server, the replicated copy on the secondary server takes the load, and the application stays up and people still have access. High availability design also applies to the HSMs that you are using. Having at least two HSMs configured in a network-based high availability configuration means that even if one HSM fails or the link to the data center with the HSM in it fails, the CA servers can still get to their key material on the secondary HSM.

Business continuity is much broader than just disaster recovery. Business continuity looks at the overall business operations, including everything from people, both data center and office locations, and the application. Business continuity should be addressing a much larger scope of support than just the recovery of the data and hardware.

7.5 DISASTER RECOVERY

Disaster recovery planning is the low-level step-by-step procedure on what to do to recover your PKI system to a functioning state once a disaster hits. You may not be able to prepare a step-by-step guide on how to react to every kind of disaster, but you must list the roles and responsibilities and the people who will get you back to normal.

1. It is important to assign roles for who does what in the event of a disaster. It is essential to have backup individuals assigned to each of the roles. In the event of a disaster, you never will know who will be unavailable. The skills and capabilities of the primary and secondary people for each role need to be matched to the effort; for example, software installation, hardware recovery, or HSM configuration.
2. Each of the disaster recovery team members needs to have their responsibilities documented on paper and available online. You never know what resources will be available in the event of a disaster, so better to have planned ahead in the first place. Team members need to know what they are expected to do, what their limits are, and who to escalate to if they get stuck.

Here are a few of the roles and responsibilities to consider for your team depending on the size and complexity of your PKI operations:

- The disaster recovery event manager initiates the DR call, activates the disaster recovery plan, coordinates all members of the DR team, and communicates the status to the management to engage other resources as needed.
- The database administrator (DBA) assesses damage and corruption to the PKI database and performs the recovery plan as needed. The DBA will plan the recovery of the database and any repairs necessary to enable the CA to issue certificates and work with the primary PKI engineer to coordinate the CA communications to the database.
- The network engineer is responsible for the restoration of the data network and works with the hardware engineer to ensure servers are communicating with HSMs and databases. He or she may need to work with the firewall engineers if failing over to a remote site to verify firewall rules.
- The PKI HSM engineer verifies the key material in the failover HSM and works with the network engineer to ensure connectivity between the HSM and the CAs.
- The primary PKI engineer manages any reconfiguration of the CA needed with the failover and verifies that the CA is up and functioning. He or she also verifies all CRL and OCSP information to ensure that the current certificate validity information is being presented to the network.

As you implement your disaster recovery plan, it is important to always prioritize your actions and recover the most important parts of your PKI operations first. The analysis and work you did on your business continuity plan will help you decide which aspects of your PKI operations are the most important. Your disaster recovery plan needs to incorporate the BC priorities. What PKI operations do you need to have up and running immediately, which comes second, and which operations can wait?

It is nice to know that not every emergency you experience will be a full-blown disaster. Minor emergencies will need to have a different set of priorities than a major catastrophe. Therefore, it is important to list the priorities according to the type of emergency. One classification system you could use might be the following:

- Severity 3, Service Interruption: This is a type of disaster recovery lasting a short period of time, usually less than 24 hours.
- Severity 2, Minor Disaster: This is a type of disaster recovery that lasts more than 24 hours but less than four days.
- Severity 1, Major Disaster: This is a type of disaster recovery that will take all your resources and will probably be at least four days before you can get back up and run as normal.

Your PKI operations should have a regular full inventory of servers, HSMs, software, and all your backup data. A full set of network and architectural diagrams will significantly aid in any DR situation you find yourself in. The inventory and diagrams are important to have in the event of a disaster because you need to know how much you have lost in order to recover the data. You would be surprised at how many engineers make changes to the infrastructure saying they are going to get to update the documentation, only to find out in a disaster situation that the documentation is out of date. Trying to trace back what changes were made last during an actual outage is not the best time to do so. People are stressed, some people will not be available, and you have many far more important things to do on your DR list. Your PKI inventory should be more than just the number, brand, and model numbers of your equipment. You should also include software versions, updates and patches, who updated them last, and a current list of suppliers and your contacts at each of those hardware vendors. Do not forget to include network diagrams, security architectures, and data flow or E/R diagrams if you have them. Keep copies of your inventory online and accessible, store them safely off-site, and remember to update all copies whenever you do an inventory update.

As was indicated in the introduction section to BC and DR, your DR plan should include regular training and testing. The team responding to the outage needs to know what to do and what is expected of them; they cannot be reading the plan for the first time when the disaster strikes. Just having a plan written and out on a file server will be worthless if no one understands how to use the plan. Engineers come and go from an organization; it is important to bring new members of the team up to speed on their role in the DR plan and have them practice their parts before an actual event takes place. All disaster recovery team members should be cross-trained as much as possible with other roles, and as indicated earlier, you need to have at least one alternate for each role. We now focus on DR plan areas of special consideration for PKI systems.

SPECIAL NOTE 7-9 DR/BC CERTIFICATE REVOCATION

Disaster recovery must include the ability of the PKI to generate CRL information.

OCSP responders, CRLs, and sometimes delta CRLs are used by subscribers to determine if a certificate has been revoked or if it is still considered valid. Most software applications will fail when they cannot determine the revocation status of a certificate, unless revocation checking has been disabled, which is a very poor practice. Just like certificates, CRLs have a finite period during which they are valid. Once the CRL expires, an application checking the revocation status of a certificate against the expired CRL will fail. A disaster related to a certification authority's ability to update its CRL information can have very large consequences all throughout the organization and outside of the company to its customers as well. A disaster situation of a PKI system not able to generate and maintain CRL information could lead to multiple disaster situations in other departments. The problem being that until the PKI system provides the CRL information online, the other departments will still be in a failed state even if they have implemented their disaster recovery plans, which is why it is so vital for the disaster recovery plan for your PKI to be carefully crafted and thoroughly tested.

You should put the CRL capabilities toward the top of your priority list of features to recover in a disaster situation. Checking on the currently posted CRL and determining how long that CRL will be valid is very important. The closer that CRL is to expiration, the more pressure you are under to produce a new CRL and get that new CRL posted so that all the subscribers can get to it to check the status of their certificates. Prioritizing the CRL signing capability near the top of your DR priority list will prevent turning the PKI disaster into a companywide disaster situation.

If the PKI still has CRL issuing capabilities and the disaster recovery looks like it will take a very long time, an option is to increase the lifetime of the CRL and publish the longer-lived CRL while the rest of the disaster recovery takes place. This can provide more time for the disaster recovery process and avoid any other downstream complications for your subscribers. You need to understand that this action will increase the time until subscribers have up-to-date information on their certificates. You will have to weigh the longer-exposure risk with all the applications and subscribers not being able to get to the CRL at all.

SPECIAL NOTE 7-10 DR/BC CERTIFICATE ISSUANCE

Disaster recovery must include the ability of the CA to issue certificates.

You may end up with a situation in your PKI disaster that results in a CA (or pair of CAs issuing the same type of certificates) that can no longer issue certificates. This situation could result in different severities depending on the types of certificates the CAs were issuing. A SEV 1 disaster may be a CA that issues short-lived certificates for a firewall or VPN concentrator; a SEV 3 disaster may be a CA that issues an infrequently used type of certificate like a Secure/Multipurpose Internet Mail Extensions (S/MIME) certificate that only a few of the employees have. Recovery from this situation could be from several of different possibilities:

1. Copy the certificate template to another operational CA and begin issuing certificates from the new CA. This may or may not be an option depending on how complicated the enrollment process is and if there is a way to redirect users to the new CA.
2. Restore all the backup data, restore the database, and bring the CA operational again. This assumes that you have not suffered any loss of the CA's key material or HSMs that were holding the CA's private key.
3. If there is no recovery from the disaster, (1) generate new key material in the HSM, (2) move to the CA that signed the failed CA and issue a new CA certificate, and (3) load the CA software with the new certificate and point the CA to the key material in the HSM. This is an extreme step, but if all other options have failed, this may be your only course of action.

SPECIAL NOTE 7-11 DR/BC CA DATABASE

Disaster recovery must include the recovery of the CA database.

Having the CA function separated into clustered CA application servers, clustered CA database servers, and high availability configured HSM to hold the CA's private key material makes a highly redundant, highly reliable system. Unfortunately, if something goes wrong with the CA's database, all the information on every certificate issued, every certificate that has been revoked, and all requests successful, pending, and failed are at risk. If the CA was configured for key archival and recovery, the CA database will contain the private keys for the certificates that were issued. This may hold the entire organizations' private encryption keys for S/MIME encrypted mail or Microsoft's Encrypting File System (EFS) file and folder encryption. Loss of this database resource could set the company back years of effort if all the information had to be recreated. Having regular backups that have been tested by restoring them in a full DR drill will minimize but not eliminate the risk of a failed database. The restoration of the backup files may result in some data loss since the last backup but will be far less devastating than losing the entire CA database to a hardware or disk issue that corrupts the database or the log files.

7.6 AFFILIATIONS

Sometimes the decision to build in-house your own PKI versus outsource some of your PKI may be based on functionality like the need for browser-recognized TLS certificates, or the decision may be purely on cost. Other factors that may come into play with the insource versus outsource decision may be your company's requirement to maintain total control over all critical aspects of your operations like security and authentication services. Many organizations will not depend on a third-party organization due to the complex legal issues involved with liability if something goes wrong. Other organizations, especially smaller organizations, are more likely to outsource some or all of the PKI responsibilities due to the cost of the hardware, software, and secure facilities, lack of technical PKI personnel, or lack of legal support.

For example, an organization may elect to outsource the CA services to a commercial CA that provides the organization's name on the certificates but retains the RA function in-house to ensure that the company's authentication standards are maintained under close control. Another example may be to outsource the RA function to an external provider that is already set up and operating providing an authentication service to be securely connected to the insourced CA for actual certificate issuance. Several different options exist for insourcing and outsourcing of the PKI components; the proper balance must be struck for each organization depending on the priorities of that particular organization.

Unless you are a very large organization with significant resources, developing your PKI infrastructure will probably need an external commercial CA to supplement your capabilities. Using an external commercial CA for Internet-facing websites that need to be protected with TLS certificates is a common use of an external commercial CA. When evaluating a CA, it is worth considering the vendor's history of trust and security. As noted in the prior section, you can inherit a significant set of problems if your commercial CA provider is compromised.

Although price certainly plays a role in the purchasing process, if the CA is compromised, the cost savings will soon look insignificant to the costs of replacing all of the certificates issued in a disaster recovery mode. Price should only be one of many factors in selecting a commercial CA. As you look for a commercial CA, check the track record of security and evaluate them for these criteria as well:

- Annual audits from a reputable independent audit firm.
- Computer facilities that have been designed to withstand multiple cyberattacks, failover, and recover all without downtime to you the customer.
- Federal Information Processing Standards 140–2 certified cryptographic hardware-based systems for private key storage and for cryptographically signing certificates.
- All CA hardware monitored and strong access controls in place.
- Biometrics-based security for the facilities, and with dual-access controls in place for critical PKI systems.
- Dual control over the issuing of all certificates with your company's name on them.
- Persons fulfilling trusted roles should have an annual background check.
- Segregation of duties based on the PKI job responsibility.
- Multiple trusted persons should be required to perform sensitive tasks, like key ceremonies and key generation.
- Service-level agreement that the vendor offers.

When you choose your commercial CA, you should look for a company that follows a comprehensive security approach that encompasses physical, logical, network, and personnel security. Think about the processes that you went through in setting up your own PKI, and any commercial provider should have what you put in place and a whole lot more. If a commercial CA has skimped on any area of security, this should be a red flag. In addition to the physical and logical security layers, you should look at the RA, customer, and remote authentication processes and how they are set up and managed.

7.7   CRYPTO-AGILITY

As noted in this chapter, existing standards will continue to change and evolve. PKI systems must be prepared to adopt these new standards. Recent history provides a number of examples of this ever-changing environment:

- DES was approved as a federal standard in November 1976 and published on January 15, 1977, as FIPS PUB 46. DES was reaffirmed as the standard in 1983 and 1988 (revised as FIPS 46–1), and in 1993 as (FIPS 46–2). In 1999 (FIPS 46–3) described "Triple DES." On May 26, 2002, DES was superseded by the Advanced Encryption Standard (AES). On May 19, 2005, FIPS 46–3 was officially withdrawn as a standard.

- RSA-1024, which was widely used for asymmetric encryption for several years, was replaced by RSA-2048, because the shorter key length was potentially attackable. NIST recommended that commercial CAs deprecate signing digital certificates that contained RSA Public Keys of 1024 bits after December 31, 2010, and cease signing with 1024-bit keys completely by December 31, 2013.
- The hash functions RC4, MD5 and eventually SHA1 have had several vulnerabilities, leading to them being phased out. SHA1 was eventually replaced by SHA-256, requiring every PKI to make the switch, or risk exposure to hacks.
- Major web browsers deprecated support for the TLS 1.0 protocol, targeting a mid-2020 deadline for all web-facing applications to upgrade to TLS 1.2 or higher.
- The CA/B Forum mandated that the minimum key size for code signing certificates be increased to 3072 Bits on June 1, 2021.

These are just a few examples of the changing requirements that large-scale PKIs must deliver upon. Currently deployed algorithms like RSA, ECC, and AES will eventually be replaced by new standards in the not-too-distant future. It is critical for PKIs to build in the ability to quickly issue new keys and certificates reflecting current best practices in a timely fashion. See Section 10.11, "NIST PQC Program," for a discussion on Post-Quantum Cryptography.

7.8   CLOUD PKI

Moving an application from an enterprise network, sometimes called an on-premise application, to a public cloud environment is often more complicated than expected, especially when the application is PKI-enabled or the application is the PKI. The term "on-premise" versus "private" network is often used to avoid confusion with similar but distinct terms such as public/private keys, public/private PKI, and public/private networks. Some of the more non-obvious issues include the following.

1. The public cloud provider might not offer or support stronger cryptographic hardware but only weaker cryptographic software. Cryptographic software, including "appliances" that are rated at lower security levels, put the application's cryptography at a higher key compromise risk. See Section 2.5, "Cryptographic Modules," for details.
2. The public cloud provider might not offer or support an external PKI. For example, if the on-premise application uses certificates from an organization's private PKI or a public PKI, but the cloud provider cannot import the asymmetric keys and certificates, whether automatic processes or manual procedures, the application might need to be rearchitected to use another non-PKI solution.
3. The public cloud provider might not offer or support its own native PKI. For example, if the on-premise application needs certificates, but a cloud-based PKI is not available or does not provide sufficient operations, then many PKI-based security solutions such as TLS or SSH might not be reliable. In this situation, an alternate PKI should be considered.
4. The public cloud provider might not offer a traditional PKI. As noted, the cloud native PKI might not support cryptographic hardware and use cryptographic software to protect the CA private signature keys. Some cloud PKI solutions offer transitory CA services with relatively short lifecycles. For example, the root CA might use cryptographic hardware to sign the transitory CA public key certificate, but the transitory CA private key resides in ordinary memory for 24 hours or less.

Consider a hypothetical migration of a PKI-enabled on-premise application "Alice" to a public cloud. Alice interacts with another application "Bob," where both use PKI certificates. Refer to Figure 7.15 for three possible scenarios.

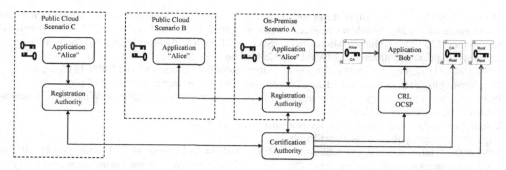

FIGURE 7.15   Cloud PKI migrations.

On-Premise Scenario A: Alice runs on-premise with a local Registration Authority (RA) that interacts with an Issuing CA. Alice generates a private/public key pair, submits a CSR to the RA, and receives a public key certificate, which is forwarded to Bob. Bob builds the certificate chain by retrieving the CA certificates and performing certificate validation, which includes interaction with the CRL or OCSP for revocation checking. Alice and Bob can now interact using Alice's certificate.

Public Cloud Scenario B: Alice runs in the public cloud but the RA runs on-premise. Alice generates her key pair and submits the CSR from the public cloud to the RA on-premise. The RA gets the certificate from the CA (e.g., public CA or private CA running on-premise), returns the certificate to Alice in the public cloud, and forwards the certificate to Bob. As usual, Bob builds the certificate chain and does certificate validation, including revocation checking. Bob is unaware that Alice runs in a public cloud and does not interact with the RA, so his interaction with the CA remains unaffected.

Public Cloud Scenario C: Alice and the RA run in the public cloud. Alice generates her key pair and submits the CSR to the RA. The RA gets the certificate from the CA, which is external to the public cloud, returns the certificate to Alice, and forwards the certificate to Bob. As usual, Bob builds the certificate chain and does certificate validation, including revocation checking. Bob is unaware that Alice or the RA runs in a public cloud and does not interact with the RA, so his interaction with the CA remains unaffected.

However, if the CA migrates to the cloud, then either the CA needs to provide CRL and OCSP external services to Bob, or Bob needs to access CRL and OCSP cloud services. Further, Bob needs access to retrieve the CA certificate from the cloud. Basically, the CA migration affects Bob such that some rearchitecting is needed. When Bob is an application, this is doable, but when Bob represents thousands of applications operated by hundreds of third-party services, the scope and scale of migrating Alice to the cloud dramatically increases.

Another impact is when the CA services are transferred from one CA to another, such as from a public PKI to a cloud native PKI, the impact to the Bobs can be problematic. One major takeaway from this book is that not all PKIs are the same. Some are highly trusted, some are less so, and some are untrustworthy such that the PKI cannot be used by a relying party. Thus, if one or more Bobs determine that the alternate PKI is untrustworthy, Bob can no longer trust Alice.

Refer to Section 9.7, "PKI Risk Assessment" and Section 9.8, "PKI Cloud Assessment," for managing risk. Also see the new Chapter 10, "PKI Industry," on the PKI Industry for details and read Section 10.12, "ASC X9 Financial PKI," for the details on the financial public key infrastructure.

NOTES

1. webobjects.cdw.com/webobjects/media/pdf/Symantec/SSL-Certificate/White-Paper-Symantec-How-To-Choose-A-Certificate-Authority-For-Safer-Web-Security.pdf

2. Microsoft SHA1, https://support.microsoft.com/en-us/topic/windows-update-sha-1-based-endpoints-discontinued-for-older-windows-devices-10b58bd9–5ba2-b23d-498b-139ce5c709af#:~:text=In%20compliance%20with%20the%20Microsoft%20Secure%20Hash%20Algorithm,will%20no%20longer%20receive%20updates%20through%20Windows%20Update
3. NIST 800-131Ar2, https://nvlpubs.nist.gov/nistpubs/SpecialPublications/NIST.SP.800-131Ar2.pdf
4. PCI, https://blog.pcisecuritystandards.org/how-the-sha-1-collision-impacts-security-of-payments
5. PCI FAQ, www.pcisecuritystandards.org/faq/articles/Frequently_Asked_Question/What-is-the-Council-s-guidance-on-the-use-of-SHA-1/
6. idge.staticworld.net/idge/insider/dis_recover-nosponsor_v1_0.pdf
7. http://csrc.nist.gov/publications/PubsSPs.html
8. NIST 800-34, http://csrc.nist.gov/publications/nistpubs/800–34-rev1/sp800–34-rev1_errata-Nov11–2010.pdf
9. www.datacenterknowledge.com/archives/2013/01/04/disaster-recovery-is-not-businesscontinuity/

8 Incident Management

This chapter discusses where and how a public key infrastructure (PKI) compromise might occur and the steps necessary to prepare for such an incident. Incident management includes preparing a PKI incident response plan and executing the plan in the event of a breach. So far in this book, we have alluded to security incidents in a variety of ways:

- Chapter 2, "Cryptography Basics," identified key compromise as a type of incident.
- Chapter 4, "PKI Management and Security," addressed incidents in the certificate policy and certificate practice statement.
- Chapter 5, "PKI Roles and Responsibilities," discussed incidents and separation of duties.
- Chapter 6, "Security Considerations," mentioned incidents relating to physical and logical security controls.
- Chapter 7, "Operational Considerations," discussed incidents affecting PKI operations including disaster recovery plans.

Incidents can originate from insider threats or external attacks, system or application misconfigurations, software or hardware failures, zero-day faults, and other vulnerabilities. Components of incident management include monitoring, response, discovery, reporting, and remediation. To begin the incident management discussion, let's first look at the areas of a PKI where a compromise might occur and the impact it has on an organization.

8.1 AREAS OF COMPROMISE IN A PKI

If we initially look at the areas that can be compromised in a PKI, it will give us an idea of how to respond if a compromise or breach occurs, and it will provide an idea of what should be in a PKI incident response plan. Because it is difficult to determine when a compromise occurred and because certificate issuance dates can be predated, any compromise puts the existing certificate population in question. We now consider the impact of compromise in various areas within another example PKI shown in Figure 8.1.

In this example, there is a single root (A) CA with two intermediate (A.1 and A.2) CA with two issuing (A.1.1, A.1.2) CA associated to intermediate (A.1) CA and another two issuing (A.2.1 and

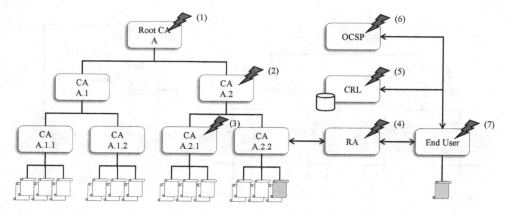

FIGURE 8.1 Potential public key infrastructure compromise points.

DOI: 10.1201/9781003425298-8

A.2.2) CA associated to intermediate (A.2) CA. End users interact with a single RA to request certificate generation or certificate revocation. Users also use either the CRL or OSCP services during certificate validation.

8.1.1 OFFLINE ROOT CA

As shown in Figure 8.2, the compromise of an offline root CA private key (A) that has two subordinate CA trees (A.1, A.1.1, A.1.2 and A.2, A.2.1, A.2.2) under this scenario negates all of the certificates issued under the hierarchy of the root CA, including all of the online issuing CA certificates and all end-user certificates that the online issuing CAs issued. This is a worst-case scenario and amounts to the most severe disaster of a PKI system.

All the CA and end-user certificates would need to be revoked, if you have the ability to issue an updated certificate revocation list (CRL) and Online Certificate Status Protocol (OCSP) capabilities available that should take top priority. Alerting all subscribers of the breach and compromise is the first order of business. Being able to alert all the relying parties of the compromise by providing revocation information on the root CA certificate should prevent any reliance on the end-entity certificates for all subscribers who are following best practices and checking the validity of the certificate chain. Being able to revoke all CA certificates and all end-entity certificates is much better in communicating the compromise. Building the completely new PKI infrastructure beginning with a new root key generation all the way down should be the second priority.

8.1.2 ONLINE INTERMEDIATE CA WITH ISSUING CAS

As shown in Figure 8.3, the compromise of an online intermediate CA private key (A.2) that has two issuing CAs (A.2.1 and A.2.2) negates all the certificates and CRLs issued under the hierarchy of the online issuing CA certificates and all of the associated end-user certificates. In this case, the root CA (A) is not compromised, and the offline root can revoke the subordinate online issuing CA (A.2) certificate and update the CRL and OCSP information. Then all the associated issuing CA certificates and all corresponding end-user certificates would need to be revoked and reissued.

The issuing CA certificates and end-user certificates are rekeyed and not renewed. When a key compromise is determined, it is rarely the case that the exact time is known. Thus, all existing certificates are considered invalid and new certificates are issued with new public keys.

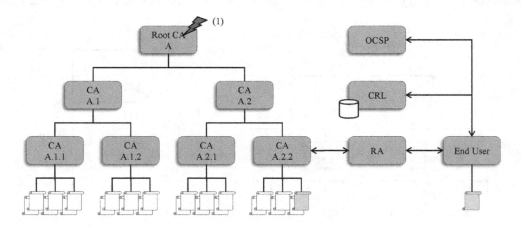

FIGURE 8.2 Root CA compromise.

8.1.3 ONLINE ISSUING CA

As shown here in Figure 8.4, the compromise of an online issuing CA private key (A.2.1) negates all of the end-user certificates issued under the hierarchy of that CA. In this case, the issuing CA (A.2) is not compromised and can revoke the subordinate online issuing CA (A.2.1) certificate and update the CRL and OCSP information with the subordinate CA revocation information. Then all the associated end-user certificates would need to be revoked and reissued.

The end-user certificates are rekeyed and not renewed. When a key compromise is determined, it is rarely the case that the exact time is known. Thus, all existing end-user certificates are considered invalid and new certificates are issued with new public keys.

8.1.4 ONLINE RA

Referring back to Figure 8.1 and looking at other areas of compromise, we can explore some of the supporting roles of the PKI. First, we will consider the compromise of an online registration authority (RA). This compromise allows unauthorized approval of counterfeit end-user certificates and puts suspicion on all end-user certificates under the hierarchy that were requested from the RA of the online issuing CA that the RA is authorized by. In this case, the RA certificate would need to be revoked, and all the associated end-user certificates requested from that RA would need to be revoked and reissued. If the time of compromise of RA is known, and that is a big if, then only the end-user certificates during that period would need to be revoked and reissued.

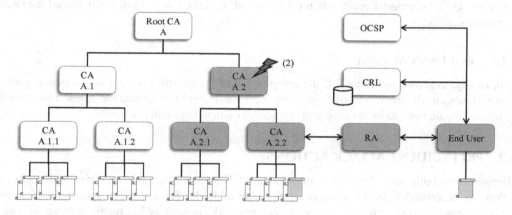

FIGURE 8.3 Online intermediate CA compromise with issuing CAs.

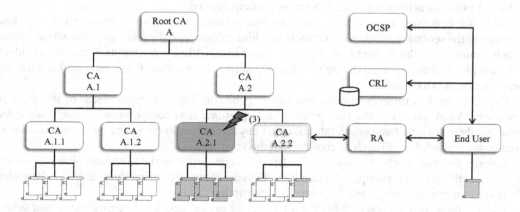

FIGURE 8.4 Online issuing CA compromise.

8.1.5 ONLINE CRL SERVICE

Again, as shown in Figure 8.1, the compromise of the CRL service allows denial of service or unauthorized addition, deletion, or modification of files. How you host CRL information may include a Hypertext Transfer Protocol (HTTP) or Hypertext Transfer Protocol Secure (HTTPS) server; this server's operating system (OS) can be susceptible to attack and compromise. You need to consider what impact there would be on internal and external relying parties.

If incorrect or no CRL information was available, what would be the impact on the users?

While a counterfeit CRL cannot have a valid signature, unless the CA was likewise compromised since the CRL is signed using the same CA private key, a relying party might (1) ignore the unavailable or invalid CRL and accept the end-user certificate, which is a poor practice, or (2) consider the certificate invalid and deny the transaction initiated by the certificate, which is a correct practice but can result in a denial of service. Ultimately, the judgment of whether to accept a partially validated certificate is a risk-based decision.

8.1.6 ONLINE OCSP SERVICE

Once again as shown in Figure 8.1, the compromise of the OCSP responder private key allows false responses to certificate status inquiries. Revoked certificates can be made valid, valid certificates can be revoked, or no status can be returned. An OCSP denial of service can also be perpetrated. The OCSP responder certificate must be revoked, new OCSP responder keys must be generated, and a new OCSP responder certificate must be issued from the CA that originally issued the OCSP responder certificate.

8.1.7 END USER'S MACHINE

And, finally, as shown in Figure 8.1, the compromise of the end-user private key, depending on its usage, allows an adversary to falsify signed messages or decrypt intercepted messages. The end-user certificate would need to be revoked and replaced with new keys and certificate.

8.2 PKI INCIDENT ATTACK ACTIONS

Microsoft has built two charts for categorizing PKI compromises with severity and suggested actions for Microsoft CAs. They are presented here in Tables 8.1 and 8.2, respectively. Note that the tables have been reformatted. The term "key integrity" is used by Microsoft to mean the key is secure and not compromised, and the term "renew" means to generate new keys and certificates. Table 8.1 provides actions when the CA server is compromised.

Table 8.1 lists three types of attacks in the first column, the known or unknown private key integrity in the second column, the severity in the third column, and the recommended actions in the fourth column. The three attacks are physical access to an offline CA, remote access to an online CA, and physical access to an online CA. Remote access to an offline CA is not feasible since no network access is available.

Key integrity has three conditions: the key is good, the key is compromised, or its status is unknown. When unknown, the best practice is to presume it is compromised. Thus, practically speaking there are only two considerations, either key integrity is known to be good, or it is considered compromised. It is difficult to confirm that the key is good.

Severity has four levels: 1 is low, 2 is moderate, 3 is important, and 4 is critical. Note that severity levels will vary. For example, Section 7.5, "Disaster Recovery," used three levels: 1 for major disaster, 2 for minor disaster, and 3 for service interruption.

The recommended actions in Table 8.1 are listed for each attack, key integrity status, and severity level. Note that some actions are the same regardless of the severity. Table 8.2 provides actions when the CA private key is known to be compromised. The first column describes the category of

TABLE 8.1

Microsoft TechNet Example Actions for Server Operating System Compromise

Attack Type	Key Integrity	Severity	Actions
Physical attack on offline CA	Known good	2	• Replace server hardware and restore backup. • Renew CA keys for entire chain. • Force new issuance of end-entity certificates.
	Unknown/compromised	1	• Retire CA server. • Complete CA server replacement and HSM reinitialization.
Remote/vulnerability attack on online CA	Known good	4	• Patch exploited vulnerability. • Use existing server hardware and restore backup.
	Unknown/compromised	3	• Patch exploited vulnerability. • Use existing server hardware and restore backup. • Revoke CA certificate and publish root CRL. • Renew CA key. • Force new issuance of end-entity certificates.
Physical attack on online CA	Known good	3	• Replace server hardware and restore backup.
	Unknown/compromised	2	• Replace server hardware and restore backup. • Revoke CA certificate and publish root CRL. • Renew CA key. • Force new issuance of end-entity certificates. • Add CA certificate to untrusted store.

TABLE 8.2

Microsoft TechNet Example Actions for Cryptographic Compromise

Category	Attack Type	Severity	Actions
Mathematic attack on offline CA	Brute force	2	• Use existing server hardware. • Renew CA keys for entire CA chain. • Use a larger key size. • Force new issuance of end-entity certificates. • Add CA certificate to untrusted store.
	Algorithm weakness	2	• Use existing server hardware. • Renew CA keys for the entire CA chain. • Use an uncompromised algorithm. • Force new issuance of end-entity certificates. • Add CA certificate to untrusted store.
Logical attack on offline CA	MTM or Shim	1	• Retire CA server. • Complete CA server replacement and HSM • reinitialization. • Force new issuance of end-entity certificates. • Revoke subordinate CAs and publish final CRL. • Add CA certificate to untrusted store.
Mathematic attack on online CA	Brute force	3	• Renew CA keys for the entire CA chain. • Use a larger key size. • Revoke CA certificate and publish root CRL. • Force new issuance of end-entity certificates. • Add CA certificate to untrusted store.
	Algorithm weakness	3	• Renew CA keys for the entire CA chain. • Use a larger key[1] size. • Revoke CA certificate and publish root CRL. • Force new issuance of end-entity certificates. • Add CA certificate to untrusted store.

(Continued)

TABLE 8.2   (*Continued*)

Category	Attack Type	Severity	Actions
Logical attack on online CA	OS vulnerability	2	• Replace server hardware and restore backup. • Revoke CA certificate and publish root CRL. • Renew CA key. • Force new issuance of end-entity certificates. • Add CA certificate to untrusted store.
	MTM or Shim	3	• Patch exploited vulnerability. • Use existing server hardware and restore backup. • Revoke CA certificate and publish root CRL. • Renew CA key. • Force new issuance of end-entity certificates.

attacks for offline and online CA. The second column describes specific types of attacks. The third column provides the severity of the attack. The fourth column recommends actions relative to the category, type, and severity of attack.

The compromise of these points within the PKI can be organized into four main categories that should be considered: (1) private key compromise, (2) private key access, (3) limited access to the private key, and (4) other attacks. We next review each of these categories.

8.2.1   PRIVATE KEY COMPROMISE

This is where an attacker has gained access to a copy of the CA or RA's private key and can fraudulently sign information, such as the following:

- CA-distributed PKCS#12 file containing the CA private key exported from the hardware security module (HSM)
- CA-issued code-signing certificate to fraudulently sign any executable code
- RA requests for certificates to obtain counterfeit certificates
- RA requests for revocations to illegally revoke legitimate certificates

Therefore, when a CA is compromised, the investigator must assume that every certificate issued by that CA is potentially compromised as well. If the CA is a root CA or an intermediate issuing CA, then all the CA certificates and all the certificates that any subordinate CA issues must also be considered to be compromised. A full private key compromise could result from an operating system compromise or a cryptographic compromise. Both compromises are covered here.

There are several attack vectors for the operating system of a CA server, and the response depends on many factors. Operating systems can be compromised physically or remotely.

Examples of physical attacks involve an attacker gaining access to a server by using the console due to the following:

- An unlocked server
- An attack against credentials
- An insider attack using stolen or known good credentials
- The use of storage media to inject an exploit or create a unique bootable operating system partition to make changes to the primary operating system drive

Both offline and online CA server types are susceptible to physical attack, whether it is by an intruder, an insider attack, or an unknowing person via a social engineering attack or infected file transfer device. If an offline CA is kept offline, it is not susceptible to remote attacks. However, online CA servers as well as web servers responsible for enrollment services or enrollment validation are susceptible. Examples of remote attacks are as follows:

- Brute force attacks against credentials to gain access using remote desktop
- Services or other remote management tools
- Utilizing an operating system vulnerability to gain access to a system
- Malware introduced by an operating system vulnerability
- An unaware person with access to the system being coerced into installing the malware

For CA servers, regardless of whether the operating system compromise is physical or remote, the severity of the compromise and the corresponding response depend on whether the private key integrity is known to be good or if the key integrity is unknown or compromised.[2]

Another attack vector that can lead to full key access is a cryptographic compromise of the underlying PKI algorithms. For each public key, there is only one mathematically unique private key, and the algorithms to generate keys, generate digital signatures, and perform encryption and decryption are well known. Researchers or persistent attackers can dedicate multiple servers and build testing algorithms to determine the private key by brute force. If a weakness is found in an algorithm used by the CA or weak keys are used, the weakness could be further exploited to identify the private key or issue certificates that appear to come from the CA.

8.2.2 Private Key Access

When an attacker or malicious insider has gained access to a CA or RA private key from an operating system compromise, the CA or RA may not have sufficient information to determine which certificates need to be revoked. This is one of the most difficult to recover from because the tendency is to keep the CA or RA in operation by just revoking the fraudulent certificates rather than revoking the CA or RA certificate and rebuilding the compromised system.

8.2.3 Limited Access to the Private Key

If an attacker gains access to a CA or RA and can request or issue certificates, but the breach was recorded at the time and date of the unauthorized certificates, then in this situation, revocation of the unauthorized certificates is possible.

8.2.4 Other Attacks

This category includes other attacks such as denial of services (DoS) and theft. DoS may block PKI services preventing the issuance of new certificates or interfere with certificate validation by obstructing access to CRL location or the OCSP responder. Theft of a CA or RA server that has access to an HSM protecting the CA or RA's private key might allow unauthorized access to the CA or RA private keys. Theft of the HSM itself might compromise the CA or RA private key depending on the sophistication of the attacker, the simplicity of the HSM, and the resources available to the attacker. Loss or theft of a remote access device might allow unauthorized access to the CA or RA systems or the HSM protecting the private keys.

So far, we have looked at PKI hierarchy compromise areas, the Microsoft PKI compromise charts, and compromise categories. Now that we understand the points that can be attacked and the compromises that could happen, it is time to look at building and maintaining an incident response plan to cope with a potential PKI compromise.

8.3   PKI INCIDENT RESPONSE PLAN

As discussed with business continuity and disaster recovery in Chapter 7, "Operational Considerations," an incident response plan allows an organization to take coordinated action when a security breach occurs. The PKI incident response team must have the correct processes and procedures in place to respond to a PKI-related incident and execute the six basic steps of any incident response plan:

Step 1: Preparation
Step 2: Detection
Step 3: Containment
Step 4: Eradication
Step 5: Remediation
Step 6: Follow-up

In August 2012, the National Institute for Standards and Technology (NIST) released an update to its Computer Security Incident Handling Guide[3] – Special Publication 800–61. This is the third revision to the guide and offers guidance on issues that have arisen since the previous release in March 2008. This current guide addresses new technologies and attack vectors and changes the prioritization criteria for incident response and facilitating information sharing. There is currently no specific section on PKI incidents, but the guide can be used as a good example for building a specific PKI incident response plan. The old NIST guide had a small set of five categories of incidents:

1. Denial of service
2. Malicious code
3. Unauthorized access
4. Inappropriate usage
5. Multiple components

The guide has taken these categories and replaced them with the new concept of an attack vector. An attack vector is how an attacker might carry out the attack. The vectors included in the updated guide are as follows:

- External/removable media: An attack executed from removable media or a peripheral device
- Attrition: An attack that employs brute force methods to compromise, degrade, or destroy systems, networks, or services
- Web: An attack executed from a website or web-based application
- E-mail: An attack executed via an e-mail message or attachment
- Impersonation: An attack involving replacement of something benign with something malicious, for example, spoofing, man-in-the-middle attacks, rogue wireless access points, and SQL injection attacks, all involving impersonation
- Improper usage: Any incident resulting from violation of an organization's acceptable usage policies by an authorized user
- Loss or theft of equipment: The loss or theft of a computing device or media used by the organization, such as a laptop or smartphone
- Other: An attack that does not fit into any of the other categories

These attack vectors can be used when building a PKI incident response plan. Each attack vector has its own characteristics about detection, containment, eradication, and remediation activities. The new NIST guide also presents a mechanism for prioritizing incidents, pointing out the need for identifying the significant attacks from the large number of minor or nuisance attacks and dealing with those incidents first.

Functional impact describes how the business functions are affected by the system and is categorized as none, low, medium, or high. Incidents with a high functional impact result in a situation where the organization is unable to provide one or more critical services to all users.

Information impact describes the sensitivity of the information breached during the incident and may be categorized as follows:

- None – If no data were breached
- Privacy breach – If sensitive personal identifying information is lost
- Proprietary breach – If trade secrets may have been compromised
- Integrity loss – If data have been modified or substituted

Recoverability impact describes the resources needed to recover from the incident and may be categorized as follows:

- Regular – If no additional resources are needed
- Supplemented – If the company can predict the recovery time but needs additional resources
- Extended – For cases where the company cannot predict recovery time
- Not recoverable – The most serious incidents when recovery is not possible

These three areas of incident prioritization can easily be adapted to the PKI environment. When a PKI area is compromised, the functional, information, and recovery impacts can be estimated based on the area of the compromise, the extent of the compromise, the business processes affected, and the corresponding information disclosed or lost.

SPECIAL NOTE 8-1 NIST 800–61

The NIST Computer Security Incident Handling Guide is an excellent tool for building or updating a PKI incident response plan.

In developing the incident response plan, it is important to use the assumption that every precaution to avoid a PKI compromise will be taken, but the incident response plan must be written with the assumption that sooner or later a breach will happen. As part of planning, the types of information protected by the certificates, the private keys, and associated symmetric keys must be known, as well as the related data breach laws. Data privacy and data breach notification laws vary by jurisdiction and industry. The relative risks must be understood when data are lost or disclosed. For example, personally identifiable information is not the same as personal healthcare information (PHI) and is not the same as payment card industry (PCI) data or even sensitive personal information. For multinational organizations that operate in different jurisdictional areas or whose customers reside in different countries, it is essential to have written in your plan what responses are required, what notifications are needed, who will take the appropriate actions, and the time frames dictated by law – basically, the PKI incident response plan needs to address who, what, when, where, and how.

SPECIAL NOTE 8-2 PKI INCIDENT RESPONSE PLAN

Organizations need a PKI incident response plan that must be regularly reviewed and rehearsed as part of best practices.

Many organizations have annual business continuity or disaster recovery tests, or even quarterly exercises. Similarly, organizations need to practice their incident response plan. If the plans are not rehearsed, there is no way of knowing if an organization is prepared for a breach or if they need to wing it when an incident occurs. Despite having a plan, an unrehearsed plan is essentially unproven, and the organization is basically unprepared. Establishing an incident response capability should include the following actions as outlined by the NIST guide:

- Developing an incident response policy in addition to the incident response plan
- Developing procedures for performing incident handling and reporting
- Setting guidelines for communicating with outside parties regarding incidents
- Selecting a team structure and staffing model
- Establishing relationships and lines of communication between the incident response team and others, both internal (e.g., legal department) and external (e.g., law enforcement agencies) groups
- Determining what services the incident response team should provide
- Staffing and training the incident response team

The time to create an incident response plan is not during or after a PKI compromise, but before anything happens. Once a PKI incident response plan is in place, the initial process is to monitor the PKI environment prior to an incident occurring.

8.4   MONITORING THE PKI ENVIRONMENT PRIOR TO AN INCIDENT

Both large and small organizations deploy a variety of security monitoring tools to keep watch over their network and applications. These tools identify what is normal and what is not and raise alerts and alarms when something amiss is detected. Defense in depth means multiple tools and layers are needed. Intrusion detection system (IDS), intrusion prevention system (IPS), and security information and event management (SIEM) all come into play when monitoring the infrastructure. What one tool might miss another might detect.

Monitoring includes active and passive scans of applications, servers, cryptographic modules, middleware, operating systems, and associated network appliances. Active scans include checking domain names and enabled Internet Protocol (IP) addresses for working ports and protocols. Only authorized ports and protocols should be enabled; they should be compliant with the Internet Assigned Numbers Authority[4] and operate current software to avoid known security flaws. Passive scans include collecting system and application logs, reviewing logs for significant events, and performing analysis for current or past attacks. Analysis might be performed in real time as events occur or after events occur, which might be hours, days, weeks, or even months. Figure 8.5 provides a conceptual framework for PKI system monitoring and its potential interface with network and application monitoring.

PKI systems such as CA and RA servers generate local operating system logs, middleware logs, cryptographic module logs, and application logs. PKI system monitoring might access the local server logs, collect logs, and also have monitoring agents on the CA and RA servers. Support staff might manage PKI system monitoring applications using local or remote workstations or even tablets, including alerts, reports, or analytical processes. PKI-related information might also be collected by other monitoring systems and forwarded to the PKI system monitoring.

For example, PKI-enabled application systems likewise generate local operating system logs, middleware logs, cryptographic module logs, and application logs. Application monitoring might access the local server logs, collect logs, and also have monitoring agents on the application servers. For example, System A does not have an application monitoring agent, but System B has an application monitoring agent. PKI-relevant logs collected by the application monitoring might be forwarded to the PKI system monitoring.

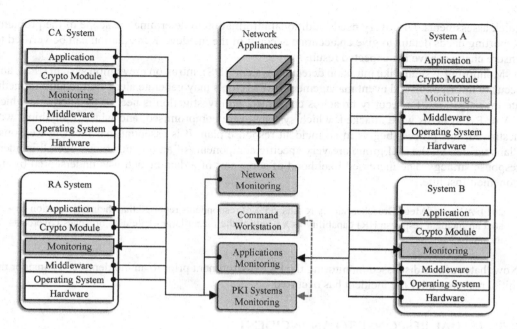

FIGURE 8.5   Monitoring tools.

As another example, network appliances, such as routers, firewalls, or switches that connect PKI systems, which support PKI-enabled applications or are themselves PKI-enabled appliances, might generate logs or send Simple Network Management Protocol traps to a network monitoring tool. PKI-relevant logs and traps collected by network monitoring might also be forwarded to the PKI system monitoring. Operating systems, middleware, and cryptographic modules might generate logs for a variety of events that would be common across all systems:

- Operating system events that generate logs include successful and failed access attempts; network connection information such as port, protocol, and IP addresses; device errors; and data management actions such as file and folder creation, modification, and deletion.
- Middleware events that trigger logs include session information such as time stamps and resource issues, including system, network, and application errors.
- Cryptographic modules might generate logs for cryptographic actions such as key generation, import, export, and usage, including signature generation for certificates and CRL and internal processing errors.
- CA application events that should generate logs include private key and certificate installation, certificate issuance, CRL issuance, and failed access attempts.
- RA application events that should generate logs include private key and certificate installation, certificate signing requests, certificate revocation requests, and failed CA interactions.
- PKI-enabled application events that should generate logs include private key and certificate installation, certificate validation failures, signature verification failures, key transport failures, and key agreement failures.
- Network appliance events that correlate to PKI events include failed connections to CA or RA systems, certificate validation failures, signature verification failures, key transport failures, and key agreement failures.

Monitoring controls support incident management by providing information for initial response, the discovery process, reporting, and ultimately remediation. Initial responses need precise data for quick assessments. Discovery needs additional information to determine the scope of the problem. Reporting needs details to give an accurate account of the incident. Remediation can be verified to ensure changes have the expected results.

Monitoring systems like intrusion detection system (IDS), intrusion prevention system (IPS), and security information and event management (SIEM) tools may generate alerts that require immediate investigation. If a security breach is confirmed, an investigation is needed to determine which CA or RA systems were attacked, which systems were compromised, and what, if anything, was destroyed; this process begins in an incident response plan. It is essential that Incident Response Plans written by the PKI group are very specific components of an organization's overall incident response strategy. The increased likelihood of some sort of a data breach was underscored by the Ponemon Institute:

> 2014: A Year of Mega Breaches survey results, 55% of respondents reported that their organization created an incident response (IR) capability as a result of the recent large-scale data breaches covered in the media.[5]

Now that we have discussed monitoring the PKI environment prior to an incident, let's consider the initial response after the incident has occurred.

8.5   INITIAL RESPONSE TO AN INCIDENT

When a PKI compromise occurs, the impact on an organization can be extremely detrimental and very quick; therefore, it is critical to respond quickly and effectively. The concept of general computer security incident response has become widely accepted and implemented. The only challenge that the PKI team has is to tailor the response to just the PKI environment. One of the benefits of having a written PKI incident response plan is that a plan gives you a way of responding to incidents in a systematic fashion so that all the appropriate actions are taken in the correct order.

Performing the initial analysis and validation of a PKI compromise can be very challenging. The NIST guide to incident response provides the following recommendations for making incident analysis easier and more effective; these can be applied directly to the PKI environment:

- *Profile networks and systems*: Profiling is measuring the characteristics of expected activity so that changes to it can be more easily identified. Examples of profiling are running file integrity checking software on hosts to derive checksums for critical files and monitoring network bandwidth usage to determine what the average and peak usage levels are on various days and times. In practice, it is difficult to detect incidents accurately using most profiling techniques; organizations should use profiling as one of several detection and analysis techniques.
- *Understand normal behaviors*: Incident response team members should study networks, systems, and applications to understand what their normal behavior is so that abnormal behavior can be recognized more easily. No incident handler will have a comprehensive knowledge of all behavior throughout the environment, but handlers should know which experts could fill in the gaps. One way to gain this knowledge is through reviewing log entries and security alerts. This may be tedious if filtering is not used to condense the logs to a reasonable size. As handlers become more familiar with the logs and alerts, they should be able to focus on unexplained entries, which are usually more important to investigate. Conducting frequent log reviews should keep the knowledge fresh, and the analyst should be able to notice trends and changes over time. The reviews also give the analyst an indication of the reliability of each source.
- *Create a log retention policy*: Information regarding an incident may be recorded in several places, such as firewall, IDPS, and application logs. Creating and implementing a log

retention policy that specifies how long log data should be maintained may be extremely helpful in analysis because older log entries may show reconnaissance activity or previous instances of similar attacks. Another reason for retaining logs is that incidents may not be discovered until days, weeks, or even months later. The length of time to maintain log data is dependent on several factors, including the organization's data retention policies and the volume of data. See NIST Special Publication 800–92 Guide to Computer Security Log Management[6] for additional recommendations related to logging.

- *Perform event correlation*: Evidence of an incident may be captured in several logs that each contains different types of data – a firewall log may have the source IP address that was used, whereas an application log may contain a username. A network IDPS may detect that an attack was launched against a particular host, but it may not know if the attack was successful. The analyst may need to examine the host's logs to determine that information. Correlating events among multiple indicator sources can be invaluable in validating whether a particular incident occurred.
- *Keep all host clocks synchronized*: Protocols such as the Network Time Protocol synchronize clocks among hosts. Event correlation will be more complicated if the devices reporting events have inconsistent clock settings. From an evidentiary standpoint, it is preferable to have consistent time stamps in logs – for example, to have three logs that show an attack occurred at 12:07:01 a.m., rather than logs that list the attack as occurring at 12:07:01, 12:10:35, and 11:07:06.
- *Maintain and use a knowledge base of information*: The knowledge base should include information that handlers need for quick referencing during incident analysis. Although it is possible to build a knowledge base with a complex structure, a simple approach can be effective. Text documents, spreadsheets, and relatively simple databases provide effective, flexible, and searchable mechanisms for sharing data among team members. The knowledge base should also contain a variety of information, including explanations of the significance and validity of precursors and indicators, such as IDPS alerts, operating system log entries, and application error codes.
- *Use Internet search engines for research*: Internet search engines can help analysts find information on unusual activity. For example, an analyst may see some unusual connection attempts targeting Transmission Control Protocol (TCP) port 22912. Performing a search on the terms "TCP," "port," and "22912" may return some hits that contain logs of similar activity or even an explanation of the significance of the port number. Note that separate workstations should be used for research to minimize the risk to the organization from conducting these searches.
- *Run packet sniffers to collect additional data*: Sometimes the indicators do not record enough detail to permit the handler to understand what is occurring. If an incident is occurring over a network, the fastest way to collect the necessary data may be to have a packet sniffer capture network traffic. Configuring the sniffer to record traffic that matches specified criteria should keep the volume of data manageable and minimize the inadvertent capture of other information. Because of privacy concerns, some organizations may require incident handlers to request and receive permission before using packet sniffers.
- *Filter the data*: There is simply not enough time to review and analyze all the indicators; at minimum, the most suspicious activity should be investigated. One effective strategy is to filter out categories of indicators that tend to be insignificant. Another filtering strategy is to show only the categories of indicators that are of the highest significance; however, this approach carries substantial risk because new malicious activity may not fall into one of the chosen indicator categories.
- Seek assistance from others: Occasionally, the team will be unable to determine the full cause and nature of an incident. If the team lacks sufficient information to contain and

eradicate the incident, then it should consult with internal resources (e.g., information security staff) and external resources (e.g., U.S. Computer Emergency Readiness Team [US-CERT], other CSIRTs, contractors with incident response expertise). It is important to accurately determine the cause of each incident so that it can be fully contained and the exploited vulnerabilities can be mitigated to prevent similar incidents from occurring.

Now that we have discussed monitoring and the initial response, including the NIST guidelines, let's consider the discovery process for the incident.

8.6 DETAILED DISCOVERY OF AN INCIDENT

PKI application monitoring will provide system logs that will typically provide sufficient operations data to allow the various monitoring and reporting systems to display trends, flag anomalies, and generate alarms. This information and the alarms can then be followed up by PKI staffing after false-positive data are discarded. What can make a PKI incident investigation challenging is the time before an incident is detected. Days, weeks, and possibly months of logs should also be inspected to determine if the compromise may have been missed some time previously. Security IDS, IPS, and SIEM tools can be used to drill down into the period before and after a suspected compromise may have taken place. This is particularly important where an attack's initial objective is to compromise a system from which further internal attacks can be initiated.

Using existing security monitoring tools with network packet capture tools can help in identifying the system or systems that may have been compromised. Network capture data can be an indispensable addition to the forensic diagnosis if a PKI compromise occurs. Network data are valuable and can provide information on interactions with other systems, unusual activity, or atypical protocol usage. There are simple passive tools available to capture, index, store, and retrieve network packet data[7]:

- Data packets passed between CA component and service tiers are a good source of irrefutable data that show exactly what transpired between the various components of the PKI service.
- Network traffic data show what communication occurred among the service tiers, and the same trace also shows what communications did not take place. This can be useful if expected communications did not occur (like a CRL update that did not take place). This lack of information can aid in understanding the root cause of the compromise or actions that were suppressed by the compromise.
- Time stamps on network data packets allow correlations between events if the system clocks are synchronized as recommended per the NIST guide.
- Network data packets can be retrieved, and session reconstruction can occur tracing the attacker's activities that might not be discovered during the initial investigation.
- Network data and host-generated logs and events can be used to cross-reference events across different host systems.

An emerging trend in incident management is automated incident management systems. These systems will automate several tasks to free up personnel to respond to serious incidents and real compromises. It is not abnormal for an organization to experience thousands of new security alerts every day. With all those warnings popping up, it is easy to understand how attacks can go undetected until it is too late. Security operations centers and cyber incident response teams are simply overwhelmed by the volume of threat activity. This is primarily because investigating and responding to many of these events consists of many labor-intensive manual efforts[8] – collecting information, creating trouble tickets, sending e-mails, and generating reports – that can occupy many of the personnel assigned to respond to actual attacks. These automated incident management systems can be tailored to the PKI environment and reduce the time and effort needed to zero in on PKI-based attacks and compromises.

These automated systems can log into potentially affected systems after an alert is generated to look for something out of the ordinary. These systems can be set to automatically look for new files, search Windows event logs, and compare them to other systems or baselines. When the analysis is complete, a PKI engineer can analyze the results or probe the systems deeper if anomalies are found. Once an attack is identified, much of the work needed to remediate it can already be started.

8.7   COLLECTION OF FORENSIC EVIDENCE

If a breach occurs in the PKI environment, it will be necessary to plan how to collect evidence for analysis without further compromising the situation and making the breach worse. The log files on CAs, RAs, and HSMs will all contribute to and contain information about what has been accessed, what processes have been run, and any connections from the outside that may have been made. The keyboard might have data in its buffers containing the last commands typed on the keyboard. Of course, there are always the permanent files, the non-PKI network and system logs discussed in the previous section, the active network connections, and the users who are currently logged on. However, there are several problems with trying to collect forensic computer evidence:

1. Once in the middle of a PKI incident, the actions taken to prevent further system compromise can alter the system state and may damage or destroy forensics data that could be used to find the attackers. Anything done on the CA system such as running diagnostic programs will make it harder to determine the actual status of the system at the time of the attack – important files might be overwritten, destroying forensic information.

2. Shutting down or disconnecting a CA, an RA, a web server, or an HSM from the network to avoid further compromise can delete or alter information that might have been important to the investigation. Any data in memory will be lost when the system gets powered off. Any network connection will likely be dropped by the other system when disconnected from the network.

3. Well-intentioned PKI operators may try and find out what is wrong and begin working on the affected system. This can be the absolute worst thing to do at the time. PKI operators should be trained to escalate first if they suspect something has been compromised as opposed to becoming a poorly trained investigator poking at the problem.

SPECIAL NOTE 8-3 PROTECT FORENSIC INFORMATION

It is highly recommended that any compromised systems be immediately isolated from all network connections to preserve forensic evidence, and if that cannot be done, then shutting down the systems is the next best thing to reduce the risk of further loss or exposure.

Most professional forensic investigators understand this dilemma and what tradeoffs must be taken in the heat of dealing with a breach. Again, dealing with a PKI breach is not the time to plan for an incident. Planning the actions taken during an incident will not necessarily make the event less stressful, but it will provide a game plan to follow in the heat of the moment. The PKI incident response plan should focus on the event as a whole and what it means to the organization, the organization's customers, the organization's reputation, and any legal issues. The technical steps to recovery, discussed later in this chapter, will be by far the easiest of the activities in the plan.

One of the most important parts of the investigative process is to maintain the security of the evidence chain. This is where a carefully structured incident response plan can really help. In the haste to find the root of the malware or cause of the breach, PKI staff can jump into many of the logs, databases, and other data files, thereby altering the information that these files contain. If the proper steps and protocol are not followed, the evidence can become compromised, leading to difficulties in finding the original source of the PKI compromise. It is important to note that compromised evidence is not going to help solve the original breach or assist with legal issues.

Keeping the PKI staff on task per the plan is an important aspect of running an incident response plan. A forensics expert can provide the step-by-step processes for investigating data sources in a way that preserves the integrity of the evidence. Further legal review of these steps will help head off any missteps that could result in contaminated evidence. Consider a PKI operator who moves a critical log or inadvertently changes the access time of a critical log file. Those actions could create doubt as to what the attacker did versus what the PKI operator did. Every breach should be investigated with the premise that a major PKI compromise could result in legal action from outside your company.

SPECIAL NOTE 8-4 ENGAGE LEGAL

Involving legal expertise as part of the PKI forensic investigation is an important aspect.

A compromise of a PKI system may affect more than just your own company. A PKI compromise needs to be evaluated with respect to whether there may be any legal action because of the event. The response, investigation, communications, and overall incident response plan need to be written with an eye to legal implications. An internal attorney would be a good review point for the incident response plan to point out where legal consequences should be the overriding concern. If your organization does not have an internal legal team, then a review by a practicing technology attorney could be worth the price. Another legal consideration is to have as much of the post-compromise investigation as possible protected under attorney-client privilege, especially when a PKI compromise significantly affects outside entities.

It may have been a generally accepted practice to have a PKI administrator or the PKI manager in charge of a forensic investigation post-compromise, but there are many good reasons to have a lawyer either as part of the team or leading the team. Many highly specialized forensic investigation companies will have legal experts who are good at looking at operating systems and digging through computer files. This is not to hamper the PKI engineers or to slow down the investigation, but to make sure that whatever is found is clearly documented in the context of the overall legal situation.

One way to reduce the potential of compromised evidence and inadvertent legal complications is to add a qualified attorney to the incident response team or even have the attorney lead the post-compromise investigation of the PKI environment. This may seem like a very expensive addition to the post-compromise cleanup, but if the attorney prevents the contamination of evidence or avoids a significant legal pitfall, the cost of adding the attorney to the team may be insignificant in comparison.

8.8 REPORTING OF AN INCIDENT

Reporting of a PKI compromise may take both an internal form and an external one. For external reporting requirements, if a PKI protects or includes PCI, HIPAA, or PHI information, then a component of the PKI incident plan must include the disclosures they are required to make under the laws and regulations governing their respective industries.[9] Examples of which are as follows:

- PCI DSS 4.0 imposes reporting requirements on organizations that store, process, or transmit credit card holder information. If the PKI compromise event included PCI data – technically called Cardholder Data (CHD) – then reporting requirements will have to be made to the relevant card brands and possibly card processors [B.7.23].

- If the PKI compromise exposed cryptographic keys that protected healthcare data, then HIPAA requires that organizations suffering a security breach notify the affected individuals as well as the Secretary of Health and Human Services.
- And many jurisdictional areas have their own breach notification laws that may require the notification of individuals as well as state governments.

One of the points made in the NIST incident response guide was that companies should share information with trusted partners. From a PKI perspective, "trust" refers to the public or private PKI provider, the RA, the subscribers, and even relying parties. Hence, trusted partners could be outsourced PKI providers, RAs both in-house and potentially outsourced, as well as any trading partners that may be affected by the certificates of the PKI compromise.

The precise set of reporting requirements facing each enterprise varies based on the types of information that are handled and the jurisdictions in which the organization operates. This is another area in which consulting an attorney well-versed in breach notification laws will come in handy in filling out the details of your incident response plan.

Another external reporting requirement that might arise is that of reporting the PKI compromise to the media. The information gathered from the investigation can be shared when it most makes sense. What may not make sense is to release small bits and pieces of the incomplete story allowing for the news media to speculate on the full extent of the problem and the damages it may have caused. Providing a full and complete press release will reduce a company's chance of appearing in multiple news cycles/stories each time a new piece of information comes out. By controlling the reports and sharing information only when it is fully vetted, a good response is much more likely, which can help minimize potentially negative media coverage. This is an area in your incident response plan to factor in your company's communications specialist rather than using one of the PKI engineers to communicate the message.

The final area of external communications is to share information with any of your customers that might be affected. Stay away from inaccurate or technical jargon-filled communications to customers. This can make the situation worse or can lead to further loss of customer trust.

Internal communications within your company will have the same requirements to be accurate as all external communications. Well-intended but misguided internal individuals may leak information outside the organization before the incident response team was prepared for an external communication. Therefore, all internal communications must be accurate, and not shared internally before the information has been fully vetted and the incident response team is prepared should an information leak occur. Other entities that may need to be included in the reporting section of an incident response plan include the following:

- Your company's Internet service provider
- Software vendors of the compromised area
- Hardware vendors including, if affected, HSM vendors
- U.S. Computer Emergency Readiness Team (US-CERT)[10]

It can be far worse to change a story later than to say you do not know and take the time to verify and validate that the information you are about to release is accurate. Balance the need for speed of information release with accuracy. A quick but inaccurate answer will not help the situation. Try to avoid a response that contains excessive jargon or many legal caveats. Find a balance and recognize that it is acceptable to say, "We don't know at this point."

NOTES

1. If the algorithm is weak, it is better to change the algorithm with a stronger key, than to reuse the same algorithm with a larger key.

2. technet.microsoft.com/en-us/library/dn786435.aspx (accessed October 2015).
3. NIST 800-61, https://nvlpubs.nist.gov/nistpubs/SpecialPublications/NIST.SP.800-61r2.pdf
4. www.internetassignednumbersauthority.org
5. www.identityfinder.com/us/Files/2014TheYearOfTheMegaBreach.pdf
6. NIST 800-92, https://nvlpubs.nist.gov/nistpubs/Legacy/SP/nistspecialpublication800-92.pdf
7. www.emulex.com/artifacts/8F743BF4-E2DB-46DC-B8EC-2744000C4177/end_sb_all_general_security.pdf
8. www.baselinemag.com/security/automated-incident-response-todays-must-have.html
9. www.techtarget.com/searchsecurity/tip/PCI-DSS-v40-is-coming-heres-how-to-prepare-to-comply
10. www.us-cert.gov/

9 PKI Governance, Risk, and Compliance

Governance, risk, and compliance (GRC) are three areas of information security used across many industries and organizations. GRC is often considered a discipline to synchronize security policies and practices across an organization's lines of business (LOBs). In this chapter, we look at GRC components as they relate to public key infrastructure (PKI), including organizational structures, audits, and risks.

9.1 PKI GOVERNANCE

Throughout the book, we have discussed various standards organizations such as the American National Standards Institute (ANSI) and the International Organization for Standardization (ISO), accreditation bodies such as the National Institute of Standards and Technology (NIST) for algorithms and cryptographic modules, and other specification sources such as the Internet Engineering Task Force (IETF). We also introduced a hypothetical PKI scenario for the ABC Corporation and reviewed the primary roles for any PKI system. In summary, we have described these topics as follows:

- In Chapter 1, "Introduction," we looked at ANSI and ISO standards organizations.
- In Chapter 4, "PKI Management and Security," we looked at the ABC Corporation's PKI internal and external hierarchies.
- In Chapter 5, "PKI Roles and Responsibilities," we looked at fundamental groups that exist for the various PKI components and participants.
- In Chapter 6, "Security Considerations," we looked at the ABC Corporation's senior management organizational chart.

In order for any organization to be successful in governing its PKI systems, there are three essential support groups whose cooperation and interactions are crucial: management, security, and audit. Each group has its own area of responsibility, but each group also supports the others. Depending on the size of an organization, some of these functions may need to be sourced from outside the organization. For example, a small organization may not have a dedicated audit department, but the audit function is still necessary; in fact, it can be argued that audit is an even more important function for small businesses versus large enterprises so that information technology (IT) and security do not make the mistake of believing that they have built an impenetrable security system.

- *Management*: The organization needs to have a management structure that enables and supports both the security and audit groups.
- *Security*: The organization needs to have a security structure that executes its functions and supports both the management and audit groups.
- *Audit*: The organization needs to have an audit structure that executes its functions and supports both the management and security groups.

In this chapter, we look at the stability, reliability, and due diligence of each group and their interactions with each other. Furthermore, we revisit our hypothetical ABC Corporation organizational chart introduced in Chapter 6, "Security Considerations." Table 9.1 provides a summary of the groups, organizational structure, and the corresponding officers and their responsibility.

DOI: 10.1201/9781003425298-9

TABLE 9.1

ABC Corporation Groups

Group	Officer	Responsibility
CEO	Zane	The chief executive officer (CEO) manages the organization. The CEO reports directly to the board of directors and has five direct reports: HR, legal, CFO, audit, and COO.
HR	Yvonne	The human resources (HR) manage all personnel benefits, including salaries, bonuses, stock options, and medical. The HR reports directly to the CEO.
CLO	Ugo	The chief legal officer (CLO) manages law, regulatory, contractual, privacy, and intellectual property issues. The CLO reports directly to the CEO.
CFO	Paula	The chief financial officer (CFO) manages revenues and expenditures for the organization. The CFO reports directly to the CEO.
Audit	Wayne	The audit group manages law, regulatory, and contractual compliance for the organization. The audit group reports directly to the CEO and has a reporting channel to the board of directors.
COO	Tony	The chief operating officer (COO) manages the daily operations of the organization. The COO reports directly to the CEO and has five direct reports: PKI, CTO, risk, Corp, CIO, and CISO.
PKI	Roger	The public key infrastructure (PKI) staff manages the internal and external CA hierarchies and all PKI systems. The PKI staff reports to the COO.
CTO	Xavier	The chief technology officer (CTO) manages information technology (IT) within the organization. The CTO reports to the COO.
Risk	Veda	The risk group manages financial, reputational, and resource issues for the organization. The risk group reports to the COO.
CSG	Sandra	The corporate security group (CSG) manages campus and building security for the organization. CSG reports to the CCO.
CIO	Oscar	The chief information officer (CIO) manages data and systems for the organization. The CIO reports to the COO.
CISO	Quincy	The chief information security officer (CISO) manages network and system access for the organization. The CISO reports to the COO.

We now discuss each of the major roles for management, security, and audit organizations. The hypothetical ABC corporate structure is used to demonstrate how different groups need to interact and complement each other.

9.1.1 MANAGEMENT ORGANIZATION

Regarding the ABC Corporation, management functions are segmented and allocated for a variety of reasons, including separation of duties. For example, hiring practices are managed by human resources (HR), but each group does the actual hiring to support their areas. Of course, HR does assist in the hiring process so it is always an activity under scrutiny. As another example, current technology is managed by the chief operating officer (COO), but new technology is researched and approved by the chief technology officer (CTO). If the COO had free reign over technology, then vendors might unduly influence decisions without the CTO being a balance. Likewise, the chief information officer (CIO) manages information, but the chief information security officer (CISO) manages the data controls. Otherwise, fewer controls often result in lower costs, which proportionally increases risk. Thus, the risk group measures and evaluates relative risks by striking a balance between vulnerabilities, processes, and controls.

But as everyone knows, the management organization is never static, hence the infamous joke about organizational charts needing time stamps to determine who reports to whom. The reality is that any organization changes its overall structure for many reasons. Human resources change: individuals are hired and fired, quit, retire, and sometimes pass away. Technology changes: new products need support staff, and decommissioned products no longer need staffing. Business changes:

new services need training, adding support staff; old services no longer need training; and staffing is eventually ended. Threats change: new vulnerabilities sometimes require new products or new staffing, whereas older vulnerabilities become obsolete or less of a threat. Vendors change: new releases replace older versions, older products are no longer supported, or product lines disappear due to mergers and acquisitions. Zero-day attacks may even necessitate temporary or permanent changes to the organizational chart to better defend against the attack. And, finally, industry trends can affect the organization: roles that were once considered indispensable either merge into others or are eliminated altogether.

From a PKI perspective, the organization needs to have a management structure that enables and supports both the security and audit groups. By enablement, we simply mean not disabling or impeding the ability of the other groups. The other groups need recognition as having the authority to perform their duties, which includes entitlement (rights), respect, and reporting capabilities to senior management. By support, we simply mean funding and staffing to do their jobs, which includes budgets for staffing, travel, training, and technology. First, let's consider management's responsibility to the various security groups.

- The CLO participates in the policy authority (PA) to address liability, warranty, intellectual property, privacy, and other business matters. As discussed in Chapter 4, "PKI Management and Security," the certificate policy (CP) and certificate practice statement (CPS) include other business and legal matters. As discussed in Chapter 5, "PKI Roles and Responsibilities," both attorneys and business managers participate in the policy authority (PA). Legal also provides contractual language for PKI agreements such as certificate authority (CA), registration authority (RA), subscriber, and relying party agreements.
- The CFO needs to ensure the COO has sufficient funds to manage the daily operations of the organization, including its PKI group, corporate (Corp) for physical security, and the CISO for logical security. Funding should be based on current needs to maintain the existing infrastructure and resources, improvements based on capacity planning, enhancements for additional functionality, remediation efforts for security vulnerabilities, and development dollars when vendor off-the-shelf solutions are unavailable.
- The COO needs to convey the importance of its security groups to the chief executive officer (CEO) to ensure funding for its PKI, corporate (Corp), and CISO. Training needs to be approved to keep knowledge current. Travel needs to be approved to manage people and systems. Technology needs to be approved to manage systems and keep hardware and software components current. As more applications become PKI enabled, the systems need to be upgraded, expanded, and extended with newer capabilities.
- The CTO needs to coordinate with the COO to ensure that technology solutions align with the PKI, corporate (Corp), and CISO security requirements. Designing, developing, or implementing solutions with inherent vulnerabilities is an antithetical approach and should be strongly discouraged. Technical solutions need to comply with security practices and should aspire to industry best practices, not just the minimal security requirements. Security should be based on the greatest common divisor and not the lowest common denominator.
- The CIO needs to collaborate with the COO and security groups for data management and related security controls. The related security controls need to address data in transit, data in storage, and even data in memory. Controls include data confidentiality, data integrity, authentication, authorization, accountability, and even nonrepudiation.
- The risk group needs to collaborate with the COO and security groups to identify and manage the relative risks. External or internal events can affect the organization. External issues include zero-day attacks, new vulnerabilities, emergency fixes, new research, vendor changes such as mergers and acquisitions or product end of life (EOL), denial of service attacks, and even law, regulatory, or contractual changes. Internal issues include

insider threats such as disgruntled employees, discontented contractors, access control failures, malware, equipment failure, data exfiltration, and even industrial espionage.

Next, let's consider the management's responsibility to the audit and risk groups. The primary duty is to provide timely information to both audit and risk.

- The board of directors (BoD) needs to accept direct reporting from the audit group without interference or influence from the COO. Obviously, the audit group needs to collaborate with all its peer groups (HR, legal, and CFO) and the technology and security groups including the risk group, to formulate the most accurate picture.
- The CLO needs to coordinate with the audit and risk groups to address compliance with law, regulatory, contractual, privacy, and intellectual property issues. Changes in any of these landscapes can adversely affect the overall security posture of the organization and inadvertently cause noncompliance issues.
- The CFO needs to provide financial information to the audit and risk groups regarding the stability and growth of the organization. Insufficient funds hamper the organization's ability to grow or even maintain a stable and reliable infrastructure, including staffing.
- The COO needs to provide operational information to the audit and risk groups regarding the resiliency and overall security of the organization. Operational failures, network outages or congestion, and system instabilities all adversely affect the organization.
- The CTO needs to provide technological information to the audit and risk groups regarding the current tactical and future strategies of the organization. Project delays, budget overruns, lack of resources, or obsolete technology can impact the organization.
- The CIO needs to provide data management information to the audit and risk groups regarding the confidentiality, integrity, and authenticity of data, systems, and communications. Data leakages, breaches, modifications, or other security incidents damage the organization.
- The risk group needs to partner with the audit group regarding legal, financial, operational, technology, and data management system issues that affect the overall security of the organization. There should be a substantial relationship between the audit group and the risk. Whereas the risk group can evaluate and prioritize issues, the audit group has direct channel to the board of directors.

For smaller organizations where the roles might overlap, the functional characteristic remains the same; however, separation of duties becomes problematic. In addition, the independence of the audit group needs to be maintained whenever possible. Privately held companies, whose owners and operators are the same individuals, typically have all management groups reporting directly to them, as there might not be the equivalent of a board of directors.

9.1.2 SECURITY ORGANIZATION

In other chapters, we have discussed various aspects of the security organization, generally looking at their respective roles and responsibilities. What we have not discussed up to this point is the overall security groups as they relate to the management and audit groups. Let's review what has been discussed so far.

- Chapter 2, "Cryptography Basics," discussed the importance of key management and the significance of using cryptographic modules, certified by accredited laboratories.
- Chapter 4, "PKI Management and Security," discussed policy and practices, including PKI participants, the policy authority (PA), physical security controls, procedural controls, personnel controls, and audit logs.

- Chapter 5, "PKI Roles and Responsibilities," discussed PKI custodians that handle cryptographic material and security managers who oversee physical security controls.
- Chapter 6, "Security Considerations," discussed physical security controls, logical security controls, audit logs, and cryptographic modules.

The security organization for the ABC Corporation includes PKI, CTO, Risk, Corp, CIO, and CISO groups reporting to the COO. Each group has their own area of responsibility that needs to be managed independently. At the same time, each group has knowledge and experience that needs to complement the other groups. In addition, the collective information, tactics, and strategy need to be shared among the groups to maintain and report on the overall security posture.

- The COO needs to coordinate each of its direct reports in order to consolidate security information. The overall security posture might be presented in a formal report to the chief offices or be summarized as a security dashboard.
- The PKI information includes the number of certificate requests, the number of certificates issued, the number of revocation requests, the number of certificates revoked, service-level statistics, and the relative numbers based on certificate types. Other pertinent information might be certificate misuse or other agreement violations.
- The CTO information includes the number of new system deployments, the number of decommissions, and the system status for patches, modifications, and changes. Other pertinent information might be cyberattacks or other security incidents.
- The risk group information includes the number of new cases, cases in progress, and remediated cases along with the relative risk levels such as high, medium, and low categories.
- The CSG information includes the number of new deployments, decommissions, and facility status. Other pertinent information might be security incidents such as intruders, vandalism, or other security incidents.
- The CIO information includes data volumes transmitted and stored, new database deployments, decommissions, and overall systems status. Other pertinent information might be data loss, data recovery, or other unplanned incidents.
- The CISO information includes access requests, new access allocations, terminated access, or other access changes. Other pertinent information might be unauthorized access attempts or other security incidents.

Information from the COO peer groups is also valuable. While the peer groups do not provide security information per se, some information is actually security related. The COO needs to determine what information is conveyed to its direct reports, what is restricted on a need-to-know basis, and what cannot be shared.

- The HR information might include recent termination of disgruntled employees or those terminated for other causes. Other pertinent information might be internal investigations of employee misconduct that might be in cooperation with the CTO, the Corp, the CIO, the CISO, or the law enforcement.
- The CLO information might include recent changes in law, regulatory, or contractual obligation that might affect the security posture. Other pertinent information might be lawsuits, privacy violations, identity theft, or intellectual properties issues such as patents, copyright, or trademark infringements.
- The CFO information might include budget cuts that affect funding. Other pertinent information might be changes in vendors or product support.
- The audit group information might include noncompliance issues that affect security policy or practices. Other pertinent information might be internal or external assessments of security programs such as the PKI systems.

As discussed in Chapter 6, "Security Considerations," the ABC Corporation might have some independence issues when looking at physical and logical security areas. The Corp reports to the COO, who reports to the CEO, who in turn reports to the board of directors (BoD). All physical security issues are dutifully reported to the COO, but only high-risk issues or incidents are typically reported to the CEO, so consequently the BoD gets edited reports. Similarly, the CTO also reports to the COO, so often the BoD gets filtered information. Furthermore, the audit group is responsible for bringing issues to the BoD, but the audit group also reports to the CEO, and its Corp and CTO peer groups might not openly share information except with the CEO. An unbiased automated security dashboard made available at the senior level including the board of directors is one mechanism that might help avoid unintended independence issues.

Another important issue facing the security organization is cryptography transitions [B.7.16]. Like any other technology, cryptography suffers from vendor and product changes. Vendors might decide that a product has an end of life and is no longer supported. Due to a merger or acquisition, competing products are often eliminated. Cryptographic products and protocols also suffer from vulnerabilities due to buggy code, poor design, or bad implementations. For example, in Chapter 4, "PKI Management and Security," we discussed the standards gap, where products, deployment, or management introduced disparities between security requirements and actual use. However, unlike other technologies, cryptography employs algorithms and key sizes that are affected by many external influences. Cryptanalysis or other research might discover a previously unknown weakness. Mathematical breakthroughs might render an existing security control obsolete. And, of course, Moore's law continues to erode key sizes as computers get faster and storage gets cheaper, which allows once-theoretical solutions to become reality.[1]

9.1.3 Audit Organization

From an information security perspective, an audit is an official inspection of an organization's controls, typically by an independent body or mostly independent group within the organization. The independence arises from either an internal audit group or an external audit group such as a certified public accounting firm. Section 9.6, "PKI Compliance," addresses the audit process, whereas this section deals with the different types of the audit organization. One of the primary governance needs for audit is its independence from senior management. For example, the accountants cannot be the financial auditors due to an inherent conflict of interest, and in a similar manner, groups managing technology cannot also be the one auditing technology or security due to interest conflicts.

There are specialized groups for internal auditors and licensed groups for information security professionals. First, let's consider an internal audit group. The Institute of Internal Auditors (IIA) definition of internal auditing states the fundamental purpose, nature, and scope of internal auditing[2]:

Internal auditing is an independent, objective assurance and consulting activity designed to add value and improve an organization's operations. It helps an organization accomplish its objectives by bringing a systematic, disciplined approach to evaluate and improve the effectiveness of risk management, control, and governance processes.

The IIA Attribute Standards address the characteristics of organizations and parties performing internal audit activities. This standard emphasizes the internal audit need for independence.[3]

- Independence and objectivity: The internal audit activity must be independent, and internal auditors must be objective in performing their work.
- Organizational independence: The chief audit executive must report to a level within the organization that allows the internal audit activity to fulfill its responsibilities. The chief audit executive must confirm to the board, at least annually, the organizational independence of the internal audit activity.

- Direct interaction with the board: The chief audit executive must communicate and interact directly with the board.
- Individual objectivity: Internal auditors must have an impartial, unbiased attitude and avoid any conflict of interest.
- Impairment of independence or objectivity: If independence or objectivity is impaired in fact or appearance, the details of the impairment must be disclosed to the appropriate parties. The nature of the disclosure will depend upon the impairment.

The IIA Performance Standards describe the nature of internal audit activities and provide criteria against which the performance of these services can be evaluated[4]:

- Resource management: The chief audit executive must ensure that internal audit resources are appropriate, sufficient, and effectively deployed to achieve the approved plan.
- Coordination: The chief audit executive should share information and coordinate activities with other internal and external providers of assurance and consulting services to ensure proper coverage and minimize duplication of efforts.
- Reporting to senior management and the board: The chief audit executive must report periodically to senior management and the board on the internal audit activity's purpose, authority, responsibility, and performance relative to its plan. Reporting must also include significant risk exposures and control issues, including fraud risks, governance issues, and other matters needed or requested by senior management and the board.
- External service provider and organizational responsibility for internal auditing: When an external service provider serves as the internal audit activity, the provider must make the organization aware that the organization has the responsibility for maintaining an effective internal audit activity.

The internal audit function might be outsourced, but it is still an internal audit group despite its performance by an external group. Outsourcing an internal audit should not be confused with hiring an external auditor. An external auditor is hired to assess or perform an evaluation for a specific purpose, such as an external audit of the PKI system for the ABC Corporation. Privately held companies whose owners and operators are the same individuals typically have an audit group reporting directly to them. When the internal audit group cannot maintain independence, an alternative is to rely on external auditors. An external audit firm is an accounting firm licensed by a national or regional association, such as the United States, Canada, and the United Kingdom:

- The American Institute of Certified Public Accountants (AICPA) is the world's largest member association representing the accounting profession, with more than 400,000 members in 145 countries and a history of serving the public interest since 1887. AICPA members represent many areas of practice, including business and industry, public practice, government, education, and consulting.[5]
- The Canadian Institute of Chartered Accountants (CICA) represents Canada's 83,000 CA professions both nationally and internationally. The CICA is a founding member of the International Federation of Accountants (IFAC) and the Global Accounting Alliance.[6]
- The Chartered Institute of Management Accountants is the world's largest and leading professional body of management accountants. We have more than 218,000 members and students operating in 177 countries. They work at the heart of business in industry and commerce and not for profit organizations.[7]
- The International Federation of Accountants (IFAC) is the global organization for the accountancy profession dedicated to serving the public interest by strengthening the profession and contributing to the development of strong international economies. IFAC is comprised of over 175 members and associates in 130 countries and jurisdictions,

representing approximately 2.5 million accountants in public practice, education, government service, industry, and commerce.[8]

Regardless of whether internal auditors, outsourced auditors, or external auditors are used to assess and evaluate the PKI system, the auditors need to be educated, knowledgeable, and experienced with at least a basic understanding of asymmetric cryptography. Auditors need to be familiar with digital signatures, digital certificates, Cas, registration authorities, and the many uses of certificates. In addition, auditors also need to understand technology, including operating systems, cryptographic products, signature algorithms, hash functions, cryptographic modules, and even removable media such as smart cards and USB tokens.

9.2   PKI RISKS

Throughout the book, we have referred to various types of risks about confidentiality, integrity, authentication, authorization, accountability, cryptography, protocols, certificates, key management, fraud, data theft, identity theft, identity fraud, legal issues, operational problems, security incidents, and other industry events.

- In Chapter 1, "Introduction," we introduced the concept of PKI Cryptonomics, including mathematics, cryptography, business, information technology, and legal risks.
- In Chapter 2, "Cryptography Basics," we discussed risks relative to cryptographic modules for FIPS 140–2 and 140–3 Mitigation of Other Attacks.
- In Chapter 4, "PKI Management and Security," we discussed various risks relative to formulating the certificate policy (CP) and certificate practice statement (CPS).
- In Chapter 5, "PKI Roles and Responsibilities," we discussed risk issues recognized by auditors, business managers, risk and compliance managers, and various agreements.
- In Chapter 6, "Security Considerations," we discussed various risk issues with regard to physical security, logical security, audit logs, and cryptographic modules.
- In Chapter 8, "Incident Management," we discussed the importance of managing and executing incident response plans.

In this chapter, we discuss several areas, including cryptography, cybersecurity, and operational risks. NIST describes cybersecurity as the ability to protect information technology infrastructure including systems and network components against attacks. Cybersecurity is basically a modern view of communications security (ComSec) that includes cryptographic security, transmission security, emissions security, and physical security controls [B.5.21] and [B.7.17]. Thus, we recognize that while cryptography is an important control within the cybersecurity field, cryptographically related risks are not the same as cybersecurity risks so we discuss them separately. Operational risks include system and network capacity issues, cost concern, and staff comprehension.

Another important risk topic is when the PKI operation is undocumented and consequently without an audit. Whether the PKI is public, private, or something in between, its operation cannot be validated without documented policy and practices. Further, the PKI cannot be trusted without an audit or at least an equivalent assessment. Subjects and Relying Parties alike cannot depend on untrusted and unknown PKI operations.

9.3   CRYPTOGRAPHY RISKS

As discussed in Chapter 2, "Cryptography Basics," symmetric and asymmetric algorithms use keys that are part of the input parameters. Key lengths, which are expressed as the number of bits, tend to be specific to the algorithm. Older algorithms usually have shorter key lengths, and Moore's law [B.7.1] continues to erode cryptographic strengths, so in response keys keep getting larger and protocols get more complicated. As the number of transistors continues to increase, the speed and computational power of computers correspondingly increase, which means exhaustive attacks or complex mathematics to determine the cryptographic key becomes more feasible.

SPECIAL NOTE 9-1 MOORE'S LAW

The number of transistors incorporated in a chip will approximately double every 24 months. Gordon Moore, Intel cofounder, 1965

Furthermore, general research is constantly in a state of flux and evolving. What might have once been an intractable problem becomes solvable. Thus, a mathematical breakthrough might render a cryptographic algorithm based on a "hard" problem almost useless overnight. For example, the Rivest–Shamir–Adleman (RSA) algorithm is based on the infeasibility of factoring large numbers into fundamental prime numbers, where the modulus (n = pq) is the public key that is a product of two large primes. Another example is the Diffie–Hellman (DH) algorithm based on the difficulty of determining discrete logarithms. Yet another example is elliptical curve cryptography (ECC) based on algebraic equations defined on the points of an elliptic curve.

General research is not limited to mathematics. For example, quantum computer technology has evolved to the extent that quantum computers are no longer considered research, but an engineering development problem. Predictively, sometime within the next 5 to 20 years, stable and reliable quantum computers[9] will become available. While quantum computers cannot execute software any more efficiently than classical computers, they are superior at solving complex linear equations, for which classical computers are inferior. Shor's Algorithm[10] running on a quantum computer can derive the asymmetric private key from the public key for RSA, Diffie–Helman, and ECC in matter of moments. The inevitability of quantum computers has been called "quantum risk," "quantum threat," and even "quantum menace."

More likely, general research might discover a new vulnerability within a cryptographic protocol that requires the standard or specification to be updated and the corresponding products to be upgraded with software patches. Alternatively, a design or implementation flaw might be discovered with a particular product that also requires a software patch. In Chapter 4, "PKI Management and Security," we introduced the standards gap where product implementations might fall short of the intended standards. Such gaps might introduce product instability or security vulnerabilities. Product upgrades became problematic when the software from one vendor is embedded in another vendor's product or included as value-added services.

Another vendor issue is product lifetime. Organizations might use products past their end of life (EOL) after vendors stop supporting products. Often, third-party services are needed to continue product use when warranties have expired and cannot be renewed. Mergers and acquisitions can also affect the product EOL. Competing products often cause an abrupt EOL for one with continuing support for another, or conversely the existing products might be replaced with a newer product altogether. Vendors might also enter bankruptcy or go out of business. Like any other technology, product EOL is inescapable; however, unlike other technologies, the cryptographic keys already in use must be managed securely. This is called a cryptographic transition [B.7.16]:

A cryptographic transition is defined as managing the passage from one security architecture to another in a methodical approach that is consistent with prudent business practices and security guidelines.[11]

Similar to product EOL, cryptographic transitions are likewise inevitable. Regardless of what causes the cryptographic transition – Moore's law, mathematical breakthrough, quantum computers, cryptographic vulnerability, or product EOL – there are common effects related to cryptography risks. These risks are potential threats to the PKI system reliability. Consequences related to cryptography risks are discussed in the following.

9.3.1 ALGORITHM ISSUES

Older algorithms that use short keys are susceptible to exhaustive key search attacks. For example, the Data Encryption Standard (DES) algorithm uses 56-bit keys. In the 1990s, the RSA Security Corporation began a series of DES Challenges for prize money, attempting to demonstrate that DES had reached the end of its lifecycle. In 1997, the DES II Challenge was completed, finding the DES key in about 140 days. Two years later in 1999, the DES III Challenge was completed in less than 24 hours. While the DES algorithm remains cryptographically reliable, its short keys are no longer viable. Consequently, Triple DES (3DES) using two or three 56-bit keys is still in use today for some applications, with migration to Advanced Encryption Standard (AES) that uses 128-bit, 192-bit, or 256-bit keys. Other symmetric algorithms have different length keys, such as Blowfish with a range of 32-bit to 448-bit keys, Cast with a range of 40-bit to 128-bit keys, RC2 with 64-bit default keys, and Skipjack with 80-bit keys.

However, not all key lengths have the same strength. NIST provides comparable algorithm strengths based on the estimated amount of work needed to break the algorithms or determine the keys (with the given key sizes) that are approximately the same using a given resource. The work factor is expressed as the bits of security or cryptographic strengths [B.5.19] shown in Table 9.2. Note that NIST only provides equivalent cryptographic strengths for algorithms it supports, so the equivalency table does not include all algorithms.

Historically, when cryptography was a controlled technology under import or export laws, even DES was restricted to 40-bit keys. This was achieved by setting 16 of the 56-bit key to a predetermined value that was specified by the governing body. As larger keys became necessary, NIST compared algorithm strengths. For example, as shown in Figure 9.1, 3DES is the DES algorithm used three times in the sequence: encrypt, decrypt, and encrypt. The keys for each function depend on whether one, two, or three keys are used. One key (1K) is the same as just DES for backward compatibility with older systems and transition purposes. Two key (2K) uses two 56-bit keys but per the NIST comparison only provides 80-bit cryptographic strength. Three key (3K) uses three 56-bit keys but only gives 112-bit strength. Thus, the key size is often determined by the algorithm and its cryptographic strength is not necessarily its length.

Conversely, looking at the rest of the table, AES key lengths are the same as its cryptographic strengths. In addition to symmetric algorithms, the table includes asymmetric and hash algorithms, and as discussed in Chapter 3, "PKI Building Blocks," symmetric, asymmetric, and hash algorithms

TABLE 9.2
Cryptographic Strength Equivalency

Cryptographic Strength	Symmetric Algorithm	Hash Algorithm	ECDSA/ECDH Algorithm	RSA/DSA/DH Algorithms
-	DES-40	-	-	-
40 bit	DES-56	-	-	-
40 bit	3DES-56	-	-	-
80 bit	3DES-112	SHA1–160	ECC-160	RSA-1024
112 bit	3DES-168	SHA2–224	ECC-224	RSA-2048
128 bit	AES-128	SHA2–256	EEC-256	RSA-3072
192 bit	AES-192	SHA2–384	ECC-384	RSA-7680
256 bit	AES-256	SHA2–256	ECC-512	RSA-15360

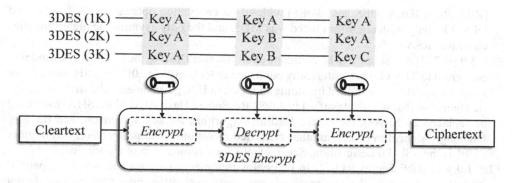

FIGURE 9.1 Overview of Triple DES (3DES) algorithm.

are typically used with data transmission protocols and key management schemes. The Secure Hash Algorithms SHA1 and SHA2 have effective cryptographic strengths that are half their hash lengths. Likewise, the cryptographic strength of elliptical curve cryptography (ECC) keys is also half of their lengths. However, the RSA algorithm, the digital signature algorithm (DSA), and the Diffie–Hellman algorithm all have much lower ratios but with the same key lengths.

Modern algorithms tend to use longer keys resistant to key search attacks, but other cryptanalysis necessitates even longer keys for some algorithms. Table 9.2 depicts larger key sizes for the RSA, DSA, DH, and ECC algorithms. For example, to achieve 80-bit cryptographic strength, the RSA, DSA, or DH key length must be 1024 bits. As noted earlier, Moore's law continually pushes for greater cryptographic strength that requires longer keys. For example, RSA-1024 was retired in 2008 by the CA Browser Forum[12] in favor of RSA-2048 for root CA, subordinate CA, and subscriber certificates. The cryptographic strengths for DSA and DH also apply.

However, the 2048-bit RSA, DSA, and DH keys are only equivalent to 112-bit cryptographic strength, the same as 3DES-3K. In order for the RSA, DSA, and DH algorithms to have the same strength as AES-128, their keys would need to be increased to 3072 bits. But bigger key sizes impact cryptographic products as the corresponding storage and buffer sizes also need to increase. And bigger key sizes also affect software performance. Eventually as stronger cryptographic strengths become necessary, the RSA, DSA, and DH key sizes become problematic. Conversely, the growth ratio between ECC, specifically ECDSA and ECDH, and the other algorithms is more optimized and more sustainable in the long run.

9.3.2 Protocol Issues

Older protocols that use older algorithms are vulnerable to exhaustive key search attacks. For example, consider the overlapping history of the Secure Socket Layer (SSL) and Transport Layer Security (TLS) protocols. SSL came first, evolved into TLS, and eventually reached its EOL. The basic protocol has remained consistent; however, changes have been made over several years to improve security and update ciphers suites.

SSL was developed by the Netscape Communications Corporation pre-1995, but the specification was never published. Dr. Taher Elgamal developed the basic protocol and is often called the Father[13] of SSL.[14] At about the same time, Netscape was in cahoots with MasterCard and others developing a new electronic commerce payments protocol that eventually evolved into the joint MasterCard and Visa Secure Electronic Transaction standard published in 1997. See Table 9.3 for a list of protocols and associated algorithms. Also see the Internet Assigned Numbers Authority (IANA) Transport Layer Security (TLS) Parameters[15] site for the TLS Cipher Suites.

SSL v2.0 [B.7.12] was submitted by Netscape as an Internet Draft to the IETF in 1995, but it was never published as a specification. The protocol included five symmetric algorithms

(RC2, RC4, IDEA, DES, and 3DES) with 40-bit encryption options for RC2, RC4, and DES. The only hash algorithm listed was MD5, and the only asymmetric algorithm allocated was RSA.

SSL 3.0 [B.7.13] was submitted by Netscape as an Internet Draft to the IETF in 1996 and was converted to TLS v1.0 but historically published as RFC 6101 in 2011 [B.3.51]. Support for several algorithms was added including Skipjack (a U.S. government–classified symmetric algorithm that was declassified in 1998), the Secure Hash Algorithm (SHA that would be replaced by SHA1), the Diffie–Hellman algorithm for key agreement, and the Key Exchange Algorithm (KEA, another classified algorithm). The protocol version number {3, 0} is the SSL 3.0 designation. See Table 9.3 for a comparison of algorithms.

TLS 1.0 was published as RFC 2246 in 1999 with a mechanism for backward compatibility to SSL; however, the two protocols have sufficient differences that the two do not interoperate. Consequently, implementations often support SSL v2.0, SSL v3.0, and TLS v1.0 protocols. Skipjack and KEA were removed from the list. Interestingly, the protocol version "3.1" number {3, 1} is used for the TLS 1.0 designation. See Table 9.3 for a comparison of algorithms.

TLS 1.1 was published as RFC 4346 in 2006 [B.3.47] with some small security improvements, clarifications, and editorial improvements. RC2–128 was removed from the list, but its 40-bit version was retained for backward compatibility. Skipjack and KEA were also removed from the algorithm list. AES was added to the list. The protocol version number {3, 2} is used for the TLS 1.1 designation. See Table 9.3 for a comparison of algorithms.

TABLE 9.3

SSL and TLS Cipher Suite Algorithms

– SSL 2.0	RFC 6101 SSL 3.0	RFC 2246 TLS 1.0	RFC 4346 TLS 1.1	RFC 5246 TLS 1.2	RFC 8446 TLS v1.3
RC2–128/40	RC2–128/40	RC2–128/40	RC2–128/40	–	–
RC2–128	RC2–128	RC2–128	–	–	–
RC4–128/40	RC4–128/40	RC4–128/40	RC4–128/40	–	–
RC4–128	RC4–128	RC4–128	RC4–128	RC4–128	–
IDEA-128	IDEA-128	IDEA-128	IDEA-128	–	–
DES-64/40	DES-64/40	DES-64/40	DES-64/40	–	–
DES-64	DES-64	DES-64	DES-64	–	–
3DES-192	3DES-192	3DES-192	3DES-192	3DES-192	–
–	Skipjack	–	–	–	–
–	–	–	AES-128	AES-128	AES-128
–	–	–	AES-256	AES-256	AES-256
–	–	–	–	–	CHACHA20
MD5	MD5	MD5	MD5	MD5	–
–	SHA1	SHA1	SHA1	SHA1	–
–	–	–	–	SHA2–256	SHA2–256
–	–	–	–	–	SHA2–384
–	–	–	–	–	POLY1305
RSA	RSA	RSA	RSA	RSA	RSA
–	DH	DH	DH	DH	DHE
–	KEA	–	–	–	–
–	–	–	–	ECDH	ECDHE
–	–	–	–	ECDSA	ECDSA
–	–	–	–	–	EdDSA

TLS 1.2 was published as RFC 5246 [B.3.48] in 2008 that contained improved flexibility, particularly for negotiation of cryptographic algorithms. The 40-bit options for RC2, RC4, and DES were removed, along with IDEA. Support for SHA2 and the Elliptic Curve Digital Signature Algorithm (ECDSA) was added. The protocol version number {3, 3} is used for the TLS v1.2 designation. See Table 9.3 for a comparison of algorithms. For details, see Section 3.2.1, "TLS v1.2 Overview."

TLS 1.3 was published as RFC 8446 [B.3.55] in 2018 with significant changes. The biggest impact was ephemeral key management, which deprecated RSA key exchange. The client and server generate DH or ECDH temporary key pairs, skip getting certificates, swap public keys, and compute a shared secret to derive the session keys. The server public key might be signed and verified using a static RSA or ECDSA public key certificate. Another change was message encryption after the Client Hello and Server Hello messages. For details, see Section 3.2.2, "TLS v1.3 Overview."

Between TLS 1.2 in 2008 and TLS 1.3 in 2018, there were more than a dozen RFCs that basically modified the TLS 1.2 protocol. Some of these changes were incorporated in TLS 1.3 while others were intentionally omitted. Further note that DHE was included in SSL 3.0 and TLS 1.0 but elliptic curve cryptography, namely ECDH and ECDHE, was introduced to TLS 1.2 via RFC 4492 in 2006. While ephemeral keys have been available for over a decade, they were optional until TLS 1.3 mandated their use.

Meanwhile, servers that continue to support aging client connections using the older SSL v2.0 or SSL v3.0 protocols endanger traffic to real-time session takeovers. Also, older protocols that support weaker ciphers or short-key options allow exhaustive key attacks or other types of cryptanalytic attacks. Thus, encrypted sessions might be recorded and decrypted at leisure to recover valuable information.

9.3.3 PRODUCT ISSUES

Manufacturers typically provide recurring updates to address software bugs, and occasionally major releases with newer functionality. Allowing products to lag behind updates might promote vulnerabilities, introduce operational instabilities, or trigger unexpected non-interoperability issues. Postponing product releases might reduce application capability or capacity. Discontinued products no longer have updates or releases, so any newly discovered vulnerability will no longer have a manufacturer fix.

Once cryptographic keys have been deployed and are in use, migrating keys from one software version to another, or from one product to another, can be problematic. Newer keys can be added to an upgraded system, but existing keys used to encrypt or sign data might need to be retained. Migrating from one cryptographic architecture to another might include new keys, longer keys, or altogether different cryptographic algorithms or protocols. Maintaining key confidentiality and integrity during a cryptography transition often includes customized and manual processes that need careful oversight by an auditor.

9.4 CYBERSECURITY RISKS

Cybersecurity is the protection of data and information technology (IT). Data protection consists of defending legitimate data from disclosure, modification, or counterfeiting during transmission, processing, and storage. IT protection consists of defending network components such as routers, firewalls, switches, and other systems from unauthorized access, misconfigurations, or denial of service attacks. The Committee on National Security Systems provides the following definition for cybersecurity with the terms "cyberspace" and "cyberattack" [B.7.17]:

- Cyberspace: A global domain within the information environment consisting of the interdependent network of information systems infrastructures including the Internet, telecommunications networks, computer systems, and embedded processors and controllers.

- Cyberattack: An attack, via cyberspace, targeting an enterprise's use of cyberspace for the purpose of disrupting, disabling, destroying, or maliciously controlling a computing environment/infrastructure or destroying the integrity of the data or stealing controlled information.
- Cybersecurity: The ability to protect or defend the use of cyberspace from cyberattacks.

Again, we recognize that while cryptography is an important control within the cybersecurity field, cybersecurity-related risks are not the same as cryptographic risks, so we discuss them separately. NIST provides a cybersecurity framework [B.5.22] that consists of three major parts: the framework core, framework profiles, and framework implementation tiers.

Framework Core: The framework core consists of five basic activities: identify, protect, detect, respond, and recover. Each activity (also called functions) can be subdivided into categories such as asset management, access controls, or detection methods. Each category can be further decomposed into subcategories, which can then be linked to information security standards and specific requirements. The activities are described as follows:

- Identify: Develop the organizational understanding to manage cybersecurity risks to systems, assets, data, and capabilities.
- Protect: Develop and implement the appropriate safeguards to ensure delivery of critical infrastructure services.
- Detect: Develop and implement the appropriate activities to identify the occurrence of a cybersecurity event.
- Respond: Develop and implement the appropriate activities to take action regarding a detected cybersecurity event.
- Recover: Develop and implement the appropriate activities to maintain plans for resilience and to restore any capabilities or services that were impaired due to a cybersecurity event.

Framework Profile: The framework profile allows an organization or specific lines of business (LOBs) to define its current state and develop its target state for remediation or enhancements.

- Current profile indicates the cybersecurity outcomes that are currently being achieved.
- Target profile indicates the outcomes needed to achieve the desired cybersecurity risk management goals.

Framework Implementation Tiers: The framework tiers are reminiscent of other maturity models that provide a structure for describing an organization's capability and consistency for some management aspects. The tiers allow an organization to describe its views on cybersecurity risk and the processes in place to manage that risk. The implementation tiers for cybersecurity risk management practices are summarized as follows:

- Tier 1: Partial – Practices are informal, and risk is managed in an ad hoc manner with limited organizational awareness.
- Tier 2: Risk informed – Practices are defined, and risk is managed within the lines of business but not with external business partners.
- Tier 3: Repeatable – Practices are formally expressed as policy managed at the enterprise level and addressing external business partners.
- Tier 4: Adaptive – Practices are continuously improved to actively adapt to a changing cybersecurity landscape managed at the enterprise level with external business partners' participation.

The PKI risks relating to cybersecurity threats/vulnerabilities are as follows:

- **Identification gaps**: When an organization has neither established nor maintained the necessary knowledge base to understand its own architecture, then protecting its PKI components much less its network components is problematic. Network ingress and egress points with external connections that poke holes through the network perimeter need to be documented. In addition, connections between internal zones within the same network likewise need to be documented, or at the very least discoverable. Understanding the architecture is a fundamental prerequisite to comprehending where and how PKI keys and certificates are deployed and where the PKI systems should be deployed.
- **Protection gaps**: As noted before, cryptography is an important safeguard within cybersecurity, but unlike other technologies, the keys need to be managed across their lifecycle. However, the use of cryptography as a cybersecurity protection mechanism often presumes the keys are magically secured by the product. Vendor defaults are not only applicable to passwords, but defaults for algorithms, key sizes, and certificates also need to be considered.
- **Detection gaps**: Cryptographic safeguards are often difficult to diagnose, too often the solution either works or not, and often a cryptographic error is indistinguishable from other errors. For example, consider certificate validation. The validation can fail for a variety of reasons – broken certificate chain, invalid signature, expired date, revoked certificate, inappropriate key usage, invalid certificate revocation list (CRL) pointer, or unavailable Online Certificate Status Protocol (OCSP) responder. However, the ability to determine the specific error is often obscured by the underlying cryptographic library such that the application can only report success or failure. Diagnostic capabilities are often a significant gap.
- **Responsiveness gaps**: When a cybersecurity event is triggered by a cryptographic error, often the underlying cause is indeterminate. As noted earlier, cryptographic diagnostic capabilities are limited, so the appropriate response can be difficult to determine. Even more problematic is the ability to ascertain when a key or certificate has been compromised. For example, in 2011 when the certificate authority DigiNotar was compromised, a counterfeit Google wild card certificate was issued and subsequently used by attackers in Iran to conduct a man-in-the-middle (MITM) attack against Google services. Until the DigiNotar compromise was discovered and the counterfeit certificate revoked, the MITM attack was undetectable.
- **Recovery gaps**: Recovering from a cybersecurity event stemming from a cryptographic error needs special consideration. Often, the only solution is to either restore the cryptographic keys from a secure backup or replace them altogether with newly generated keys. However, restoring keys is only feasible if none of the keys were compromised. Furthermore, restoring or replacing keys is only viable when the integrity of the system to be recovered can be confirmed.
- **Profile gaps**: Lacking a current profile means the group or organization has not documented its cybersecurity activities, and not having a target profile implies a lack of strategy. Without a strategy, the cybersecurity risk management program is often limited to lower tiers with immature practices and procedures.
- **Tier gaps**: Operating at lower maturity levels means the group or organization might have informal practices with undocumented procedures. Mistakes can occur, errors can be overlooked, and the staff struggles daily without repeatable processes. Managing cybersecurity to at least Tier 3 reduces common mistakes. Undertaking activities at Tier 4 with continuous improvement can reduce costs, simplify tasks, and decrease errors.

In addition to security gaps related to the NIST cybersecurity framework, there are other specific risks, including access controls, denial of service attacks, and security logs.

- **Access controls**: Person and nonperson entities logging onto network or system resource need both authentication and authorization. Authentication confirms the identity of the requesting entity, whereas authorization confirms the validity of the request. Weaknesses in either control might allow illegal access to network or system resources. The related risks include disclosed information, modified or substituted data, and malware installation. Malware can adversely affect the infected systems or provide a launch pad for other types of attacks.
- **Denial of service**: Another aspect of cybersecurity is system resiliency, the ability to keep things running when resources are under attack. Systems infected with malware might have memory or disk space overwritten with random or useless information such that legitimate processes can no longer operate. Attacks originating from network sources send high volumes of illicit requests to overrun communications bandwidth preventing legitimate processes from responding. When the attack sources are widely disseminated, such endeavors are called distributed denial of service (DDoS) attacks. Preventing any type of denial-of-service attack, whether antivirus or DDoS avoidance, is a fundamental cybersecurity activity.
- **Security logs**: Security logs include network components, application, and system-generated logs that capture mundane and significant events. Log files might be circular where new logs constantly overwrite older logs or unlimited where the files are closed daily and new files are automatically opened. In either case, if the files are not copied to a log management system, the log information is lost forever. If the logs are not analyzed for data breaches or other vulnerability trends, then the log might as well be ignored. Another area of concern is the integrity of the logs, unauthorized access might allow attackers to delete or modify logs. For high-value logs, the log server may be required to digitally sign the logs to validate their integrity at a specific point in time.

Cybersecurity and cryptography risks focus primarily on information security issues that might allow data disclosure, modification, or substitution. Data modification or substitution might further enable unauthorized network, system, or application access. However, in addition to security-related issues, there are other risks that affect the overall system operations.

9.5 OPERATIONAL RISKS

PKI operations include both PKI-enabled services and the PKI hierarchy that provide digital certificates to end entities. PKI-enabled services might include network components, computer systems, and business applications. The PKI hierarchy consists of the offline and online CA and RA systems. End entities include persons and nonperson devices, such as routers, laptops, servers, tablets, and mobile phones. Operational risks include monitoring capabilities, capacity planning, and various cost issues.

9.5.1 MONITORING

Observing and checking the status of PKI operations is an important capability that should not be overlooked. Real-time monitoring includes reporting on successful and failed operations. Reporting on successful operations provides feedback that PKI functions are working as expected. Conversely, real-time alerts and details on failed operations provide information on errors, possible misconfigurations, or potential attacks. Latency monitoring consists of analyzing system and application logs to identify problems that are not recognized with real-time monitoring.

For example, when monitoring the PKI hierarchy, tracking the number of certificates issued by the CA against the number of requests processed by the RA measures system stability. Fewer certificates might indicate an RA problem, and extra certificates suggest a CA bug or possibly fraudulent activity. However, not having real-time monitoring would overlook the certificate discrepancies. If the systems do not log the events or as discussed earlier if the logs are not collected or analyzed, the certificate discrepancies would also be overlooked.

Another example is comparing the number of valid and invalid certificates discovered using scanning tools. Certificates are typically found in "trust stores," which might occur at the system or application levels. System and application trust stores are often created automatically during installation with default keys and certificates. Alternatively, administrators might create trust stores manually to generate keys and install certificates. Reconciling trust stores against CA and RA tracking numbers is like balancing a checkbook; the number of checks, dates, and amounts can help detect errors and fraudulent activity.

As another example, when monitoring PKI-enabled services, tracking the number of successful versus failed PKI operations can measure application consistency. For instance, when one application sends a certificate to another, the receiving application needs to validate the certificate. This includes walking the certificate chain to a trust anchor, verifying each certificate signature, checking the certificate validity dates, and confirming the certificate status via the CRL or OCSP responder. However, if the certificate validation fails but the exact error is not recognized and logged, resolution becomes problematic. The worst case is when the error occurs, for example, the CRL link is invalid or the OCSP is nonresponsive, but it is ignored with the result that the certificate is falsely validated and no error is reported.

9.5.2 CAPACITY

Ensuring that PKI operations have sufficient network and system capacity enables overall reliability. Network throughput allows applications to communicate. System capabilities include memory, processing, and storage. Operating systems and applications need sufficient memory to run. Systems need sufficient processing power to run operating systems and applications. And all of them need sufficient disk space to store data. Limitations in any of these areas impact overall effectiveness and might adversely affect PKI operations.

Consider capacity planning for the PKI hierarchy. If applications cannot renew certificates, then current certificates would expire and applications would fail. New applications unable to get initial certificates would delay deployment. If individuals cannot get certificates, then virtual private network (VPN) access would be denied or secure e-mail would be disabled. If the CRL becomes unavailable or the OCSP responder goes offline, certificate validation would fail, causing widespread failures.

For example, the industry trend by browser manufactures is shorter certificate validity periods. Table 9.4 provides a summary of the Baseline Requirements[16] for the Issuance and Management

---

TABLE 9.4

Validity CAB Forum

Validity	6.3.2 Certificate Operational Periods and Key Pair Usage Periods
398 days	Subscriber Certificates issued on or after September 1, 2020, SHOULD NOT have a Validity Period greater than 397 days and MUST NOT have a Validity Period greater than 398 days.
825 days	Subscriber Certificates issued after March 1, 2018, but prior to September 1, 2020, MUST NOT have a Validity Period greater than 825 days.
1,185 days	Subscriber Certificates issued after July 1, 2016, but prior to March 1, 2018, MUST NOT have a Validity Period greater than 39 months.

of Publicly-Trusted Certificates, v1.8 from the CA/Browser Forum. Certificates issued between July 2016 and March 2018 were allowed a maximum of 39 months. However, this was shortened to 825 days for certificates issued between March 2018 and September 2020, and again to 398 days for certificates issued after September 2020.

As the certificate validity shortens, the number of issued certificates within the same timeframe proportionally increases. While the number of active certificates might remain constant, the number of expired or revoked certificates might likewise increase. Increased revoked certificate impacts CRL and OCSP services. And as the overall number of certificates increases, monitoring capacity might likewise be affected.

9.5.3 CONTINUITY

Keeping systems and applications current with security patches and software releases remediates known vulnerabilities. Zero-day attacks are always an unknown risk since by definition there is no fix available for a vulnerability that is just uncovered. Regardless, patches and releases need to be tested before being applied to production to avoid bugs in the fixes.

Many patches and software releases are large, downloaded from the Internet, and stored locally for distribution over local networks. However, the root CA should be offline, separated from the network by an air gap, so any updates need to be stored on removable media and hand carried for manual install. Regardless of whether updates are applied to online or offline systems, any software changes need to be scanned for malware before installation. Air-gapped systems are not impervious to attack; the Stuxnet malware that infected the Iranian uranium enrichment plants was somehow injected into the offline system. Rumors abound, but a USB stick carried into the facility, whether intentional or inadvertent, is the more likely scenario.

Also refer to Section 7.4, "Business Continuity," discussion on Disaster Recovery and Business Continuity (DR/BC) plans, including the NIST 800–34 Contingency Planning Guide. Business continuity includes the people, processes, and overall business operations that allow your PKI to support your organization. Disaster recovery is a subset of the overall practice of business continuity to recover your PKI in the event of a disaster.

9.5.4 RESOURCES

Resources include staffing, hardware, and software. Sufficient funds need to be allocated and managed to afford all resources. Capacity planning helps to determine resources, but unexpected incidents can easily cut into staff hours and delay development or deployment projects. For example, there have been a variety of vulnerabilities[17] and attacks[18] for SSL and TLS that necessitated remediation for PKI-enabled services. While some of these attacks were considered theoretical years ago, research experts continually poke at security protocols attempting to discover new ways of exploiting chinks in the proverbial armor.

Beyond capacity planning for the expected and unexpected are cryptographic transitions. For example, as noted in Section 9.3, "Cryptography Risks," a relatively new risk is cryptanalysis becoming available on quantum computers. Consequently, allocating resources for transitioning to Post Quantum Cryptography (PQC) algorithms is critical for avoiding PKI risk.

9.5.5 KNOWLEDGE

Research is typically done by security professionals, who focus on specific protocols or products and so build their personal knowledge. However, every person cannot possibly know the strengths and weaknesses of every PKI-related product, protocol, or algorithm; there are just too many items and things that constantly change. There are many organizations such as the NIST National Vulnerability Database[19] and the Computer Emergency Response Team[20] (CERT) that monitor cybersecurity research and publish vulnerability notices. Product manufacturers typically keep their customers informed of product issues. Groundbreaking research is typically published as a technical paper and often announced at security conferences. Nevertheless, keeping track of vulnerabilities and security patches is problematic, much less tracking research papers and getting travel funds to attend conferences.

Consequently, having unknowledgeable staff is a risky situation. Formal academic education is important, but it does not replace experience. Industry credentials are also meaningful, but again they are not a substitution for experience. Experience provides knowledge. Far too often decisions are made or actions are taken based on bad information or technical misunderstandings. Like any other technical area, it is important to retain knowledgeable staff and contribute to their continuing education, including training and conferences.

9.6   PKI COMPLIANCE

Throughout the book, we have mentioned assessments and audits, auditors, audit logs, audit mechanisms, and audit reports. In general, we have discussed the importance of audits to reassure PKI participants of its controls. In Chapter 1, "Introduction," we included auditors in the intended audience for this book and their reliance on industry standards:

- Auditors and assessors are responsible for verifying compliance to information and security policy, standards, practices, and procedures. Risk can be better identified and managed when the evaluator has a solid understanding of general cryptography, specifically PKI, and related key management. Furthermore, compliance includes not just the organization's internal security requirements but also external influences such as regulations, international and national laws, and contractual responsibilities.
- Auditors and security professionals expect applications to execute properly and to be managed properly according to industry standards.

In Chapter 2, "Cryptography Basics," the FIPS 140–3 Roles, Services, and Authentication includes audit functions in the crypto officer role and the operational environment describes audit mechanisms and audit reports:

- Role assumed to perform cryptographic initialization or management functions (e.g., module initialization, input/output of cryptographic keys and CSPs, and audit functions).
- For Security Level 2, audit mechanisms must also exist.
- For Security Level 3 audit reports, in addition to the audit requirements for Security Level 2, the initiator of a trusted path, and any attempts to use a trusted path, must be captured.

In Chapter 4, "PKI Management and Security," we discussed the security professional and auditor's reliance on the certificate policy (CP) and certificate practice statement (CPS) written in the RFC 3647 [B.3.41] format. The CP and CPS numbering scheme and content must be kept consistent in order for security assessment and audits to be performed:

- RFC 3647 §5.4 Audit Logging Procedures subsection addresses audit log management that includes the events, access controls, confidentiality and integrity controls, and analysis. Audit logs will capture the event, along with a copy of the stepwise procedures, to fully document the event.
- RFC 3647 §5.5 Records Archival subsection addresses audit log archive processes including access controls, confidentiality and integrity controls, and backup and recovery.
- RFC 3647 §6 Technical Security Controls addresses requirements and rules for protecting system and network components including hardware, software, applications, and

information objects. Applications include access controls and audits logs for system administrators, application administrators, application managers, and application users.

- RFC 3647 §6.8 Time Stamping subsection addresses time stamps for messages, transaction processing, and audit logs.
- RFC 3647 §8 Compliance Audit and Other Assessment segment addresses internal and external security audits, assessments, and evaluations.

In Chapter 8, "Incident Management," we discussed organizational issues where we described the importance of the management, security, and audit groups to the enterprise and their respective roles and responsibilities to the enterprise. The audit group responsibilities include evaluation and assessments of the PKI systems for compliance to the certificate policy and certificate practice statement (CP and CPS) and PKI industry standards. In addition, the PKI audit function might be provided by internal auditors, outsourced auditors, or external auditors. In this chapter, we now discuss the audit evaluation criteria, gap assessments, and the actual audit process.

9.6.1 Evaluation Criteria

Historically, third-party service provider audits were already in place, called Statement on Auditing Standards (SAS) No. 70 Service Organizations.[21] From about 1995 to 2010, the SAS 70 became the audit standard for data centers hosting CAs. However, the SAS 70 audit did not include evaluation criteria. Rather, it was originally intended as an auditor-to-auditor report to address what was called service carve outs. Figure 9.2 shows a graphical representation.

For example, when an auditor performs an assessment of an organization that has outsourced some of its services to an external provider, the auditor cannot always evaluate the external provider. Thus, the organization's auditor relies on the service auditor's SAS 70 report of the external provider. The organization's auditor carves out the organization's services in his or her report by relying on the second auditor's SAS 70 report. The audit scope is depicted as a subset of the organization such that the whole organization is not within its scope. In addition, the carved-out portion is shown as the SAS 70 report of the service provider. The two audits are typically done by different auditors, usually from different auditing firms.

Subsequently in late December 1997, the X9F5 Standards Workgroup[22] was established to address a new work item introduced into ASC X9 to develop PKI policy and practices for the financial services industry, which became X9.79 published in 2001. During the X9.79 development effort, the original IETF specification describing the certificate policy (CP) and certificate practice statement (CPS) was published in 1999. While X9.79 was in development, the X9 project was brought to the attention of the AICPA and CICA as part of their WebTrust program. The auditing standard was aligned with the ANSI standard, but ironically the WebTrust standard was published six months before the X9.79 standard due to the ANSI balloting process. Figure 9.3 provides a graphical overview of the various AICPA, ANSI, IETF, and ISO standards.

Consequently, the X9.79 standard was submitted to ISO by the United States and transformed into the international standard ISO 21188, which was published in 2006. Subsequently, in 2008, the

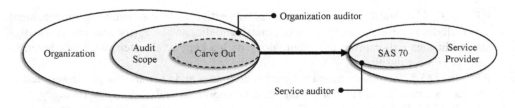

FIGURE 9.2   Audit scope carve out.

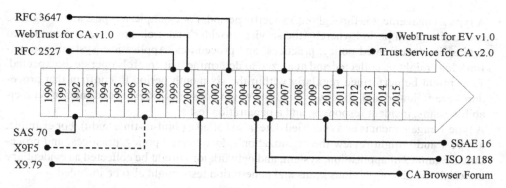

FIGURE 9.3 Audit Standards Timeline.

original ANSI standard X9.79 Part 1: Practices and Policy Framework was retired, and ISO 21188 was formally adopted by the United States. Eventually, the auditing standard was revised per the ISO 21188 standard and the renamed Trust Services v2.0 was published in 2011:

- March 1999: RFC 2527 Internet X.509 Public Key Infrastructure Certificate Policy and Certification Practices Framework
- August 2000: AICPA/CICA WebTrust[SM/TM] Program for Certification Authorities, Version 1.0
- January 2001: X9.79 Public Key Infrastructure (PKI) – Part 1 Practices and Policy Framework
- November 2003: RFC 3647 Internet X.509 Public Key Infrastructure Certificate Policy and Certification Practices Framework
- May 2006: ISO 21188 Public Key Infrastructure for Financial Services – Practices and Policy Framework
- March 2011: Trust Service Principles and Criteria for Certification Authorities, Version 2.0

Since the SAS 70 did not specify evaluation criteria but had become the de facto standard for service provider audits, the WebTrust for CA auditing standard was often used when the service provider was a CA. The auditor would specify within the SAS 70 report that its scope was based on the WebTrust for CA standard. This approach satisfied the various CA licensing programs that specified the need for a SAS 70 audit without identifying any general information security or other PKI-specific requirements.

Meanwhile, the earlier WebTrust v1.0 was adopted by four browser manufacturers as the de facto auditing standard – Apple, Google, Microsoft, and Mozilla. Each manufacturer requires a successful audit of the CA before its root certificate is added to its browser. The adoption of WebTrust (also called CA Trust) rapidly expanded and became licensed in two dozen countries, including Australia, Belgium, Brazil, Canada, China, Colombia, Denmark, Germany, Hong Kong, Hungary, Israel, Japan, Korea, Malaysia, Mexico, the Netherlands, Poland, Singapore, Spain, Switzerland, Taiwan, the United Kingdom, the United States, and the Middle East region.

In 2010, the AICPA Auditing Standards Board published Statement on Standards for Attestation Engagements No. 16 Reporting on Controls at a Service Organization (SSAE 16).[23] This standard, which provides the requirements and guidance for a service auditor reporting on a service organization's controls, supersedes the guidance for service auditors in SAS 70. SSAE 16 enables a service auditor to perform two types of engagements addressing the presentation fairness of management's description of the service organization's system and the suitability of the design and operating effectiveness of the controls to achieve the related control objectives.

- A type 2 engagement is throughout a specific period. For example, a type 2 audit might be over a six-month period whereby the service provider's controls are observed and tested against its documented policy, practices, and procedures. Application, system, and network logs might be collected and analyzed to determine that controls operate as expected. Tests might be performed regularly within the six-month period to confirm that procedures are followed and effective. The tests might consist of external and internal vulnerability scans, incident responses, and a penetration test.
- A type 1 engagement is as a specified date (also called a point-in-time audit). For example, a type 1 audit might review the organization's documented policy, practices, and procedures. Samples of application, system, and network logs might be collected as evidentiary material. Results of previous scans and penetration tests might also be included.

The Trust Services for CA might be bundled with the SSAE 16 as a combined audit, or the CA audit might be performed separately, as an independent audit. However, not all CAs rely on the WebTrust or Trust Services for CA; some organizations rely on ISO 21188. Since the Trust Services for CA was realigned with ISO 21188, the evaluation criteria are the same. Meanwhile, the Trust Services for CA are not the only audit criteria available for certification authorities.

Five years after the WebTrust for CA standard was published by the AICPA/CICA, the Certificate Authority Browser Forum[24] (CAB Forum) was established in 2005 as an initiative among commercial CA and browser software vendors to address SSL/TLS certificates. In 2007, the CAB Forum adopted the WebTrust for Certification Authorities – Extended Validation Audit Criteria (WebTrust for Extended Validation [EV]) Guidelines. EV certificates are issued by CA based on extended authentication procedures, and browsers display information when an EV certificate is used to establish an SSL/TLS connection. According to the EV rules, a CA either issues EV certificates or it does not; however, it cannot do both. Table 9.5 shows the various alternatives available to public (external) and private (internal) CAs.

For Use Case (1), a public CA that issues EV certificates must undergo both a Trust Services for CA audit and a WebTrust for EV audit. If the public CA does not issue EV certificates, as in Use Case (2), then only the Trust Services for CA audit is needed. Alternatively, depending on the jurisdictional and contractual requirements as shown in Use Case (3), an ISO 21188 assessment might suffice. However, other CA programs such as the Federal Public Key Infrastructure[25] (FPKI) might provide their own audit requirements and evaluation criteria.

For Use Case (4), a private CA does not issue EV certificates since the extended authentication procedures are for issuing certificates to external entities and not internal entities. Therefore, since the private CA and other internal entities are part of the same organization, a private CA does not need a WebTrust for EV audit. Nevertheless, a private CA should undertake either a Trust Service for CA audit as shown in Use Case (4) or an ISO 21188 assessment as shown in Use Case (5) as a best practice. Also note that any of the audit standards can also be used to do an assessment. In the next two sections, we will discuss the commonalities and differences between assessments versus audits.

TABLE 9.5
Certificate Authority Audit Options

Use Case	CA Assessment	CA Audit	EV Audit
(1) Public CA	-	Trust Services CA	WebTrust EV
(2) Public CA	-	Trust Services CA	-
(3) Public CA	ISO 21188	-	-
(4) Private CA	-	Trust Services CA	-
(5) Private CA	ISO 21188	-	-

9.6.2   GAP ASSESSMENT

In general, an assessment differs from an audit in its purpose and report style. The purpose of an assessment is to determine conformity with evaluation criteria and identify control gaps, if any, for subsequent remediation. Conversely, the purpose of an audit is to determine compliance with the same evaluation criteria and essentially provide a pass or fail score. An assessment is often performed in preparation for an audit. The audit report provides an objective comparison between actual controls versus requirements. Consequently, the assessment report provides not only the objective comparisons but also recommendations for tactical and strategic remediation. Furthermore, unlike audits, the assessment report might include subjective opinions about industry best practices and information security trends.

Another difference between an audit and an assessment is the scope of the effort. Figure 9.4 provides a PKI example showing a root CA operating offline and four CAs operating online consisting of a subordinate CA with three specific CAs for issuing TLS, VPN, and code sign certificates. Audits tend to be more costly than assessments due to professional fees and staff resources. Additionally, the audit scope is typically the whole PKI hierarchy, as shown in Figure 9.4. On the other hand, the assessment scope can be more narrowly focused, such as only addressing the offline PKI components, the online PKI components, or even a specific CA as shown in Figure 9.4. Thus, the PKI can be assessed in a piecemeal fashion versus an all-encompassing audit. Furthermore, the time frames for assessments might be shorter due to the abbreviated scope. Additionally, the assessment might be done in parallel with different teams versus an audit being performed by an audit team.

Yet another difference is when assessments can be used. Assessments can be done before or after the audit. An assessment can be done to prepare for an audit. The assessment identifies control gaps that can be remediated before the actual audit commences. The assessment can also be done after the audit if deficiencies are found per the audit. The deficiencies need remediation, and an assessment can corroborate that the problem has been fixed prior to the next audit. Again, the scope of the assessment can be reduced to address only the remediation.

Now that we have discussed the purpose of assessments versus audits, let's consider the assessment process. As discussed in Chapter 8, "Incident Management," audits might be performed by internal auditors, outsourced auditors, or external auditors. On the other hand, assessments might be done by internal PKI staff, internal auditors, or external security professionals. Regardless of who does the assessment, it is important to have a process to achieve consistent results. Figure 9.5 provides an overview of the tasks and general timeline.

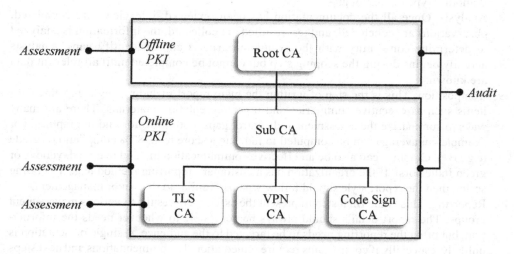

FIGURE 9.4   Assessment scope.

Although each step is described as a sequence of tasks, there are numerous overlaps, and many tasks begin before the previous ones are completed. While the assessment process might vary based on the organization's culture or assessor's experience, the tasks presented here are well proven:

1. Scope: The first step of any assessment is to define its scope. This includes ascertaining the evaluation criteria to be used and the target of the evaluation. Determining test cases is part of the scope definition. The scope will determine the work plan.

2. Resources: The second step is to determine the necessary staffing and computer resources for the assessment. The scope will help determine who is needed, what is needed, and when things are needed. The resources available will help estimate the timeline needed for the assessment work plan.

3. Kickoff: An important part of the assessment is the kickoff meeting. All the participants are informed of the assessment work plan, their respective roles and responsibilities, and the overall timeline. One possible outcome of the kickoff is that the scope needs to be updated and resources need to be revised.

4. Documentation: The relevant documentation is reviewed. This includes policies, practices, and procedures, along with any product specification or operating manuals. Ideally, the documentation is provided prior to the kickoff meeting and as input to help define the scope in the first step. Unfortunately, it is more common that the actual existence of any documentation is discovered during the kickoff meeting. Even worse, documentation is often found lacking, missing, or obsolete, which is a control gap unto itself.

5. Interviews: The relevant personnel are interviewed to corroborate the documentation, in particular the PKI practices and procedures. This step is to determine whether the documented procedures are actually followed and effective. Differences between reality and fiction are also a control gap.

6. Observations: The assessor observes actual PKI events being performed to corroborate both documentation and interviews. This step is to identify any further gaps between actual processes and documentation or the staff's understanding. Lack of knowledge, misconceptions, or other misunderstandings are another type of control gap.

7. Testing: Testing goes beyond observations to determine if procedures are effective and complete. Test cases often include error conditions to exercise recovery procedures, troubleshooting, and problem solving. The inability to recognize and handle error conditions is another type of control gap.

8. Analysis: Once all the documentation has been reviewed, interviews are completed, observations are concluded, and test resulted are collected, the information is analyzed to determine conformity with the evaluation criteria and to identify gaps. Analysis actually begins during the scoping step but cannot be completed until all relevant data are known.

9. Composition: This is the step of writing the main report including any complementary items such as executive summaries and other presentation materials. There are many ways to summarize the assessment and control gaps, both in words and in graphics. For example, an average can be computed to indicate a score (e.g., 87% compliant) or grade (e.g., B+). Graphics can also be an effective communication method (e.g., red, yellow, or green indicators). If the organization has a customary reporting method (e.g., 1–5 rating scale), then the report style should follow what is familiar to the senior management.

10. Reporting: This is the final step to present the assessment results to various management groups. The report details should always be accessible to whoever needs the information, but often the reporting needs to be targeted to the audience. A single presentation is unlikely, especially if control gaps require remediation. Recommendations and next steps are often tricky topics that need to be addressed in the presentations.

The assessment report needs to clearly state the scope of the assessment, identifying not only which PKI components were included but also which ones were out of scope. The report also needs to provide contact information, date information, documentation references, including the basis of the evaluation criteria, and an executive summary providing overall compliance, gap summary, and high-level remediation recommendations. The analysis details also need to be provided that might be in numbered paragraph or table format. Table 9.6 is an example of a table format.

The first column defines which PKI component is being assessed; the second column echoes the evaluation criteria from the corresponding standard (e.g., ISO 21188, Trust Services for CA, or WebTrust for EV). The third column describes the controls in place based on the documentation, interviews, observations, and tests. The fourth column gives both a graphical display for quick viewing and a numerical score of the compliance per each control objective. Again, the report format might differ and should use a style familiar to the senior management.

9.6.3 Audit Process

Not surprisingly, the audit process is very similar to the assessment process. However, a fundamental difference for the audit is the formal representation of the information provided by the PKI staff. Although the same information is provided for both an assessment and an audit and has identical technical value, its representation by management has a significant difference. For the assessment, the technical information represents a best effort to document the PKI operations. Conversely, for the audit, the same information is management's representation of the PKI operations. It is a common practice for auditors to request a formal management representation letter that states all significant information has been provided, in all material respects, and no deficiencies remain undisclosed. Essentially, the management's representation letter is an affirmation that any and all information is accurate and complete.

Therefore, a misstatement in any documentation, interview, observation, or test result might be an audit finding that renders a noncompliant decision. On the other hand, the same misstatement might merely be a typo, misunderstanding, or simple oversight that does not significantly affect the assessment. Thus, assessments tend to be far more forgiving than audits. Basically, audits reflect the information provided versus what might actually be in place.

The audit process consists of the same basic tasks as shown in Figure 9.5, for the same fundamental reasons. There are similarities and differences among the tasks:

1. Scope: The first step of any audit is also the scope definition. For audits, this is extremely important as the scope also determines costs when outsourced or external auditors are used. If the audit scope differs from the previous gap assessments, there might be unforeseen issues that arise late in the audit process.
2. Resources: The second step is likewise determining resources. However, unlike assessments, unavailable resources affecting the completion date of the audit might also affect costs. Differences between the audit scope and any previous gap assessments will likely impact the necessary resources.
3. Kickoff: The kickoff meeting is another important aspect of the audit process since often the organization or its personnel are unfamiliar with the audit process.

TABLE 9.6
Assessment Gap Report

PKI Component	Control Objective	Actual Control	Evaluation Score	
Root CA	Control Objective #1	Description #1	☒☒☒☒☒	100%
Root CA	Control Objective #2	Description #2	☒☒☒☐☐	60%
Root CA	Control Objective #3	Description #3	☒☐☐☐☐	20%

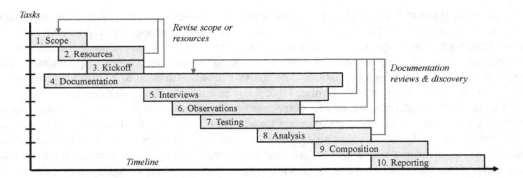

FIGURE 9.5 Assessment process.

4. Documentation: As much material that can be provided to the auditor prior to the kickoff meeting is critical. This allows the auditor to better prepare for the kickoff meeting and set expectations for the various roles and responsibilities.

5. Interviews: It is not uncommon for audit interviews to be somewhat adversarial. Often, interviewees will answer questions as briefly as possible (e.g., yes, no) without elaboration to avoid what is perceived as telling too much. Unfortunately, such attitudes can increase the interview length and the number of interviews when additional or conflictual information is later discovered.

6. Observations: Witnessing PKI events is a common auditor activity. Similar to assessors, auditors watch for knowledgeable personnel who follow procedures as written.

7. Testing: Depending on the scope of the audit, testing might not be included. Often, the audit scope is limited to observations of the production system.

8. Analysis: Once all the information has been collected, auditors analyze the data to determine compliance with the evaluation criteria.

9. Composition: This is the writing of the auditor report and auditor letter. The auditor report contains the analysis details. The auditor letter is addressed to the client and only contains a general statement that the audit is satisfactory without providing any analysis details. The auditor will also retain all work papers developed or collected during the audit, but the auditor work papers are not shared with the client.

10. Reporting: This is the final step of the audit. The auditor report and letter are provided to the client with the mutual understanding that the audit report is kept confidential, but that the audit letter might be shared with others. Some audits might also provide a website seal with a URL to the audit letter.

The report and letter style will be based on the auditor's format. The auditor's format might be based on its own firm's customary reporting style or the auditing standard. Presentations to senior management and to other groups are usually the responsibility of the client and typically not provided by the auditor. The audit letter is normally provided by the organization to subscribers or relying parties either via the auditor website seal or the organization's CP and CPS site.

The authors believe that audit best practices should include the audit team reviewing the PKI's actionable Crypto-Agility plan. Does the PKI have the ability to respond to changing cryptographic standards with the ability to update CP and CPS documents, build and implement certificate profiles, and begin issuing new certificates in a timely response to potential large scale international attacks against the infrastructure.

We strongly recommend that any PKI system undergo an annual audit. Furthermore, if the PKI system has never completed an audit, a gap assessment must be performed in preparation for the first audit. As cryptography and cybersecurity evolves, so will the evaluation criteria; therefore, the audit results will vary over time. Thus, each audit provides a measurement in time of the PKI system's overall security status.

9.7 PKI RISK ASSESSMENT

Risk assessments are an integral part of governance and compliance. As noted in Section 9.2, "PKI Risks," we refer to various types of PKI risks throughout the book, focusing on cryptographic risks in Section 9.3, "Cryptography Risks," cybersecurity risks in Section 9.4, "Cybersecurity Risks," and operational risks in Section 9.5, "Operational Risks," but this chapter discusses the actual risk assessment.

- Chapter 1, "Introduction," established the phrase "PKI Cryptonomics," which included business, legal, security, technology, and cryptography areas. Consequently, each of the areas contributes to the overall PKI operations, such that any unaddressed risk in one area can adversely affect the whole. Thus, risk assessments need to address all five areas.
- Chapter 5, "PKI Roles and Responsibilities," introduced PKI risk assessments as part of the auditor role and responsibilities. In addition to verifying that participants follow documented procedures, auditors along with the organization also perform security and risk assessments of any or all PKI components. Generally speaking, verifying that the PKI operations are compliant with its policy, practices, and procedures is the baseline for any assessment or audit. But this presumes that the documented procedures are both sufficient and adequate. Conversely, a risk assessment can determine if the policy, practices, and procedures are indeed sufficient and adequate, or if an undocumented risk or new vulnerability exists.

Note that the NIST 800-30 Guide for Conducting Risk Assessments [B.5.35] can be helpful. Further, the CNSSI-4009 Glossary [B.7.17] provides the following definitions, listed here in alphabetical order.

Term	Definition
Countermeasure	Actions, devices, procedures, or techniques that meet or oppose (i.e., counters) a threat, a vulnerability, or an attack by eliminating or preventing it, by minimizing the harm it can cause, or by discovering and reporting it so that corrective action can be taken.
Impact Level	The magnitude of harm that can be expected to result from the consequences of unauthorized disclosure of information, unauthorized modification of information, unauthorized destruction of information, or loss of information or information system availability.
Information System (IS)	A discrete set of information resources organized for the collection, processing, maintenance, use, sharing, dissemination, or disposition of information.
Risk	A measure of the extent to which an entity is threatened by a potential circumstance or event, and typically a function of (1) the adverse impacts that would arise if the circumstance or event occurs; and (2) the likelihood of occurrence.
Risk Assessment	The process of identifying, prioritizing, and estimating risks. This includes determining the extent to which adverse circumstances or events could impact an enterprise. Uses the results of threat and vulnerability assessments to identify risk to organizational operations and evaluates those risks in terms of likelihood of occurrence and impacts if they occur. The product of a risk assessment is a list of estimated, potential impacts and unmitigated vulnerabilities.
Risk Mitigation	Prioritizing, evaluating, and implementing the appropriate risk-reducing controls/countermeasures recommended from the risk management process.
Risk Tolerance	The defined impacts to an enterprise's information systems that an entity is willing to accept.
Threat	Any circumstance or event with the potential to adversely impact an IS through unauthorized access, destruction, disclosure, modification of data, and/or denial of service.
Vulnerability	Weakness in an IS, system security procedures, internal controls, or implementation that could be exploited.

Note that while Risk Mitigation refers to "controls/countermeasures" and the Glossary provides a definition for Countermeasure, the more common risk term is "control." And while the Glossary uses the adjective "controlled" with many other definitions, the Glossary does not define the term "control." For the purposes of this book, the term "control" means a product, process, or procedure that reduces a risk. Note that "product" includes a specific technology (e.g., digital signature) or general solution (e.g., event logs) provided by a product. Generally speaking, a risk can be quantified by the relative threat, based on a vulnerability, its likelihood (probability) of occurring, and the impact if the threat occurs or the vulnerability is exploited.

This risk formula describes an "equation" to compute a Risk score. Some risk models use a numeric range while others use a descriptive range. For example, the lowest risk might be "1" while the highest risk might be "5" using a 1-to-5 range. Some risk practitioners prefer a more granular scale, so to avoid fractional scores such as "2" versus "2.5" larger scales such as 1-to-10 or even 1-to-100 are used. Larger numbers allow bigger differences between numbers, which can imply greater significance, such as "40" versus "50" suggests a much higher risk. Thus, each variable (Threat, Vulnerability, Likelihood, and Impact) gets a value which when "multiplied" or some other mathematical operation, the Risk score is computed.

In addition to the five PKI areas discussed in Chapter 1, "Introduction," for business, legal, security, technology, and cryptography, each with its own associated risks, operating a PKI entails specific risks inherent to the PKI itself. Using the NIST Special Publication 800–37 Risk Framework [B.5.34], an organization can begin to understand these risks and their potential impact. A non-exhaustive list of some risks, in no particular order, that come with the operation of a PKI that should be included in a risk assessment are as follows:

1. Are the encryption keys/certificates being used for their intended purpose?
   PKI operations staff design and implement secure processes for the request and delivery of encryption keys and certificates. A WebTrust Audit will validate and verify the approach implemented and the practices of the PKI; however, these PKI processes can be circumvented by Systems Administrators, who legitimately request encryption keys and/or certificates and install them in different servers or multiple locations. Another possible risk happens when a system administrator requests a non-approved key or certificate for use (weaker key strength, incorrect algorithm, or a certificate with differing validity periods). While not every situation can be anticipated, PKI staff can reduce these risks by educating system administrators and verifying a random sampling of keys and certificates after they are installed in their intended systems.

2. Were encryption keys or certificates stolen?
   Evaluating the risks of stolen encryption keys and certificates should also be considered as part of the PKI risk assessment. The various types of encryption keys and certificates being issued should be considered for the impacts if the credentials are stolen. As an example, if an SSL/TLS certificate and private key were stolen, an attacker could impersonate the organization's website and potentially steer customers to the fraudulent site. A significant impact would result in the theft of a code signing certificate and private key which could be used to sign malware to infiltrate the organization and attack further systems. The organization should consider other types of certificates being issued like VPN certificates and API keys used to receive instructions and accounting information from various trading partners.
   If the risk assessment determines a significant likelihood of certificates and private keys being stolen, the organization should consider storing the private keys for high-value certificates in hardware (HSMs) rather than the easier-to-attack software storage of private keys.
   Storing large groups of private keys all in a centralized key management system makes an extremely tempting target for the more sophisticated attacker. Organizations using

automated key management tools must undertake a risk assessment of the compromise of that centralized key management tool. If all the certificates and private keys housed within the automated key management tool were to be compromised, how could the organization recover from such a breach and what procedures would be followed?

3. Are irrecoverable encryption keys a risk?

   Even encryption keys and certificates being used for their intended purpose can present a risk to the organization. Encryption keys designed for encrypting e-mail (SMIME) or encryption keys intended for encrypting files, if not backed up, could result in information being encrypted but unrecoverable. This risk should be considered when updating the organization's policies and procedures to reflect adequate encryption key backup for critical information resources. Malicious employees could intentionally encrypt information and exit the organization.

4. What is the risk of issuing certificates to an unintended subscriber?

   Within Chapter 5, "PKI Roles and Responsibilities," the process of creating policies and procedures to identify the intended subscribers of a PKI was emphasized. Organizations operating large PKIs with multiple types of certificates being issued to different types of subscribers can make for a very complex environment. A comprehensive PKI risk assessment should consider the possibilities even with good policies and procedures in place of individual certificates being issued to unintended subscribers. The likelihood and impact of each type of certificate issued should be considered when performing a risk assessment. Consider, for example, the low likelihood, high impact of an RA Certificate being issued to an unintended subscriber versus the higher likelihood, low impact of an SMIME certificate being issued to an unintended subscriber. As the organization performs a PKI risk assessment, these possibilities and others should be considered, and actions planned for identification and remediation of certificates being issued to unintended subscribers.

5. What potential staffing risks exist?

   Large and complex PKI operations can require staff with very specific backgrounds and skills. If PKI staff quit or are fired, can they be replaced in a reasonable timeframe? What impacts could result in not having sufficient PKI staff for upcoming efforts? Critical staffing shortages may result in the inability for dual controlled functions to take place or require substituting other roles into trusted PKI roles for activities such as key generation and PKI administrative changes. What long-term threats might these staffing shortages pose to the organization?

6. What is the impact of a failure to renew certificates in a timely fashion?

   Even a small PKI can issue hundreds if not thousands of individual certificates. A large PKI operating in a large organization could easily reach into the hundreds of thousands if not millions of certificates. Having this many certificates active leads to a problem of tracking the information associated with the validity periods of the individual certificates issued. There exist many commercial and public domain certificate tracking software packages that can help organizations keep track of their certificates and when individual certificates expire. These software packages can send reminders to system administrators for the renewal of the individual certificates on the systems they're responsible for. Even with these reminders, system administrators and individuals can forget to renew their certificates before an expiration occurs.

   The risks associated with certificates expiring may vary from a smaller impact of a single SMIME signature on an e-mail not validating to a much larger impact of an SSL/TLS certificate protecting an online banking system expiring that could impact thousands if not hundreds of thousands of individual customers trying to access their banking information. The PKI risk assessment should consider both the impact and likelihood of these situations occurring and the risks that the organization faces by having critical certificates expire.

As noted at the beginning of this chapter, risk assessments are an integral part of any governance and compliance program, including PKI operations. Risks might be self-identified by any business, legal, security, technology, or cryptography group. However, risk assessments are part of the auditor role, including internal auditors, third-party auditors, and possibly industry regulators such as the Federal Financial Institutions Examination Council[26] (FFIEC).

9.8   PKI CLOUD ASSESSMENT

Prior to migrating or operating a Cloud PKI, discussion with internal and external auditors can save a great deal of time and effort during the audit process. Cloud environments are considered to have "shared responsibilities" between the Cloud Service Provider (CSP) and the Cloud Service Customer (CSC). Another consideration is the organization's cloud architecture. An organization with a multi-cloud architecture, using more than one CSP, or a hybrid-cloud architecture, using both a private and public cloud, might have different roles and responsibilities. Hence, mapping roles and responsibilities for in-house versus cloud-based resources can avoid confusion and prevent findings in a WebTrust Audit.

For example, controls designed for in-house HSM management will need to be significantly reworked for organizations that will be taking advantage of cloud-based HSMs. Further, the HSM options and services offering will vary depending on the CSP. Many cloud providers offer "audit accounts" without the ability to make changes to the PKI for internal auditors who will be observing the controls implemented in-house as well as cloud based.

NOTES

1. Intel Corporation. 50 Years of Moore's Law, www.intel.com/content/www/us/en/silicon-innovations/moores-law-technology.html (accessed October 2015).
2. The Institute of Internal Auditors. Definition of internal audit, https://na.theiia.org/standards-guidance/mandatory-guidance/Pages/Definition-of-Internal-Auditing.aspx (accessed October 2015).
3. The Institute of Internal Auditors. Attribute standards, https://na.theiia.org/standards-guidance/attribute-standards/Pages/Attribute-Standards.aspx (accessed October 2015).
4. The Institute of Internal Auditors. Performance standards, https://na.theiia.org/standardsguidance/performance-standards/Pages/Performance-Standards.aspx (accessed October 2015).
5. American Institute of Certified Public Accountants, www.aicpa.org (accessed October 2015).
6. Canadian Institute of Chartered Accounts, www.cica.ca (accessed October 2015).
7. Chartered Institute of Management Accounts, www.cimaglobal.com (accessed October 2015).
8. International Federation of Accountants, www.ifac.org (accessed October 2015).
9. GRI, https://globalriskinstitute.org/mp-files/2022-quantum-threat-timeline-report-dec.pdf
10. MIT News: The beginning of the end for encryption schemes? https://news.mit.edu/2016/quantum-computer-end-encryption-schemes-0303
11. Jeff Stapleton, Ralph Poore. Cryptographic Transitions, Regional 5 Conference, IEEE. http://ieeexplore.ieee.org/xpl/login.jsp?tp=&arnumber=5507465&url=http%3A%2F%2Fieeexplore.ieee.org%2Fxpls%2Fabs_all.jsp%3Farnumber%3D5507465 (accessed October 2015).
12. CA/Browser Forum. Ballot 22 – RSA 1024 Retirement, https://cabforum.org/2008/12/29/ballot-22-rsa-1024-retirement/ (accessed October 2015).
13. Network World. Father of SSL, www.networkworld.com/article/2161851/security/father-of-ssl--dr--taher-elgamal-finds-fast-moving-it-projects-in-the-middle-east.html (accessed October 2015).
14. Network World. Father of SSL, www.networkworld.com/article/2181968/security/father-of-ssl-says-despite-attacks--the-security-linchpin-has-lots-of-life-left.html (accessed October 2015).
15. IANA TLS, www.iana.org/assignments/tls-parameters/tls-parameters.xhtml
16. Baseline Requirements CAB Forum, https://cabforum.org/wp-content/uploads/CA-Browser-Forum-BR-1.8.4-redline.pdf
17. Attacks on SSL, NCC Group, www.isecpartners.com/media/106031/ssl_attacks_survey.pdf (accessed October 2015).
18. Bodo Möller, Thai Duong, Krzysztof Kotowicz, Google. This poodle bites: exploiting the SSL 3.0 fallback, www.openssl.org/~bodo/ssl-poodle.pdf (accessed October 2015).

19. National Institute of Standards and Technology. National vulnerability database, https://nvd.nist.gov/ (accessed October 2015).

20. Computer Emergency Response Team, Carnegie Mellon University, www.cert.org/ (accessed October 2015).

21. SAS 70 Overview, http://sas70.com/sas70_overview.html (accessed October 2015).

22. Accredited Standards Committee X9 Inc., Financial Services Industry, www.x9.org (accessed October 2015).

23. American Institute of CPAs. Statements on standards for attestation engagements, http://www.aicpa.org/Research/Standards/AuditAttest/Pages/SSAE.aspx (accessed October 2015).

24. CA Browser Forum, https://cabforum.org (accessed October 2015).

25. Federal Public Key Infrastructure, [id] Management.Gov, www.idmanagement.gov/federal-public-key-infrastructure (accessed October 2015).

26. FFIEC, www.ffiec.gov/

10 PKI Industry

This book describes Public Key Infrastructure (PKI) as an operational system employing cryptography, information technology, business rules, specific use cases, and legal matters. Whereas both cryptography and information technology are reasonably consistent across the PKI industry, the business rules, use cases, and legal matters vary among different industry groups. Many of the relevant standards organizations are discussed in Chapter 1, "Introduction," along with a history of the associated industry standards in Chapter 3, "PKI Building Blocks," including ITU-T, PKCS, ASC X9, and IETF. As shown in Figure 10.1, this chapter looks at a long history of PKI industry trends relating to PKI policy and practices.

Academia The first publicly available research paper was the Diffie–Helman "New Directions in Cryptography" [B.7.6] published in 1976. This was quickly followed by the RSA "A Method for Obtaining Digital Signatures and Public-Key Cryptosystems" [B.7.5], which introduced the famous "Alice and Bob" characters. However, the United Kingdom's Government Code Head Quarters (GCHQ) declassified James Ellis' earlier 1970 research on non-secret encryption in 1977 [B.7.24]. Taher Elgamal, known as the father of SSL, published the Elgamal digital signature algorithm [B.7.25] paper in 1984. Two researchers, Martin Miller and Neal Koblitz, published independent papers on Elliptic Curve Cryptography (ECC), "Uses of Elliptic Curves in Cryptography" in 1985 [B.7.7] and "Elliptic Curve Cryptosystems" in 1987 [B.7.8]. And two researchers, Miklós Ajtai and Cynthia Dwork, published a paper on lattice-based cryptography, "A Public-Key Cryptosystem with Worst Case/Average Case Equivalence" in 1997 [B.7.27]. Thus, in order of publication:

- Diffie–Hellman
- RSA (Rivest-Shamir-Adleman)
- Elliptic Curve Cryptography (ECC)
- Lattice-based cryptography

ITU-T The International Telecommunication Union (ITU), formerly known as the International Telegraph and Telephone Consultative Committee (CCITT), telecommunications standardization sector (ITU-T), published the original X.509 recommendation as the Blue Book Volume VIII Fascicle VIII.8 from the CCITT 9th Plenary Assembly located in Melbourne, Australia, in November 1988 and republished as X.509 v1 the same year. X.509 v2 was released in November 1993 five years later, and X.509 v3 with certificate extensions was released in August 1997. There were five

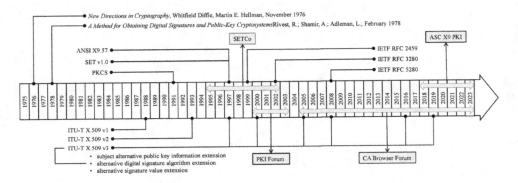

FIGURE 10.1 PKI industry trends.

DOI: 10.1201/9781003425298-10

more updates in 2003, 2005, 2008, and 2016. The current standard with new v3 extensions for Subject Alternative Public Key Information and Alternative Digital Signature Algorithm was published in October 2019.

SETCo MasterCard and Visa published the initial version of Secure Electronic Transaction (SET) version 0.0 in June 1996, followed by version 1.0 in May 1997, which refers to X.509 v3 (1993) certificates. SETCo was an organization created and staffed by MasterCard and Visa to manage the SET specification and Root CA. KPMG performed assessments of the various brand-level CA that operated under the SETCo Root CA, while the WebTrust CA auditing standard was under development and before its worldwide adoption.

PKI Forum The PKI Forum was publicly announced in January at the RSA 2000 Conference as a new industry consortium to promote PKI interoperability. With over 140 attendees, the expectation of 25 participants was exceeded. Its charter was an advocacy group to promote industry standards but not develop standards. Its focus was the then-current IETF specification RFC 2459 Internet X.509 Public Key Infrastructure Certificate and CRL Profile. After two successful years, the PKI Forum was merged into the Organization for the Advancement of Structured Information Standards (OASIS) in 2002.

CA Browser Forum The CA Browser Forum (also called the CA/Browser or CAB Forum) membership are certification authorities (CA), browser manufacturers, and other application vendors that use X.509 certificates. Founded in 2005, their focus is on SSL/TLS certificates, Extended Validation (EV) SSL certificates, Code Signing certificates, and Secure/Multipurpose Internet Mail Extensions (S/MIME) certificates. The CAB Forum manages various Baseline Requirements and Guidelines for web-based services.

ASC X9 PKI The Accredited Standards Committee X9, as discussed in Section 1.3, "Standards Organizations," was accredited by ANSI in 1974 for banking operations, and now develops national standards and fosters international standards for the financial services industry. The X9 committee established an X9F Data and Information Security subcommittee PKI Study Group in June 2018 to determine strategy and tactics for the financial services industry.

The following chapters provide a more in-depth discussion of many relevant PKI groups and their efforts, including their similarities, interactions, and dissimilarities. These groups and many individuals helped shape the PKI industry as we know it today. Some no longer exist, while others will continue to influence the PKI industry in the immediate future. Any omission of other groups or individuals is unintentional, merely by-product of the authors' experience and knowledge.

10.1 ITU-T X.509

The International Telecommunication Union (ITU), formerly the International Telegraph and Telephone Consultative Committee (CCITT), as part of its Series X: Data Communication Networks standards, published the initial X.509 The Directory: Authentication Framework in 1988 establishing public key certificates.

- X.509 v1 was published in 1988 with basic signed certificate fields.
- X.509 v2 was published in 1993, which introduced two optional unique identifiers: issuer (*issuerUniqueIdentifier*) and subject (*subjectUniqueIdentifier*).
- X.509 v3 was published in 1997, which introduced extensions composed of three fields: an extension identifier (extnId), critical (Boolean) flag, and the value (extnValue). The identifier is an object identifier (OID), which is globally unique. The critical flag indicates whether the extension must be processed or can be ignored if the OID is unrecognized. The value syntax and semantics depend on the OID meaning.

The X.509:1997 edition defined many of the certificate and certificate revocation list (CRL) extensions still in use today, but not all have widespread adoption. Each subsequent X.509 edition remained as v3 but with clarifications, additions, and further recommendations. Note that in Chapter 3, "PKI Building Blocks," we provided Table 3.1 with an overview of a typical X.509 certificate. However, certificates will vary among CA and applications.

Note that the IETF published its own adaptation of the X.509 standard, namely RFC 2459 (1999), RFC 3280 (2002), and RFC 5280 (2008) as profiles of the X.509 v3 certificate and X.509 v2 certificate request list (CRL) for use on the Internet. The profiles include the ISO/IEC/ITU-T and ANSI extensions that may be useful in the Internet PKI. The profiles are presented in the 1988 Abstract Syntax Notation One (ASN.1) rather than the 1997 ASN.1 syntax used in the most recent ISO/IEC/ITU-T standards. As noted in Chapter 3, "PKI Building Blocks," the Authority Info Access (AIA) is an IETF-defined extension.

The X.509:2019 edition added three alternative extensions: an alternate subject public key, an alternate certificate signature algorithm, and an alternate certificate signature.

Extension OID	Extension Name and Description
2.5.29.72	*subjectAltPublicKeyInfo*: a subject's alternative public key information to be used instead of the information provided in the *subjectPublicKeyInfo* component;
2.5.29.73	*altSignatureAlgorithm*: an alternative signature algorithm to be used instead of the algorithm specified in the signature component; and
2.5.29.74	*altSignatureValue*: an alternative digital signature to be checked instead of the native digital signature.

The OID arc 2.5.29 *certificateExtension* (id-ce) is defined as joint-iso-itu-t (2), directoryservices (5), certificateExtension (29) with three new extensions:

- *subjectAltPublicKeyInfo* (72)
- *altSignatureAlgorithm* (73)
- *altSignatureValue* (74)

This allows a public key certificate to contain two different keys and signatures: the *native* subject public key and certificate signature, and an *alternative* subject public key and certificate signature. The concept is to enable cryptographic transitions from older algorithms in the native fields to newer algorithms in the alternative extensions. However, the alternative extensions can also be used for backward compatibility with newer algorithms in the native fields and older algorithms in the alternative extensions. Further, the native fields and alternative extensions might offer cryptographic options negotiable between the subject and the relying party.

Another interesting public key certificate extension is the private key usage period, with similar *notBefore* and *notAfter* attributes as the public key validity field. This extension indicates the usage period of the private key corresponding to the public key. It is applicable only for private key used for creating digital signatures. Further, for multiple cryptographic algorithm public key certificates, the native private key usage period also applies to the alternative private key. However, this extension is rarely used. The private key usage period extension was explicitly disallowed in RFC 3280 but RFC 5280 neither deprecates nor recommends its use for the Internet PKI.

10.2 EMV INTEGRATED CIRCUIT CARD (ICC)

In 1993, the three major credit card brands, EuroPay, MasterCard, and Visa (EMV), began discussions with the goal of standardizing a global SmartCard-based replacement for mag-stripe credit and debit cards. The effort and resulting specification were named EMV after the original participants. Note that EuroPay eventually merged with MasterCard in 2002. This risk-based PKI deployment was intended to secure face-to-face card bank card transactions and eliminate some of the largest targets for bank card fraud. Where SET addressed "card not present" transactions, EMV addressed "card present" activity.

The second book *Security Without Obscurity: A Guide to Cryptographic Architectures* provides several illustrations, including EMV Payment Cards [B.7.28].

The EMV smartcard (ICC) payment card is an alternative to the legacy magnetic stripe (magstripe) payment cards. EMV payment "chip and PIN" card specifications were available as early as 1994, but worldwide adoption was slow for several reasons. First, there was no smartcard infrastructure; point-of-sale (POS) terminals and automated teller machines (ATMs) only had magstripe readers. Second, the costs associated with replacing legacy POS, ATM, and magstripe cards was another hurdle that had to be overcome. Consequently, hybrid cards with both legacy magstripe and ICC have been issued.

The EMV specification uses PKI but because of early technical limitations of storage and processing power, shorter asymmetric keys are used and X.509 certificates are not used. However, EMV claims to follow the usual practice of certificates to validate the source of issuer and card public keys [EMV Issuer and Application Security Guidelines].

A certificate is a form of digital signature designed to validate the origin and integrity of a public key. A certificate consists of a public key concatenated with other related data and signed with the private key of a trusted entity known as a Certification Authority (CA). Any entity with a trusted copy of the CA's Public Key can then verify all certificates generated by that CA and thereby obtain trusted copies of other users' public keys.

In the EMV environment, the Payment System acts as a Certification Authority and creates Issuer Public Key certificates by signing each issuer public key. Issuers act as Certification Authorities and create ICC Public Key certificates by signing each ICC Public Key. The Payment Systems CA's Public Keys are distributed to the terminals through the acquirers for verifying issuer certificates, thereby yielding trusted copies of issuers' public keys, used in turn to verify ICC Public Keys.

An EMV card authenticates itself to the merchant terminal and vice versa to establish a secure "terminal-to-chip card" communication. That is the first step in securing an EMV transaction. The terminal sends the transaction information including the merchant data, type of merchant, transaction amount, date/time, and other supporting information to the chip on the EMV card. The EMV card uses that information along with an incrementing counter to create a cryptogram that is unique to the transaction. The card and cryptogram can be verified by the card issuer as part of the authorization transaction. The transaction counter used to create the cryptogram prevents transaction replay and subsequently reduces merchant errors or unintentional duplicate billing.

As shown in Figure 10.2, the EMV PKI is managed by the individual card brands with additional authentication incorporated into the EMV card to enable terminal-to-card mutual authentication.

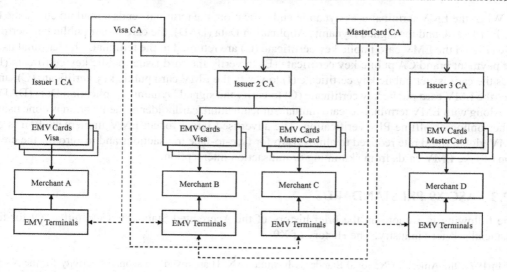

FIGURE 10.2   EMV PKI.

Each brand (X, Y) manages its own domain where issuers might only offer one brand (e.g., issuer 1 offers brand X, issuer 2 offers brand Y), while others offer both (e.g., issuer 2 offers brand X and Y). Each issuer manages its EMV card portfolio, which might be used at various merchant locations with EMV terminals.

- The **payment brand** (e.g., MasterCard, Visa) has a CA private key (b) and public key certificate (B); the payment brand CA private key (b) is used to sign the card issuer public key certificate (I).
- The **card issuer** (e.g., financial institution) has an issuer private key (i) and public key certificate (I) provided by the payment brand CA; the card issuer private key (i) is used to sign the EMV card public key certificate (C).
- Each **EMV card** has a unique card private key (c) and public key certificate (C) provided by the card issuer; thus, the card issuer is its own EMV card CA, and the card issuer signs Static Application Data (SAD) installed on the EMV card.
- The **acquirer** (or merchant) installs the payment brand CA public key certificate (B) into the EMV terminal.

When the EMV terminal uses static authentication, the signed SAD and card issuer public key certificate (I) are sent from the EMV card to the terminal. The terminal uses the payment brand CA public key certificate (B) to verify the card issuer public key certificate (I), and then uses the card issuer public key certificate (I) to verify the signed SAD. Note that Certificate Revocation List (CRL) checking is optional and Online Certificate Status Protocol (OCSP) is not supported. Merchants can still check payment card status using the Restricted Card List (RCL) for low transaction amounts or online authorization for higher amounts. Note that the issuer private key (i) is used to sign both the EMV card public key certificate (C) and the EMV card Static Application Data (SAD), which is not allowed with X.509 certificates.

SPECIAL NOTE 10-1 EMV KEY REUSE

Note that within a PKI the CA signs the subscriber certificate and the subscriber signs the data; however, EMV allows the Issuer to sign both the card certificate and the authentication data with the same keys, which is a bad cryptographic practice.

When the EMV terminal uses dynamic authentication, the terminal sends a random challenge to the EMV card, and the signed Dynamic Application Data (DAD), the card issuer public key certificate (I), and the EMV card public key certificate (C) are returned to the terminal. The terminal uses the payment brand CA public key certificate (B) to verify the card issuer public key certificate (I), uses the card issuer public key certificate (I) to verify the EMV card public key certificate (C), and uses the EMV card public key certificate (C) to verify the signed Dynamic Application Data (DAD).

Along with EMV terminal-to-card mutual authentication, cardholder authentication is done using either online or offline PIN verification. The advertised target for an EMV implementation is an EMV global fraud rate reduced to almost zero for face-to-face transactions and to zero for the creation of fake EMV cards from skimming or transaction interception.

10.3   ASC X9 PKI STANDARDS

The following is a quote on the brief history of the Accredited Standards Committee X9 for the financial services industry: The History of X9[1]

In 1974, the American National Standards Institute (ANSI) approved the scope of activity for the X9 Standards Committee on Banking, as "Standardization for Facilitating Banking Operations." The X9

Standards Committee operated as part of the American Bankers Association (ABA) and concentrated on check standards.

In June, 1976, the X9 Standards Committee approved expansion of its membership to include vendors, insurance companies, associations, retailers, regulators, and others in the financial services area. With this approval, the name was changed to X9, Financial Services.

ANSI first granted X9 official accreditation in 1984 as a standards development organization for the financial services industry. An accreditation X9 proudly still holds today and the official committee name became the Accredited Standards Committee X9, Financial Services. In 2001, X9 separated from the ABA and was incorporated under a 501c(6) nonprofit designation for associations. The name changed slightly to Accredited Standards Committee X9, Financial Services Inc. ("ASC X9"). ASC X9 operates under its own procedures as well as those prescribed and approved by the American National Standards Institute (ANSI).

ASC X9 participates in the development of international standards for the global financial services industry through the ISO Technical Committee for Financial Services TC68. ASC X9 is the USA Technical Advisory Group (TAG) to TC68 under the International Organization for Standardization (ISO), of Geneva, Switzerland. In this role, X9 holds the USA vote on all ISO standards of TC68 or its subcommittees SC2, SC8, and SC9. X9 further provides subject matter experts to develop international standards. ASC X9 also provides the secretariat function to TC68.

As the use of cryptography expanded in the financial sector, ASC X9 was busy analyzing and developing standards for PKI deployment. Numerous X9 standards documented elsewhere in this publication were developed by volunteers using their expertise and vision to facilitate secure deployment and interoperability of encryption techniques. Under ASC X9 direction, the needs of the financial sector were addressed through ASC X9 standards.

- ANSI X9.30 Public Key Cryptography Using Irreversible Algorithms for the Financial Services Industry
  - Part 1: The Digital Signature Algorithm (DSA) (Revised)
  - Part 2: The Secure Hash Algorithm (SHA1) (Revised)

These two X9.30 standards were published in 1995 and updated in 1997 to coincide with the NIST standards FIPS 180–1 Secure Hash Algorithm (1995) and FIPS 186 Digital Signature Algorithm (1994). However, since X9 standards are copyrighted and the FIPS content could not be explicitly included, the two X9.30 standards were withdrawn by X9. Accordingly, the X9 Registry was created to recognize the adoption of other standards such as NIST FIPS.

- ANSI X9.31 Digital Signatures Using Reversible Public Key Cryptography for the Financial Services Industry (rDSA)

When the company Security Dynamics acquired the RSA company in 1995, the RSA algorithm patent lawsuit was settled. This allowed the X9F1 workgroup to reactivate the development of the X9.31 standard, which included the RSA digital signature algorithm. The X9.31 standard was published in 1998 and added as a reference to the NIST standard FIPS 186–1 Digital Signature Standard (1998). However, ANSI administratively withdrew the X9.31 standard in 2008 because it aged ten years without a review. Consequently, the FIPS 186–5 revision (2019) noted the X9.31 withdrawal and added its own RSA Digital Signature Algorithm section.

- ANSI X9.42 Public Key Cryptography for the Financial Services Industry: Agreement of Symmetric Keys Using Discrete Logarithm Cryptography

The X9.42 standard was published in 2003, reaffirmed in 2013, and ballot revision in 2022. This X9.42 standard and NIST Special Publication 800–56A both include Diffie–Hellman and Menezes-Qu-Vanstone (MQV) key establishment schemes. NIST 800–56A was published in 2006, revised in 2010, 2013, and 2018. Key agreement consists of two parties exchanging public keys, computing a shared secret using their own private key and the other's public key, and deriving one or more symmetric keys from the shared secret.

- ANSI X9.44 Public-Key Cryptography for the Financial Services Industry Key Establishment Using Integer Factorization Cryptography

The X9.44 standard was published in 2007, reaffirmed in 2017, and ballot revision in 2022. This X9.44 standard and NIST Special Publication 800–56B specify key-establishment schemes using integer factorization cryptography (in particular, RSA). NIST 800–56B was published in 2009, with revisions in 2014 and 2018. Key transport consists of one party encrypting a symmetric key using the other party's public key, and the other party decrypting the symmetric key using the private key, so each party has the symmetric key. Key agreement consists of one party encrypting a random number using the other party's public key, and the other party decrypting the random number using the private key, such that each party derives a symmetric key using the random number.

- X9.45 Enhanced Management Controls Using Digital Signatures and Attribute Certificates

The X9.45 standard was published in 1999 but withdrawn by X9 in 2011. This standard described the use of attribute certificates and other mechanisms defined in X9.57 Certificate Management, to allow the verifier (e.g., recipient) of a signed document or transaction to determine whether the document or transaction can be considered authorized according to the rules and limits agreed to by the parties to the transaction. Attribute certificates had limited industry adoption.

- ANSI X9.55 Public Key Cryptography for the Financial Services Industry: Extensions to Public Key Certificates and Certificate Revocation Lists

The X9.55 standard was published in 1997, submitted to ISO TC68, adopted as ISO 15782–2 in 2003, and X9.55 withdrawn by X9 in 2007. The X9.55 and ISO 15782–2 standards specify extensions to the definitions of public key certificates and certificate revocation list in ANSI X9.57 Certificate Management. Meanwhile, ISO 15782 Certificate Management for Financial Services – Part 2: Certificate extensions was published in 2003, revised in 2009, merged into ISO 21188 in 2018, and consequently withdrawn by ISO in 2018.

- ANSI X9.57 Public Key Cryptography for the Financial Services Industry: Certificate Management

The X9.57 standard was published in 1977, submitted to ISO TC68, adopted as ISO 15782–1 in 2003, and X9.55 withdrawn by X9 in 2007. The X9.55 and ISO 15782–1 standards specify extensions to the definitions of public key certificates and certificate revocation list in ANSI X9.57 Certificate Management. Meanwhile, ISO 15782 Certificate Management for Financial Services – Part 1: Public key certificates was published in 2003, revised in 2009, merged into ISO 21188 in 2018, and consequently withdrawn by ISO in 2018.

- ANSI X9.62 Public Key Cryptography for the Financial Services Industry: The Elliptic Curve Digital Signature Algorithm (ECDSA)

The X9.62 standard was published in 1998 and revised in 2005 but administratively withdrawn by ANSI in 2016. Regrettably, the X9F subcommittee, the X9F1 workgroup, and the X9.62 project editor did not keep up with ANSI bureaucracy. Further, once ANSI has withdrawn a standard, the number cannot be reactivated or reused. Fortunately, a renumbered X9.142 revision was published in 2020.

- ANSI X9.63 Public Key Cryptography for the Financial Services Industry Key Agreement and Key Transport Using Elliptic Curve Cryptography

The X9.63 standard was published in 2001 and revised in 2011 and 2017. The ANSI action to administratively withdraw X9.62 was avoided for X9.63 by X9 submitting a Project Initiation Notification System (PINS) to ANSI in a timely manner.

- ANSI X9.68 Digital Certificates for Mobile/Wireless and High Transaction Volume Financial Systems: Part 2: Domain Certificate Syntax

The X9.68–2 standard was published in 2001 but withdrawn by X9 in 2011 as part of a general clean up on unadopted standards. The original concept was an abbreviated X.509 certificate profile for bandwidth constrained wireless devices with limited computational capacity. But as mobile phones improved and wireless got faster, the need was overtaken by events. Note that X9.68–1 was a placeholder but was never developed or published.

- ANSI X9.79 Public Key Infrastructure (PKI) – Part 1: Practices and Policy Framework

The X9.79–1 standard was published in 2001, submitted to ISO TC68, adopted as ISO 21188 in 2006, and consequently withdrawn by X9 in 2006. ISO 21188 was revised in 2018. Meanwhile, X9.79–1 was adopted by the AICPA and CICA auditing standard WebTrust for CA version 1.0 in 2000 and version 2.0 in 2011 changed to ISO 21188. Further, ISO/IEC JTC1 adopted ISO 21188 for ISO/IEC 27099 Information Technology – Public Key Infrastructure – Practices and Policy Framework in 2022. Both X9.79–1 and ISO 21188 have been popular and successful.

- ANSI X9.79 Public Key Infrastructure (PKI) – Part 4: Asymmetric Key Management for the Financial Services Industry

The X9.79–4 standard was published in 2013 for the management and security of asymmetric keys protecting financial information. This standard's asymmetric key management lifecycle has been recognized by many other standards and organizations. Note that the middle parts 2 and 3 were placeholders, but the X9F5 workgroup plans on completing the series.

- ANSI X9.98 Lattice-Based Polynomial Public Key Establishment Algorithm for the Financial Services Industry

This X9.98 standard was published in 2010 and revised in 2017. The development of this standard pre-dated the NIST 2016 post-quantum cryptography (PQC) call for algorithms and the 2022 Round 3 selections, which include lattice-based cryptography.

Large financial institutions, smaller regional banks, and credit unions have the business requirement to communicate with their operations centers, branch facilities, and third-party service providers. All the financial data must be securely managed without unauthorized disclosure, interception, alteration, or other compromise. Encrypted communication channels facilitate that communication using X9 standards and communication channels fitting the business and technical needs of each individual institution.

Even before there was widespread use of the Internet, remote banking and access to financial services was already developing. X9 was charged by ANSI and the financial industry to develop a standard for Secure Remote Access to Financial Data. This effort X9.49 started in 1994 and evolved as the Internet broadened its reach. The X9 ANSI Standard X9.117 successor stands today and continues to evolve to meet the requirements for secure home banking, electronic bill payment and other electronic financial services.

To provide a *risk-based* standard to establish trust in the emerging PKI industry, X9 was tasked with standardizing policies and operational practices that support financial institutions and other PKI users trust in the public key deployments that meet those standards. X9.79 was developed to provide a standard for Certificate Policies and practices. It was strong enough to be accepted as ISO 21188, the ISO standard for financial PKI. This standard was used as the baseline for the development of WebTrust CA described elsewhere.

Of particular interest to the financial sector and the history of ATM security was the development of public key techniques for the secure distribution of ATM symmetric keys. These keys are required by X9 and ISO standards for the protection of Personal Identification Numbers (PINs) used in ATM account access and withdrawal transactions. Several different ATM manufacturers, software and cryptographic hardware vendors, and consultants came together at the urging and leadership of MasterCard, Visa, Diebold, and ACI software (of Omaha, NE) to develop a set of common requirements that provided a risk-based security environment, interoperability, and an open development environment. The methodology was submitted to ASC X9 to be developed into an extension of the existing X9.24 standard for PIN Security and encryption key management.

The ASC X9 standards development work continues to support the financial community. Standards working groups are involved in almost every aspect of financial services operation, interoperability, and security. X9 standards range from Magnetic Ink Character Recognition (MICR) encoding through Fast Payments, secure access to financial services, encryption techniques and security services. The X9 forward vision and related research continues including in-depth research and development of plans for addressing risk in a Quantum Computing environment and beyond.

10.4   SECURE ELECTRONIC TRANSACTIONS (SET)

Early in 1995, along with the popularization of the Word Wide Web and newfangled browsers such as Mosaic and Netscape, the industry began to demand a method of securing the emerging e-commerce industry. After a few failed attempts at providing a successful joint specification, Master-Card and Visa released *Secure Electronic Transactions (SET)* in June 1996. SET was a risk-based, transaction-oriented implementation of PKI, the first in history. The specification was published as three books: (1) Business Description [21], (2) Programmer's Guide [22], and (3) Formal Protocol Definition [23]. After operating worldwide for six years, SET was decommissioned in 2002.

When SET was developed, the rise of e-commerce also saw the rise in fraud based on phony "merchants" setting up websites pretending to sell merchandise at deep discounts. But their purpose was to collect credit card data and use it for their own fraud or for selling the information to organized crime syndicates. This was an important focus of SET – to reduce or eliminate the risk of merchant fraud by verifying the validity of merchants involved in e-commerce and tracing their relationship with the merchant's bank and card association. A Visa card-based transaction could only be processed under Visa's segment of the SET PKI.

The SET public key implementation was multifaceted. One PKI use was based on protecting specific sensitive transaction data, including the credit card information used in the transaction. Another was the authentication of the parties associated with the transaction through the use of public key certificates. The subordinate architecture of the PKI allowed individual participants in SET such as MasterCard and Visa the opportunity to manage their SET PKI environment, including who would operate their PKI, geographically diverse management options, security requirements for participation, internal organization management, registration, and other critical matters. The SET publication was three books:

- Book 1: *Business Description* [SET] by Bill Poletti, Tony Lewis, Jeff Stapleton
- Book 2: *Programmer's Guide* [SET]
- Book 3: *Formal Protocol Definition* [SET]

As shown in Figure 10.3, SET also forced the participating organizations into developing a common SET Root CA. The SET Root CA was located in a secure wing of an R&D facility in the Battelle Institute campus across the street from Ohio State University in Columbus, OH. It was only accessed under tight security controls managed by a disinterested third party with several layers of security and enforced dual occupancy requiring both Visa and MasterCard presence in the room. The SET Root CA software was custom-developed such that the "m of n" method was used, which ensured both MasterCard and Visa would be forced to participate in any SET Root signing events.

The SET Root CA Team would meet at that facility as the needs required, but at least once per year for the renewal of the Root CA keys and certificate. Individual key components and security tokens were stored locally and were the separate responsibility of MasterCard and Visa. Though the SET Root CA certificate had a seven-year life, its private key use period was limited to one year. This was based on the longest useable certificate life of the subordinate certificates that could exist under a given SET root.

Shortly after the release of SET, MasterCard and Visa independently developed security and operational requirements for participation. Visa used its PIN Security Compliance Program as its model for security requirements. MasterCard had no such program so developed its security compliance program from scratch. Both programs were established to address the specific financial and reputational risks associated with e-commerce. That risk profile was higher than communication risk under TLS.

When released in its initial draft, SET was analyzed by the best cryptanalysis and security experts in the world. Except for a social engineering attack, no cryptographic or successful operational attacks were even discovered. It was considered to absolutely secure transactions and fully met its business requirements. SET was an important public key-based specification because:

1. There was a specific business case developed around an identified financial risk.
2. It was application-specific with embedded cryptographic operations.
3. It managed participation through PKI chaining.
4. It authenticated multiple parties.
5. It was a deep and robust business-based PKI hierarchy.
6. It established a risk-based security compliance program based on the needs of the financial sector.
7. It helped launch e-commerce by proving the security of Internet-based financial transaction protection.
8. It solved the business problem of credit card compromise in non-face-to-face electronic transactions.

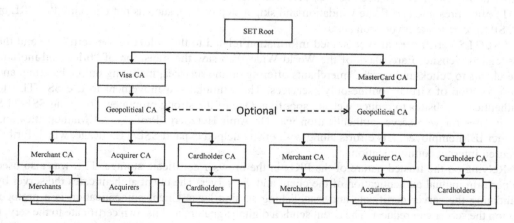

FIGURE 10.3 SET PKI hierarchy.

SET marked the beginning of application risk-based Internet security initiatives. SET provided proof that e-commerce could be fully secured and safe for consumers. That was its ultimate goal. However, its decommission in 2002 was partly due to its complexity, the separation of Visa and MasterCard brand-level certificates, the lack of other brand participation (e.g., Amex, Discover, JCB), the problematic issuance of cardholder certificates, and an alternative solution call Secure Socket Layer (SSL).

10.5 SECURE SOCKET LAYER (SSL)

As discussed in Chapter 3, "PKI Building Blocks," the PKI Protocol SSL was invented by Dr. Taher Elgamal, Chief Scientist at Netscape, known as the Father of SSL. The initial intent of SSL was to secure communication between a web server and a client browser over the Internet. During the same period when Taher was designing SSL, Netscape was also collaborating with MasterCard to develop a new payments protocol, which eventually became the Secure Electronic Transaction (SET).

During one of the SET development sessions, Taher drew two boxes on the whiteboard labeled server and client, and began drawing a sequence of process flows, explaining his thoughts. After he finished, Taher turned to us and said something like, "I was thinking of call it Secure Socket Layer, what do you think?" Basically, we had just witnessed the draft SSL 0.1 protocol. Note that SET ran its course from 1995 to 2002, while the IETF published TLS in 1999 to replace SSL. Thus, SET began with SSL and ended with TLS when SET was decommissioned in 2002.

A core feature of SSL is server authentication: the server authenticates itself to the client using a digital certificate based on the assumption that a recognized PKI issued the certificate to the legitimate owner or operator. Basically, the server sends its SSL certificate to the client, the client validates the certificate, and then, trusting the server RSA public key, returns an encrypted random number. The server and the client both use the random number and other exchanged information to determine a shared secret from which both derive the session keys, one for data encryption and the other for data integrity. Chapter 3, "PKI Building Blocks," describes the SSL and TLS protocols in greater detail.

The server certificate is issued and signed by a recognized Certificate Authority (CA) from a trusted PKI. The client is expected to (i) verify that the URL matches the certificate subject name and (ii) validate the certificate chain including validity (expiration) dates, key usage, and revocation status. For browsers, the CA certificates are installed by the browser manufacturer per a CA audit program, such as the auditing standard WebTrust CA. Early days, some browsers didn't verify the subject name, so any certificate was accepted. Even today, some browsers allow the user to override a certificate problem, alerting the user but asking the user to proceed with a simple yes or no click. Other non-browser clients such as web services, mobile devices, and even the Internet of Things (IoT) often presume certificate validation and skip a step or two, such as not checking the CRL or OCSP for certificate revocation status.

SSL/TLS certificates also contained information related to the holder of the certificate and the associated website. Early days of the World Wide Web saw the transition of "brick-and-mortar" merchants to "click-and-mortar" merchants offering online services, including online banking, and the evolution of virtual "online-only" services. That stimulated a movement to use SSL/TLS to authenticate websites to reduce website spoofing. One of the strong proponents of using SSL/TLS certificates for web server authentication was Dr. Amir Herzberg, Professor of Mathematics and former IBM employee. His efforts along with others helped expand SSL/TLS usage, which further secured Internet communication.

Relying on the trusted nature of the PKIs in the browser certificate storage, TLS was also used to perform mutual authentication of the client and the server. The client authenticates the server by validating the server certificate and establishing session keys. Client authentication is a protocol option the server can request. The client sends a digital signature and its own certificate to the server. The server authenticates the client by validating the client certificate and the client digital signature.

TLS offers mutual authentication as well as an option to stop communication if the parties failed authentication. This became a useful tool for securing remote employee access to company resources.

An interesting technique was developed to even further secure server access using SSL/TLS. By clearing server certificate cache and installing a single or small number of issuing CA certificates, enabling required mutual authentication with session fail when authentication fails, TLS could be turned into an access control tool. The only client systems that could access the server would be those using certificates issued under the CA certificates installed on the server. All other clients would be refused under the "session fails when authentication fails" TLS option. This technique was known as "Private Isolated Root Mutual Authentication" or PIRMA developed in 1999 and increased in use in academic research environments. This technique was communication-oriented and was application transparent.

Note that there was no transaction risk analysis associated with SSL/TLS. SSL/TLS are communication protocols and a method of authentication. The data content of the SSL/TLS encrypted packets are agnostic to the protocols; the information can be anything from financial payment transactions to surfing the Internet for cat videos. Realistically, payment applications address transaction risks independent of the communications protocols.

The impact on the PKI business environment was to stimulate the establishment of commercial Certification Authorities that performed background checks and issued certificates based on the degree of background checks and applicant authentication. Several CA dominated the market. The most successful at the time was Silicon Valley-based Verisign.

The market for SSL/TLS certificates exploded in the late 1990s. And with an increasing understanding of asymmetric encryption and PKI, application designs using PKI were starting to gain traction. This led to a rise in the number of private Certification Authorities aimed at limited use and focused on specific applications.

For the SSL/TLS certificates to operate successfully, browsers were required to embed the Root or issuing CA in their certificate cache and to perform certificate authentication when presented with a server certificate. This requirement pulled the browser manufacturers into the picture led by Netscape but soon followed by others. Eventually the CA Browser Forum evolved to establish PKI operating rules along with the adoption of the WebTrust CA auditing standard led by KPMG within the American Institute for Certified Public Accounts (AICPA) and the Canadian Institute of Chartered Accountants (CICA).

Note that SET involved a complex interaction of three certificates between the cardholder, merchant, and payment gateway. However, cardholder certificates were never fully adopted, so SET was basically reduced to protecting the credit card transaction between the merchant and payment gateway. Coincidently, SSL with client authentication (also called mutual authentication) where the merchant is the client (browser) and the payment gateway is the server, was functionally equivalent to SET but without the burden of brand-driven certificates.

10.6 PKI FORUM

The PKI Forum charter was an advocacy group that promoted industry standards but did not develop standards. The initial focus was the then current IETF specification RFC 2459, and as noted in Section 10.1, "ITU-T X.509," the specification is an Internet profile of the ITU-T X.509 standard. The forum held its kickoff meeting at the RSA 2000 Conference. The expected 25 attendees were exceeded by the approximately 140 attendees. During the next three years, the PKI Forum published numerous PKI Notes. Eventually, the PKI Forum merged with OASIS PKI in March 2003, where the PKI Notes[2] white papers are publicly posted.

- PKI Note: US Healthcare, March 2001
- CA-CA Interoperability, March 2001
- PKI Interoperability Framework, March 2001

- PKI Note: PKI Policy White Paper, March 2001
- PKI Note: Biometrics, May 2001
- PKI Note: CA Trust, July 2001
- PKI Note: Smart Cards, April 2002
- PKI Note: PKI Basics – A Business Perspective, April 2002
- PKI and Financial Return on Investment, August 2002
- AKID/SKID Implementation Guideline, September 2002
- Understanding Certification Path Construction, September 2002
- PKI Note: PKI Basics – A Technical Perspective, November 2002

Coincidently, with regard to WebTrust CA audits, three industry issues were identified and brought to the attention of the PKI Forum: PKI assurance levels, PKI cross-certification, and PKI subordination. Consequently, a special PKI Security Issues meeting was held in June 2002 in Washington, DC, where fireworks ensued. Reportedly a CA's reputation for issuing low-cost SSL certificate lacking identity verification was the crux of the PKI assurance levels issue. The heated discussion allegedly led to allegations of tortious interference, the act of interfering with someone's business by making a false claim that ultimately damages the business. Meeting minutes were promised, but none were distributed. What did occur was a Department of Justice investigation. All records and e-mails pertaining to the meeting were collected but apparently the matter resolved itself without criminal prosecution.

Meanwhile, the PKI Forum merged with the OASIS PKI in March 2003. Soon afterwards, the first three meetings of the CA Browser Forum were held in 2005, located in New York City, Kanata, Ontario, and Scottsdale Arizona. Ultimately the Extended Validation (EV) Guidelines for SSL/TLS Certificates were published in June 2007. In addition to the CA Browser Forum members, representatives of the Information Security Committee (ISC) of the American Bar Association (ABA) Section of Science & Technology, Law (STL), and the Canadian Institute of Chartered Accountants (CICA) developed the EV certificates.

Whether the development of the EV Guidelines was a direct consequence of the PKI Security Issues meeting or merely an influence is debatable. The EV Guidelines basic purpose is to provide a higher assurance level for the identity of the legal entity that controls a web site. The EV scope includes code signing certificates. The initial EV Guidelines v1.0 was published in 2007 and the current EV Guidelines v1.8.0 was published in November 2022. However, some industry experts[3] argue that EV certificates have outlived their usefulness.

10.7   AMERICAN BAR ASSOCIATION (ABA)

The American Bar Association (ABA) published two significant papers: the Digital Signature Guidelines (DSG) and the PKI Assurance Guidelines (PAG). Specifically, the ABA's Information Security Committee (ISC) researched legal, business, and technical aspects of securing electronic commerce and of protecting information and critical infrastructures within computer systems and networks, such as the Internet. Another area of interest was the legal standing of digital signatures, certificates, and PKI. The ABA ISC published the Digital Signature Guidelines (DSG) in 1996 and the PKI Assurance Guidelines (PAG) in 2003.

1996: Digital Signature Guidelines (DSG) Legal Infrastructure for Certification Authorities and Secure Electronic Commerce [B.7.24]
The DSG proposes a safe harbor which will:

(1) *minimize the incidence of electronic forgeries,*
(2) *enable and foster the reliable authentication of documents in computer form,*
(3) *facilitate commerce by means of computerized communications,* and

(4) *give legal effect to the general import of the technical standards for authentication of computerized messages.*

The DSG provides a PKI tutorial, terminology definitions, and general principles for certification authorities (CA), subscribers, and relying parties. The relationships between the CA, subscribers, and relying parties are described from a legal perspective.

- *The relationship between a certification authority and subscriber may be primarily contractual, whereby a subscriber and certification authority will agree to reinforce and enhance the subscriber's digital signature capability in exchange for a fee or other consideration.*
- *The duties of a certification authority to a third party relying on a certificate are rooted mainly in legal proscriptions against fraud and negligent misrepresentation.*
- *The duties of a subscriber to a person who relies upon the subscriber's certificate and digital signatures verified using that certificate, rest upon principles of both contract and tort.*

The DSG describes reliance on certificates and digital signatures as six legal requirements.

1) **Digitally signed message is written**: A message bearing a digital signature verified by the public key listed in a valid certificate is as valid, effective, and enforceable as if the message had been written on paper.
2) **Satisfaction of signature requirements**: Where a rule of law requires a signature, that rule is satisfied by a digital signature, which is affixed by the signer with the intention of signing the message, and verified by reference to the public key listed in a valid certificate.
3) **Unreliable digital signatures**: Unless otherwise provided by law or contract, the satisfaction of signature requirements (requirement 2) does not apply to a digital signature if a relying party either (a) knows that the signer breached a duty prescribed in the subscriber requirements or (b) assumes the risk that the digital signature is invalid per the reasonableness of reliance (requirement 4).
4) **Reasonableness of reliance**: The relying party understands (a) the subscriber certificate, (b) the importance of the digital signature, and (c) the course of dealing between the relying person and subscriber.
5) **Digitally signed originals and copies**: A copy of a digitally signed message is as effective, valid, and enforceable as the original of the message.
6) **Presumptions in dispute resolution**: In resolving a dispute involving a digital signature, it is rebuttably presumed that (a) the information in a valid certificate is correct, (b) the public key used to verify the signature belongs to the certificate subscriber, (c) the message associated with the verified signature has not been altered, (d) the certificate is issued by a valid CA, and (e) the signature was generated before it was time-stamped.

2003: PKI Assurance Guidelines (PAG) Guidelines to Help Assess and Facilitate Interoperable Trustworthy Public Key Infrastructures [B.7.25]

The PAG was developed as a sequel to the DSG over a five-year period, providing recommendations for assessing and facilitating interoperable trustworthy public key infrastructures. At the time, the literature addressing the means and methods for assessing PKIs and concerning PKI in general were considered relatively sparse. Further, the increasing reliance on PKI services and products created a commensurately rising demand for information about PKIs and how to assess their quality. Since its publication in 2003, the reliance on PKI and public key certificates has continued to increase over the past two decades.

In this book, Chapter 1, "Introduction," describes PKI as an operational system that employs cryptography, information technology (IT), information security (cybersecurity), legal matters, and business rules – see Figure 1.1 PKI Cryptonomics. The importance of legal issues, as reflected in the CP/CPS discussion in RFC 3647 §9 "Other Business and Legal Matters," cannot be understated. Legal areas include confidentiality of business information, privacy of personal information, intellectual property rights, representations and warranties, disclaimers of warranties, limitations of liability, indemnities, term and termination, notifications and communications, dispute resolution procedures, and applicability of governing law. For the financial services industry, governing law, regulatory guidance, and contractual obligations are equally applicable.

SPECIAL NOTE 10-2 RELYING PARTY AGREEMENTS

The original 50-dollar reimbursement limit on fraudulent credit card transactions provided by the card brands and merchants, often quoted in many older PKI-relying party agreements, is insufficient and immaterial for today's diverse retail payments and wholesale settlements.

The PAG covers a wide variety of legal areas relating to the original CP/CPS provisions and expands issues such as initial identification, certificate lifecycle management, physical security, records management, key management, technical security, certificate profiles, and administrative controls. An important distinction is made between technical nonrepudiation versus legal nonrepudiation.

When a PKI is intended to support digital signatures for the purpose of authenticating a transaction or a communication that needs to be attributed to a particular subscriber, the digital signature does not by itself result in legal "nonrepudiation." When a subscriber attempts to repudiate a transaction or communication, there may be factual and legal questions and disputes that, if not settled, will need to be resolved in litigation, arbitration, or other alternative dispute resolution mechanism, in order to determine whether the attempted repudiation is ultimately successful. The unique value of PKI is its technological ability to provide robust factual inferences of nonrepudiation, through cryptography, that will serve to provide credible evidence sufficiently strong to persuade a disinterested third party (the ultimate dispute resolution authority), that a subscriber originated a particular transaction or communication. Once the legal proceedings produced a final judgment to that effect, then legal nonrepudiation has occurred. [B.7.25]

We therefore conclude that legal nonrepudiation (1) depends on technical nonrepudiation as its foundation, with (2) sufficient evidence to persuade an independent third-party authority (judge, jury, or arbitrator) of a consistent and uninterrupted chain of evidence, and (3) an unambiguous documented process for assessing the first and second stipulations.

10.8 WEBTRUST CA

WebTrust® for CA is an auditing standard managed by the Chartered Professional Accountants (CPA) Canada that provides an evaluation framework for auditing and reporting on CA's control environments and compliance with industry standards. The "WebTrust CA" auditing standard addresses the following critical services:

- Leverages international auditing, reporting, and auditor independence standards
- Maintains a list of WebTrust® licensed practitioners
- Maintains current audit principles and criteria for various PKI programs
- Provides a WebTrust® seal program for the WebTrust® reports
- Provides a mechanism for reporting on compliance with specific PKI standards or general CP/CPS requirements
- Develops and publishes PKI-specific audit guidance

Historically, the WebTrust® for CA auditing standard was a collaboration between the American Institute of Certified Public Accountants (AICPA), the Canadian Institute of Chartered Accounts (now the CPA Canada), and the Accredited Standards Committee X9 for the Financial Services Industry. The collaboration subsequently expanded to the ISO Technical Committee 68 Financial Services per the relationship with ASC X9.

2000: AICPA and CICA published WebTrust CA 1.0 based on the X9.79 requirements and recommendations, while the draft standard was undergoing ASC ballots and ANSI public review. Basically, Al Van Ranst (KMPG) brought the X9.79 draft to the attention of the AICPA/CICA workgroup. The X9.79 requirements and recommendations became the basis for the WebTrust CA evaluation criteria.

2001: ANSI published X9.79 PKI Practices and Policy Framework when the ASC ballots and the ANSI public review were completed. X9.79 was later renamed to PKI – Part 1: Practices and Policy Framework as other parts were added to the standard.

2005: CA Browser Forum adopts WebTrust CA. This provided browser manufacturers assurance that before they allowed a root CA certificate to be deployed with a browser, the CA operations were consistent with its CP/CPS and industry standards. Microsoft was the first browser manufacturer to embrace WebTrust CA and the other browser manufacturers quickly followed.

2006: ISO TC68 published ISO 21188 PKI for Financial Services – Practices and Policy Framework. ASC X9 submitted X9.79 as a USA contribution to TC68 which became ISO 21188. Once published, ISO 21188 was adopted by ASC X9 and X9.79 was formally withdrawn. Recently, the X9F5 working group is updating ISO 21188 with ANSI notes with plans to republish under its original X9.79 name.

2007: CICA published WebTrust CA Extended Validation (EV) 1.0 stemming from the PKI Forum incident with regard to PKI assurance levels. EV certificates are cryptographically the same as any other certificate except the CA performed "extended validation" of the subject's identity for the certificate request, including stronger authentication and authorization methods. The CA Browser Forum now defines three assurance levels for TLS certificates from low to highest assurances:

- Domain Validation (DV) certificates
- Organizational Validation (OV) certificates
- Extended Validation (EV) certificates

2014: CPA Canada published WebTrust CA 2.0 for SSL, Code Sign, and Extended Validation (EV) based on ISO 21188. As noted, the X9.79 standard was submitted to ISO TC68 as a USA submission and became ISO 21188.

2018: ISO TC68 updated ISO 21188. The revision included the merger with two previous PKI-related international standards: ISO 15782–1 originally ANSI X9.57 and ISO 15782–2 originally ANSI X9.55 domestic standards. The two previous ISO standards were officially withdrawn.

2022: ISO/IEC JTC1 developed ISO/IEC 27099 PKI Practices and Policy based on ISO 21188. Initially, JTC1 attempted to transfer the ISO standard from TC68 with the argument that PKI was generic and therefore belonged to an information security group. However, TC68 gave the counter argument that the financial services industry needed its own PKI standard. Thus, JTC1 decided to write their own ISO/IEC based on the existing ISO standard.

As a result of broad SSL/TLS deployment and the risk-based SET PKI development, there was diversity of the security and basic operating environment requirements for Certification Authorities. Some CAs operated under very strict security and control, others not so much. The latter particularly applied to public CA operations issuing TLS/SSL certificates.

- **Domain Validation (DV):** A Domain Validated SSL certificate is issued after proof that the owner has the right to use their domain is established. This is typically done by the CA sending an e-mail to the domain owner (as listed in a WHOIS database). Once the owner responds, the certificate is issued. Many CAs perform additional fraud checks to minimize issuance of a certificate to a domain that may be similar to a high-value domain (e.g., Micros0ft.com, g00gle.com, b0fay.com).
- **Organizational Validation (OV):** For Organizational Validation SSL certificates, CAs must validate the company name, domain name, and other information through the use of public databases. CAs may also use additional methods to ensure the information inserted into the certificate is accurate. The issued certificate will contain the company name and the domain name for which the certificate was issued. Because of these additional checks, this is the minimum certificate recommended for e-commerce transactions as it provides the consumer with additional information about the business.
- **Extended Validation (EV):** for Extended Validation SSL certificates, CAs only issue EV certificates once an entity passes a strict authentication procedure. These checks are much more stringent than OV certificates.

All three models (DV, OV, and EV) remain in use today. However, the IETF decision to migrate from TLS static public keys for key establishment (e.g., RSA key transport, Diffie–Hellman and ECDH key agreement) to ephemeral keys (e.g., DHE and ECDHE) has undermined the importance for EV certificates. Note the TLS server's ephemeral public key is signed by the server and verified using the TLS server's public key certificate for digital signatures, but the TLS client's ephemeral public key has no such protection. Also, the CA Browser Forum's commitment toward shorter TLS service certificates has further eroded the significance for EV certificates.

10.9   CA BROWSER FORUM

The CA Browser Forum was established to address industry concerns regarding web-based server certificates and code-signing certificates, the former being TLS certificates to establish secure connections between a browser and a web service, and the latter being authenticatable code downloaded to a browser. The scope of the forum has expanded to include certificates for Secure/Multipurpose Internet Mail Extensions (S/MIME) and Network Security. Historically, the first CA Browser Forum meetings occurred in 2005, roughly two years after the PKI Forum merged with OASIS, with the CA Browser Forum publication of the Extended Validation (EV) Guidelines in 2007.

The Server Certificate Working Group (SCWG) manages the Baseline Requirements, Extended Validation Guidelines, and other acceptable practices for the issuance and management of SSL/TLS server certificates used for authenticating servers accessible through the Internet. The SCWG does not address certificates intended to be used primarily for code signing, S/MIME, timestamping, VoIP, IM, or Web services, nor "private" PKI are where the Root CA Certificate is not distributed by any Application Software Supplier (e.g., browser vendors). Recognized audit standards include:

- WebTrust for CAs v2.0 (or newer),
- ETSI EN 319 411–1 or ETSI EN 319 411–2, which includes normative references to ETSI EN 319 401 (or latest versions), or
- Government PKI programs (e.g., Federal PKI,[4] DoD PKI[5])

The Code Signing Certificate Working Group (CSCWG) was chartered to work on requirements applicable to Certification Authorities that issue code signing certificates. The CSCWG manages the Baseline Requirements for the Issuance and Management of Publicly-Trusted Code Signing Certificates.

The S/MIME Certificate Working Group (SMCWG) manages requirements applicable to Certification Authorities that issue S/MIME digital certificates used to sign, verify, encrypt, and decrypt e-mail. Additionally, the SMCWG may address identity validation for natural persons and legal entities in the context of S/MIME certificates.

The Network Security (NetSec) Working Group (NSWG) authored the Network and Certificate System Security Requirements (NCSSR). The NSWG charter expired in June 2018 but a new Network Security Subcommittee (NetSec Subcommittee) manages the NCSSR. Recognized audit standards include ETSI 101 456, and ETSI TS 102 042.

2007: CA Browser Forum published the Guidelines for the Issuance and Management of Extended Validation [EV] Certificates version 1.0 was published in June 2007. The EV Guidelines provide the minimum requirements that a Certification Authority (CA) must meet in order to issue Extended Validation Certificates ("EV Certificates"). Information about the certificate subject (e.g., TLS server, code-sign service) might be displayed to the relying party (e.g., end user) by proprietary software (e.g., browser) authenticating the website. The current EV Guidelines version 1.8.0 was published in November 2022.

2011: CA Browser Forum adopted the Baseline Requirements version 1.0 for the Issuance and Management of Publicly-Trusted Certificates, describing technologies, protocols, identity-proofing, lifecycle management, and auditing requirements, necessary (but not sufficient) for the issuance and management of Publicly-Trusted Certificates. The current Baseline Requirements version 1.8.6 was published in December 2022.

2012: CA Browser Forum incorporated the Baseline Requirements into its Extended Validation (EV) Guidelines. Specifically, the EV Guidelines version 1.4 dated May 2012 explicitly references the Baseline Requirements but without denoting its version, rather generically providing the *www.cabforum.org* link. The corresponding Baseline Requirements version 1.0 was published in November 2011, six months before the EV Guidelines were published, and its successor version 1.1 was published in September 2012, four months afterward. Presumably, the reader needs to obtain the latest version of any document.

2013: CA Browser Forum published the Network and Certificate System Security Requirements (NCSSR) version 1.0 in January 2013. These network requirements are in addition to the other baseline requirements and apply to all publicly trusted CA and Delegated Third Parties. The current NCSSR version 1.7 was published in April 2021.

2019: CA Browser Forum published the Baseline Requirements Code Signing Certificates version 1.2 in August 2019. These Baseline Requirements describe a subset of the requirements that a CA must meet to issue Publicly-Trusted Code Signing Certificates. The Code Sign Baseline Requirements references both the Publicly-Trusted Certificates Baseline Requirements and the Network and Certificate System Security Requirements per the *www.cabforum.org* link. The current Code Sign Baseline Requirements version 3.2.0 was published in October 2022.

Note that the CA Browser Forum and its four workgroups do not address every possibly PKI or certificate use case. Each workgroup has a well-defined charter, and the Server Certificate Working Group (SCWG) explicitly states items that are out of scope for the SCWG. Other areas such as financial services or healthcare have their own needs.

10.10 CLOUD SECURITY ALLIANCE (CSA)

According to the history[6] of the Cloud Security Alliance, the call to action for secure cloud computing began in November 2008 at an ISSA CISO Forum in Las Vegas. Later that same year in December, the CSA was founded and it was incorporated in 2009. The Cloud Controls Matrix (CCM) was first published in 2010 along with the Certificate of Cloud Security Knowledge (CCSK) credential. The Security, Trust and Assurance Registry (STAR) registry program was launched two years later in 2012. The CSA in cooperation with the International Information System Security Certification Consortium[7] (ISC2) established the Certified Cloud Security Professional (CCSP) credential.

The CSA Security Guidance for Critical Areas of Focus in Cloud Computing is an official study guide for the CCSK credential. This guideline refers to encryption 120 times but not general cryptography, remarks about key management 11 times, but only mentions certificates three times without addressing PKI or any of its components. As shown in Table 10.1, encryption is referenced in 10 of the 14 security cloud domains and not just in Domain 11: Data Security and Encryption.

Conversely, digital certificates are only mentioned once in Domain 12: Identity, Entitlement, and Access Management for privileged user management, and twice in Domain 14: Related Technologies for mobile applications, relating to application programming interface (API) access, and both certificate pinning and validation inside mobile applications. Other PKI components (CA, RA, PA, CRL, OCSP) and processes such as certificate validation and revocation are not addressed.

The Cloud Controls Matrix (CCM) is organized into 17 control domains. Note that the CSA Security guide was grouped into 14 cloud domains, so there appears to be some inconsistency between the two documents. Regardless, each CCM control domain is subdivided into control specifications, each with its own control title and control ID (e.g., A&A-01, A&A-02). As shown in Table 10.2 altogether, there are 200 control IDs for the 17 control domains.

The fifth CCM control domain Cryptography, Encryption & Key Management (CEK) has 21 control IDs (CEK-01 through CEK-21) that address some aspects of cryptography and key management.

- Data Encryption CEK-03 refers to data-at-rest and data-in-transit but does not mention any security protocols (e.g., TLS, SSH, IPsec) or certificates.
- Key Generation CEK-10 refers to industry-accepted cryptographic libraries but does not provide any examples (e.g., OpenSSL, WolfSSL, Bouncy Castle) or mention any security protocols or certificates.
- Key Purpose CEK-11 refers to secret and private keys but does not use the terms "symmetric" or "asymmetric cryptography," or mention key pairs, public keys or certificates.
- Key Revocation CEK-13 refers to cryptoperiod, key compromise, and departure (entity is no longer part of the organization) but does not mention PKI, CRL, or OCSP.
- Key Destruction CEK-14 refers to HSM but does not address the NIST Cryptographic Module Validation Program (CVMP) or any other evaluation process.

TABLE 10.1
CSA Security Cloud Domains

Domain	Encryption	Certificates
1. Cloud Computing Concepts and Architectures	-	-
2. Governance and Enterprise Risk Management	Encryption	-
3. Legal Issues, Contracts and Electronic Discovery	Encryption	-
4. Compliance and Audit Management	-	-
5. Information Governance	Encryption	-
6. Management Plan and Business Continuity	Encryption	-
7. Infrastructure Security	Encryption	-
8. Virtualization and Containers	Encryption	-
9. Incident Response	-	-
10. Application Security	Encryption	-
11. Data Security and Encryption	Encryption	-
12. Identity, Entitlement, and Access Management	-	Certificates
13. Security as a Service	Encryption	-
14. Related Technologies	Encryption	Certificates

TABLE 10.2

CSA Cloud Controls

Control	Encryption	Certificates
1. Audit & Assurance (A&A)	-	-
2. Application & Interface Security (AIS)	-	-
3. Business Continuity Management and Operational Resilience (BCR)	-	-
4. Change Control and Configuration Management (CCC)	-	-
5. Cryptography, Encryption & Key Management (CEK)	Encryption	-
6. Datacenter Security (DCS)	-	-
7. Data Security and Privacy Lifecycle Management (DSP)	-	-
8. Governance, Risk and Compliance (GRC)	-	-
9. Human Resources (HRS)	-	-
10. Identity & Access Management (IAM)	-	Certificates
11. Interoperability & Portability (IPY)	-	-
12. Infrastructure & Virtualization Security (IVS)	-	-
13. Logging and Monitoring (LOG)	-	-
14. Security Incident Management, E-Discovery, & Cloud Forensics (SEF)	-	-
15. Supply Chain Management, Transparency, and Accountability (STA)	-	-
16. Threat & Vulnerability Management (TVM)	-	-
17. Universal Endpoint Management (UEM)	-	-

The tenth CCM control domain Identity & Access Management (IAM) has 16 control IDs (IAM-01 through IAM-16) that address some aspects of cryptography and certificates.

- Segregation of Privileged Access Roles (IAM-09) refers to administrative access for encryption and key management but does not mention PKI or certificates.
- Strong Authentication (IAM-14) mentions digital certificates for system identities but does not mention PKI, validity periods, CRL, or OCSP.

Nevertheless, there are many PKI issues and considerations when it comes to cloud computing and deployment. Consider the scenario when the hypothetical ABC Corporation wants to deploy an application with some cloud service provider (CSP). Some providers offer PKI services (CSP PKI) and some support external PKI services, either from the cloud subscriber's private PKI (ABC PKI) or from third-party public PKI (3RD PKI). Further, we extend the scenario whereby the ABC application interacts with another application from the XYZ Corporation, and the XYZ application needs to validate the ABC certificate. For the purposes of this scenario, we assume the ABC certificate chain consists of the ABC application certificate (ABC), an issuing CA certificate (ICA), and a root CA certificate (RCA). See Figure 10.4 Cloud PKI scenario for an overview of three cases, ABC PKI, the CSP PKI, and the third-party 3RD PKI.

First, consider the case when the ABC application, as a PKI subject, gets its certificate from the ABC private PKI and the XYZ application, as a relying party, accepts the certificate.

- Either the ABC application generates its own asymmetric public/private key pair and submits a CSR to the ABC PKI to get its certificate, or possibly the ABC PKI provisions the asymmetric key pair for the ABC application and sends the certificate and private key using a secure delivery method.
- The XYZ application needs to trust the CA certificates so that they can be used for certificate validation. This might be accomplished by the XYZ Corporation relying on an

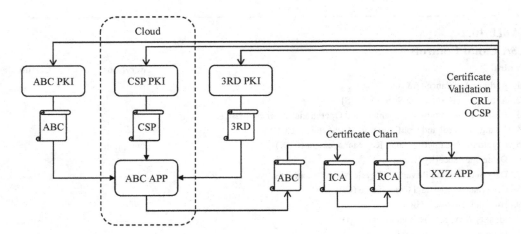

FIGURE 10.4 Cloud PKI scenario.

independent third-party audit (e.g., WebTrust CA) of the ABC PKI, an independent third-party PKI program (e.g., CA Browser Forum) that recognizes the ABC PKI, or working directly with the ABC Corporation.

- The XYZ application needs to store the CA certificates so that they can be accessed quickly and securely for certificate validation. Note that the CA certificates might be "pinned" and therefore the XYZ application needs the ability to change and pin the new CA certificates prior to certificate expiration of the old CA certificates.
- The XYZ application needs access to the ABC PKI revocation services, either its CRL or OCSP responder, for certificate validation.
- The XYZ application needs to receive or possibly store the ABC application certificate for message authentication, and it might whitelist the certificate for authorization.

Second, consider the case when the ABC application, as a PKI subject, gets its certificate from the CSP public or private PKI and the XYZ application, as a relying party, accepts the certificate.

- Either the ABC application generates its own asymmetric public/private key pair and submits a CSR to the CSP PKI to get its certificate, or possibly the CSP PKI provisions the asymmetric key pair for the ABC application and sends the certificate and private key using a secure delivery method.
- The XYZ application needs to trust the CA certificates so that they can be used for certificate validation. This might be accomplished by the XYZ Corporation relying on an independent third-party audit (e.g., WebTrust CA) of the CSP PKI, an independent third-party PKI program (e.g., CA Browser Forum) that recognizes the CSP PKI, or working directly with the CSP.
- The XYZ application needs to store the CA certificates so that they can be accessed quickly and securely for certificate validation. Note that the CA certificates might be "pinned" and therefore the XYZ application needs the ability to change and pin the new CA certificates prior to certificate expiration of the old CA certificates.
- The XYZ application needs access to the CSP PKI revocation services, either its CRL or OCSP responder, for certificate validation.
- The XYZ application needs to receive or possibly store the ABC application certificate for message authentication, and it might whitelist the certificate for authorization.

Third, consider the case when the ABC application, as a PKI subject, gets its certificate from a third-party (3RD) public PKI and the XYZ application, as a relying party, accepts the certificate.

- Either the ABC application generates its own asymmetric public/private key pair and submits a CSR to the 3RD PKI to get its certificate, or possibly the 3RD PKI provisions the asymmetric key pair for the ABC application and sends the certificate and private key using a secure delivery method.
- The XYZ application needs to trust the CA certificates so that they can be used for certificate validation. This might be accomplished by the XYZ Corporation relying on an independent third-party audit (e.g., WebTrust CA) of the 3RD PKI, an independent third-party PKI program (e.g., CA Browser Forum) that recognizes the 3RD PKI, or working directly with the 3RD PKI.
- The XYZ application needs to store the CA certificates so that they can be accessed quickly and securely for certificate validation. Note that the CA certificates might be "pinned" and therefore the XYZ application needs the ability to change and pin the new CA certificates prior to certificate expiration of the old CA certificates.
- The XYZ application needs access to the 3RD PKI revocation services, either its CRL or OCSP responder, for certificate validation.
- The XYZ application needs to receive or possibly store the ABC application certificate for message authentication, and it might whitelist the certificate for authorization.

Remember that the ABC application, as a PKI subject, has a direct relationship with the CA and its owners, the ABC Corporation, agrees to abide by the subject agreements declared in the CPS and subscriber agreement. Also recall that the XYZ application, as a relying party, accepts the certificates and therefore the XYZ Corporation implicitly agrees to abide by the relying party agreements declared in the CPS and subscriber agreement. Recognize that "CPS" is the certificate practice statement and "CSP" is the cloud service provider. Abbreviations are helpful, but there are only so-many letters in the alphabet and often the notations are too similar.

Another issue is whether a cloud-deployed CA is using an HSM to protect its private signature keys. For our scenario, this relates not only to a CSP PKI but possibly to the ABC PKI or 3RD PKI deployed in the cloud. If the CSP provides the CA then presumably it would use its own HSM to manage its PKI; however, some CSPs rely on cryptographic software for general key management so the PKI subscriber and relying party need to be aware and confirm the CSP PKI is using HSM to protect the CA private keys. Accordingly, if another entity has deployed its CA into the cloud, since most CSPs do not allow hardware deployment into their data centers, there are limited options for protecting the CA private signature keys.

- *Cloud HSM* is a common CSP service offering to "rent" access to an HSM deployed in the CSP data center. Network latency is relatively low as the application and HSM typically run in the same cloud data center.
- *Customer HSM* is a lessor CSP service offering to allow access between a cloud-deployed application (the CA) and an HSM deployed in a collocated data center. Network latency is higher than cloud HSM as the application and HSM might not run in the same collocated data center, or the application might be relegated to the collocated data center.
- *External HSM* is a rare CSP service offering to allow access between a cloud-deployed application and an HSM deployed in an external data center. Network latency is the highest as the application runs in the CSP data center, but the HSM runs in the external data center, which might be many miles apart from each other.

Yet another issue for a cloud-deployed CA is capacity. Microservices are a popular approach for managing scalability, where new instances can be "spun up" or "spun down" whenever and wherever the demand occurs within the cloud. However, if the issuing CA is "micro-serviced," there are benefits and drawbacks to this cloud practice.

- One benefit is that a micro-CA can be spun-up when needed and spun-down when the demand decreases to a normal amount.
- But one drawback is that if the micro-CA generates its CA key pairs, then it needs to obtain its CA certificate from its superior CA in real-time. But since root CA is operated offline, this implies the PKI is at least three tiers: the issuing micro-CA, at least one intermediate CA, and the root CA. The micro-CA needs to get its CA certificate from an online superior CA within seconds for the microservice to be useful.
- Another drawback is that the validity of the micro-CA certificate is problematic. For example, if the micro-CA has an operational period of one day, it would not be feasible for the micro-CA certificate to expire at the end of the day, unless all of the application certificates it generated had the same short lifecycle.
- Alternatively, the micro-CA certificate could use the X.509 Private Key Usage Period extension to lengthen its own validity period. The application certificates generated by the micro-CA could then have a longer validity period (e.g., one year) and the micro-CA certificate could have the same or longer validity period, but this private key might only have a 24-hour usage period. However, this extension is rarely used today and so might cause systematic failures with existing applications.
- An additional drawback relates back to the HSM issue. The micro-CA might not have access to an HSM. HSM access is typically done carefully to avoid any mistakes that might enable intentional or inadvertent access to cryptographic keys. Thus, allowing a micro-CA to generate certificates without protecting its private key within an HSM does not follow industry standards and best practices.

From a general perspective, cloud cryptography and key management is problematic today and has higher risk and as financial applications migrate to the cloud, the risks will increase. The risks associated with cloud PKI are even more problematic, especially considering the cryptanalytical threat from quantum computers and the inevitable cryptographic transition to post-quantum cryptography (PQC).

10.11 NIST PQC PROGRAM

The National Institute of Standards and Technology (NIST), established in 1901 and now part of the U.S. Department of Commerce, was directed by Congress to address the United States' lagging measurements infrastructure. At the time, the United Kingdom, Germany, and other economic rivals were ahead of the United States. For example, the American Foundrymen's Association turned over the task of producing samples of standardized iron to NIST in 1905. Today, NIST measurements support the smallest of technologies (e.g., nanoscale) to the largest and the more complex of human-made creations (e.g., skyscrapers, global communication systems). The NIST laboratory programs include communications technology, engineering, information technology, materials measurements, and physical measurements.

Relative to PKI is the NIST Post-Quantum Cryptography (PQC) program, initiated by the NSA announcement that Suite B cryptography would be replaced by a new "yet to be determined" quantum-resistant algorithm suite. There have been many articles [B.7.25] and blogs on the "quantum menace" but what is the quantum threat? Chapter 1, "Introduction," explained the difference between cryptography versus cryptanalysis, and Chapter 9, "PKI Governance, Risk, and Compliance," mentioned quantum computers. Basically, quantum computers rely on quantum mechanical effects, namely quantum entanglement and quantum superposition, to program quantum bits (qubits) with complex linear equations to solve problems that are infeasible on today's regular computers. While the math is understood and regular computers can be programmed, it would take hundreds to millions of years to find the answer, whereas a quantum computer can find the answer in minutes or hours. Today the problems are estimated without finding the exact answer.

2015: NSA[8] Suite B Cryptography: NSA's Information Assurance Directorate (IAD) protects and defends national security information and information systems. *IAD recognizes that there will be a move, in the not distant future, to a quantum resistant algorithm suite. Based on experience in deploying Suite B, we have determined to start planning and communicating early about the upcoming transition to quantum resistant algorithms. Our ultimate goal is to provide cost effective security against a potential quantum computer. We are working with partners across the USG, vendors, and standards bodies to ensure there is a clear plan for getting a new suite of algorithms that are developed in an open and transparent manner that will form the foundation of our next Suite of cryptographic algorithms.*

Historically, the NSA maintained two algorithm suites: Suite A for classified algorithms strictly for use by the Department of Defense (DoD) consisting of the military branches (Army, Air Force, Navy, Marines, and Coast Guard), and Suite B for unclassified algorithms for use by DoD and its military branches, and its coalition partners. Basically, Suite A are NSA algorithms and Suite B are NIST algorithms. Suite B consisted of NIST-approved industry algorithms such as RSA, Diffie–Helman, and elliptic curve cryptography (ECC) with sufficient key sizes. The NSA essentially deprecated Suit B with a warning that the inevitable threat from quantum computers is significant.

2016: NIST[9] Call for Proposals: *solicit, evaluate, and standardize one or more quantum-resistant public-key cryptographic algorithms. These next generation public-key cryptographic algorithms would be added to the existing FIPS 186–4 Digital Signature Standard (DSS), as well as special publications SP 800–56A Revision 2, Recommendation for Pair-Wise Key Establishment Schemes Using Discrete Logarithm Cryptography, and SP 800–56B, Recommendation for Pair-Wise Key-Establishment Schemes Using Integer Factorization Cryptography.*

For documentation, NIST[10] published Internal Report (NISTIR) 8105 *Report on Post-Quantum Cryptography* in April 2016. Note that sometimes the "IR" is referred to as an Interagency Report versus an Internal Report, but presumably they are interchangeable terms.

2017: NIST[11] Round 1: Candidates. NIST received 82 submissions from industry, consisting of 23 digital signature algorithms, and 59 key establishment methods (KEM) algorithms. However, only 69 of the 82 were acceptable per the submission requirements.

For information, NIST[12] published an Information Report (NISTIR) 8240 *Status Report on the First Round of the NIST Post-Quantum Cryptography Standardization Process* in January 2019.

2019: NIST[13] Round 2: Candidates. NIST reduced the 69 candidates to 26 algorithms consisting of 17 KEM algorithms, and 9 digital signature algorithms.

For information, NIST[14] published an Information Report (NISTIR) 8309 *Status Report on the Second Round of the NIST Post-Quantum Cryptography Standardization Process* in July 2020.

2020: NIST[15] Round 3: Candidates. NIST further reduced the 26 candidates to 15 algorithms but grouped them into a Finalist list and an Alternate list. Altogether there were seven finalists and eight alternates.
- Round 3 Finalists included 7 algorithms consisting of 4 KEM algorithms and 3 digital signature algorithms. The finalists would be standardized in NIST documents.
- Round 3 Alternates included eight algorithms consisting of five KEM algorithms and three digital signature algorithms. The alternates would likely be standardized in NIST documents.

2022: NIST[16] Round 3: Selections. NIST announced the selected four algorithms from the Round 3 Candidates on July 5, 2022, consisting of one KEM algorithm and three digital signature algorithms.

- CRYSTALS-KYBER was selected from the Round 3 Finalists as the KEM algorithm.
- CRYSTALS-DILITHIUM was selected from the Round 3 Finalists as the first digital signature algorithm.

NIST[17] provided rationalization for choosing the Cryptographic Suite for Algebraic Lattices (CRYSTALS) algorithms: *CRYSTALS-KYBER (key-establishment) and CRYSTALS-Dilithium (digital signatures) were both selected for their strong security and excellent performance, and NIST expects them to work well in most applications.*

- FALCON was selected from the Round 3 Finalists as the second digital signature algorithm. NIST provided rationalization: *FALCON will also be standardized by NIST since there may be use cases for which CRYSTALS-Dilithium signatures are too large.*
- SPHINCS+ was selected from the Round 3 Alternates as the third digital signature algorithm. NIST provided rationalization: *SPHINCS+ will also be standardized to avoid relying only on the security of lattices for signatures. NIST asks for public feedback on a version of SPHINCS+ with a lower number of maximum signatures.*

2022 NIST Round 4: Candidates. NIST announced on July 5, 2022, further evaluation of four KEM algorithms: BIKE, Classic McEliece, HQC, and SIKE. However, within the next month of August, the SIKE algorithm was broken[18] using a regular single-core personal computer. The NIST site was updated in September with a note and link that the SIKE teams acknowledge that SIKE [Supersingular Isogeny Key Encapsulation] and SIDH [Supersingular Isogeny Diffie–Hellman] are insecure and should not be used.

For information, NIST[19] published an Information Report (NISTIR) 8413 *Status Report on the Third Round of the NIST Post-Quantum Cryptography Standardization Process* in July 2022; however, this report was withdrawn two months later in September 2022.

2022: NIST[20] Call for Proposals: *for Additional Digital Signature Schemes for the Post-Quantum Cryptography [PQC] Standardization Process.*

NIST is primarily interested in additional general-purpose signature schemes that are not based on structured lattices. For certain applications, such as certificate transparency, NIST may also be interested in signature schemes that have short signatures and fast verification. NIST is open to receiving additional submissions based on structured lattices, but is intent on diversifying the post-quantum signature standards. As such, any structured lattice-based signature proposal would need to significantly outperform CRYSTALS-Dilithium and FALCON in relevant applications and/or ensure substantial additional security properties to be considered for standardization.

Since the time this second edition was updated, the NIST PQC program will have continued to evolve, but this is always true for cryptography. Advancements in cryptology[21] has been around for 4,000 years since the Egyptian priesthood used character substitution with hieroglyphics, and it has evolved from monoalphabetic (e.g., Caesar cipher) through polyalphabetic (e.g., Vigenère cipher) to binary structures (e.g., Feistel ciphers) and mathematical constructs. As cryptanalysis and computing power continue to evolve, so too will cryptography evolve with older algorithms being replaced by newer algorithms. It is, after all, a world where cryptographic transitions are inevitable [B.7.16].

Note that during the writing of this second edition, NIST released three of the four Round 3: Selections as draft Federal Information Processing Standard (FIPS) in August 2023 for public comment period due November 22, 2023.

- FIPS 205 Stateless Hash-Based Digital Signature Standard (CRYSTALS-KYBER)
- FIPS 204 Module-Lattice-Based Digital Signature Standard (CRYSTALS-Dilithium)
- FIPS 203 Module-Lattice-Based Key-Encapsulation Mechanism Standard (SPHINCS+)

10.12 ASC X9 FINANCIAL PKI

Financial systems are reliant on PKIs, where the PKIs can be either public or private. However, these PKIs are frequently designed for general use across many diverse industries rather than being focused on the financial services industry, a highly regulated industry. Consequently, PKI users rely on these general-use PKIs for specialized protection. Accordingly, the X9 executive committee approved establishing the X9F PKI Study Group for the following tasks:

1) Analyzed how various PKIs are being used in the financial services community through a collection of existing and trending Use Cases
2) Made recommendations and proposed new standards, where X9 can lead the financial services community in the use of PKI technologies
3) Explored the feasibility of developing an X9-sponsored PKI for its members

The X9F PKI Study Group will research, analyze, and formulate recommendations relating to PKI policy and practices for the financial services industry. Further, other X9F workgroups will continue to maintain and develop PKI-related ANSI standards and will coordinate development of international PKI standards with ISO TC68/SC2/WG8[22] PKI workgroup and the ISO/IEC JTC1/SC27 Information Security subcommittee.

Note that numerous industry groups have established their own PKI systems, including military, healthcare, EMV chip cards, the Society for Worldwide Interbank Financial Telecommunications (SWIFT), the European Identity, Authentication and trust Services (eIDAS), the CA Browser Forum, and many others. Therefore, it is not surprising that X9, accredited by ANSI for developing national standards for the financial services industry and the ISO TC68 secretariat, has taken steps to address the inconsistent and conflicting PKI systems affecting financial services.

10.12.1 X9 FINANCIAL PKI ORIGINS

In 2018, a proposal was developed and presented to X9 to analyze the need for one or more PKIs to address the specific needs and risks in the financial sector. The proposal was approved, and the Public Key Infrastructure Study Group (PKI SG) was created. An organizational meeting was held in late 2018 during an X9 "all hands" meeting. The goals of a *risk-based X9 PKI* were as follows:

- Improve end-user access to financial services and information.
- Reduce Financial Institution and end-user operating costs through secure implementation of electronic business processes.

- Provide a financial sector solution to address the risks and vulnerabilities of the existing PKI models to Quantum Computing attacks.
- Provide a common point of trust to the financial industry that requires a secure environment consistent with the higher risk associated with Financial transaction activity
- Define the handling, usage, and limitations of cryptographic tools
- Flexibility to address specific use cases that may have additional requirements beyond what is covered in the X9 PKI Certificate Policy.

The first phase of PKI SG efforts began with the identification and analysis of financial use cases. The SG created a report that identified 27 PKI use cases in the Financial Sector that could be addressed with one or more X9 PKIs. The data, usage volumes, and risk profiles for many of these use cases varied greatly. The study group findings were submitted to the X9 Board of Directors who approved the report and selected six use cases, three as the top priority and three others for attention, as follows:

1) Secure e-commerce transactions
2) Cryptographic key exchange and refresh
3) DLT blockchain
4) Secure remote banking
5) POS and ATM transaction communication security
6) Financial aggregator/compilation services

For the overall PKI and in consideration of each use case, the X9 PKI would mitigate the vulnerabilities of Quantum Computing Risks. Only those techniques and algorithms would be allowed in the design and implementation of the various X9 PKI(s). X9 published its first Information Report on Quantum Computer Risk in 2019 [B.1.23] along with the Technical Report TR-50 Quantum Techniques in Cryptographic Message Syntax (CMS) and a revision to the [B.1.24] Information Report on Quantum Computer Risk in 2022.

An important consideration for the X9 PKI was that the PKI(s) and support management should be designed such that additional applications could be supported without major changes to the PKI components or policies. These requirements and use cases were the development focus as the PKI analysis moved to the next phase, the creation of an overarching Certificate Policy (CP) that would apply to all use cases. Because the CP had to be designed as a "one size fits all" document, there is a stated provision that certain use cases may have their own CP extensions and policy modifications. This was done to support specific requirements and to address operation and risk differences between use cases.

Once the Certificate Policy was completed, work began on the risk-based business case description of the PKI and its operational components. Early in the process, it was decided that the X9 PKI would fall under and be a separate organization from ASC X9 with staff approved and appointed by ASC X9. This organization would be responsible for managing X9 PKI services by handling some services internally and outsourcing other services. Management of all aspects of the PKI would be carried out by the X9 PKI organization. The X9 PKI organization would also be responsible for changes to the Certificate Policy, participation management, reviewing all participant application information including, but not limited to, CP compliance assessments.

As various use cases are addressed, the X9 PKI organization is responsible for assessing risk, operational requirements and vulnerabilities, and determining what extensions and modifications are required for that use case with regard to the Certificate Policy. Updates, modifications, or addendums will be published as needed, in addition to the mandatory five-year review cycle imposed by the ANSI and ISO standardization procedures.

10.12.2 PKI Architecture Models

Chapter 4, "PKI Management and Security," provided an example PKI hierarchy for the ABC Corporation, with separate internal and external PKI; see Figure 4.6. Each example PKI has its own root CA, one or more intermediate CA, sometimes called subordinate CA, and several issuing CA systems. For the purposes of this discussion on financial PKI architecture models, intermediate CA are called subordinate CA.

This chapter denotes root CA by "R_X," where "x" is the organization, either "A" for Alice or "B" for Bob. The intermediate CA are denoted by "S_X" using "S" for subordinate to distinguish from the issuing CA, and the issuing CA are denoted by "I_X" so each PKI hierarchy is $R \Rightarrow S \Rightarrow I$, where the issuing CA generates entity "E_X" certificates. Figure 10.5 shows separate siloed PKI for Alice and Bob, where each certificate is shown with the subject public key and the certificate signature. The arrow direction indicates the higher CA signing the lower CA certificate.

Note that the CA public key terms (I_A, S_A, R_A) were chosen to be the same as the CA signature terms (I_A, S_A, R_A) to visually reinforce that the CA public key is used to verify the CA signature. Note that the first position versus the second position in the certificate expression determines the meaning of public key versus signature.

For example, Alice's certificate chain for some entity E_A is shown as the certificate expression using square brackets: $[E_A, I_A] \Leftarrow [I_A, S_A] \Leftarrow [S_A, R_A] \Leftarrow [R_A, R_A]$ where:

- $[E_A, I_A]$ is the end entity certificate with its E_A public key and the issuing CA signature I_A, noting that other certificate information discussed in Chapter 3, "PKI Building Blocks," see Table 3.1 Basic X.509 Certificate.
- $[I_A, S_A]$ is the issuing CA certificate with its I_A public key (not to be confused with the I_A signature in the end entity certificate) and the subordinate CA signature S_A.
- $[S_A, R_A]$ is the subordinate CA certificate with its S_A public key (not to be confused with the S_A signature in the issuing CA certificate) and root CA signature R_A.
- $[R_A, R_A]$ is the root CA certificate with its R_A public key (not to be confused with the R_A signature in the subordinate CA certificate) and root CA signature R_A (not to be confused with the R_A public key in its own signed certificate).

Similarly, Bob's certificate chain for another entity E_B is shown likewise as the certificate expression: $[E_B, I_B] \Leftarrow [I_B, S_B] \Leftarrow [S_B, R_B] \Leftarrow [R_B, R_B]$, where Bob's root CA signed its own certificate and the subordinate CA certificate, the subordinate CA signed the issuing CA certificate, and the issuing CA signed the end entity certificate.

Any relying party that trusts Alice's root CA can validate an end entity certificate from Alice's issuing CA as follows: $[E_A, I_A] \Rightarrow [I_A, S_A] \Rightarrow [S_A, R_A] \Rightarrow [R_A, R_A]$, where the R_A public key verifies the S_A certificate, the S_A public key verifies the I_A certificate, the I_A public key verifies the E_A certificate, such that the E_A public key can now be used for its intended purpose. The relying party that trusts Alice's root CA can only validate the end entity certificate for the certificate chain for Alice's PKI but not Bob's PKI since they do not share any common certificates.

Any relying party that trusts Bob's root CA can validate an end entity certificate from Bob's issuing CA as follows: $[E_B, I_B] \Rightarrow [I_B, S_B] \Rightarrow [S_B, R_B] \Rightarrow [R_B, R_B]$, where the R_B public key verifies the S_B certificate, the S_B public key verifies the I_B certificate, the I_B public key verifies the E_B certificate, such that the E_B public key can now be used for its intended purpose. The relying party that trusts

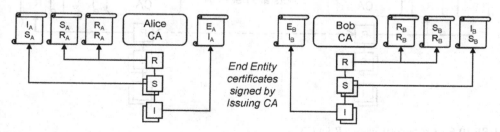

FIGURE 10.5 Silo CA.

Bob's root CA can only validate the end entity certificate for the certificate chain for Bob's PKI but not Alice's PKI since they do not share any common certificates.

SPECIAL NOTE 10-5 SILO PKI

Any relying party that only trusts Alice's PKI cannot validate an entity certificate from Bob's PKI because there is no common CA certificate. Likewise, any relying party that only trusts Bob's PKI cannot validate an entity certificate from Alice's PKI without a common CA certificate. Therefore, Alice's and Bob's siloed PKI cannot interoperate with each other or any other PKI.

Chapter 5, "PKI Roles and Responsibilities," provided an overview of PKI interactions using PKI subordinate certification (see Figure 5.3), PKI cross-certification (see Figure 5.4), and PKI bridge (see Figure 5.5). This chapter provides a more detailed analysis of the three PKI architectures being explored by the X9F PKI Study Group; in particular, we describe cross-certification, third party, and bridges at the root CA, at the subordinate CA, and at the issuing CA levels.

Figure 10.6 Cross-certification Root CA provides an overview between Alice and Bob. Alice generates a root crossover certificate $[R_B, R_A]$ containing Bob's root CA public key signed by her root CA, where the first letter indicates the public key owner and the second letter denotes the certificate signer. Similarly, Bob generates a root crossover certificate $[R_A, R_B]$ containing Alice's root CA public key signed by his root CA, where the first letter indicates the public key owner and the second letter denotes the certificate signer.

Any relying party that trusts Alice's root CA can now validate an end entity certificate from Bob's issuing CA as follows: $[E_B, I_B] \Rightarrow [I_B, S_B] \Rightarrow [S_B, R_B] \Rightarrow [R_B, R_A] \Rightarrow [R_A, R_A]$, where the R_A public key verifies the R_B certificate, the R_B public key verifies the S_B certificate, the S_B public key verifies the I_B certificate, the I_B public key verifies the E_B certificate, such that the E_B public key can now be used for its intended purpose.

Any relying party that trusts Bob's root CA can now validate an end entity certificate from Alice's issuing CA as follows: $[E_A, I_A] \Rightarrow [I_A, S_A] \Rightarrow [S_A, R_A] \Rightarrow [R_A, R_B] \Rightarrow [R_B, R_B]$, where the R_B public key verifies the R_A certificate, the R_A public key verifies the S_A certificate, the S_A public key verifies the I_A certificate, and the I_A public key verifies the E_A certificate, such that the E_A public key can now be used for its intended purpose.

Figure 10.7 (Cross-certification subordinate CA) shows another option between Alice and Bob. Alice generates a subordinate crossover certificate $[S_B, S_A]$ containing Bob's subordinate CA public key signed by her subordinate CA, where the first letter indicates the public key

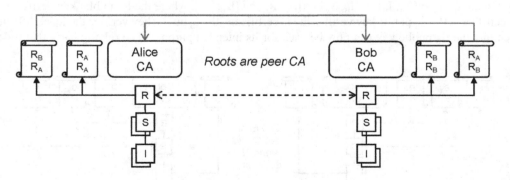

FIGURE 10.6   Cross-certification Root CA.

owner and the second letter denotes the certificate signer. Likewise, Bob generates a subordinate crossover certificate $[S_A, S_B]$ containing Bob's subordinate CA public key signed by his subordinate CA, where the first letter indicates the public key owner and the second letter denotes the certificate signer.

Any relying party that trusts Alice's root CA can now validate an end entity certificate from Bob's issuing CA as follows: $[E_B, I_B] \Rightarrow [I_B, S_B] \Rightarrow [S_B, S_A] \Rightarrow [S_A, R_A] \Rightarrow [R_A, R_A]$, where the R_A public key verifies the S_A certificate, the S_A public key verifies the S_B certificate, the S_B public key verifies the I_B certificate, and the I_B public key verifies the E_B certificate, such that the E_B public key can now be used for its intended purpose.

Any relying party that trusts Bob's root CA can now validate an end entity certificate from Alice's issuing CA as follows: $[E_A, I_A] \Rightarrow [I_A, S_A] \Rightarrow [S_A, S_B] \Rightarrow [S_B, R_B] \Rightarrow [R_B, R_B]$, where the R_B public key verifies the S_B certificate, the S_B public key verifies the S_A certificate, the S_A public key verifies the I_A certificate, and the I_A public key verifies the E_A certificate, such that the E_A public key can now be used for its intended purpose.

Figure 10.8 (Cross-certification issuing CA) shows an alternative between Alice and Bob. Alice generates an issuing crossover certificate $[I_B, I_A]$ containing Bob's issuing CA public key signed by her issuing CA, where the first letter indicates the public key owner and the second letter denotes the certificate signer. Likewise, Bob generates an issuing crossover certificate $[I_A, I_B]$ containing Bob's issuing CA public key signed by his issuing CA, where the first letter indicates the public key owner and the second letter denotes the certificate signer.

Any relying party that trusts Alice's root CA can now validate an end entity certificate from Bob's issuing CA as follows: $[E_B, I_B] \Rightarrow [I_B, I_A] \Rightarrow [I_A, S_A] \Rightarrow [S_A, R_A] \Rightarrow [R_A, R_A]$, where the R_A public key verifies the S_A certificate, the S_A public key verifies the I_A certificate, the I_A public key verifies the I_B certificate, and the I_B public key verifies the E_B certificate, such that the E_B public key can now be used for its intended purpose.

Any relying party that trusts Bob's root CA can now validate an end entity certificate from Alice's issuing CA as follows: $[E_A, I_A] \Rightarrow [I_A, I_B] \Rightarrow [I_B, S_B] \Rightarrow [S_B, R_B] \Rightarrow [R_B, R_B]$, where the R_B public key verifies the S_B certificate, the S_B public key verifies the I_B certificate, the I_B public key

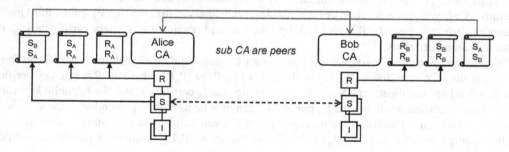

FIGURE 10.7 Cross-certification subordinate CA.

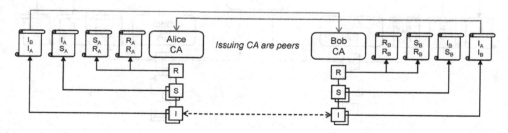

FIGURE 10.8 Cross-certification issuing CA.

verifies the I_A certificate, and the I_A public key verifies the E_A certificate, such that the E_A public key can now be used for its intended purpose.

SPECIAL NOTE 10-6 CROSS CERTIFICATION PKI

Any relying party that only trusts Alice's PKI can validate an entity certificate from Bob's PKI because of their cross-certification. Likewise, any relying party that only trusts Bob's PKI can validate an entity certificate from Alice's PKI because of their cross-certification. However, Alice and Bob cannot interoperate with any other PKI.

Figure 10.9 (Third party at root CA) provides an overview between Alice and Bob. Alice and Bob are issued certificates from a third-party CA for interoperability with compatible certificate policy and practices. This allows participation with other PKI domains with subsidiary certificates from the same third party. Subsidiary certificates are often done at the root CA level, but realistically the subsidiary can occur at any level within the PKI hierarchy. Alice submits a CSR with her R_A public key and obtains a subsidiary certificate $[R_A, P]$ from a third party. Likewise, Bob submits a CSR with his R_B public key and obtains a subsidiary certificate $[R_B, P]$ from the same third party.

Any relying party that trusts the third party root CA can validate an end entity certificate from Alice's issuing CA as follows: $[E_A, I_A] \Rightarrow [I_A, S_A] \Rightarrow [S_A, R_A] \Rightarrow [R_A, P] \Rightarrow [P, P]$, where the P public key verifies the R_A subsidiary certificate, the R_A public key verifies the S_A certificate, the S_A public key verifies the I_A certificate, and the I_A public key verifies the E_A certificate, such that the E_A public key can now be used for its intended purpose.

Any relying party that trusts the third-party root CA can validate an end entity certificate from Bob's issuing CA as follows: $[E_B, I_B] \Rightarrow [I_B, S_B] \Rightarrow [S_B, R_B] \Rightarrow [R_B, P] \Rightarrow [P, P]$, where the P public key verifies the R_B subsidiary certificate, the R_B public key verifies the S_B certificate, the S_B public key verifies the I_B certificate, and the I_B public key verifies the E_{AB} certificate, such that the E_{AB} public key can now be used for its intended purpose.

Figure 10.10 (Third party at subordinate CA) shows another option between Alice and Bob. Alice submits a CSR with her SA public key and obtains a subsidiary certificate $[S_A, P]$ from a third party. Likewise, Bob submits a CSR with his SB public key and obtains a subsidiary certificate $[S_B, P]$ from the same third party.

Any relying party that trusts the third-party root CA can validate an end entity certificate from Alice's issuing CA as follows: $[E_A, I_A] \Rightarrow [I_A, S_A] \Rightarrow [S_A, P] \Rightarrow [P, P]$, where the P public key verifies the S_A subsidiary certificate, the S_A public key verifies the I_A certificate, and the I_A public key verifies the E_A certificate, such that the E_A public key can now be used for its intended purpose.

Any relying party that trusts the third-party root CA can validate an end entity certificate from Bob's issuing CA as follows: $[E_B, I_B] \Rightarrow [I_B, S_B] \Rightarrow [S_B, P] \Rightarrow [P, P]$, where the P public key verifies

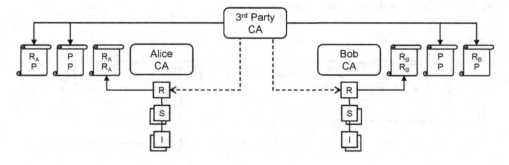

FIGURE 10.9   Third party at root CA.

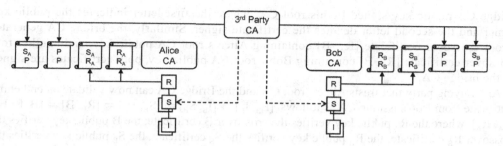

FIGURE 10.10 Third party at subordinate CA.

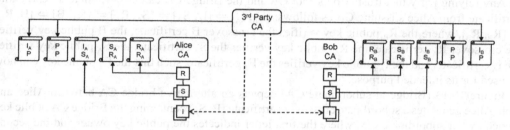

FIGURE 10.11 Third party at issuing CA.

the S_B subsidiary certificate, the S_B public key verifies the I_B certificate, and the I_B public key verifies the E_{AB} certificate, such that the E_{AB} public key can now be used for its intended purpose.

Figure 10.11 (Third party at issuing CA) shows an alternative between Alice and Bob. Alice submits a CSR with her I_A public key and obtains a subsidiary certificate $[I_A, P]$ from a third party. Likewise, Bob submits a CSR with his I_B public key and obtains a subsidiary certificate $[I_B, P]$ from the same third party.

Any relying party that trusts the third-party root CA can validate an end entity certificate from Alice's issuing CA as follows: $[E_A, I_A] \Rightarrow [I_A, P] \Rightarrow [P, P]$, where the P public key verifies the I_A subsidiary certificate, and the I_A public key verifies the E_A certificate, such that the E_A public key can now be used for its intended purpose.

Any relying party that trusts the third-party root CA can validate an end entity certificate from Bob's issuing CA as follows: $[E_B, I_B] \Rightarrow [I_B, P] \Rightarrow [P, P]$, where the P public key verifies the I_B subsidiary certificate, and the I_B public key verifies the E_{AB} certificate, such that the E_{AB} public key can now be used for its intended purpose.

SPECIAL NOTE 10-7 THIRD-PARTY PKI

Any relying party that trusts the third-party PKI can validate an entity certificate from Alice's PKI, Bob's PKI, or any other PKI who cooperates with the third-party PKI. Hence, Alice and Bob can interoperate with each other and any other PKI who cooperates with the third-party PKI, but each PKI must operate with a common certificate policy.

Figure 10.12 (Bridge at root CA) depicts a bridge CA between Alice and Bob. Alice generates a root crossover certificate $[B, R_A]$ containing the Bridge CA public key signed by her root CA, where the first letter indicates the public key owner and the second letter denotes the certificate signer. Likewise, Bob generates a root crossover certificate $[B, R_B]$ containing the

Bridge CA public key signed by his root CA, where the first letter indicates the public key owner and the second letter denotes the certificate signer. Similarly, the bridge CA generates a root crossover certificate $[R_A, B]$ containing Alice's root CA public key, and another root crossover certificate $[R_B, B]$ containing Bob's root CA public key, both certificates are signed by the bridge CA.

Any relying party that trusts Alice's root CA and the Bridge CA can now validate an end entity certificate from Bob's issuing CA as follows: $[E_B, I_B] \Rightarrow [I_B, S_B] \Rightarrow [S_B, R_B] \Rightarrow [R_B, B] \Rightarrow [B, R_A] \Rightarrow [R_A, R_A]$, where the R_A public key verifies the crossover B certificate, the B public key verifies the crossover R_B certificate, the R_B public key verifies the S_B certificate, the S_B public key verifies the I_B certificate, and the I_B public key verifies the E_B certificate, such that the E_B public key can now be used for its intended purpose.

Any relying party that trusts Bob's root CA and the Bridge CA can now validate an end entity certificate from Alice's issuing CA as follows: $[E_A, I_A] \Rightarrow [I_A, S_A] \Rightarrow [S_A, R_A] \Rightarrow [R_A, B] \Rightarrow [B, R_B] \Rightarrow [R_B, R_B]$, where the R_B public key verifies the crossover B certificate, the B public key verifies the crossover R_A certificate, the R_A public key verifies the S_A certificate, the S_A public key verifies the I_A certificate, and the I_A public key verifies the E_A certificate, such that the E_A public key can now be used for its intended purpose.

Figure 10.13 (Bridge at subordinate CA) depicts an alternative bridge CA between Alice and Bob. Alice generates a subordinate crossover certificate $[B, S_A]$ containing the Bridge CA public key signed by her subordinate CA, where the first letter indicates the public key owner and the second letter denotes the certificate signer. Likewise, Bob generates a subordinate crossover certificate $[B, S_B]$ containing the Bridge CA public key signed by his subordinate CA, where the first letter indicates the public key owner and the second letter denotes the certificate signer. Similarly, the bridge CA generates a subordinate crossover certificate $[S_A, B]$ containing Alice's subordinate CA public key, and another subordinate crossover certificate $[S_B, B]$ containing Bob's subordinate CA public key, both certificates are signed by the bridge CA.

Any relying party that trusts Alice's root CA and the Bridge CA can now validate an end entity certificate from Bob's issuing CA as follows: $[E_B, I_B] \Rightarrow [I_B, S_B] \Rightarrow [S_B, B] \Rightarrow [B, S_A] \Rightarrow [S_A, R_A] \Rightarrow [R_A, R_A]$, where the R_A public key verifies the S_A certificate, the S_A public key verifies the crossover

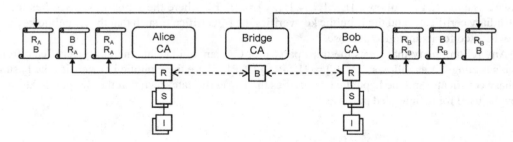

FIGURE 10.12   Bridge at root CA.

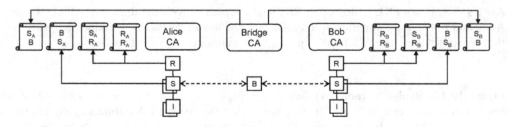

FIGURE 10.13   Bridge at subordinate CA.

B certificate, the B public key verifies the crossover S_B certificate, the S_B public key verifies the I_B certificate, and the I_B public key verifies the E_B certificate, such that the E_B public key can now be used for its intended purpose.

Any relying party that trusts Bob's root CA and the Bridge CA can now validate an end entity certificate from Alice's issuing CA as follows: $[E_A, I_A] \Rightarrow [I_A, S_A] \Rightarrow [S_A, B] \Rightarrow [B, S_B] \Rightarrow [S_B, R_B] \Rightarrow [R_B, R_B]$, where the R_B public key verifies the S_B certificate, the S_B public key verifies the crossover B certificate, the B public key verifies the crossover S_A certificate, the S_A public key verifies the I_A certificate, and the I_A public key verifies the E_A certificate, such that the E_A public key can now be used for its intended purpose.

Figure 10.14 (Bridge at issuing CA) depicts another alternative bride between Alice and Bob. Alice generates an issuing crossover certificate $[B, I_A]$ containing the Bridge CA public key signed by her issuing CA, where the first letter indicates the public key owner and the second letter denotes the certificate signer. Likewise, Bob generates an issuing crossover certificate $[B, I_B]$ containing the Bridge CA public key signed by his issuing CA, where the first letter indicates the public key owner and the second letter denotes the certificate signer. Similarly, the bridge CA generates an issuing crossover certificate $[I_A, B]$ containing Alice's issuing CA public key, and another issuing crossover certificate $[I_B, B]$ containing Bob's issuing CA public key, both certificates are signed by the bridge CA.

Any relying party that trusts Alice's root CA and the Bridge CA can now validate an end entity certificate from Bob's issuing CA as follows: $[E_B, I_B] \Rightarrow [I_B, B] \Rightarrow [B, I_A] \Rightarrow [I_A, S_A] \Rightarrow [S_A, R_A] \Rightarrow [R_A, R_A]$, where the R_A public key verifies the S_A certificate, the S_A public key verifies the I_A certificate, the I_A public key verifies the crossover B certificate, the B public key verifies the crossover I_B certificate, and the I_B public key verifies the E_B certificate, such that the E_B public key can now be used for its intended purpose.

Any relying party that trusts Bob's root CA and the Bridge CA can now validate an end entity certificate from Alice's issuing CA as follows: $[E_A, I_A] \Rightarrow [I_A, B] \Rightarrow [B, I_B] \Rightarrow [I_B, S_B] \Rightarrow [S_B, R_B] \Rightarrow [R_B, R_B]$, where the R_B public key verifies the S_{AB} certificate, the S_B public key verifies the I_B certificate, the I_B public key verifies the crossover B certificate, the B public key verifies the crossover I_A certificate, and the I_A public key verifies the E_A certificate, such that the E_A public key can now be used for its intended purpose.

SPECIAL NOTE 10-8 BRIDGE PKI

Any relying party that trusts the bridge PKI can validate an entity certificate from Alice's PKI, Bob's PKI, or any other PKI who cooperates with the bridge PKI. Hence, Alice and Bob can interoperate with each other and any other PKI who cooperates with the bridge PKI, but each PKI must operate with a common certificate policy.

Note that X9 has developed a "common" Certificate Policy as a set of mutually agreed upon PKI controls between Alice, Bob, and any other X9 approved PKI participant. As noted, updates,

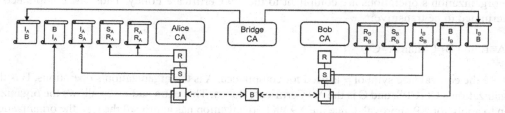

FIGURE 10.14 Bridge at issuing CA.

modifications, or addendums to the X9 Certificate Policy will be published as needed, in addition to the mandatory five-year review cycle per ANSI and ISO standardization procedures. The PKI architecture models will likely be revised as needed or per a similar review cycle.

10.12.3   X9 Financial PKI Program

The X9 Financial PKI Program increases the assurance level for any relying party using an X9 approved PKI within the financial services industry. The PKI study group report presented to the X9 Board of Directors in 2019 identified 27 use cases, and several more have been recognized including wholesale banking and settlement networks. Each use case might use one or more PKI architecture models, possibly with an initial deployment and migrating to a target state architecture, depending on its business, legal, security, and technology needs. Regardless of the use case and its PKI architecture, the X9 approval process will be consistent.

Currently, when an independent auditor performs an audit of a PKI, see Section 10.8, "Web-Trust CA," the goal is to confirm that the CA is operating according to its published policy (e.g., Certificate Policy) and practices (e.g., Certificate Practice Statement). The auditor will review the CP/CPS and any supplemental documentation, including the organization's subscriber agreements, relying party agreements, and cybersecurity procedures. The auditor will inspect the facility and the physical security measures, including alerts, alarms, guards, and logs. The auditor will conduct interviews with staff to confirm that the operations are conducted as documented. The auditor will observe actual operations, possibly execute tests, or review previous tests, including vulnerability scans, penetration testing [B.1.18] and other security metrics.

An average audit is done over a period of time, anywhere from several months to a full year, or possibly longer if remediation is needed. Unlike some programs where the report is due and the results can be "pass or fail," there is no such thing as a "bad" audit report. The auditor will only provide a "good" audit report if and when the CA meets the agreed upon minimal requirements, although some audit reports may include recommendations for improvement. Further, the audit report is sensitive such that it is only provided to the audited organization with a copy of the report, the audit letter, and the associated workpapers kept by the audit firm. The audited organization may opt to share the report with others, but typically only the audit letter is provided, which states when the audit occurred, what criteria was used (e.g., WebTrust CA), who was organization audited, and the name of the audit firm. Handwritten signatures from representatives of both the organization and the firm are included with the audit letter, but the exact names of the auditor and the organization participants are not provided. Those details are in the audit report and the associated workpapers.

X9 chose to avoid reinventing the audit wheel and rely on existing programs. Note that other assessment programs, such as QSA for PCI DSS and QPA for PCI PIN, manage their own program, but X9 determined that the WebTrust CA program, also recognized by the CA Browser Forum, was sufficient with one minor extra step. That extra step is when the auditor compares the organization's CP/CPS to the X9 Certificate Policy and opines on its compliance. The basic idea is that if the WebTrust CA audit of the organization's operations indicates that they are compliant to its own CP/CPS, and if the organization's CP/CPS are compliant to the X9 Certificate Policy, then the organization's operations are compliant to the X9 Certificate Policy. Thus, the compliance is determined to be transitive:

If $A \equiv B$ and $B \equiv C$ than $A \equiv C$

Where the equivalence symbol $\equiv$ is used for compliance, A is the organization's operations, B is the organization's CP/CPS, and C is the X9 Certificate Policy. This extra audit step allows the organization to apply for X9 approval. Once the X9 PKI organization has approved the CA, the organization can then participate in the corresponding PKI use case and architecture.

SPECIAL NOTE 10-9 X9 FINANCIAL PKI

The adoption of the X9 financial PKI will be an interesting industry trend to watch, both nationally and internationally.

Initially, the X9 approval recognition is basically a letter from the X9 PKI organization to the audited organization recognizing its status. The audited organization will be permitted to use the X9 PKI logo on its website and associated documentation. Likely joint press releases will be issued, promoting both the X9 Financial PKI program and the audited organization. Further, the audited organization may include the X9 PKI object identifier (OID) in its relevant certificates, depending on the use case and PKI architecture.

NOTES

1. History of X9, https://x9.org/history-of-x9/
2. OASIS PKI, www.oasis-pki.org/whitepapers.html
3. Troy Hunt, www.troyhunt.com/extended-validation-certificates-are-dead/
4. Federal PKI, https://playbooks.idmanagement.gov/fpki/
5. DoD PKI, https://public.cyber.mil/pki-pke/
6. CSA History, https://cloudsecurityalliance.org/about/history/
7. ISC2, www.isc2.org/
8. NSA Suite B, https://web.archive.org/web/20150815072948/www.nsa.gov/ia/programs/suiteb_cryptography/index.shtml
9. NISTPQCAlgorithms, https://csrc.nist.gov/news/2016/public-key-post-quantum-cryptographic-algorithms
10. NISTIR 8105, https://nvlpubs.nist.gov/nistpubs/ir/2016/NIST.IR.8105.pdf
11. NIST Round 1, https://csrc.nist.gov/Projects/post-quantum-cryptography/post-quantum-cryptography-standardization/round-1-submissions
12. NISTIR 8240, https://nvlpubs.nist.gov/nistpubs/ir/2019/NIST.IR.8240.pdf
13. NIST Round 2, https://csrc.nist.gov/Projects/post-quantum-cryptography/post-quantum-cryptography-standardization/round-2-submissions
14. NIST 8309, https://nvlpubs.nist.gov/nistpubs/ir/2020/NIST.IR.8309.pdf
15. NIST Round 3, https://csrc.nist.gov/Projects/post-quantum-cryptography/post-quantum-cryptography-standardization/round-3-submissions
16. NIST Round 3 Selection, https://csrc.nist.gov/Projects/post-quantum-cryptography/selected-algorithms-2022
17. NIST CRYSTALS, https://csrc.nist.gov/News/2022/pqc-candidates-to-be-standardized-and-round-4
18. Schneier SIKE, www.schneier.com/blog/archives/2022/08/sike-broken.html
19. NISTIR 8413, https://csrc.nist.gov/publications/detail/nistir/8413/archive/2022-07-05
20. NIST PQC Digital Signature, https://csrc.nist.gov/csrc/media/Projects/pqc-dig-sig/documents/call-for-proposals-dig-sig-sept-2022.pdf
21. PCI SSC Advances in Cryptology, www.youtube.com/watch?v=-xLk0TgLdpE
22. ISO TC68/SC2/WG8, www.iso.org/committee/49670.html

Bibliography

B.1   ASC X9 FINANCIAL SERVICES

This section lists the Accredited Standards Committee (ASC) X9 references. ASC X9 is accredited by the American National Standards Institute (ANSI) as the standards developer for the financial services industry. ASC X9 is also the U.S. Technical Advisory Group (TAG) to ISO Technical Committee 68 Financial Services and the TC68 Secretariat. X9 standards and technical reports can be found at the www.x9.org site.

Formally, X9 standards are designated as "ANSI X9," whereas X9 reports are labeled as "ASC X9" since, while they are developed and approved using the X9 ballot process discussed in Section 1.3, "Standards Organizations," reports are not publicly reviewed by ANSI.

Note that for backward compatibility with the first edition of this book, the newer references are appended to the previous list.

1. ANSI X9.19 Financial Institution Message Authentication (Retail).
2. ANSI X9.24 Retail Financial Services: Symmetric Key Management:
   • Part 1: Using Symmetric Techniques.
   • Part 2: Using Asymmetric Techniques for the Distribution of Symmetric Keys.
   • Part 3: Derived Unique Key Per Transaction [DUKPT]
3. ANSI X9.30 Public Key Cryptography Using Irreversible Algorithm:
   • Part 1: Digital Signature Algorithm (DSA).
   • Part 2: Secure Hash Algorithm (SHA).
4. ANSI X9.31 Digital Signatures Using Reversible Public Key Cryptography for the Financial Services Industry (rDSA).
5. ANSI X9.42 Public Key Cryptography for the Financial Services Industry: Agreement of Symmetric Keys Using Discrete Logarithm Cryptography.
6. ANSI X9.44 Public Key Cryptography for the Financial Services Industry: Key Establishment Using Integer Factorization Cryptography.
7. ANSI X9.55 Public Key Cryptography for the Financial Services Industry: Extensions to Public Key Certificates and Certificate Revocation Lists.
8. ANSI X9.57 Public Key Cryptography for the Financial Services Industry: Certificate Management.
9. ANSI X9.62:2005 Public Key Cryptography for the Financial Services Industry: The Elliptic Curve Digital Signature Algorithm (ECDSA).
10. ANSI X9.63:2017 Public Key Cryptography for the Financial Services Industry – Key Agreement and Key Transport Using Elliptic Curve Cryptography.
11. ANSI X9.68–2:2001 Public Key Cryptography for the Financial Services Industry – Part 2: Digital Certificates for High Transaction Volume Financial Systems.
12. ANSI X9.69:2023 Framework for Key Management Extensions.
13. ANSI X9.73:2023 Cryptographic Message Syntax (CMS)
14. ANSI X9.79 Public Key Infrastructure (PKI):
   • Part 1:2001 Practices and Policy Framework.
   • Part 4:2013 Asymmetric Key Management.
15. ANSI X9.95:2022 Trusted Time Stamp Management and Security.
16. ANSI X9.8–1:2019 / ISO 9564–1:2017 Financial services – Personal Identification Number (PIN) Management and Security – Part 1: Basic Principles and Requirements for PINs in Card-Based Systems

17. ANSI X9.84:2018 Biometric Information Management and Security for the Financial Services Industry
18. ANSI X9.111:2018 Penetration Testing within the Financial Services Industry
19. ANSI X9.117:2020 Mutual Authentication for Secure Remote Access
20. ANSI X9.122:2020 Secure Customer Authentication for Internet Payments
21. ANSI X9.141:2021 Financial and Personal Data Protection and Breach Notification Standard
    - Part 1: Data Protection
    - Part 2: Breach Notification
22. ASC X9 Information Report X9.IR01:2019 Quantum Computing Risks to the Financial Services Industry https://x9.org/quantum-computing/
23. ASC X9 Technical Report X9.TR-50:2019 Quantum Techniques in Cryptographic Message Syntax (CMS) https://x9.org/quantum-computing/
24. ASC X9 Information Report X9.IR01:2022 Quantum Computing Risks to the Financial Services Industry https://x9.org/quantum-computing/

B.2 EUROPEAN TELECOMMUNICATION STANDARDS INSTITUTE (ETSI)

This section lists the European Telecommunications Standards Institute (ETSI) references. ETSI standard and technical specifications (TS) can be found at the www.etsi.org site.

1. TS 101 862 v.1.3.1: Qualified Certificate profile.
2. TS 101 903 v.1.2.2: XML Advanced Electronic Signature.

B.3 INTERNET ENGINEERING TASK FORCE (IETF)

This section lists the Internet Engineering Task Force (IETF) references. IETF request for comment (RFC) specifications can be found at the www.ietf.org site.

Note that for backward compatibility with the first edition of this book, newer references are appended to the previous list.

1. RFC 1113: Privacy Enhancement for Internet Electronic Mail: Part I – Message Encipherment and Authentication Procedures, J. Linn, August 1989.
2. RFC 1114: Privacy Enhancement for Internet Electronic Mail: Part II – Certificate-based Key Management, S. Kent and J. Linn, August 1989.
3. RFC 1115: Privacy Enhancement for Internet Electronic Mail: Part III – Algorithms, Modes, and Identifiers, J. Linn, August 1989.
4. RFC 1421: Privacy Enhancement for Internet Electronic Mail: Part I – Message Encryption and Authentication Procedures, J. Linn, February 1993.
5. RFC 1422: Privacy Enhancement for Internet Electronic Mail: Part II – Certificate-Based Key Management, S. Kent, February 1993.
6. RFC 1423: Privacy Enhancement for Internet Electronic Mail: Part III – Algorithms, Modes, and Identifiers, D. Balenson, February 1993.
7. RFC 1424: Privacy Enhancement for Internet Electronic Mail: Part IV – Key Certification and Related Services, B. Kaliski, February 1993.
8. RFC 1824: The Exponential Security System TESS: An Identity-Based Cryptographic Protocol for Authenticated Key-Exchange, H. Danisch, August 1995.
9. RFC 2025: The Simple Public Key GSS-API Mechanism (SPKM), C. Adams, October 1996.
10. RFC 2246: The Transport Layer Security (TLS) Protocol v1.0, T. Dierks and C. Allen, January 1999.
11. RFC 2313 PKCS #1: RSA Encryption v1.5, B. Kaliski, March 1998.

12. RFC 2314 PKCS #10: Certification Request Syntax v1.5, B. Kaliski, March 1998.
13. RFC 2437 PKCS #1: RSA Cryptography Specifications v2.0, B. Kaliski and J. Staddon, October 1998.
14. RFC 2459: Internet X.509 Public Key Infrastructure Certificate and CRL Profile, R. Housley, W. Ford, W. Polk, and D. Solo, January 1999.
15. RFC 2510: Internet X.509 Public Key Infrastructure Certificate Management Protocols, C. Adams and S. Farrell, March 1999.
16. RFC 2511: Internet X.509 Certificate Request Message Format, M. Myers, C. Adams, D. Solo, and D. Kemp, March 1999.
17. RFC 2527: Internet X.509 Public Key Infrastructure Certificate Policy and Certification Practices Framework, S. Chokhani and W. Ford, March 1999.
18. RFC 2528: Internet X.509 Public Key Infrastructure: Representation of Key Exchange Algorithm (KEA) Keys in Internet X.509 Public Key Infrastructure Certificates, R. Housley and W. Polk, March 1999.
19. RFC 2559: Internet X.509 Public Key Infrastructure Operational Protocols – LDAPv2, S. Boeyen, T. Howes, and P. Richard, April 1999.
20. RFC 2585: Internet X.509 Public Key Infrastructure Operational Protocols – FTP and HTTP, R. Housley and P. Hoffman, May 1999.
21. RFC 2587: Internet X.509 Public Key Infrastructure LDAPv2 Schema, S. Boeyen, T. Howes, and P. Richard, June 1999.
22. RFC 2692: Simple Public Key Infrastructure (SPKI) Requirements, C. Ellison, September 1999.
23. RFC 2693: Simple Public Key Infrastructure (SPKI) Certificate Theory, C. Ellison, B. Frantz, B. Lampson, R. Rivest, B. Thomas, and T. Ylonen, September 1999.
24. RFC 2797: Certificate Management Messages over CMS, M. Myers, X. Liu, J. Schaad, and J. Weinstein, April 2000.
25. RFC 2847: LIPKEY – A Low Infrastructure Public Key Mechanism Using SPKM, M. Eisler, June 2000.
26. RFC 2898: PKCS #5: Password-Based Cryptography Specification v2.0, B. Kaliski, September 2000.
27. RFC 2985: PKCS #9: Selected Object Classes and Attribute Types v2.0, M. Nystrom and B. Kaliski, November 2000.
28. RFC 2986: PKCS #10: Certification Request Syntax Specification v1.7, M. Nystrom and B. Kaliski, November 2000.
29. RFC 3029: Internet X.509 Public Key Infrastructure: Data Validation and Certification Server Protocols, C. Adams, P. Sylvester, M. Zolotarev, and R. Zuccherato, February 2001.
30. RFC 3039: Internet X.509 Public Key Infrastructure: Qualified Certificates Profile, S. Santesson, W. Polk, P. Barzin, and M. Nystrom, January 2001.
31. RFC 3156: MIME Security with OpenPGP, M. Elkins, D. Del Torto, R. Levien, and T. Roessler, August 2001.
32. RFC 3161: Internet X.509 Public Key Infrastructure: Time Stamp Protocol (TSP), C. Adams, P. Cain, D. Pinkas, and R. Zuccherato, August 2001.
33. RFC 3278: Use of Elliptic Curve Cryptography (ECC) Algorithms in Cryptographic Message Syntax (CMS), S. Blake-Wilson, D. Brown, and P. Lambert, April 2002.
34. RFC 3279: Algorithms and Identifiers for the Internet X.509 Public Key Infrastructure Certificate and Certificate Revocation List (CRL) Profile, W. Polk, R. Housley, and L. Bassham, April 2002.
35. RFC 3280: Internet X.509 Public Key Infrastructure: Certificate and Certificate Revocation List (CRL) Profile, R. Housley, W. Polk, W. Ford, and D. Solo, April 2002.
36. RFC 3281: An Internet Attribute Certificate Profile for Authorization, S. Farrell and R. Housley, April 2002.

37. RFC 3370: Cryptographic Message Syntax (CMS) Algorithms, R. Housley, August 2002.
38. RFC 3379: Delegated Path Validation and Delegated Path Discovery Protocol Requirements, D. Pinkas and R. Housley, September 2002.
39. RFC 3447: Public Key Cryptography Standards (PKCS) #1: RSA Cryptography Specifications v2.1, J. Jonsson and B. Kaliski, February 2003.
40. RFC 3628: Policy Requirements for Time Stamping Authorities (TSAs), D. Pinkas, N. Pope, and J. Ross, November 2003.
41. RFC 3647: Internet X.509 Public Key Infrastructure: Certificate Policy and Certification Practices Framework, S. Chokhani, W. Ford, R. Sabett, C. Merrill, and S. Wu, November 2003.
42. RFC 3709: Internet X.509 Public Key Infrastructure: Logotypes in X.509 Certificates, S. Santesson, R. Housley, and T. Freeman, February 2004.
43. RFC 3739: Internet X.509 Public Key Infrastructure: Qualified Certificates Profile, S. Santesson, M. Nystrom, and T. Polk, March 2004.
44. RFC 3766: Determining Strengths for Public Keys Used for Exchanging Symmetric Keys – Best Current Practice (BCP) 86, H. Orman and P. Hoffman, April 2004.
45. RFC 3779: X.509 Extensions for IP Addresses and AS Identifiers, C. Lynn, S. Kent, and K. Seo, June 2004.
46. RFC 3820: Internet X.509 Public Key Infrastructure (PKI) Proxy Certificate Profile, S. Tuecke, V. Welch, D. Engert, L. Pearlman, and M. Thompson, June 2004.
47. RFC 4346: The Transport Layer Security (TLS) Protocol v1.1, T. Dierks and E. Rescorla, April 2006.
48. RFC 5246: The Transport Layer Security (TLS) Protocol v1.2, T. Dierks and E. Rescorla, August 2008.
49. RFC 5746: Transport Layer Security (TLS) Renegotiation Indication Extension, E. Rescorla, M. Ray, and N. Oskov, February 2010.
50. RFC 5280: Internet X.509 Public Key Infrastructure Certificate and Certificate Revocation List (CRL) Profile, D. Cooper, S. Santesson, S. Farrell, S. Boeyen, R. Housley, and W. Polk, May 2008.
51. RFC 6101: The Secure Sockets Layer (SSL) Protocol Version 3.0, A. Freier, P. Karlton, and P. Kocher, August 2011.
52. RFC 6960: X.509 Internet Public Key Infrastructure Online Certificate Status Protocol – OCSP, S. Santesson, M. Myers, R. Ankney, A. Malpani, S. Galperin, and C. Adams, June 2013.
53. RFC 6962: Certificate Transparency, B. Laurie, A. Langley, and E. Kasper, June 2013.
54. RFC 2560: X.509 Internet Public Key Infrastructure Online Certificate Status Protocol – OCSP, M. Myers, R. Ankney, A. Malpani, S. Galperin, and C. Adams, June 1999.
55. RFC 8446 The Transport Layer Security (TLS) Protocol Version 1.3, August 2018.

B.4 INTERNATIONAL ORGANIZATION FOR STANDARDIZATION (ISO)

This section lists the International Organization for Standardization (ISO) references. ISO standards and technical reports can be found at the www.iso.org site.

Note that for backward compatibility with the first edition of this book, newer references are appended to the previous list.

1. ISO/IEC 7810:2019 Identification Cards – Physical Characteristics.
2. ISO/IEC 7816 Identification Cards – Integrated Circuit Cards.
   • Part 1:2011 Cards with Contacts – Physical Characteristics.
   • Part 2:2007 Cards with Contacts – Dimensions and Location of the Contacts.
   • Part 3:2006 Integrated Circuit Cards with Contacts and Related Interface Devices.

- Part 4:2020 Organization, Security and Commands for Interchange.
- Part 5:2004 Registration of Application Providers.
- Part 6:2016 Interindustry Data Elements for Interchange.
- Part 7:1999 Interindustry Commands for Structured Card Query Language (SCQL).
- Part 8:2021 Commands for Security Operations.
- Part 9:2017 Commands for Card Management.
- Part 10:1999 Electronic Signals and Answer to Reset for Synchronous Cards.
- Part 11:2022 Personal Verification Through Biometric Methods.
- Part 12:2005 Cards with Contacts – USB Electrical Interface and Operating Procedures.
- Part 13:2007 Commands for Application Management in a Multi-Application Environment.
- Part 15:2016 Cryptographic information application.

3. ISO/IEC 9797 Information Technology – Security Techniques – Message Authentication Codes (MACs):
   - Part 1:2011 Mechanisms using a Block Cipher.
   - Part 2:2021 Mechanisms using a Dedicated Hash-Function.
   - Part 3:2011 Mechanisms using a Universal Hash-Function.

4. ISO 11568 Banking – Key Management (Retail):
   - Part 1:2005 Principles.
   - Part 2:2012 Symmetric Ciphers, Their Key Management and Life Cycle.
   - Part 3:1994 Key Life Cycle for Symmetric Ciphers [Withdrawn]
   - Part 4:2007 Asymmetric Cryptosystems – Key Management and Life Cycle.
   - Part 5:1998 Part 5: Key Life Cycle for Public Key Cryptosystems [Withdrawn]

5. ISO 13491 Banking – Secure Cryptographic Devices (Retail):
   - Part 1:2016 Concepts, Requirements and Evaluation Methods.
   - Part 2:2017 Security Compliance Checklists for Devices Used in Financial Transactions.

6. ISO/IEC 14443 Identification Cards – Contactless Integrated Circuit Cards – Proximity Cards:
   - Part 1:2018 Physical Characteristics.
   - Part 2:2020 Radio Frequency Power and Signal Interface.
   - Part 3:2018 Initialization and Anticollision.
   - Part 4:2018 Transmission Protocol.

7. ISO/IEC 15408 Information Technology – Security Techniques – Evaluation Criteria for IT Security.
   - Part 1:2022 Introduction and General Model.
   - Part 2:2022 Security Functional Components.
   - Part 3:2022 Security Assurance Components.
   - Part 4:2022 Framework for the Specification of Evaluation Methods and Activities.
   - Part 5:2022 Pre-Defined Packages of Security Requirements.

8. ISO 15782 Banking – Certificate Management.
   - Part 1:2009 Public Key Certificates [Withdrawn].
   - Part 2:2001 Certificate Extensions [Withdrawn].

9. ISO 16609:2022 Financial Services – Requirements for Message Authentication Using Symmetric Techniques.

10. ISO 17090 Health Informatics – Public Key Infrastructure:
    - Part 1:2021 Overview of Digital Certificate Services.
    - Part 2:2015 Certificate Profile.

- Part 3:2021 Policy Management of Certification Authority.
- Part 4:2020 Digital Signatures for Healthcare Documents.
- Part 5:2017 Authentication using Healthcare PKI credentials.

11. ISO 21188:2018 Public Key Infrastructure for Financial Services – Practices and Policy Framework.
12. ISO/IEC 19790:2012 Information Technology – Security Techniques – Security Requirements for Cryptographic Modules.
13. SO/IEC 24759:2017 Information Technology – Security Techniques – Test Requirements for Cryptographic Modules.
14. ISO/IEC TR 15446:2017 Information Technology – Security Techniques – Guidance for the Production of Protection Profiles and Security Targets.
15. ISO/IEC 18045:2022 Information Security, Cybersecurity and Privacy Protection – Evaluation Criteria for IT Security – Methodology for IT Security Evaluation.
16. ISO/IEC TR 19791:2010 Information Technology – Security Techniques – Security Assessment of Operational Systems.
17. ISO/IEC TR 20004:2015 Information Technology – Security Techniques – Refining Software Vulnerability Analysis under ISO/IEC 15408 and ISO/IEC 18045.
18. ISO/IEC 29128:2011 Information Technology – Security Techniques – Verification of Cryptographic Protocols.
19. ISO/IEC 29192 Information Security – Lightweight Cryptography.
    - Part 1:2012 General.
    - Part 2:2019 Block Ciphers.
    - Part 3:2012 Stream Ciphers.
    - Part 4:2013 Mechanisms using Asymmetric Techniques.
    - Part 5:2016 Hash-Functions.
    - Part 6:2019 Message Authentication Codes (MACs).
    - Part 7:2019 Broadcast Authentication Protocols.
    - Part 8:2022 Authenticated Encryption.

20. ISO/IEC 27099:2022 Information Technology – Public Key Infrastructure – Practices and Policy Framework.
21. ISO/IEC 9594 Information Technology – Open Systems Interconnection.
    - Part 1:2020 The Directory: Overview of Concepts, Models and Services.
    - Part 2:2020 The Directory: Models.
    - Part 3:2020 The Directory: Abstract Service Definition.
    - Part 4:2020 The Directory: Procedures for Distributed Operation.
    - Part 5:2020 The Directory: Protocol Specifications.
    - Part 6:2020 The Directory: Selected Attribute Types.
    - Part 7:2020 The Directory: Selected Object Classes.
    - Part 8:2020 The Directory: Public-Key and Attribute Certificate Frameworks.
    - Part 9:2020 The Directory: Replication.
    - Part 10: Use of Systems Management for Administration of the Directory [Withdrawn].
    - Part 11:2020 Protocol Specifications for Secure Operations.

B.5 NATIONAL INSTITUTES OF STANDARDS AND TECHNOLOGY (NIST)

This section lists the National Institute of Standards Technology (NIST) references. Federal Information Processing Standards Publications (FIPS PUB) are available at the NIST http://csrc.nist.gov/publications/PubsFIPS.html site, and NIST Special Publications are available at the http://csrc.nist.gov/publications/PubsSPs.html site.

Note that for backward compatibility with the first edition of this book, newer references are appended to the previous list.

1. FIPS PUB 46–3: Data Encryption Standard (DES), 2005.
2. FIPS PUB 113: Computer Data Authentication, 2008.
3. FIPS PUB 140–2: Security Requirements for Cryptographic Modules, 2001.
4. FIPS PUB 180–4: Secure Hash Standard (SHS), 2012.
5. FIPS PUB 186–4: Digital Signature Standard (DSS), 2013.
6. FIPS PUB 197: Advanced Encryption Standard (AES), 2001.
7. FIPS PUB 198–1: The Keyed-Hash Message Authentication Code (HMAC), 2008.
8. NIST Special Publication 800–32 Introduction to Public Key Technology and the Federal PKI Infrastructure, 2001 [Withdrawn].
9. NIST Special Publication 800–38A: Recommendation for Block Cipher Modes of Operation: Three Variants of Ciphertext Stealing for CBC Mode, 2001.
10. NIST Special Publication 800–38B: Recommendation for Block Cipher Modes of Operation: The CMAC Mode for Authentication, 2005.
11. NIST Special Publication 800–38C: Recommendation for Block Cipher Modes of Operation: The CCM Mode for Authentication and Confidentiality, 2004.
12. NIST Special Publication 800–38D: Recommendation for Block Cipher Modes of Operation: Galois/Counter Mode (GCM) and GMAC, 2007.
13. NIST Special Publication 800–38E: Recommendation for Block Cipher Modes of Operation: The XTS-AES Mode for Confidentiality on Storage Devices, 2010.
14. NIST Special Publication 800–38F: Recommendation for Block Cipher Modes of Operation: Methods for Key Wrapping, 2012.
15. NIST Special Publication 800–38G: Recommendation for Block Cipher Modes of Operation: Methods for Format-Preserving Encryption, 2013.
16. NIST Special Publication 800–56A: Recommendation for Pair-Wise Key-Establishment Schemes Using Discrete Logarithm Cryptography, 2013.
17. NIST Special Publication 800–56B: Recommendation for Pair-Wise Key-Establishment Schemes Using Integer Factorization Cryptography, 2014.
18. NIST Special Publication 800–56C: Recommendation for Key Derivation through Extraction-then-Expansion, 2011.
19. NIST Special Publication 800–57: Recommendation for Key Management:
    - Part 1: General (Revision 3), 2012.
    - Part 2: Best Practices for Key Management Organization, 2005.
    - Part 3: Application-Specific Key Management Guidance, 2015.
20. NIST Special Publication 800–67: Recommendation for the Triple Data Encryption Algorithm (TDEA) Block Cipher, 2012.
21. NIST Interagency Report 7298: Glossary of Key Information Security Terms, Revision 2, May 2013.
22. NIST Framework for Improving Critical Infrastructure Cybersecurity v1.0, February 12, 2014.
23. FIPS 196 Entity Authentication using Public Key Cryptography, October 2015 [Withdrawn].
24. NIST Special Publication 800–29A Comparison of the Security Requirements for Cryptographic Modules in FIPS 140–1 and FIPS 140–2, September 2018 [Withdrawn].
25. NIST Special Publication 800–34 Revision 1 Contingency Planning Guide for Federal Information Systems, November 2010.
26. NIST Special Publication 800–52 Revision 2 Guidelines for the Selection, Configuration, and Use of Transport Layer Security (TLS) Implementations, August 2019.
27. NIST Special Publication 800–61 Revision 2 Computer Security Incident Handling Guide, August 2012.

28. NIST Special Publication 800–63–3 Digital Identity Guidelines, March 2020.
29. NIST Special Publication 800–77 Revision 1 Guide to IPsec VPNs, June 2020.
30. NIST Special Publication 800–92 Guide to Computer Security Log Management, September 2006.
31. NIST Special Publication 800–102 Recommendation for Digital Signature Timeliness, September 2009.
32. NIST Special Publication 800–107 Revision 1 Recommendation for Applications using Approved Hash Algorithms, August 2012.
33. NIST Special Publication 800–113 Guide to SSL VPNs, July 2008.
34. NIST Special Publication 800–37 Rev. 2 Risk Management Framework for Information Systems and Organizations: A System Life Cycle Approach for Security and Privacy.
35. NIST Special Publication 800–30 Rev. 1 Guide for Conducting Risk Assessments.
36. FIPS PUB 140–3: Security Requirements for Cryptographic Modules, March 2019.

B.6   PUBLIC KEY CRYPTOGRAPHY STANDARDS (PKCS)

In his 1991 paper, "An Overview of the PKCS Standards," Dr. Burt Kaliski published the Public Key Cryptography Standards (PKCS) through RSA Data Security, Inc. for developers of computer systems employing public key technology to maintain compatibility with the Privacy-Enhanced Mail (PEM) standards, extend the PEM scope, and promote PKI interoperability.

See Table 3.2 Public Key Cryptography Standards for more details on PKCS.

1. PKCS #1: Recommendations for the RSA Algorithm.
   - PKCS #2: Encryption of Message Digests.
   - PKCS #4: RSA Key Syntax.
2. PKCS #3: Diffie–Hellman Key-Agreement Standard.
3. PKCS #5: Password-Based Encryption Standard.
4. PKCS #6: Extended-Certificate Syntax Standard.
5. PKCS #7: Cryptographic Message Syntax (CMS) Standard.
6. PKCS #8: Private Key Information Syntax Standard.
7. PKCS #9: Selected Object Classes and Attribute Types.
8. PKCS #10: Certification Request Syntax Standard.
9. PKCS #11: Cryptographic Token Interface Standard (Cryptoki).
10. PKCS #12: Personal Information Exchange Syntax.
11. PKCS #13: Elliptic Curve Cryptography Standard.
12. PKCS #14: Pseudo-Random Number Generation.
13. PKCS #15: Cryptographic Token Information Syntax Standard.

B.7   MISCELLANEOUS

This section lists miscellaneous references.

Note that for backward compatibility with the first edition of this book, newer references are appended to the previous list.

1. Moore's Law and Intel Innovation, Intel Corporation, www.intel.com/content/www/us/en/history/museum-gordon-moore-law.html (accessed October 2015).
2. Security without Obscurity: A Guide to Confidentiality, Integrity, and Authentication, J.J. Stapleton, CRC Press/Auerbach Publications, May 2014.
3. The Codebreakers: The Comprehensive History of Secret Communication from Ancient Times to the Internet, D. Kahn, Scribner Macmillan Library Reference, Simon & Schuster, New York.

4. Handbook of Applied Cryptography (HAC), A.J. Menezes, P.C. van Oorschot, and S.A. Vanstone, CRC Press, Boca Raton, FL.

5. A method for obtaining digital signatures and public key cryptosystems, R. Rivest, A. Shamir, and L. Adleman, Communications of the ACM, 21(2):120–126, February 1978.

6. New directions in cryptography, W. Diffie and M.E. Hellman, IEEE Transactions on Information Theory, 22(6):644–654, 1976.

7. Uses of elliptic curves in cryptography, V. Miller, Advances in Cryptology: CRYPTO, 85:417–426, 1985.

8. Elliptic curve cryptosystems, N. Koblitz, Mathematics of Computation, 48(177):203–209, 1987.

9. How to share a secret, A. Shamir, Communications of the ACM, 22(11):612–613, 1979.

10. Common criteria protection profile: Cryptographic modules, security level "Enhanced," BSI-CC-PP-0045, endorsed by the Bundesamt für Sicherheit in der Informationstechnik.

11. Common Criteria Protection Profile: CWA 14167-4 Cryptographic Module for CSP Signing Operations, CMCSO-PP-0309, www.ssi.gouv.fr

12. The SSL Protocol v2.0, K.E.B. Hickman, Netscape Communications Corp, April 1995.

13. The SSL Protocol v3.0, A.O. Freier and P. Karlton, Netscape Communications, P.C. Kocher, Independent Consultant, November 1996.

14. PKI Assessment Guidelines (PAG v1.0), Information Security Committee, Electronic Commerce Division, Section of Science & Technology Law, American Bar Association, Chicago, IL, 2003, Product Code 5450032.

15. WebTrust® for Certification Authorities – Extended Validation Audit Criteria v1.4, 2013. CPA Ontario, www.cpaontario.ca 3400-130 King St W, Toronto ON M5X2A2.

16. Cryptography Transitions, J. Stapleton and R. Poore, Institute of Electrical and Electronics Engineers (IEEE), 2006. https://ieeexplore.ieee.org/document/5507465

17. Committee for National Security Systems Instruction No. 4009 (CNSSI-4009) National Information Assurance (IA) Glossary, April 2010. https:// www.cnss.gov/cnss/

18. A concise history of public key infrastructure, J. Stapleton, ISSA Journal, 10(9):27–30, September 2012.

19. PKI under attack, J. Stapleton, ISSA Journal, 11(2):33–40, March 2–13.

20. X.509 Information Technology – Open Systems Interconnection – The Directory: Public Key and Attribute Certificate Frameworks, International. https:// www.itu.int/rec/T-REC-X/e

21. MasterCard, Visa: Secure Electronic Transaction (SET) Specification – Book 1: Business Description, v1.0, May 1997.

22. MasterCard, Visa: Secure Electronic Transaction (SET) Specification – Book 2: Programmer's Guide, v1.0, May 1997.

23. MasterCard, Visa: Secure Electronic Transaction (SET) Specification – Book 3: Formal Protocol Definition, v1.0, May 1997.

24. Digital Signature Guidelines (DSG), Information Security Committee, Electronic Commerce Division, Section of Science & Technology Law, American Bar Association, Chicago, IL, 1996, ISBN 1-57073-250-7.

25. PKI Assessment Guidelines (PAG), Information Security Committee, Electronic Commerce Division, Section of Science & Technology Law, American Bar Association, Chicago, IL, 2003, Product Code 5450032.

26. Quantum Cryptography: Myths, Legends, and Hypothesis, Jeff Stapleton, ISSA Journal, Volume 18, Issue 5, May 2020

27. A public-key cryptosystem with worst case/average case equivalence, M. Ajtai, C. Dwork, In Proc. 29th ACM Symposium on Theory of Computing, 1997, 284–293.

28. Security without Obscurity: A Guide to Cryptographic Architectures, Jeff Stapleton, CRC Press/Auerbach Publications, July 2018

Index

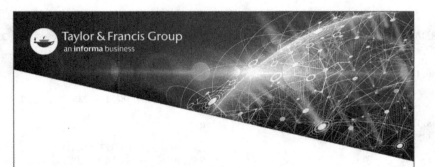